STUDIES IN INDIAN LITERATURE AND PHILOSOPHY

Johannes Adrianus Bernardus (Hans) van Buitenen

STUDIES IN INDIAN LITERATURE AND PHILOSOPHY

COLLECTED ARTICLES OF

J.A.B. van Buitenen

EDITED BY

LUDO ROCHER

AMERICAN INSTITUTE OF INDIAN STUDIES

MOTILAL BANARSIDASS

Delhi Varanasi Patna

Bangalore Madras

First Published: 1988

MOTILAL BANARSIDASS
Bungalow Road, Jawahar Nagar, Delhi 110 007
Branches
Chowk, Varanasi 221 001
Ashok Rajpath, Patna 800 004
24 Race Course Road, Bangalore 560 001
120 Royapettah High Road, Mylapore, Madras 600 004

ISBN: 81-208-0458-9

PRINTED IN INDIA
BY JAINENDRA PRAKASH JAIN AT SHRI JAINENDRA PRESS, A-45 NARAINA INDUSTRIAL AREA, PHASE I, NEW DELHI 110 028 AND PUBLISHED BY NARENDRA PRAKASH JAIN FOR MOTILAL BANARSIDASS, DELHI 110 007.

CONTENTS

FOREWORD

As the obituaries by J. Gonda and Daniel H. H. Ingalls make clear, Professor J. A. B. ("Hans") van Buitenen's death removed from the ranks of America's scholars one of the nation's outstanding Sanskritists and classical Indologists. It is a testimony to Hans's intellectual energy that, after his death, his students, colleagues, and friends took upon themselves the completion of tasks Hans himself, had he lived longer, would have wanted to complete. This volume represents one such task. The articles in this volume, collected from a variety of scattered sources, span primarily the early and middle years of Hans's extraordinary career. They reflect the wide range of Hans's interests and repeatedly demonstrate the rich qualities of his mind.

The production of this volume has involved the cooperation of many people to whom we, in the American Institute of Indian Studies, are immensely grateful. One scholar deserves to be singled out for our special gratitude—the volume's editor, Professor Ludo Rocher. Professor Rocher's painstaking scrutiny of the details of this project establish a model for thoughtful editing. All of us owe him a deep debt of thanks.

July 1987

JOSEPH W. ELDER
President
American Institute of Indian Studies

OBITUARY*

by

J. Gonda

Hans van Buitenen, Distinguished Service Professor of Sanskrit and Indic Studies at the University of Chicago, and a corresponding member of this Academy, died on September 21, 1979, in Champaign, Illinois, at the age of fifty-one.

Johannes Adrianus Bernardus van Buitenen was born in The Hague, on May 21, 1928. He attended elementary school and high school in his hometown, and on June 20, 1946, successfully passed final examination A at the R.C. Gymnasium. While still a high school student he developed a keen interest in things Oriental generally and in India in particular. In this he seems to have been primarily influenced by the window display and the general inventory of his neighbor across the street, who ran the well known Oriental Bookshop on the Noordeinde. As with almost all Dutch Sanskritists, neither his family nor his immediate environment determined his choice of a discipline, which he had already decided as a schoolboy. He managed to get in touch with Dr. Ali Beth, then a classics teacher in one of the high schools in The Hague; she introduced him to the rudiments of Sanskrit during his last years in high school.

I will never forget the first time I met him: he appeared, at 1:00 p.m., during my office hour, on the first day of the academic year 1946-47. Without concern for what the future might hold, he briefly explained that he wanted to study Sanskrit, and told me what he had done thus far. When he heard that an advanced class was to meet at four o'clock, he said he would like to attend. The fact that, until then, he had only read texts in transliteration did not deter him; he went to the waiting room in the railway station, learned the script, and at 4:00 p.m. he read and translated the text as well as any other student. Thus he always was: unusually talented, efficient, sure of what he wanted,

*Translated by the editor from Jaarboek van de Koninklijke Akademie van Wetenschappen, 1979.

capable of expeditious and concentrated work under any circumstances, ready to seize any chance or opportunity that might come along, prepared, if need be, to bend men and things to his will at the opportune moment, all without ostentation or grandstanding. He passed his examinations in a minimum of time, cum laude. Besides Indian literature, he studied Arabic, Persian, Old and New Javanese, and classical philosophy. Even though he was not to work in any of those fields later on, his oeuvre has definitely benefited from this broadening of his horizon. In later life he also acquired a knowledge of Russian, sufficient to evaluate a Mahābhārata translation in that language.

The ease with which he studied foreign languages did not, however, turn him into a linguist. Early on —and this proved to be permanent—his interest appeared especially directed to two areas of Indology, the philosophico-theological and narrative literatures. While still a student he prepared a complete translation of the Vetālapañcaviṃśatikā, the well-known twenty-five vampire stories from the Kathāsaritsāgara, in elegant Dutch, well suited to the subject. It was published by Brill in Leiden, in 1952, under the title *Sprookjes van een spook*. For his Ph.D. dissertation he chose the Gītābhāṣya by the philosopher-theologian Rāmānuja (ca. 1100). Thirty years ago this extremely important figure still stood, in the minds of many Indologists, in the shadow of his predecessor, Śaṅkara. Briefly put, his contribution consists in having demonstrated that the basic texts of Vedānta, which Śaṅkara had interpreted in a strictly monistic and atheistic way, can with equal validity be explained theistically, and can be combined with specific religious convictions, in this case a belief in Viṣṇu as the Supreme Being. This combination of Vedānta philosophy with the theism of Vaiṣṇava theology has contributed much to the spread of the former, and has deeply influenced Indian culture in the course of the centuries. Curiously enough, Rāmānuja's second most important work, his commentary on the Bhagavadgītā, had been totally neglected. It is this book, though, more than any other, that allows us to understand the actual religious basis of his system. It is this book that shows us both the intellectual acuteness and the religious depth with which the author interpreted the basic values of the Bhagavadgītā for his contemporaries and for future generations. We are in van Buitenen's debt for having made this work available in an abbreviated translation—abbreviated for financial reasons, but based on a complete translation he had prepared earlier—, together with a detailed introduction and notes. His book met with wide, international appreciation, and as early as 1958 it appeared in a second, Indian edition.

He was awarded the Ph.D. degree, cum laude, on October 23, 1953. The evening of the same day he hosted a party which was also a farewell reception for his friends and relatives, was married early the next morning, and by noon was on his way to India. There he participated in the preparation of the *Encyclopedic Dictionary of Sanskrit*, a major project of the Deccan College Research Institute in Poona, comparable to the European *Thesaurus Linguae Latinae,* but broader in scope and range. When he arrived, about twenty Indian scholars were working on the project. On the occasion of an internal reorganization he was soon entrusted with a position of leadership. He became an Assistant Editor with full responsibility for the lexicography of at least one quarter of the total enterprise, Vedānta philosophy and kāvya—the extensive branch of Sanskrit literature which, among other things, is characterized by its striving for perfection of form and display of learning. Not only could he demonstrate here his talents as an organizer, since he supervised a number of research assistants, he also had an opportunity for the first time to develop his didactic skills. To quote from one of his letters, he learned to correct errors by people who ought to have known better. In the course of his stay in India, from 1953 to 1956, he found time to travel in the South of the subcontinent; while there he became the first scholar to conceive the idea of photographing and tape-recording the Vedic ritual which remains partly alive in that region. He was able to secure American financial support for this work, and, at the same time, established his first contacts with the United States. He also succeeded, not without difficulty, in obtaining permission from the organizers to film and tape-record the solemn performance, in Poona, of a large Vedic ceremony, the Vājapeya, an event that may not often be repeated in the future. Though he hired assistants for the technical parts, he prepared himself the elaborate commentary and documentation; in order to do so he had to familiarize himself with a field which was practically new to him: the complex

Vedic ritual. The final product —the first film of its kind—has an extraordinary documentary value.

In those years he also found time to write and publish a few articles and, as a follow-up on his Ph.D. dissertation, a thick book, a critical edition with annotated translation of Rāmānuja's *Vedārthasaṃgraha* (Poona 1956), another work by the Vaiṣṇava philosopher who was so congenial to him. Here again he remained faithful to the principles which were to be characteristic of his later work. That is, once more he played the role of a pioneer: this "Summary of the Meaning of the Veda," a work of primary importance, in which the author refutes his opponents theologically as well as philosophically, was practically unknown in the West; even in India it was no longer a source of inspiration. Van Buitenen clearly demonstrated that the study of such philosophical works too, must rest on a sound philological basis. He also used an old Sanskrit commentary, since he was rightly convinced that Western scholars, all too often to their own detriment, overlook traditional Indian interpretations provided by people who are within the scholastic traditions of the authors.

In 1957-58 van Buitenen accepted an invitation to go to the United States, right at the time when there was, in that country, a growing general awareness that it was necessary to bridge the gap in the study, first, of the living languages, but also of the classical languages of South and Southeast Asia. He became "associated with the Indian Studies Program," traveled and consulted with colleagues, visited universities which intended to start or expand Indic studies, and noticed with satisfaction that, in spite of a shortage of Sanskritists, other scholars such as religionists, sociologists, and political scientists, realized the need for thorough philological training. He participated actively in setting up a graduate program which, with Sanskrit philology at the core, brought together a number of other disciplines, and he was soon entrusted with part of its operation.

Besides playing some role in the preparation of the Critical Pali Dictionary in Copenhagen—an enterprise which obviously failed to enthuse him, since one could not see the end of it—, he was from 1959 to 1961 Reader in Indian philosophy at Utrecht. It soon became clear that he had no permanent interest in this position, which had been created especially for him. He had outgrown our country and made little effort to reassimilate himself. English had become his language at home. As a result, in 1961 he enthusiastically accepted an appointment in Chicago, where he soon reached the highest level. In a short period of time he helped to make Chicago into a center of primary importance. His presence stimulated his colleagues and collaborators, with whom he formed a most active team, and he trained good students, American and foreign. Thus he became the founder and, for the first ten years, the Chairman of the Department of South Asian Languages and Civilizations. He was deeply respected by the staff and by the students, not only, to quote one of his colleagues, because of "his unique combination of uncompromising scholarship and insistence on the truth," but also because of his "deep feeling for people," a quality which, there as well as here earlier, he tried very hard to hide.

In the meanwhile his scholarly work went on. As early as 1957 he completed a critical edition and translation of another undeservedly neglected work, the commentary (bhāṣya) on the Brahmasūtras by the philosopher Bhāskara. Later he also brought out a *Source Book of Advaita Vedānta* (Honolulu 1971), in collaboration with E. Deutsch.

In 1962 he published a penetrating study of the Maitrāyaṇīya-upaniṣad (The Hague), a text which until then had puzzled scholars, for it gave the impression of an odd mixture of old ritual symbolism, old upaniṣadic teachings, and relatively late, partly Buddhist, philosophical themes. He showed that we have here, in fact, a series of repeatedly expanded and recast short texts, arranged around an old prose upaniṣad; that the teachings of the various component parts can be clearly identified; and that the redactor who, by means of interpolations, tried to introduce a coherence which did not exist, has failed in his attempt to produce a homogeneous whole. Even those fellow scholars who object to certain details in his argument, agree that this publication is superior to any other on this kind of issue.

Another book, published in Poona in 1968, followed up on his Vājapeya work: a study of the Vedic Pravargya ritual, once more a neglected subject. He tried to demonstrate, not without success, that this remarkable ceremony, which is properly regarded as an originally distinct milk cult, contains elements of non-brahmanic origin, and that its original intent was to strengthen the sun by boiling milk in a red-hot pot.

Following up on his Rāmānuja studies he published in Madras, in 1971, the first critical edition, with translation and a detailed introduction, of the Āgamaprāmāṇyam, by Rāmānuja's predecessor Yāmuna. It is the oldest apologetics of the Vaiṣṇava Pāñcarātra religion and philosophy. Although the religion is still practised today, copies of this extremely difficult text had become rare, and commentaries and earlier translations seem not to exist. No wonder that the author earned much gratitude among Indian scholars and prominent Vaiṣṇavas interested in their cultural heritage.

In addition to the above, the translations from the narrative literature, for the benefit of a larger audience, which he had started as a student, also received a sequel. I think here of his *Tales of Ancient India* (Chicago 1959) and *Two Plays of Ancient India* (Chicago 1964, second edition 1968), both in most readable and delicately shaded English, with a keen eye for internal differences in the style of the plays, part of the translation even in rhymed verses, yet always faithful to the originals. The elaborate introductions, replete with apt formulations, bear testimony not only to his close familiarity with the content and cultural background of the literature in question, but also to a deep awareness of its esthetic value. Moreover, they contain interesting ideas on the peculiarities of Indian theatre and the characters in the plays, as well as original contributions to our knowledge of the storytellers' techniques, the share of truth and fantasy in their works, the specific nature of these literary genres, and noteworthy though as yet unproven suggestions on the intentions of the playwrights: in short, important contributions to historical research on literature.

Finally, in 1967, van Buitenen conceived the idea of translating into English, on the basis of the new critical edition, the Mahābhārata, the great Sanskrit epic, eight times as long as the Iliad and the Odyssey combined. He completed half of it. Three large volumes, representing five of the eighteen parvans, were published in 1973, 1975, and 1978 (University of Chicago Press). To quote an authoritative American critic, they are written in "the most polished, readable, and absorbing English." Indeed, even I who have never been able to muster much admiration for translations, enjoy reading page after page in these volumes. Some have wondered what motivated him to invest so much time in such a protracted enterprise. After all, there already existed two complete English translations, though in abominable English, and totally inadequate from a philological standpoint. I suggest the following answer. First, there was a need for him to exercise his stylistic skills, a challenge to do better than any predecessor, and a change from his other activities. Whatever else he had to do, he translated thirty double verses every day. According to the preface of the latest volume he counted on being ready by 1983. But there is more. Just as his philosophical work was primarily directed toward essentially neglected important works by great thinkers, just as many of the stories he translated treated themes of Indian literature which had become less well-known—for instance, the trials and tribulations of that forgotten figure in cultural life, the merchant—, in the same way he was attracted to the Mahābhārata because, from the end of the nineteenth century onward, Western Sanskritists had treated it in a stepmotherly fashion, in spite of its enormous importance for the past twenty centuries of Indian history. In addition, there was the satisfaction, by means of a good translation, to make this encyclopedia of Hinduism in the broadest sense of the word, available to practitioners of other disciplines—sociologists, cultural anthropologists, historians, historians of literature—and, thus, to produce a work that would be useful for studies far beyond his own sphere and competence. I mention only in passing that the copious introductions to these volumes contain many valuable contributions to our knowledge of the Mahābhārata, the composition of the text, the motivation and craftsmanship of the poets, and the psychology of the main characters.

Hans van Buitenen earned the respect of his colleagues and friends in Chicago. His death deprived them of a natural central figure. Appreciation of his wise judgment in scholarly and administrative matters led, in the course of years, to his membership in many societies and committees in and outside the University, in the board of directors of the International Association of Sanskrit Studies, the Association for Asian Studies, and the American Academy for the Study of Religion. In 1975 he was honored by the Association of Indians in America and became a member of the American Academy of Arts and Sciences. At that very time thought was given to calling him back to the Netherlands. When he was approached about this, however, he intimated that he was not prepared to leave Chicago. From his point of view it was a wise decision. He would have had to abandon the pace, the dimensions, and the opportunities across the Atlantic, with which he had identified himself quite naturally and inevitably, right from the beginning. Also—and this is a free quote—, he was unwilling to surrender what his American investment in time and energy was to yield him in the form of prospects for new projects and undertakings. He could not foresee at the time that he would have to do so anyway, soon and forever.

OBITUARY*

by

DANIEL H.H. INGALLS

Johannes Adrianus Bernardus van Buitenen was born into a family of Roman Catholic diamond merchants in The Hague on May 21, 1928. Twelve years later the family was living under the German occupation, without diamonds, without sufficient food, without anything solid except Dutch tenacity to keep them alive. During the occupation years Johannes attended Gymnasium and distinguished himself, I am told, in Latin and Greek. After the end of the war he went to study at the University of Utrecht. At first, like many Hollanders of prewar days, he aimed at a career in the East Indies. So his language studies spread to Old Javanese, Arabic, Persian, and Sanskrit. It was partly the loss of the Dutch Empire but more a matter of personal taste that changed his goal in mid course. Two subjects in his curriculum fascinated him: the works of Plotinus, which he studied under C.J. de Vogel and Sanskrit language and literature,, where his teacher was the great Jan Gonda. Gonda was to remain van Buitenen's ideal of scholarship throughout his life. It is these interests that explain van Buitenen's doctoral thesis "Ramanuja and the Bhagavadgita." For many years his work was heavily concentrated on Sanskrit theology and metaphysics.

At the age of 24, within one year, Hans received his doctorate, was appointed an assistant to Gonda, married a wife, and then set off to India with her, where he found work on the Sanskrit dictionary project at Poona. For the deadly task of word gathering he chose the Vedarthasamgraha, and in the course of his three year stay, he made a critical text and translation of that work, prefacing it with the best analysis the work has yet received. The study of Visistadvaita led him on to the Bhedabheda and that is how I came to know him.

He wrote me a letter. He had heard from Katre that I had been

*Newsletter of the American Oriental Society, Number 4, September 1961.

working on Bhaskara, also that I knew the whereabouts of a fragment of Bhaskara's Gitabhasya. Could I tell him what I was planning to do so that we would not duplicate each other's work; and would I tell him about the mysterious fragment?

In 1956 van Buitenen received a Rockefeller Fellowship to work on Bhaskara with me at Harvard. He arrived in Cambridge in November; his wife, Corrie, and the children just before Christmas. That year we saw each other almost every day as we worked on Bhaskara. Originally he was to edit and translate the Brahmasutrabhasya and I was to do the Gitabhasya. Later I gave the Gitabhasya material to him so that he could do the whole.

Next year came a job offer from the University of Chicago, where Hans was to broaden out widely from his conservative background under the stimulus of a group of singularly creative Indianists. There in time he came under the influence of Milton Singer, McKim Marriott, and Edward Dimock. The first effect of the new vision was to prompt him to an omniverous reading of Sanskrit literature; no longer theology and metaphysics, but epics, poems, plays, stories, everything. The 'winter readings' grew into his "Tales of Ancient India," which of all his translations I like on stylistic grounds the best. He catches the sly humor of the tales to perfection.

The trial at Chicago was a success. But the van Buitenens had to leave the U.S. for a two year period in order to obtain permanent visas. Back in Holland, Hans had an appointment as lecturer at Utrecht, once more under Gonda. I think these may have been the happiest two years in his life.

The family returned to Chicago in 1961, and Hans published his Maitreyopanisad translation and continued to work on Bhaskara. He advanced rapidly, from Associate to Full Professor in two years. But then administrative work and family problems drained most of his energy. There was a divorce. The Bhaskara was shelved, never to be mentioned again to me by word or by letter after 1966.

When Hans did finally get back to his scholarly life he had found a new love. He wrote me in November '66: "For the last year I have been talking myself in and out of an attack on the Mahabharata and I believe it is worth a serious try. I have no illusions about the size of the try and can only hope that it won't take me into my grave."

It would be easy to catch at this remark and call it a premonition. But I do not think that the Mahabharata took Hans into the grave. I think rather that it kept him alive for thirteen years. Other things, of course, he took pleasure in: reading and teaching; and he must have enjoyed helping other scholars or he would not have been so generous with his carefully garnered time. For Edward Dimock he worked through all the Sanskrit verses of the Caitanyacaritamrta. For Cornelia Dimmitt, with whom he did the *Classical Hindu Mythology* he translated several hundred pages of Puranic texts. But when hurt by family griefs, when harried by administrative duties and correspondence, when, as often, he was lonely, and when in the last years he was in increasing pain from bad health, it was his translation of the Mahabharata, the great purpose of his life, that kept him happy.

He has left us three massive volumes of translation of the Mahabharata, the best for accuracy that has yet been produced. The style suffers from his insistence on a strict rendering of every epithet and vocative and from his attempt to turn the tristubh stanzas into English verse. But test the translation by the difficult passages. Take the Hymn to the Asvins or the Uttarayayati from the First Book. If you have marked your Bharata, as I have mine, with little exes in the margin of passages which you don't understand, see how many exes you can erase after reading van Buitenen's translation. Hans had read more widely in Sanskrit than any other western Sanskritist that I have known personally; and he had a retentive linguistic memory. Unlike most translators of Sanskrit he would not be misled by dictionary meanings; he would remember the words from their actual usage. I wish he had reached the Twelfth Book, where his wide knowledge of Indian philosophy and his sure sense of the language would have elucidated many a thorny passage that will defy the efforts of lesser scholars for many years. Fortunately he had some good pupils. Perhaps the mantle will pass, as it passed from Elisha to Elijah.

In May 1979 van Buitenen remarried; four months later, on September 21st, Johannes van Buitenen died.

This is the ideal of scholarship that van Buitenen adopted early in his life: "The example of strict scientific method, of many-sided learnedness and untiring helpfulness is the example that shall be my ideal." Throughout his often unhappy life van Buitenen always had the strength to live up to that ideal. Those who knew him personally and those who read his books will be eternally grateful.

EDITOR'S INTRODUCTION

Our paths have crossed in several ways, over a period of three decades, on three continents. I first met Hans van Buitenen in 1948, when I joined him and J.C. Heesterman in a weekly Vedic class conducted by Professor Gonda at the University of Utrecht. Five years later, upon my arrival at the Deccan College in Pune, I found a letter from Hans announcing that he and his wife Corrie were on their way to the same destination. We were to live and work on the same campus for about one year and a half, including six weeks at the end of my stay when I enjoyed the hospitality of the van Buitenen bungalow. One day in 1956 Hans came to see me at the old India Office Library in Whitehall; that evening I saw him off at the Victoria air terminal for his first departure to the United States. Finally, when my turn came, in 1966, to move across the Atlantic, Hans van Buitenen became a welcome source of information on the many questions a newcomer wanted to ask one who had been in that position ten years earlier.

It was while walking back from the memorial service for Hans at the University of Chicago that Edward C. Dimock, the then President of the American Institute of Indian Studies, suggested that I edit a collection of Hans' articles as an Institute publication. Even though the completion of this volume was unduly delayed, I am happy to present here, in easily accessible form, twenty-seven articles originally published in fourteen different scholarly journals and collaborative volumes.

Hans' untimely death left us without a complete and up-to-date list of his publications. The collection of articles in this volume is the outcome of one outdated curriculum vitae and consultations with a number of friends who might possess off-prints of articles that were unknown to me. I can only hope that I did not miss anything important.

Rather than organize the articles by topics, I decided to arrange them strictly in chronological order, at least in chronological order of their publication. In addition to the fact that later articles often refer to or build on earlier ones, this approach will enable the reader to follow van Buitenen's gradually shifting scholarly interests. Also, a number of articles were direct by-products of book-length publications, all of which are discussed in the two obituary notes above.

The articles reprinted in this volume cover a period of twenty-five years, from 1954 to 1979. They were published in a variety of volumes each of them presenting their own idiosyncrasies. I did not consider it the editor's duty—or even right—either to interfere with the author's changing style or to introduce uniformity of presentation which was not there in the original publications. Except for a few minor adaptations which could not be avoided and for correcting obvious misprints, all articles are reprinted exactly as they were first published. The original page numbers are inserted in bold type and in brackets.

I thank Professor Elder for writing a prefatory note to the volume, and Professors Gonda and Ingalls for allowing me to include—in the first case also to translate—the obituaries they wrote soon after Hans van Buitenen's death. I also thank the editors and publishers of van Buitenen's articles for permission to reproduce these here; the original places of publication and credit lines, wherever required, are indicated in the Contents. Thanks are also due to Mrs Kushla Sar for preparing a first version of the Index. Finally, this volume would never have been completed without the dynamic support of the Director of the American Institute of Indian Studies, Dr. Pradeep R. Mehendiratta. For this, as for so many favors over the years, many, many thanks.

1

NOTE ON *KATHAM . . KATHAM*

It may be worthwhile to draw the attention to a curious construction in Rāmānuja's Śrībhāṣya 1, 1, 1 which reads:[1] *nanu ca sakalabhedanivṛttiḥ pratyakṣaviruddhā katham iva śāstrārthajanyavijñānena kriyate/kathaṃ vā rajjur eṣā na sarpa iti jñānena pratyakṣaviruddhasarpanivṛttiḥ kriyate/tatra dvayoḥ pratyakṣayor virodha iha tu pratyakṣamūlasya śāstrasya pratyakṣasya ceti cet tulyayor virodhe kathaṃ bādhyabādhakabhāvaḥ.*

The question is how to translate the two interrogative sentences *katham iva . . kriyate/kathaṃ vā . . kriyate.* At a first glance nothing would seem to be anomalous. So Rangacharya and Varadaraja Aiyangar[2] translate literally: "However, it may be asked—how is that cessation of all distinctions, which is contrary to perception, accomplished by the knowledge that is derived out of the scriptures?—or, how (for instance) by means of the knowledge "this is a rope, not a serpent," is the destruction of the serpent perception effected—(the destruction) that has to contradict what is actually perceived." This literal translation is not only unreadable but incomprehensible at that. It suggests that two unconnected questions are being put, but this suggestion is belied by the second part of the objection *tatra . . pratyakṣasya ca,* which refers to both sentences in a direct connexion and puts them in opposition to each other. Thibaut[3] appears to have avoided an unsatisfactory translation like this but not without silently assuming an irregularity in the text: he treats the second interrogative *katham*-sentence as a counter-question in reply to the first sentence: "But, an objection is raised: "How can knowledge . . ." "How then, we rejoin, can the knowledge . . ."," while with the *tatra*-sentence the first objector proceeds. But then the first *katham*-sentence should have been followed by *iti cet.* Either we have to account for so singular and irregular an omission, or to reject the translation; but [**138**] both

Lacombe[4] and Otto[5] follow Thibaut silently and leave the irregularity unaccounted for.

I would propose another translation which is better in keeping with the context. The passage under discussion forms a vital part of the so-called Great Pūrvapakṣa. The *Pūrvapakṣin*, an advaitin, states his view that Brahman is the sole reality, that all plurality is illusory and brought about by nescience, and that this nescience is annulled by true knowledge: "Brahman alone, being mere, non-differentiated spirituality, is true; all the rest is untrue. Untrue is, by definition, an object of which a notion has been conceived that subsequently can be annulled by exact knowledge of the real nature of that object".[6] To illustrate this he draws the following comparison: "So is untrue, for example, the snake that is conceived to exist in an object that in reality is a rope."[7] Follows a selection of śruti and smṛti quotations which demonstrate the sole existence of Brahman, etc. At this point Rāmānuja introduces a question: *nanu ca* etc. The most consistent translation of the two interrogative sentences would be, not to separate them as if they were unconnected, still less to distribute them over two speakers, but to treat them as one interrogative sentence bearing upon the one comparison drawn by the advaitin: "How can you put both in the same class, the annulment of plurality and that of the snake? Both contradict the evidence of sense-perception, but one is effected by scriptural knowledge and the other by perceptual knowledge. In the latter case, therefore, perception contradicts perception, whereas in the former the scriptures, deriving from perception, contradict perception."

The point which Rāmānuja wants to make is that the advaitin has to account for his comparison of two distinct sources of knowledge both of which—it is the *tertium comparationis*—appear to be capable of annulling only knowledge from one source: scriptural and perceptual knowledge both annul perceptual cognitions. To this sense the advaitin replies by pointing out that the *tertium* is the invalidity of both perceptual knowledge and the cognition of a snake: on one plane perceptual truth annuls perceptual error, and on the other the scriptural truth annuls all erroneous perception. In this passage the most fundamental epistemological difference between advaita and viśiṣṭādvaita is neatly indicated by a play of question and counter-question [**139**], and to solve the problems involved Rāmānuja will in his Great

Siddhānta develop his theory of knowledge on the basis of differentiation.

So the above translation, though inevitably "free", should not be considered a mere paraphrasis. If we accept this sense of the passage we have to adopt a differentiated meaning of *katham* (*iva*) .. *kathaṃ* (*vā*) in the sense of "How can this be so as that?" "How can both be comparable?", i.e., emphatically they cannot.[8] I may draw an analogy with the well-known construction *kva* (*ca*) .. *kva* (*ca*) expressing "disproportion" or incongruity.[9] Finally the conspicuous use of the stylistic figure of *chiasmus* indicating opposition should also be noted.

As far as I know a nuance like this has not been recorded. That of course weakens my case which rests entirely upon the context; however, the context seems suggestive enough to put the case *sub judicibus*.

NOTES

1. P. 18 of V. S. Abhyankar's edition, Bombay 1914.
2. M. Rangacharya and M. B. Varadaraja Aiyangar, *Vedānta-Sūtras with Śrī-Bhāṣya*, I, Madras 1899, p. 33.
3. George Thibaut, *Vedānta-Sūtras with the Commentary of Rāmānuja*, S.B.E. XLVIII (Oxford 1904), p. 24; the quotes are mine.
4. Olivier Lacombe, *La Doctrine morale et métaphysique de Rāmānuja* (Paris 1938), p. 22.
5. Rudolf Otto, *Siddhānta des Rāmānuja* (Tübingen 1923), p. 30.
6. *nirviśeṣacinmātraṃ brahmaiva satyam anyat sarvaṃ mithyā ... / mithyātvaṃ nāma pratīyamānatvapūrvakayathāvasthitavastujñānanirvartyatvam*, Śrībhāṣya 1, 1, 1, p. 15.
7. *yathā rajjvādyadhiṣṭhānakasarpādeḥ*, Śrībhāṣya, 1. c.
8. *katham* as a particle introducing a rhetorical question with negative reply implied or expected has this function especially when followed by particles like *iva*. The development of the sense suggested here out of an oratorical "how is this so: how is that so!" is easy to follow semantically.
9. Louis Renou, *Grammaire sanscrite* (Paris 1930), p. 512.

2

VĀCĀRAMBHAṆAM

Uddālaka's teaching in the sixth prapāṭhaka of the Chāndogya is easily the most celebrated Upaniṣad text, not only in India ancient and modern, but also in the West, where the expression *tat tvam asi*, in the somewhat biblical rendering of Thou art That, is often considered a formula that sums up the entire Indian philosophy. Yet there is no śruti text of which the meaning has been disputed so vehemently as Uddālaka's sadvidyā. The oldest interpreters of the Chāndogya Up. of whose commentaries we have some fragments left, Ṭaṅka the Vākyakāra and Dramiḍa the Bhāṣyakāra,[1] show that already at their time there was a controversy between those who considered that *sat* was *brahman* without qualities and those who held that *sat* was *brahman* with qualities.[2] Correlated with this question whether *sat* or *brahman*[3] as the causa prima possesses qualities or not is the question whether its effect, the phenomenal world of individual souls and of matter has a proper and distinct reality or not. The problematic relation between the absolute, permanent and perfect that is cause and the relative, impermanent and imperfect that is effect has remained the fundamental problem of Vedānta: the discussion of this problem has always taken the form of a commentary on Uddālaka's teaching ever since the Sūtrakāra had formulated his solution in Uddālaka's terms.[4] Modern research[5] has made it plausible that the Sūtrakāra [158] adhered to the view of *pariṇāma* which admits an inner causal transformation of the absolute into the relative: this was the view, incidentally, that was also adhered to by the oldest Vedāntins Ṭaṅka and Dramiḍa.[6] The logical difficulties implicit in the pariṇāma view must have been recognized early; it was Bhartṛhari, the author of the Vākyapadīya, who apparently for the first time availed himself of the ancient notion of *vivarta* to describe the causal process as somehow illusory, not real, only in appearance so.[7] Though it would seem not yet by Śaṅkara himself,[8] the same view was formulated in advaita-vedānta. Other Vedāntins, however, took a different stand. Bhāskara still represents the more ancient view that the causal change takes really place within the qualified brahman, whereas Yāmuna[9] and more systematically Rāmānuja[10] integrated a Sāṃkhya doctrine and maintained that *pariṇāma* only takes place within matter, which, though real and eternal in itself, is inseparably dependent on God of whom it constitutes the body. Madhva took the same stand but denied Rāmānuja's body-soul identity. Within Vedānta we distinguish thus a great variety of views which are all read into and proved from the sadvidyā passage *vācārambhaṇaṃ vikāro nāmadheyaṃ mṛttiketyeva satyam*,[11] which, according to the Sūtras (2, 1, 14 *tadananyatvam ārambhaṇaśabdādibhyaḥ*) declares that the world, the effect, is no other than its cause, *sat* or *brahman*.

What was Uddālaka's own view? It is summed up in 6, 8, 7: when all products are successively dissolved in their causes, an ultimate prime cause remains to which all the rest can be reduced: *sa ya eṣo 'ṇimā etadātmyam idaṃ sarvaṃ tat satyaṃ sa ātmā:* it is the irreducible minimum in which all this ultimately consists, the *satya:* it is the ātman.[12] The term *satya* refers us to the passage quoted above where it is stated that in clay products 'clay' is *satya* and that the product, a pitcher, bowl etc. is *vācārambhaṇaṃ vikāro nāmadheyam*. The crucial term is *vācārambhaṇaṃ*. Usually it is taken adjectively with *nāmadheyam:* "the effect is (just) a name deriving from [159] speech". One objection is that the word-order rather reads "the name is the effect", another that according to Uddālaka himself speech or *vāc* is a later product instead of a cause as *ārambhaṇa* would suggest; the last objection is that a tangible and serviceable object like a clay pitcher is *not* only another name of clay, as the old Commentators realized better than many translators.[13] Name must mean here what later on is termed *nāmarūpe* "name and form", which, in 6, 3, 2, describes the products or creatures that are "separated out of" (*vyā√kṛ-~ vikāra*) the materia prima[14].

The meaning of *ārambhaṇa*, too, could be specified if we follow up a contextual connexion that is suggested by Rāmānuja and stated expressly by Madhva.[15] Commenting on *advitīyam* Rāmānuja[15a] declares that the term conveys that there is no second *adhiṣṭhātṛ* side by side with *sat* (equated with a personal God) which is the material cause. He refers in this connexion to Taittirīya Br. 2, 8, 9, 6: *kiṃ svid vanaṃ ka u sa vṛkṣa āsīd yato dyāvāpṛthivī niṣṭatakṣuḥ / manīṣiṇo manasā pṛcchated u tad yad adhyatiṣṭhad bhuvanāni dhārayan.* This question is answered *brahma vanaṃ brahma sa vṛkṣa* etc. The urgency of this reference—which inspired Rāmānuja's use of the term *adhiṣṭhātṛ* for *nimittakāraṇam*—becomes clear when we study the context of the Ṛgveda sūkta from which TaittBr. has taken the question: 10, 81, 4. There it is an illustrative repetition of a preceding question (2) *kíṃ svid āsīd adhiṣṭhā́nam ārámbhaṇaṃ katamát svit kathā́sīt / yáto bhū́miṃ janáyan Viśvákarmā ví dyā́m ā́urṇon mahinā́ viśvácakṣāḥ* "whatever was the standing-place, which the basis and how was it by which Viśvakarman, when producing the earth, put the sky apart by his power, he who sees all?" We remark in passing that in st. 7 Viśvakarman is styled *vācaspáti*, "lord or possessor of *vāc*". We may compare 10, 129 where it is said that that which is *sat* sprang from that which is not *sat*, and that sages who reflect discovered, after searching in their hearts, that sat is fastened to asat (4 cd): *satό bándhum ásati níravindan hṛdí pratī́ṣyā kaváyo manīṣā́.* Whether one would take this last statement as one reply to the question of 10, 81 or not, it cannot be denied that the three hymns 10, 129, 72, and 81 are, with many others, ever so many speculations and formulations of one cosmogonic myth of which the evolution and elaboration can be pursued throughout the Brāhmaṇas and the Upaniṣads. It would seem that this one myth of the creation of the many out of the one had two basic forms, one in which the creation was imagined [160] to proceed from a personal and divine progenitor, and another in which the notions of *sat* and *asat*, standing respectively for "this which is here, the world" and "that which is other than that, its matrix and origin," took the place of creator. Often enough both forms are so interlinked that we can hardly distinguish them. Uddālaka's formulation, so it seems, is an elaboration of 10, 129.[16] But even in this latter hymn, where a tendency to do away with divine progenitors is conspicuous, the shade of a demiurge makes a hesitant come-back at the end, if only to have his assistance at and knowledge of sat's origination questioned. In 10, 72, 2 it is Brahmaṇaspati who superintends this origination: *bráhmaṇas-*

pátir etā́ sám̧ karmā́ra ivādhamat / devā́nām̧ pūrvyé yugé 'sataḥ sád ajāyata. This hymn again reminds us strongly of 10, 81 where it reads (3) *sám̧ bāhúbhyām̧ dhámati sám̧ pátatrair dyā́vābhū́mī janáyan devá ékaḥ.* This one god is Viśvakarman who has not only the appellation *vācaspáti* in common with Brahmaṇaspati,[17] but other features as well: both as the contexts show represent in some respect the sun,[18] who separates sky and earth after their nocturnal union, and in this are strongly reminiscent of the anonymous deity of 10, 129 who "watches from the far-away sky."[18a]

This context of interconnected speculations on a cosmogonic myth must have inspired Rāmānuja and Madhva to their explanatory references which, possibly, might already have been given in ancient commentaries. More obvious must the same connexions have been to Uddālaka himself who lived in a *milieu* of thinkers who tried out ever new and more comprehensive formulations of this myth. To my mind there can be little doubt that his use of the term *ārambhaṇa* was inspired by its place in the entire idea-complex concerning the emergence of the many from the one and should as far as possible to explained within this idea-complex.

The same mythical context throws light on the meaning of *vāc* in *vācārambhaṇam.* We are justified to make at least a distinction[19] between this **[161]** *vāc* and the *vāc* which is described in ChUp. 6, 5, 3-4 as the subtlest—that is no doubt the first—product of *tejas*: We remarked in passing that Viśvakarman and Brahmaṇaspati have corresponding functions within this context, and that both are called *vācaspati.* In this as in other respects they are comparable to Prajāpati who is also described as the husband of *vāc*, and consequently even identified with *vāc.*[20] Instructive is a passage in Kāṭhaka Saṃhitā 12, 5: *prajāpatir vā idam āsīt tasya vāg dvitīyāsīt tām̧ mithunam̧ samabhavat sa garbham adhatta sāsmād apākramat semāḥ prajā asṛjata sā prajāpatim eva punaḥ prāviśat*[21] etc. *Vāc* as the first product (literally; *vāc* is ejaculated)[22] of the creator, the second one to exist side by side with him as his partner in creation (we recall Uddālaka's emphatic *advitīyam eva*), is personified as a progenitrix. Scharbau[23] goes too far when he comments on this and similar passages that "mit dem Logos (i.e. *vāc*; I would object to this term) ist also eine objektive, metaphysische Substanz gemeint" which supposes a differentiation between power and matter which is not yet recognized; but he is nearer to the mark when he continues: "Er (i.e. Logos) ist das Brahman als Urwort, als Uroffenbarung des göttlichen (the term is unfortunate) ātman". There is enough evidence to show that *vāc* represents at least one of the aspects of *brahman* as the powerful and creative word,[24] and the progenitive and creative function of *vāc/brahman* may partly account for the importance of the concept of *brahman* in later thought where the notion of permanent underlying stability with the typically Indian association of (material) cause will remain fundamental.

[162] We shall not be far astray when we interpret *vācārambhaṇaṃ* on the basis of this cosmogonic context. The *ārambhaṇa* and *adhiṣṭhāna*, the forest and the tree on which Viśvakarman vācaspati stood when creating was identified with *vāc/brahman*. The *vikāra* "that which is separated out of the underlying stuff that is the material cause", that which appears as name-and-form, derives from (*ārambhaṇa-*) *Vāc* as the creating word of the creator, that force with which he is able to create. Uddālaka, who insists emphatically on the uniqueness of the first cause that is *sat*, must have conceived of this *vāc* as the power of creation of *sat*. But *vāc* is no longer projected outside the first cause as a partner (*sat* is *advitīyam*). It would seem that the fundamental doctrine of the Vedāntins that the material cause and the operative cause (*nimittakāraṇa*, which would correspond to *vāc*) are identical reflects Uddālaka's view accurately.

NOTES

1. The present writer has collected the available fragments of both these *pūrvācāryas* of Rāmānuja in an appendix to his study of the Vedārthasaṃgraha, which will be out shortly.

2. Fragment XV, quoted *Vedārthasaṃgraha*, Paṇḍit Ed. p. 143, *yuktam/ tadguṇakopāsanāt* "(also with regard to the sadvidyā) it is appropriate, for meditation is on an object (or: *brahman*) that has those qualities" (Ṭaṅka's Vākya); *yady api saccitto na nirbhugṇadaivataṃ guṇagaṇaṃ manasānudhāvet tathāpy antarguṇām eva devatāṃ bhajate* "although one, when meditating on the sadvidyā, does not pursue with one's thoughts the multitude of qualities (of the daharavidyā, ChUp. 8, 1, 5) that are negative (*apahata-pāpmā*, etc.) or divine (*satyakāmaḥ satyasaṃkalpaḥ*), still one lovingly cognizes the Deity as having inner qualities" (Dramiḍa's bhāṣya).

3. We shall not touch here on the disputable equation *sat*=*brahman* of Vedānta.

4. BrS. 2, 1, 14.

5. Dasgupta, *Indian Philosophy* II, p. 36 ff; V. S. Ghate, *The Vedānta* (Poona 1926=*Les Brahma-Soutras et leurs cinq commentaires*, Thesis Paris

1918) who, however, has committed the methodological error of not considering Bhāskara's bhāṣya, which represents a much more ancient Vedānta than any other bhāṣya does.

6. Fragment XII, quoted, Bhāskara's Brahmasūtrabhāṣya ad 1, 4, 25, *pariṇāmas tu syād dadhyādivat* "there is an inner causal change, as in the case of curds (turning into butter: ChUp. 6, 6, 1) etc."; cf. also the indirect testimony of the Sarvajñātman's presentation, Fragment XVIII and the discussion in Ch. II of Introduction of my *Vedārthasaṃgraha.*

7. Paul Hacker, *Vivarta*, Studien zur Geschichte der illusionistischen Kosmologie und Erkenntnistheorie der Inder (Ak. Wissensch. und Lit. Abh. Geistes etc. Kl., 1953, nr 5), p. (13) ff.

8. Hacker, o.c. p. (24) ff. who describes Śaṅkara's cosmology als "eine Art *illusionistischer Pariṇāmavāda*".

9. Yāmuna, Saṃvitsiddhi, (in: Siddhitraya, Chaukhamba Skt. Ser. 10, Benares 1900), p. 82, beginning *jñānādi* etc.

10. Vedārthasaṃgraha, p. 28 ff; Ś. Bh. 2, 1, 15.

11. ChUp. 6, 1, 3.

12. For Uddālaka's concept of the ātman cf. ChUp. 5, 17.

13. Rāmānuja, for instance, availing himself of one of the many senses of the term, renders *vācā* with *vyavahāreṇa* "practical purpose" which expresses the initiating or actuating function of language.

14. ChUp. 6, 2, 1 *sadevedamagra āsīdekamevādvitīyam* "the *sat* was here (idam adverbially) at first, alone without a partner".

15. Madhva (ad BrS. 2, 1, 14) refers directly to RV 10, 81, 2 in connexion with *ārambhaṇa,* the expression proving that God needed no other instrument; Ghate is too rash in considering it irrelevant (p. 81).

15a. *Vedārthasaṃgraha*, p. 55 ff.

16. More details on this point *Vedārthasaṃgraha*, Intr., Ch. I.

17. E.g. MS. 2, 6, 6.

18. For this solar aspect of both Viśvakarman and Brahmaṇaspati, cf. Macdonell, *Vedic Mythology*, §§ 39 and 36.

18a. Ad RV. 10, 125 (to Vāc), 7 *ahám̐ suve pitáram asya mūrdhán máma yónir apsú antáḥ samudré | táto ví tiṣṭhe bhúvanā́nu víśvotā́mā́m̐ dyā́m̐ varṣmáṇopa spṛśāmi.* Geldner remarks that the father, born from Vāc, is the *ádhyakṣa* in the Supreme Heaven of 10, 129, 7c.

19. Curiously enough, *vāc* here is not the first product of all as one might expect, its cause being *tejas* which is the first of the "colours" or "aspects" that constitute the self-creating *sat*, but the third, after *prāṇa* from water, and *manas* from food; yet, other texts like Śat. Br. 10, 6, 5, 5 *so 'kāmayata—dvitīyo ma ātmā jāyeteti, sa manasā vācaṃ mithunaṃ samabhavad*—where *manas* "desire" reminds us of *manas* RV. 10, 129, 4b—warn us that the relation of *vāc* also as progenitrix with *manas* is very intimate.

20. Cf. ŚBr. 5, 1, 5, 6; Viśvakarman identified with Prajāpati ŚBr. 8, 2, 1, 10; 8, 2, 3, 13.

21. "Prajāpati verily was here; his partner was Vāc; he copulated with her and impregnated her; thereupon she separated from him and bore these creatures; then again she united with Prajāpati".

22. Interesting is what Neumann, *Ursprungsgeschichte des Bewusstseins*

(Zürich 1949), p. 39 has to say about the creative power of all that goes out of the body.

23. Carl Anders Scharbau, *Die Idee der Schöpfung in der Vedischen Literatur* (Stuttgart 1932), p. 127.

24. Identifications are numerous, and it is tempting to explain BhG. 14, 3-4 in this context: *mama yonir mahad brahma tasmin garbhaṃ dadhāmy aham/ saṃbhavaḥ sarvabhūtānāṃ tato bhavati bhārata // sarvayoniṣu kaunteya mūrtayaḥ saṃbhavanti yāḥ / tāsāṃ brahma mahad yonir ahaṃ bījapradaḥ pitā //* "I use the great *brahman* as the womb in which I beget an embryo: therefrom proceeds the origination of all beings: all bodies that originate in all wombs have in the great brahman their womb and in me their impregnating father:" evidently God is here conceived still as *prajāpati*, and his female counterpart is *brahman*~*vāc*. Even BrS. 1, 1, 1-3 may be reminiscent *athāto brahmajijñāsā, janmādy asya yataḥ, śāstrayonitvāt* "therefore now the exegesis of the *brahman*, from which this (world) has its birth etc., because it has its womb (origin) in *śāstra*," where *śāstra* would be *brahman* as primarily the (pro-) creative, revelatory and sacral Word dealing with its content the *brahman*, cause and foundation of the Universe.

3

THE ŚUBHĀŚRAYA PRAKARAṆA (VIṢṆU PURĀṆA 6, 7) AND THE MEANING OF *BHĀVANĀ*

I

AN exegetical passage in Rāmānuja's *Śrībhāṣya* ad *Vedānta Sūtras* (1, 1, 1), so far unsatisfactorily explained, proves, on further investigation, to give rise to a number of interesting questions which it may be worthwhile to discuss here. The passage[1] is entirely devoted to the elucidation of the term *praty-astamita-bheda*, occurring in *Viṣṇu Purāṇa* (6, 7, 53) which was quoted before[2] by the advaitin *pūrvapakṣin* in support of his thesis that *śruti* and *smṛti* deny the existence of difference or diversity (bheda) in the universe. As it is very unlikely that a convinced advaitin would ever quote the *Viṣṇu Purāṇa* as an authority to be reckoned with[3], Rāmānuja must have had a reason of his own to include this quotation in the 'Objection' and consequently in the 'Refutation'. This reason will be found in the apparent 'monistic' flavour of this śloka, which moreover occurs in a context that must have enjoyed a certain amount of popularity in Vaiṣṇavitc circles, if only [4] because of the detailed anthropomorphous description of the God Viṣṇu in the immediate sequel.[4] His attempts to introduce this purāṇa as an authoritative text corroborating the tenets of Viśiṣṭādvaita particularly in their application to religious life,[5] made it necessary for Rāmānuja to explain any seemingly incompatible portions satisfactorily. The discussed śloka[6] reads:

प्रत्यस्तमितभेदं यत् सत्तामात्रमगोचरम् ।
वचसामात्मसंवेद्यं तज्ज्ञानं ब्रह्मसंज्ञितम् ॥

"It is that pure being, in which all differentiations have disappeared, inexpressible by language and knowable only to the soul, that is the knowledge called Brahman." It is evident that a 'satisfactory' explanation of this śloka necessitated a consistent interpretation of the whole context—for which, indeed, a serious need might have been felt, for this context, however clear generally, is rather obscure in details.

Viṣṇu Purāṇa (6, 7), after an introductory survey of dharma, leads up to a discussion of yoga, which again seems to serve only to introduce the description of the manner and form in which *Viṣṇu* should be contemplated. Starting from 6, 7, 27, a first distinction is made between a *yogayuj 'débutant* in yoga' and a completely concentrated yogin (viniṣpanna-samādhi); then the mediate members of yoga (yama, niyama, [5] āsana, prāṇāyāma and pratyāhāra) are enumerated quickly and succinctly—so succinctly indeed that the marked characteristics of this *Tantric variant* of yoga remain in the dark. That this passage is inspired by Tantra, more precisely the Pāñcarātra Tantra, seems to me to be beyond question. Compare, for instance, with *Viṣṇu Purāṇa* (6, 7, 40) प्राणायामः स विज्ञेयः सबीजोऽबीज एव च, *Ahirbudhnya Saṃhitā*[7] (32, 52 ff.) where the *mantra's* (=bīja-s) are described which accompany the stages of *prāṇāyāma*. In stanza 42:

तस्य चालम्बनवतः स्थूलरूपं......... ।
आलम्बनमनन्तस्य योगिनोऽभ्यसतः स्मृतम् ।।

(Construe: तस्य चालम्बनवतो योगिनोऽभ्यसत आलम्बनम् अनन्तस्य स्थूलरूपं स्मृतम्) *ananta* probably stands for a *mantra*[8] and *ālambana* means the 'support' which the yogin finds in that *mantra* in one of its three aspects, here its 'gross' (sthūla) one. For these aspects cf. *Ahirbudhnya Saṃhitā* (51, 9) स्थूलः सूक्ष्मः परश्चेति भावो मन्त्रे त्रिधा स्थितः and for the *sthūla* aspect cf. 51, 10, and especially 51, 11.

Having established the Pāñcarātra tenor of this portion, we may now turn to the following passages with the suspicion that there too certain Tantric elements will, or at least may, appear. The text proceeds: "When the breath is brought under control with *prāṇāyāma* and the senses with *pratyāhāra*, the yogin must put his mind (cetas) on the auspicious [6] substratum (śubhāśraya)", whereupon the question arises: what is that *śubhāśraya?* (stanzas 45-46). The next *yogāṅga* after *pratyāhāra* is, of course, *dhāraṇā* (*Yogasūtra* 3, 1), from the root *dhṛ* (with suffix) 'to have something held or supported' by, or on, an *ādhāra* 'a hold, a support', or its synonym *āśraya*. In other words: which object of the mental fixation called *dhāraṇā* is really pure? The reply is: brahman. The exact meaning of this brahman is then further explained, but in a rather paradoxical way: first, brahman is said to be twofold, then the universe is said to be threefold. Brahman has two aspects (rūpa), *mūrta* and *amūrta*, respectively minor and major;[9] whereas the universe consists in three *bhāvanās*, respectively *brahman*, *brahma-karman*, and *karman*, or rather one *bhāvanā* (or bhāva-bhāvanā, stanzas 49, 51) with these three aspects. At first this tripartition seems to be an elaboration of the dichotomy of brahman in *mūrta* and *amūrta*; *brahma-bhāva* corresponding to *amūrta*, *karma-bhāva* to *mūrta*, and *ubhaya-bhāva* to the intermediate link, the three of them constituting the entire universe. But this rarefied atmosphere of abstract conception is suddenly invaded by mythology: to *brahma-bhāva* correspond such beings as *Sanandana* (so brahma is the god Brahmā); to *karma-bhāva* correspond the creatures, god, men etc.; and to *ubhaya-bhāva* such beings as Hiraṇyagarbha, or Brahmā himself. Then again two stanzas follow, definitely advaitic in tone (stanza 52-53), to be followed again by a passage in which the mythology is resumed and utilized as supplying the material [7] for an ultimate inventory of the universe classified under three *śaktis* of a supreme personal being, Viṣṇu.

Before we can attempt to establish some order here, we must determine the meaning of *bhāvanā* and *bhāva*. The commentators on *Viṣṇu Purāṇa* (6, 7, 46 ff.)[10] take it as more or less synonymous with *dhāraṇā*. If so, *bhāva* is synonymous with *ādhāra* or *āśraya*, the object of the process called *dhāraṇā/bhāvanā*. In the loose language of a purāṇa aiming at popularizing, *bhāvanā* would also stand for *bhāva* and be simultaneously the action and its object. This explanation is not entirely satisfying: in stanza 50, *Sanandana* etc. are 'connected' with (yuta) the *bhāvanā*, which could perhaps pass; but that the *bhāvanā* should 'exist' (vidyate) in other beings is definitely odd. The subject would be the yogin; the objects of his *bhāvanā* cannot be the subjects.

In stanza 59 the three *bhāvanās* are components of Hari's embodied form, and in stanza 67 the yogin is said to pass beyond the *bhāvanās* if he bases his *citta* on the *śubhāśraya*. Finally in stanza 79 the *dhāraṇā* is the fixation on the *mūrta* form (*i.e.* the three *bhāvanās* together) of the Lord. We have, therefore, to look for another interpretation before we can arrive at the full connotation that this term had for the author.

It is tempting to connect this passage with *Ahirbudhnya Saṃ-*

hitā (51, 9) स्थूलः सूक्ष्मः परश्चेति भावो मन्त्रे त्रिधा स्थितः [8] 'there are three *bhāvas* in a *mantra*, a gross, a subtle and a transcendent one'. *Bhāva* is described in 51, 8-9:

तारको नाम यो भावः सारः सर्वगिरामयम् ।
प्रभवन्ति ह्यतः शब्दा भावं पुष्णन्ति च स्वकम् ॥

"The *tāraka i.e.* the *Oṃ* syllable, is the 'essence of denotation' of all words: it is the germ (hence *bīja*) out of which the 'denotative words' develop and to which they return; they derive their proper 'denotations' from this *bīja*". The word standing for the thing it denotes and all words for all things, it follows that the *bīja* in which they are contained, is brahman in its 'verbal' aspect: *śabda-brahman.* So it is not surprising that in itself, encompassing in its essence all its evolutions, it is similarly threefold: transcendent, subtle and gross. Here, we meet again the ancient upaniṣadic speculations about *Vāc* in the Sāṃkhyan guise.[11]

Bhāva, provisorily rendered by 'denotation', is at once the fundamental sense residing in the word, not modified by subject and object, as well as the word's bearing on this sense. On the other hand it carries such ontological notions as 'being' and 'becoming'. The sharp distinction that we instantly make between 'ontology' and 'linguistics' was not so self-evident to the ancient Indians, used to synthetize rather than analyse and assuming word and 'denoted entity' to form an indiscernible unity, for whom glottogony coincided with cosmogony.

On the strength of these general considerations, occasioned by the definite connexion we established between part of the same context and certain concepts and practices described [9] in the *Ahirbudhnya Saṃhitā*, we are justified to explain other parts of this context tentatively in the terms of a consistent correspondence so long as we have no other means to explain them independently.

The *Ahirbudhnya Saṃhitā* (51, 10) explains what these three 'phases' of *bhāva* are:

स्थूलः संसर्गजो योऽर्थः सूक्ष्मः पदविभावितः ।
अप्रमेयादिभिर्भावैरक्षरार्थः परः स्मृतः ॥

"The gross phase is the denoted thing in relation with the word; the subtle phase of *bhāva* is manifested[12] in the word as such; the transcendent phase is that of the *Oṃ* as the indestructible principle, beyond the [subtle] *bhāvas* which are already metempirical etc.[13] In other words: even as the universe lies articulated as a mere presence in the Supreme Being during *pralaya*, is differentiated as potentiality in the subtle phase in which it is cause, and is completely articulated in actuality in the phenomenal world of *cit* in conjoint creation with *acit*, in which it is effect, so the *mantra* is dissolved in its indestructible essence *Oṃ* which is eternal, enters on potentiality by becoming word, and actualizes itself completely by being denotative (cf. *Ahirbudhnya Saṃhitā* 51, 11-13).

When we see our *Viṣṇu Purāṇa* context in this perspective, we see more clearly in what sphere the connotation of *bhāvanā* lies. It is that potency that gives rise to *bhāva* in the above wide sense; it is the efficient force creatively operating in the universe and manifesting itself in three orders of **[10]** being (bhāva) which, on the 'material' plane, are classes of beings hierarchically ordered in the process of creation, and on the 'verbal' plane more or less[14] corresponding evolutionary phases of transcendent denotative potency latent in the primeval Word, which manifests itself in a second phase as definite potentiality and in a third phase as complete 'actualities' (padārthas). As *bhāva* is the internal object of *bhāvanā*, *bhāva-bhāvanā* and *bhāvanā* may be considered synonymous.

Though so far we may have been justified in trying to establish the meanings of *bhāva/bhāvanā*[15] by adducing illustrative material from the *Ahirbudhnya Saṃhitā* we are, in my opinion, not entitled to go further and identify the three *bhāvas* of the *Viṣṇu Purāṇa* with the three *bhāvas* of the *Ahirbudhnya Saṃhitā*. We may be intrigued by the analogy between '*para—sūkṣma—sthūla*', and '*brahma-karman—brahman—karman*', and by the analogous evolutionary process of which they mark the principal moments: '*śuddha-sṛṣṭi—śuddhāśuddha-sṛṣṭi—aśuddha-sṛṣṭi*',[16] and 'Brahmā the Creator—Sanandana, etc., as mediators of creation—gods, men, etc., as the creatures'. We may point out that *sthūlaṃ rūpam* again **[11]** occurs in stanza 55 and *para* throughout. Yet, no more than an analogy can be recognized here. Besides, the fact that, in stanza 56, Vāsudeva is put on an equal with Hiraṇyagarbha and the gods,[17] while in systematized Pāñcarātra he is the Supreme Being, tells against pressing the analogy too much.

The three *bhāvanās* constitute the *mūrta* aspect of god; the *amūrta* is described in stanza 52-53, the *mūrta* in stanza 54-59.

Immediately afterwards it is declared that the entire universe with its *śaktis* is of Viṣṇu. These *śaktis* are three: *parā*, *aparā* (or kṣetrajña) and *tṛtīyā* (or karman or avidyā). It would seem that here another Tantric triad is hinted at: Lakṣmī as Viṣṇu's transcendent *śakti*,[18] *bhūti-śakti* and *kriyā-śakti*. This triad and the *bhāvanā-traya* do not tally entirely, for Hiraṇyagarbha of the *ubhaya-bhāva* (stanza 51) is, in stanza 67, of the *kṣetrajña-śakti*. Then it should be noted that in stanza 69 without any transition we are referred back to stanza 47 and the author after his digression returns to the point: on what should the *yogayuj* and the complete yogin concentrate? The yogin on the *amūrta*, the *yogayuj* on the *mūrta*, to purify his soul. Then there is some more confusion: in stanzas 75-79 there is no question further of *amūrta*, but only of the *mūrta*, which at last is defined as the *śubhāśraya*; yet, according to stanza 76 this *mūrta* is beyond the three *bhāvanās* by which this *mūrta* is constituted according to stanza 59. But since then the theory of the *śaktis* intervened; so we are to understand **[12]** that, since all beings connected with the three *bhāvanās* are embodied beings, *i.e.* subject to *karman*, whereas the universe is God's plaything and no result of *karman* (stanza 71-72) so that God himself is beyond *karman*, it follows that God's body—the universe—is also beyond *karman* in as far as it is God's body.

Concluding we can say this much: in this *prakaraṇa* two different conceptions, both possibly or probably to be traced to an early form of Pāñcarātra, have been wedded. On the one hand the conception of a 'material' universe in which a certain efficient force is operating, manifesting itself in three orders to beings hierarchically placed on the scale of evolution; on the other hand the conception of three *śaktis* of which one seems transcendent and the other two operate in the two orders of soul and matter. Besides, there is the dichotomy, suggestive of early Vedānta, between *mūrta* and *amūrta*, the former of which comprises the *bhāvanā-traya*. Finally the three *śaktis* are contained in an essentially personal Supreme Being—in its *mūrta* aspect—which constitutes the *śubhāśraya*.

II

At this point we may compare the interpretation which Rāmānuja puts on this *prakaraṇa.* In all three of his major works (*Vedārtha-saṃgraha, Śrībhāṣya* and *Gītā-bhāṣya*) he refers to the *bhāvanā-traya*, always in this connexion: that Brahmā etc. are subject to *karman* (bhāvanā-trayānvayād) 'because they are associated with, or included among, the three *bhāvanās*'.

In *Vedārtha-saṃgraha* (Paṇḍit ed., pp. 189-190):

तदेतद्ब्रह्मादीनां[19] भावनात्रयान्वयेन कर्मवश्यत्वम् ।

[13] Rāmānuja refers to our *Viṣṇu Purāṇa* text. He is less casual in his *Gītā-bhāṣya* 10, 3:

तथा भावनात्रयान्तर्गतत्वात् । 'यो ब्रह्माणं विदधाति' इति श्रुतेः ।
तथान्येऽपि केचिदणिमाद्यैश्वर्यं प्राप्ताः[20] ।

Veṅkaṭanātha, commenting on this passage, borrows all his ideas from Rāmānuja himself who, in *Śrībhāṣya* (1, 1, 1), devotes a few pages to the entire *śubhāśraya-prakaraṇa.* After my analysis above compare Rāmānuja's synthesis.

His interpretation is briefly as follows:

Brahman (= Viṣṇu) has two forms or aspects (rūpa), *mūrta* and *amūrta. Mūrta*, called *para*, is identical with the *parā śakti*; *amūrta*, called *apara*, with the *aparā śakti*. The *amūrta* is the *ātma-svarūpa*,[21] *i.e.* the individual *ātman* in its essential nature, '*disjoined*' from *prakṛti*. The *mūrta* is the *kṣetrajña i.e.* the ātman 'conjoined' with *prakṛti*. The *kṣetrajña* as such implies the third *śakti*, the one called *karman* or ignorance. So the latter two *śaktis*, *kṣetrajña* and *prakṛti*, constitute together the *amūrta rūpa*. Brahman (= Viṣṇu) has these two *rūpas*, because ultimately he is the immanent ātman (antarātman) and Inner Ruler (antaryāmin) of ātman and *prakṛti*. The three *śaktis*, since they coincide with the two *rūpas*, are therefore founded on him; being their foundation, he is the *śubhāśraya*. He is this *śubhāśraya* in his embodied form, that is, as the one whose body is constituted by the universe. This embodied form or *mūrtaṃ rūpam* is not the above *mūrta* (= kṣetrajña + prakṛti) but an entirely different one: the form exclusively proper to God. The [14] *bhāvanā-traya* is reduced to not more than an indication of *kṣetrajña;* all three fall under the second *śakti* or *kṣetrajña*.

To add up: 1. two *rūpas* a. *mūrtam* b. *amūrtam* 2. three *śaktis* = two *rūpas*, the latter two coinciding with the *mūrta* 3. three *bhāvanās*, all coinciding with the *kṣetrajña* or second *śakti* 4. one *mūrtam rūpam of* Viṣṇu alone.

I add a translation of this passage, because Thibaut's rendering is not always complete and correct.

In the above text (*Viṣṇu Purāṇa*) the term *pratyastamita-bheda* asserts that the essential nature of the individual ātman, even when it is conjoined with a particular development of *prakṛti* into a body—god, man etc.—remains 'beyond language'[22] (*viz.* because it is free from the differences of the body, for language describes by the differences of body), 'knowable only unto itself'[23] 'definable only as being' (*i.e.* as being and knowledge)[24] and beyond the ken of the mind of a *yogayuj.*[25] The term does not negate the real existence of the phenomenal world.

—But how do we know that?

—In the *prakaraṇa* under discussion it is declared that yoga is the only remedy for the *saṃsāra.*[26] After having enumerated the stages of yoga up to the withdrawal of the senses,[27][15] the text then proceeds—in order to say what the *śubhāśraya* is so as to make the *dhāraṇā* succeed—to state that the Supreme Brahman Viṣṇu has two aspects, to be denoted by the word *śakti,* which are distinguished as *mūrta* and *amūrta.* Then the text propounds that the *kṣetrajña,* which is 'enveloped by a third *śakti,* ignorance called *karman*'[28] (*i.e.* which is differentiated by *acit*)[29] is distinguished as *mūrta* and is not *śubha* because it falls under three *bhāvanās.*[30] Then it denies that the second aspect[31] or *amūrta,* which is separated from *acit* and thus free from 'the ignorance called *karman*' (that means: having only the form of knowledge) and which is [16] distinguished as *amūrta*[32] would then be the *śubhāśraya*; the reasons for this denial are that this *amūrta* is the accomplished yogin's object of meditation[33] and is not to be resorted to by the *yogayuj*[34] and that it is not pure in itself.[35]

So there are 1. the *amūrtaṃ rūpam,* which has the form of the supreme *śakti*; 2. the *mūrtaṃ rūpam,* which has the form of the second *śakti* called *kṣetrajña*; 3. the third *śakti,* which is the reason that the ātman (which is the supreme *śakti* by itself) takes on the nature of *kṣetrajña.*[36] So, that form of the Lord which is the substratum of all these three *śaktis* is the *śubhāśraya*;[37] and that is an embodied form exclusively proper[38] to Himself, as established by Vedānta texts such as *āditya-varṇam.*[39]

To conclude, in our *prakaraṇa* the text *praty-astamitabhedaṃ yat* serves the purpose of asserting that the completely purified essential nature of the individual ātman cannot be the *śubhāśraya.*

Follow quotations from *Viṣṇu Purāṇa*[40] and *Viṣṇu-dharmottara Purāṇa*.[41]

[17] We note in this remarkable piece of exegesis that Rāmānuja, by identifying the *amūrtaṃ rūpam* (which according to stanza 53 is unequivocally called 'brahman') with the essence of the individual ātman,[42] arrives at a consistent interpretation. All the rest follows. Incidentally this enables him to distinguish the *mūrtaṃ rūpam* of God from the *mūrtaṃ rūpam* of the *kṣetrajña*. That this *mūrtaṃ rūpam* is exclusively proper to God, Rāmānuja no doubt concludes from stanza 70 रूपमन्यद्धरेर्महत् where *anyat* is taken absolutely, 'different from anything else'. Unfortunately Rāmānuja omits to explain the striking contradiction between this stanza and stanza 54. In stanza 54 विष्णोः परं रूपमरूपम्, the *amūrta* of stanzas 52-53 (= ātman, according to Rāmānuja), is stated to be *viśva-rūpa-vairūpya-lakṣaṇaṃ* 'defined as the variety of forms of him whose forms are infinite': the same is said of the *mūrtaṃ rūpam* in stanza 70. But probably Rāmānuja would take *vairūpya* in stanza 54 to mean 'formlessness'.

However attractive Rāmānuja's distinction between the two *mūrtas* be, it cannot be maintained. On the other hand it is clear that the author of the *Viṣṇu Purāṇa* is himself searching for a reinterpretation of the *mūrta* of the beginning of this *prakaraṇa*. Via the introduction of the *śaktis* (which he must have felt to stand in some relation to both the *rūpas* and the three *bhāvanās*) he arrives at *mūrta* as Viṣṇu's supernal and universal body, after which he forgets all about the *amūrta*. But he has left some traces of the stages of his progress to synthesis, a synthesis which was finished by Rāmānuja.

[18] But it remains dark in which sense Rāmānuja takes *bhāvanā*. Though we have no other evidence than the casual mention of *bhāvanā-traya*, as proof of Brahmā's subjection to *karman*, we may venture a guess, based on the very occurrence of the term in Rāmānuja's commentary on *Bhagavad-gītā* 10, 3. There is nothing in this śloka which occasions the mention of *bhāvanā-traya*. But I have found time and again that Rāmānuja never elaborates more than it is quite necessary. Now we find in *Bhagavad-gītā* 10, 5 *bhāva* 'mental disposition', general term covering the various qualities summed up in stanzas 4 and 5. Rāmānuja defines this *bhāva* as *mano-vṛtti* (specified *pravṛtti-nivṛtti-hetu* to suit the context) 'function of the mind'. If we may assume that Rāmā-

nuja anticipated this *bhāva*[43] by introducing the term *bhāvanā-traya* in his comment on 10, 3 we could establish for *bhāvanā* the meaning of 'that which occasions a *bhāva* or *mano-vṛtti*' which, when seen against the background of the *Viṣṇu Purāṇa* context, may stand for 'category (Brahmā etc.; Sanandana etc.; creatures), constituent of the universe, as object of the reflective mind'.

However this may be, in another passage of the *Gītā-bhāṣya* we find an indication of the way in which Rāmānuja regarded the *dhāraṇā* of *Viṣṇu Purāṇa* 6, 7, *viz.* in his *Bhāṣya* on *Bhagavad-gītā* (2, 61/64/68). There the *jñāna-niṣṭhā* is under discussion: Rāmānuja connects 2, 61 with *Viṣṇu Purāṇa* 6, 7 and interprets *matparaḥ* as चेतसः शुभाश्रयभूते मयि मनोऽवस्थाप्य and quotes *Viṣṇu Purāṇa* (6, 7, 72-73); [19] the same connexion is pointed out *ad* 2, 64 and 68. From Rāmānuja's comments on these three stanzas it is evident that he regards the *dhāraṇā* on the *śubhāśraya*, not as yogic concentration on God himself preparatory to full realization of His glory (this is only possible through *bhakti-yoga*) but as a preparatory stage of the process leading to the realization of the individual ātman, which itself is again propædeutic to the ultimate attainment of God in *bhakti*.

NOTES

1. Edition Abhyankar (Bombay 1914), pp. 69 ff; further references are to this edition.
2. *ibid.*, p. 14.
3. Dr. V. Raghavan directs my attention, however, to Śaṅkara, *Brahma-sūtra-bhāṣya* 1, 3, 30 where *Viṣṇu Purāṇa* 1, 5, 59-60 is quoted; meanwhile it is not impossible that Rāmānuja had in mind *Brahma-siddhi*, p. 26, line 15: *praty-astamita-sakala-viśeṣaṃ tattvam* etc., Rāmānuja was demonstrably familiar with Maṇḍana's theories.
4. *Viṣṇu Purāṇa* (6, 7, 80 ff.), which, incidentally, served as the model for Rāmānuja's evocation (*Vedārtha-saṃgraha*, Paṇḍit edition (Kāśī, 1894), pp. 244 ff).
5. I shall elaborate on this and allied questions in a forthcoming study of the *Vedārtha-saṃgraha;* suffice it here to refer to *Vedārtha-saṃgraha*, p. 179.
6. Which, in the devotional Gītā Press edition (Gorakhpur 2009/1953), is significantly underlined as particularly edifying.
7. The *Ahirbudhnya Saṃhitā*, ed. by F. O. Schrader (Adyar, 1916).
8. Possibly the Sudarśana-mahā-mantra, cf. *Ahirbudhnya Saṃhitā*, 17, [1] ध्यायिनां सुखदं नित्यं सुदर्शनाख्यम् ।
9. *Apara* and *para;* these terms return to qualitfy the first two *śaktis* in

6, 7, 61—this double form ascribed to Brahman is no doubt taken from such passages as *Bṛhad Āraṇyaka Upaniṣad* (2, 3, 1):

द्वे वाव ब्रह्मणो रूपे मूर्तं चैवामूर्तं च ।

10. Wilson, *Viṣṇu Purāṇa*, V. (London 1870) renders *bhāvanā* by 'apprehension of spirit' and quotes the commentaries: "The term is *bhāvanā*, defined as a 'function to be engendered by knowledge' *jñāna-janyaḥ saṃskāraḥ* (Ratnagarbha). . . it is also termed *bhāva-bhāvanā* 'apprehension of the being, the existence, or substantiality of the object, the thing contemplated', भाव-भावना—भावो वस्तु तद्विषया भावना (Śrīdhara)."

11. For particulars see Maryla Falk, *Nāma-rūpa and Dharma-rūpa* (Calcutta 1943).

12. Note in *vibhāvita* the causative form, and cf. *bhāvanā*.

13. I make *bhāvaiḥ* refer to the subtle 'meanings' which are already beyond the ken of the intellect; the transcendent *bhāva* is necessarily single.

14. 'More or less' because both triads do not tally completely, though they would seem analogous; see further on.

15. But without exhausting its full connotation: there are *karma-mīmāṃsā* associations as well, particularly in the use of *bodha* and *adhikāra* which remain obscure but suggest, in connexion with such notions as *karman, bhāva, bhāvanā* that the *karma-mīmāṃsā* also contributed some ideas to these syncretistic conceptions: hardly surprising since ritualism prevails in Tantra. On *bhāvanā* in *karma-mīmāṃsā*, see V. A. Ramasvami Sastri's paper, *The Mīmāṃsaka conception of bhāvanā* (*Vāk*, no. 1).

16. I refer to F. O. Schrader, *Introduction to Pāñcarātra* (Adyar 1916); cf. also *śuddha* stanza 75—and *aśuddha*—stanza 77.

17. It is however remarkable that Sudarśana's *Tātparya-dīpikā* ad *Vedārtha saṃgraha* (pp. 188-189) quotes this stanza with a significant variant: हिरण्यगर्भो भगवान् वासवोऽथ प्रजापतिः where *Viṣṇu Purāṇa* (Gītā Press) reads *vāsudevaḥ prajāpatiḥ*. Vāsudeva is at any rate quite unexpected here.

18. In passing we may note that the relation between Viṣṇu and his transcendent *śakti* Lakṣmī is described as that between *bhavat* and *bhāva*, Schrader, *o. c.* p. 30.

19. So rather than as suggested in my *Rāmānuja on the Bhagavad-gītā* (the Hague 1953), note 415.

20. These *anye* according to Veṅkaṭanātha, refer to the class Sanandana, etc.

21. See notes 29 and 32.

22. *agocaram/vacasāṃ* (*Viṣṇu Purāṇa*, 6, 7, 53).

23. *ātma-saṃvedyam—Viṣṇu Purāṇa*=Rāmānuja—*sva-saṃvedyam*, for brahman is here ātman; for this equation cf. note 42.

24. *jñāna-sattā* in *jñāna-sattaikalakṣaṇam* taken as *dvandva* explaining *Sattāmātram. . .taj jñānaṃ* (*Viṣṇu Purāṇa*, 6, 7, 53) cf. also *Vedārtha-saṃgraha* (Paṇḍit ed.) p. 10. which the commentator correctly compares with this *Viṣṇu Purāṇa śloka*.

25. न तद्योगयुजा शक्यं चिन्तयितुम् (*Viṣṇu Purāṇa* 6, 7, 55).

26. क्लेशानां च क्षयकरं योगादन्यन्न विद्यते (*Viṣṇu Purāṇa*, 6, 25).

27. *Viṣṇu Purāṇa* 6, 7, 27-45.

28. *Viṣṇu Purāṇa* 6, 7, 61-62.

29. *Acit* 'non-spiritual, material component of the universe, sum-total of the evolutions of *prakṛti*', conjoined with which the spiritual component (*cit*, sum-total of individual *ātmans*) becomes *kṣetrajña* or *bhoktṛ*. I prefer the rendering 'spiritual' to Thibaut's and Srinivasachari's usual 'sentient' because strictly speaking sentiency is of *prakṛti*.

30. Thibaut omits this clause; O. Lacombe (*La doctrine morale et métaphysique de Rāmānuja*=annotated translation of *Śrībhāṣya* 1, 1, 1) renders (following Raṅgāchārya and Varadarāja Aiyaṅgār's note 100 in *Śrībhāṣya* translated, vol. I (Madras 1899?) *bhāvanā-trayānvayād:* "à peine de tomber nécessairement dans l'une de trois (fausses) conceptions" and annotates (Note 586) "d'après le *Viṣṇu Purāṇa* (VI, vii) ces trois fausses conceptions semblent être 1. que l'âme individuelle se confond avec le Brahman; 2. qu'elle n'a pas à rechercher de fin transcendant au fruit de ses actes; 3. que par la seule voie de l'acte elle arrive à se confonde avec le Brahman"; but I fail to see how the Indian and French translators arrive at this description. Meanwhile my own notes on *bhāvanā, Rāmānuja on the Bhagavad gītā* (p. 122, n. 415), in which I rendered *bhāvanā* 'category to be reflected upon', following the commentary on *Viṣṇu Purāṇa* (supra, note 1, p. 6) should also be modified.

31. *dvitīyam*, from *Viṣṇu Purāṇa*, 6, 7, 69.

32. That is *ātma-svarūpa*—'the individual ātman in its essential form'.

33. *Viṣṇu Purāṇa* 6, 7, 69.

34. *Viṣṇu Purāṇa* 6, 7, 55.

35. Taken from *Viṣṇu-dharmottara Purāṇa* quoted below (cf. n. 41).

36. तथा तिरोहितत्वाच्च शक्तिः क्षेत्रज्ञसंज्ञिता (*Viṣṇu Purāṇa*) 6, 7, 33.

37. *Viṣṇu Purāṇa* 6, 7, 70.

38. See below.

39. *Śvetāśvatara Upaniṣad* 3, 8.

40. Respectively 6, 7, 55; 69 ab (correct the locus, in Abhyankar p. 70 and Lacombe; Note 589, accordingly); 69 cd; 70 ab. Note the significant *varia lectio* 'paraṃ padaṃ' for the expletive *mahāmate* in Gītā Press edition; on *paraṃ* (*paramaṃ*) *padaṃ* see Rāmānuja's detailed discussion, *Vedārtha saṃgraha* p. 225 ff.

41. *Viṣṇu-dharmottara Purāṇa* 104, 23-26, according to Raṅgāchārya and Varadarāja Aiyangār.

42. I may refer to my *Rāmānuja on the Bhagavad-gītā*, pp. 34-35, where the equation brahman=ātman in the *Gītā-bhāṣya* is discussed.

43. Which, of course, is not identical with the *bhāva* of *Viṣṇu Purāṇa:* it would be the object of the *manovṛtti*. The connexion suggested here would be associative rather than logical, but association plays an important part in commentarial literature.

4

ON ATHARVAVEDA 10, 8, 43*b*

puṇḍárīkaṃ návadvāraṃ tribhír guṇébhir ā́vṛtam /
tásmin yád yakṣám ātmanvát tád vaí brahmavído viduḥ //

The interpretation of *b* has long been a bone of contention. It is agreed on all hands that the "lotus of nine doors" represents the human, i.e. male, body with the nine orifices, here especially of the cosmic Person. "Lotus" is a favourite mysterious name for the body of the Puruṣa (BĀUp. 2, 3, 6: *tasya haitasya puruṣasya rūpam..yathā puṇḍarīkam;* ChUp. 8, 1, 1 *atha yad idam asmin brahmapure daharaṃ puṇḍarīkaṃ veśma* etc.), associated with the sun (cf. ChUp. 3, 1, 1 *asau vā āditya devamadhu* etc.), as well as with water (cf. our hymn AthV. 10, 8, 34, and lotus is a water-flower), and lies no doubt at the root of the popular conception of Brahmā's origination in the lotus on the navel of Viṣṇu (cf. MBh. 12, Cr. Ed. 175, 15 *tatas* tejomayaṃ divyaṃ padmaṃ *sṛṣṭam svayaṃbhuvā* etc.). So far there is no difficulty. Meanwhile we note that both terms *puṇḍarīka* and *navadvāra* are used metaphorically.

The crux is the meaning of *guṇa.* Garbe in his edition of Sāṃkhyatattvakaumudī,[1] records previous explications and gives one of his own: "mit drei Schnüren (d.i.dreifach) umhüllt," this triple covering referring to skin, nails and hair. Keith, *Sāṃkhya System,* p. 19, follows Garbe. Ultimately both follow Boethlingk-Roth, s.v. *guṇa,* who explain *tribhir guṇebhir* as *triguṇa,* a rare usage of guṇa outside the numerical compound that is well attested, and render the clause "dreifach verhüllt". Whitney-Lanman[2] explain that 'the three guṇas' [rendered "strands" in translation] are probably the three temperaments familiar under that name later; reference is to the three *doṣas* or humours, *vāta, pitta* and *kapha.* Both Garbe's and Whitney-Lanman's translations give a purely physiological explanation, to which *navadvāra* may have led them. Prosaic explanations usually sound sensible; but the fact remains that their interpretations are wholly conjectural and in fact far-fetched. Besides, there is not really anything in the stanza or the hymn that favours physiology, not even *navadvāra*: the nine doors represent the organs and functions and objects of hearing, seeing, smelling, speaking, [78] and eating, impregnating and secreting, which all have a virtually metaphysical import in this age of thought.

Others are prepared to accept the three *guṇas* as "universal constituents" in a sense akin to that of Sāṃkhya etc. Within the entire cosmological context this interpretation is certainly more plausible, although the exact connotation of *guṇa* here will be difficult to establish. The best case has been presented by Senart,[3] whose remarks on *tantu/sūtra/guṇa* are persuasive. His interpretation of *āvṛtam*,[4] however, is less convincing. He compares AthV. 10, 2, 31-32, where it is said that "within the town of the gods with nine gates there is a golden divine flower-cup surrounded by light; this cup has three spokes on which it is thrice firmly established". (. . *návadvārā devā́nāṃ pū́r. . tásyāṃ hiraṇyáyaḥ kóśaḥ svargó jyótiṣā́vṛtaḥ // tásmin hiraṇyáye kóśe tryàre trípratiṣṭhite/ tásmin yád yakṣám ātmanvát* etc., as in 10, 8, 43; note again ChUp. 8, 1, 1. .*daharaṃ puṇḍarīkam veśma, daharo 'sminn antarākāśa*, which inspired Mahānār Up. 10, 7; 11,7). The comparison is indeed apt, but does not explain why in 10, 8, 43 the *puṇḍarīka* is covered by *guṇas*, which is different from being surrounded by light or firmly fixed on three spokes.

I may quote another parallel from a Mokṣadharma text, which, I think, hails from the same milieu of thinkers as our AthV. passages; 12,210 reads

uṣṇīṣavān yathā vastrair tribhir bhavati saṃvṛtaḥ /
saṃvṛto 'yaṃ tathā dehī sattvarājasatāmasair //12//

The next line declares that these *guṇas*, styled *hetu* "cause, starting-point", surround the tetrad:

tasmāc catuṣṭayaṃ vedyam etair hetubhir āvṛtam.

This tetrad cannot be identified with the four conditions, waking, dreaming, dreamless sleep and *turīya*, of the MāṇḍUp. 2-7, which is at the basis of Nīlakaṇṭha's interpretation (ad ib., 1, with advaitic variants[5]) followed by Deussen-Strauss.[6] For one thing, the *turīya* at least is definitely beyond the *guṇas*. We may connect[7] the epical *catuṣṭaya* with the *catuṣ*-[79] *pād* of our hymn (10, 8, 21) in the creation myth where the Person, originally without quarters, becomes *catuṣpād* "having four quarters", when he has created the bright sky; the meaning of *catuṣṭaya* is apparently "four components of the universe", earth, atmosphere, sea and sky (ChUp. 4, 6, 3), or the four quarters of the sky (ChUp. 4, 5, 2; cf. also 4, 7, 3; 4, 8, 3; 3, 18, 2 has *vāk/agni*; *prāṇa/vāyu*; *cakṣuḥ/āditya*; *śrotra/ diśaḥ*), etc. *Catuṣṭaya* in these senses would be strictly subject to *guṇas*.

There are other reminiscences and correspondences in a series of comparisons: the three-spoked *kośa*, in the eight-wheeled town of the gods (AthV. 10, 2, 31 and 10, 8, 43):

> *etāvad etadvijñānam etad asti ca nāsti ca* /
> *tṛṣṇābaddhaṃ jagat sarvaṃ cakravat parivartate* //32//

both the lotus and the *tantu*:

> *bisatantur yathaivāyam antasthaḥ sarvato bise* /
> *tṛṣṇātantur anādyantas tathā dehagataḥ sadā* //33//

the *sūtra* on which in AthV. 10, 8, 37[8] all is strung:

> *sūcyā sūtraṃ yathā vastre saṃsārayati vāyakaḥ* /
> *tadvat saṃsārasūtraṃ hi tṛṣṇāsūcyā nibaddhyate* //34//

It is clear that old metaphors and images are here reinterpreted in the terms of the more recent conception of *tṛṣṇā*.

We should not forget that originally *guṇa* as a universal component or constituent was also a metaphor: "strand", three of which are required to twine a rope, or plait a tress. The three-piece turban may quite plausibly also have been an ancient comparison for the *guṇas*: threads and cloth will remain associated with the *guṇas* throughout the philosophical literature, especially threads and clothes of different colours, which are rudiments of the three *rūpas* of ChUp. 6, 4 and SvetUp. 4, 5.[9] I think we have good reason to believe that the three pieces tied into one turban were also of different colours. As is well-known, the [80] turban is a wrapping of one long piece (up to six yards) of cloth. On inquiry I found that in certain parts of India, esp. Gujarāt, three pieces of cloth are occasionally tied into one turban, always three and always of different colours, called *pāghḍī* in Surat.[10] Does the epic author refer to some such fashion of turban? Another[11] interpretation is possible: a man with a turban is wrapped in three cloths: turban-cloth, upper-cloth and under-cloth. In any case, the comparison may well point to a natural explanation of *tribhir guṇebhir āvṛtam*: the Puruṣa's cosmic body, likened to a lotus, with its nine orifices, likened to doors, is wrapped in its components, as if wrapped in a three-piece turban, or a three-piece dress. We have a delightful vision of the three *guṇas* tied into a gaudy turban on the head of the cosmic Puruṣa. But this after all is the kind of naturalistic imagery in which the ancient thinkers and poets themselves delighted.

NOTES

1. Abh. Bayer. Ak. Wiss. XIX, p. 529.
2. *Atharva-Veda Saṃhitā*, II, p. 601.
3. *Rajas et la théorie indienne des trois guṇas*, J. As. 1915, p. 151 ff.
4. *āvṛtam* was Keith's main difficulty: "if the reference is to be taken as to the constituents in the sense of the Guṇas of the Sāṃkhya philosophy, is is clear that the expression is inaccurate, since the three constituents make up nature, and the passage would say that the body was covered with nature, instead of consisting of nature," *Sāṃkhya System*, p. 19.
5. *catuṣṭayaṃ pūrvoktaṃ dṛṣṭāntabhūtaṃ svapnasuṣuptyākhyaṃ dvayaṃ dārṣṭāntikaṃ ca saguṇanirguṇabrahmabhāvākhyaṃ dvayam iti catuṣṭayam*, (Poona ed.)
6. *Vier philosophische Texte des Mahābhāratam*, (Leipsic 1906), p. 266-67.
7. As I think we must: the *catuṣpād* of AthV.10, 8, 21 should be distinguished from the four quarters (three hidden, one revealed) of RV. 1, 164, 45; 10, 90, 3-4; AthV. 2, 1, 2 (the four conditions of MāṇḍUp. 2-7, three metempirical, one empirical, are akin), and connected with the four quarters of ChUp. 3 and 4 as quoted; although in 4 each quarter is again in divided into four, it is clear from 3, 18, 2 that this is a device to account for 3 rival macrocosmic tetrads and 1 microcosmic one simultaneously. Meanwhile, to complicate matters, it would seem that the *catuṣṭaya* of MBh. 12, 210, 1 (*na sa veda paraṃ brahma yo na veda catuṣṭayam*) is different from that of st. 13 (S 12, 197, 199 and Cr. Ed. read *dharmam* for *brahma*); but the first half-śloka, 1 ab, stands completely isolated, and I take it that it is interpolated (from a marginal gloss just on *catuṣṭaya* in 13? It reads like a quotation); 1 cd is evidently a make-shift.
8. *yo vidyāt sūtraṃ vitataṃ yasminn otāḥ prajā imāḥ/sūtraṃ sūtrasya yo vidyāt sa vidyād brāhmaṇaṃ mahat.*
9. *lohita*, *śukla* and *kṛṣṇa*, corresponding resp. to the sun, the waters (i.e. rain from the clouds) and food (i.e. the wet soil in the rainy season when the sowing is done); later on the order was: white—*sattva* ("bright"); red—*rajas* (on account of its constant association with *rāga*, which forced not only the meaning of "passion" but also of "redness" on *rajas*); and black—*tamas*. The *rūpāṇi* of ChUp. 6, 4 are almost invariably explained by Indian commentators to refer, not to the guṇas, but the 5 elements. The only passage I have come across where the connexion with the guṇas is recognized is MBh. 12, 302, 46, where *rūpāṇi* shows that the author refers to ChUp., not to ŚvetUp.
10. From Dr. H. D. Sankalia of the Deccan College.
11. Deussen-Strauss prefer the three-piece turban: "gleichwie einer, der einen Turban tragt, sein Haupt mit drei Tuchstreifen umwickelt, etc".

5

NOTES ON *AKṢARA*

One of the several intriguing terms which play a not insignificant role in the period of thought before the Sāṁkhyakārikās and then fall into desuetude after this landmark has been passed is *akṣara*. In an original, but sometimes controversial study, *Akṣara; a Forgotten Chapter in the Indian Philosophy*, Modi[1] has shown the relative importance of this term in the later Upaniṣads, the Gītā and the Epic. It is not my intention here to enter upon a discussion of Modi's views but to study the term and its significance before the period at which he starts and to point out a background of associations which, in my opinion, will help us to understand the scope of the concepts later to be described by *akṣara*.

The etymology of the word *na kṣaratīti* has never been seriously questioned. An alternative etymology mentioned by Patañjali,[2] from *AŚ* with a suffixed *sara*—, has not found acceptance. Yet, it is interesting to note this derivation of the etymologically transparent term, not because it would be important in itself, but because it betrays a measure of dissatisfaction with the etymology "unflowing" of *akṣara* "syllable".

That the word started its career as an adjective, meaning "not flowing away, unperishing", seems obvious. But already in the most ancient source, the Ṛgveda, the word is used in a specialized sense exclusively associated with Vāc, and Bergaigne for one would render the word everywhere with "syllable".[3] When, however, the word occurs in later texts where no special associations with Vāc are immediately apparent, all scholars prefer to return to the "etymological sense" and translate "indestructible, eternal" and variants, thereby separating it from *akṣara* "syllable". Is this separation really justified? In other words: does the later *akṣara* not continue the older *akṣara* "syllable"?

This 'later' *akṣara* may be dated from BĀUp. 3, 8. We note, however, that this is the only occurrence in the older Upaniṣads where the [205] meaning "eternal principle" is preferred. Let us consider the other occurrences, BĀUp. 5, 2, 1; 3, 1; 5, 1; 5,3; 14, 1-3; ChUp. 1, 1, 1; 5; 6; 7; 9; 10; 3, 6-7; 4, 1; 4-5; 2, 10, 3-4; 23, 3; 8, 3, 5. In all these passages *akṣara* occurs in the sense of "syllable"; we may distinguish a more special sense, side by side with that of "any of the syllables into which a given word is analysed", namely "the syllable par excellence", the syllable *OM*. This is the same distinction as made by the author of the Gītā: *girām asmy ekam akṣaram* "I am the one syllable among all words" (10, 25), and; *akṣarāṇām akāro 'smi* "I am the A among the syllables" (10, 33).

The one *akṣara* OM is, in ChUp. 1, equated with the udgītha: *om ity etad akṣaram udgītham upāsīta/ om ity udgāyati* (1, 1, 1) "know that the udgītha is this syllable OM, (for) the udgātar sings the udgītha as OM." This equation udgītha = OM, which is repeatedly made, is of special interest; it cannot be completely explained by the fact that the udgītha begins with OM: the prastāva ends with this ubiquitous syllable; the equation with OM the udgītha is much more frequent than, e.g., with *ṛc*, though all mantras sung at the sacrifices end and almost dissolve in OM. The special identity of OM with the udgītha is, I think, better explained by the peculiar way in which certain sāmans are chanted, the so-called *aniruktagāna* "the singing of the unpronounced (syllables)". This is customary with the three pavamānasāmans which are chanted at the three soma pressings of the Agniṣṭoma: each syllable of the udgītha is substituted by the sound O. For instance the first udgītha of the bahiṣpavamānasāman, which is chanted at the prātaḥsavana, reads *pávamānāyéndave abhí devā́ṁ íya*—(RV. 9, 11, 1) or in Sāmavedic notation *pa*^{1}*va*^{2}*māna*^{3}*ye*^{1}*nda*^{2} *ve a*^{3}*bhi*^{2} *de*^{3}*va*^{1}*m iya*^{2r}—(SV. 651; 763), but is sung: OM o 2 o 2 o^{1r} o^{r} o^{r} o o 2 o o^{1} o^{r} o^{r} o o^{2}.1212. When one hears it chanted, it sounds like one long-drawn repetition of the initial OM , which it may well have been originally. I would consider it probable that the special significance of the otherwise mysterious equation udgītha = OM is to be understood from this peculiar mode of singing the udgītha at the soma pressings.

After this equation has been enlarged upon and the supremacy of the udgītha established, the speculations of this Chāndogya chapter are pushed farther and the *word* udgītha, which is of course identical with the *thing*, is analysed into its syllables *ud-gī-tha*. But we are to remember that the udgītha is really the supreme and that this analysis is therefore of the supreme as 'represented' by the udgītha. The akṣara *ut-* is equated with prāṇa (cf. also 1, 1, 5; this equation has its natural explanation in the fact that the Chandogas, much more than the Ṛgvedic and Yajurvedic priests require breath while singing), sky, sun (cf. 1, 3, 1) **[206]** and Sāmaveda; the akṣara *gī* is equated with vāc (=*gīr*), atmosphere, wind and Yajurveda; the akṣara *tha* with anna, earth, fire and Ṛgveda.

These triads are fundamental classes of creation. They inventorize creation, which is thus represented as being finally reducible to the three syllables of the word *udgītha* which is also the one syllable OM. The reduction of all things to a triadic scheme which itself is reduced again to one ultimate, from which therefore all things derive, is characteristic of the cosmogonical and cosmological speculations of this age.[4] That here these triads of akṣaras and their correspondents are ultimately resolved in the unit OM, the akṣara *par excellence*, may already be clear from the context, but it is more explicitly stated elsewhere in the same upaniṣad.ChUp. 2, 23, 3-4 reads: *prajāpatir lokān abhyatapat / tebhyo 'bhitaptebhyas trayī vidyā saṃprāsravat / tām abhyatapat / tasyā abhitaptābhyā etāny akṣarāṇi saṃprāsravan bhūr bhuvaḥ svar iti / tāny abhyatapat / tebhyo 'bhitaptebhya oṃkāraḥ saṃprāsravat / tad yathā śaṅkunā sarvāṇī parṇāni sarvā vāk saṃtṛṇṇā / oṃkāreṇa saṃtṛṇṇāny evam oṃkara evedaṃ sarvam oṃkāra evadaṃ sarvaṃ /* That which is the last to "flow out" when the worlds etc. have been brooded by the creator, is the sap or juice, *rasa* or the essence. The syllable OM is the ultimate essence of all that is, because it is the basis of all speech: here we have to understand by "speech" primarily the sacred language of the Veda which is fundamental to the sacrifice which maintains the order of the universe.

Another version of this episode is found in JaimUpBr. 1, 10,[5] where it appears as an exegetical paraphrases of RV. 1,164, 41-42, which we shall discuss later: (1) *sā pṛthaksalilaṃ kāmadughākṣiti prāṇasaṃhitaṃ cakṣuśśrotraṃ vākprabhūtaṃ manasā vyāptaṃ hṛdayāgram....sahasrākṣaram ayuta-dhāram amṛtaṃ duhānā sarvān imān lokān abhi vikṣaratīti* "she, the milch-cow of desires, yielding (as milk) the elixir of immortality in separate waves, imperishable, compounded with Breath, possessed of Sight and Hearing, abundant in Speech, pervaded by Mind, having the heart as its top, consisting of a thousand akṣaras and ten thousand streams, flows out in all directions into all these worlds."[6] Then this text **[207]** continues: (2) *tad etat satyam akṣaraṃ yad om iti / tasminn āpaḥ pratiṣṭhitā apsu pṛthivī pṛthivyām ime lokāḥ / yathā sūcyā palaśām saṃtṛṇṇāni syur evam etenākṣareṇeme lokās saṃtṛṇṇāḥ*" "this is the *satyam akṣaram*, the OM: on it the waters are founded, on the waters the earth, on the earth these worlds: just as leaves are struck on a pin,[7] so are the worlds stuck on this akṣara." It is clear that the "cow of desires yielding immortality" is no one but Vāc herself who is frequently described as a cow. A parallel is furnished by ChUp. 1, 3, 5: *dugdhe 'smai rāg dohaṃ yo vāco doho 'nnavān annādo bhavati ya etāny evaṃ vidvān udgīthākṣarāṇy upāsta udgītha iti:* "Vāc yields milk—which is the milk of Vāc herself—to him, and rich in food and eating food will be he, who knowing thus recognizes these akṣaras of the udgītha, namely *ud-gī-tha*, for what they really are."

We find in the JaimUpBr. text just quoted that the akṣara OM is equated with satyam: *tad etat satyam akṣaraṃ yad OM*, which can also be rendered: "*this akṣara, viz. OM, is the satyam*"; both this translation and the one given above amount to the same equality of satyam and the akṣaram. We find that similar things are said of both. In one text the three vyāhṛtis, *bhūḥ, bhuvaḥ* and *svaḥ*, are derivates of udgītha = OM; elsewhere the three are connected with *satyam* in a comparable manner. In BĀUp. 5, 5, 1 a creation myth starts with the Waters, which beget satyam or satyam brahman,[8] which begets Prajāpati, who begets the gods. The gods know only satyam. This satyam is syllabized into *sa-ti-yam,* the first and last syllables of which are true (*satyam*) while the middle one is untrue (*anṛtam*). The same notion is to be found in ChUp. 8, 3, 5 where of satyam, syllabized *sat-ti-yam, sat* and *yam* are said to be immortal and *ti* to be mortal: as a matter of fact, the *ti* does not exist really: satyam is just *sat-yam*. But the point is, of course, to analyze the supreme called satyam into three syllables which can support a triadic scheme: to the three syllables corresponds the triad of *bhūḥ*, *bhuvaḥ*, and *svaḥ*. Then this text adds another complication: this triad constitutes the One Puruṣa, both macrocosmically as the person in the sun and microcosmically **[208]** as the person in the eye. But this notion too refers us back to comparable speculations about the udgītha in ChUp. 1, 6, 6-7.

This connexion of the tripartite OM = akṣaram = satyam with the Puruṣa myth is certainly not an accidental result of ever more comprehensive speculations about the Supreme One. As the BĀUp. 2, 3 has it: the Name of the puruṣa is *satyasya satyam.*[9] Similarly akṣara is connected with the microcosmic person in the eye in JaimUpBr. 1, 43, 7-9.[10] How closely all these conceptions are associated is shown by the connexions of the BĀUp. passage in 5, 14. Here still another Supreme is posited, the Gāyatrī metre. This metre consists of four feet or pādas of eight syllables, which are counted to comprise respectively earth, atmosphere and sky (*bhūmiḥ, antarikṣam, diauḥ∼bhūḥ, bhuvaḥ, svaḥ*), the three Vedas (*ṛco, yajūṃṣi, sāmāni*) and three *prāṇas* (*prāṇaḥ, apānaḥ, viānaḥ*): these three triads constitute three pādas of the Gāyatrī. The fourth pāda is described as follows: *athāsyā etad eva turīyaṃ darśataṃ pādaṃ parorajā ya eṣa tapati* "its fourth beautiful foot is the one who shines beyond space"[11] and further on: *saiṣā gāyatrī etasmiṃs turīye darśate pade parorajasi pratiṣṭhitā / tad vai tat satye pratiṣṭhitam".* "This gāyatrī is based on this beautiful foot which is beyond space: that foot again is based on satyam." The one who shines beyond space is no doubt the person in the sun. The passage recalls ChUp. 3, 12 where basically the same speculation is found which is, however, more faithful[12] **[209]** to its ultimately Ṛgvedic prototype: *Gāyatrī vā idaṃ sarvaṃ bhūtaṃ yad idaṃ kiṃ ca / vāg vai gāyatrī vāg vā idaṃ sarvaṃ bhūtaṃ gāyatri ca trāyate ca.* The gāyatrī is sixfold: all beings; vāc; earth; body; heart; prāṇas; but also four-footed, which no doubt refers to such divisions as explained in the above BĀUp. passage. The ChUp. quotes the Ṛgveda (10, 90, 3): *etā́vān asya mahimā́ 'to jyā́yāṃś ca pū́ruṣaḥ / pā́do 'sya vī́śvā*[13] *bhūtā́ni tripā́d asyāmṛtaṃ diví //* "so far goes its greatness; the puruṣa is greater than it still: all beings make up one foot (or quarter) of him: three feet (or quarters) are immortal in heaven." This description of the Puruṣa is elsewhere given of Vāc (1. 164, 45) *catvā́ri vā́k párimitā padā́ni tā́ni vidur brāhmaṇā́ yé manīṣíṇaḥ / gúhā trī́ṇi níhitā néṅgayanti turī́yaṃ vācó manuṣyā vadanti //* "Vāc is measured in four feet: the keepers of the brahman who are wise know these feet: three, put away in hiding, do not stir; the fourth foot of Vāc is spoken by men." It would seem that the Puruṣa has succeeded to some of the functions of

Vāc when his association with Vāc became more significant in cosmogonical speculations. We see how Vāc is described as the female partner of the creator, Prajāpati, Vācaspati, Bṛhaspati, while at the same time his identity with Vāc is confirmed.

It is significant that in the above sūkta 1,164 akṣara is used several times in connexion with Vāc: (24) *gāyatréṇa práti mimīte arkám arkéna sā́ma traíṣṭubhena vākám / vākéna vākáṃ dvipádā́ cátuṣpadā 'kṣáreṇa mimate saptá vā́ṇīḥ //* "With the *gāyatrī* foot he measures the *arka*, with the *arka* the *sāman*, with the *triṣṭubh* foot the *vāka*, with the two-foot and four-foot *vāka* the recitation, with the syllable the seven voices." (39) *ṛcó akṣáre paramé vyòman yásmin devā́ ádhi víśve niṣedúḥ / yás tán ná véda kíṃ ṛcā́ kariṣyati yá ít tád vidús tá imé sám āsate //* "What will he do with the hymns who does not know the syllable of the hymn, which is the highest heaven where the gods all live? Only those who know it are sitting together here." (41-42) *gaurír mimāya salilā́ni tákṣaty ékapadī dvipádī sā cátuṣpadī / aṣṭā́padī návapadī babhūvúṣī sahásrākṣarā paramé vyòman // tásyāḥ samudrā́ ádhi ví kṣaránti téna jívanti pradíśaś cátasraḥ / tátaḥ kṣaraty akṣáraṃ tád víśvam úpa jīvati //* "The buffalo cow has lowed, building lakes, having become one-footed, two-footed, four-footed, eight-footed, nine-footed—with a thousand syllables in the highest heaven: on the seas that flow out from her do [**210**] all four world-quarters live: therefrom flows the Syllable: on it lives everything."

As Bergaigne already remarked[14] there is no reason to assume for *akṣara* in 42c another meaning than it has in *sahásrākṣarā;* Geldner, who apparently cannot believe in the metaphysical significance of the speculations on metres and syllables,[15] prefers to render the second *akṣára* more appropriately with "das Unvergängliche". The Indian exegetes differ: Yāska and Sāyaṇa prefer "water", Sāyaṇa elsewhere "syllable".[16] The author of the Jaim-UpBr. text quoted above patently takes *akṣára* in 42c as "syllable", though it is doubtful whether the Ṛgvedic poet had already the syllable OM in mind. A comparison of the Jaim UpBr. exegesis is interesting: *gaurī* is paraphrased with *kāmadughā;* in *pṛthag-salilam* we have doubtless to recognize the RV. *salilāni,* the "lakes" or "pools" anticipating the variously footed metres summed up in the sequel. It is exceedingly tempting to see in *akṣiti* a corruption of RV. *tákṣatī.* The attributes *prāṇasaṃhitam* etc. certainly mean to explain *ekapadī,* though we may be at a loss to explain some of these explanations.[17] On the other hand it would seem that the JaimUpBr. author understood *sahásrākṣarā* as "having a thousand streams", as the explicative or associative *ayutadhāram* would suggest. The expression *sahásrākṣarā paramé vyòman* in the sūkta is interesting: the recurring expression *akṣáre paramé vyòman,*[18] to be explained either as "in the syllable which is the highest heaven" or as "which is *in* the highest heaven" is probably at the root of it.

It is clear that the above upaniṣadic texts continue old speculations about an *akṣara* that had already in Ṛgvedic "times" been more or less **[211]** clearly articulated as an ultimate and supreme principle without losing its significance "syllable". Sometimes the akṣara is conceived as a sort of hypostatised Word, as in 1, 164, 39, sometimes as the simplest measure of recited mantras, as in ib. 24, sometimes as the essence of life as in ib. 42: but these distinctions are ours, not the Ṛgvedic priest's. Elsewhere the syllable is the prime utterance of Vāc, as in 3, 55, 1 ab: *uṣásaḥ pū́rvā ádha yád vyūṣúr mahád ví jajñe akṣáraṃ padé góḥ* / "When the ancient dawns first dawned the great Syllable was born in the footstep of the cow." Here another association of akṣara with the sun is hinted at. The footstep of the cow is also the step or foot of metrical Vāc. That the syllable, as the common denominator of the sacred mantras, can represent the universal order which is based on the sacrifice, is almost a matter of course: so we read in 6, 16, 35-36; *gárbhe mātúḥ pitúṣpitā vididyutānó akṣáre* / *sī́dann ṛtásya yónim ā́* // *bráhma prajā́vad ā́bhara jā́tavedo vícarṣaṇe*/ *ágne yád dīdáyad diví* // "Thou that art shining in the syllable, the womb of your mother,[19] as your father's father, sitting in the womb of the ṛtam, fetch thou, O excellent Agni Jātavedas, the child-bearing bráhman which radiates in heaven." Evidently we have to regard the womb of the mother, the womb of the *ṛtam* and the heaven in which brahman radiates as parallel expressions: we see how easily and naturally *akṣara*, *ṛtam* = *satyam* and *brahman* in its ancient sense of powerful sacred utterance could be juxtaposed and be substituted for one another, as we see happen frequently in later texts.

It cannot be doubted that the "etymological" meaning "unflowing, imperishable" was constantly in the mind of the priests speculating about the syllable. It is this deliberately sought polysemy characteristic of Vedic poetry which perhaps reveals best the mentality behind the speculations on Vāc: it is not mere abstract theorizing to reduce the Universe to its order, the order to the sacred Word and the Word to its metre and ultimate unit of syllable, but the immediate experience of the composing poet himself. It cannot be accidental that the supremacy of Vāc was upheld by priest-poets who themselves attempted—and with what success—to express ever more meanings by ever more pregnant words. With a beautiful stanza like *uṣásaḥ pūrvā áddha yád vyūṣúr mahád ví jajñe akṣáraṃ padé góḥ* the poet could express not only the dawns of the first day, the first step of a cow at dawn to the river, the primacy of the syllable of the first revelation of the sacrificial world-order, but even his [**212**] own start on composing a new song while driving his cow to the river at dawn! The resulting obscurity is not an obscurity for its own sake; it is the expression of layer upon layer of identities.

The etymological speculations on akṣara suggest that its derivation[20] was more a hindrance than a help to thought. Akṣara is conceived both as the sap or essence that "flowed out" and as the ultimate term of an ascending series which is no longer "flowing out" into an ulterior essence. But the last is always the first, and from the "unflowing" flow out the first seeds of creation. In JaimUpBr. 1, 1 we read *athaikasyākṣarasya rasaṃ nāśaknod ādātum / om ity etasyaiva seyaṃ vāg abhavat / om eva nāmaiṣā / tasyā u prāṇa eva rasaḥ* etc. "He (Prajāpati) could not take the sap of this akṣara. Of this akṣara, viz. OM, Vāc came to be: Vāc is in fact OM. Her sap is Breath". Elsewhere, in 1, 23, there is an attempt to push further; but there is nothing beyond the "irreducible imperishable Syllable': (1) *ayam evedam agra āsīt / sa u evāpy etarhi /* (2) *sa yas sa ākāśo vāg eva śā / tasmād ākāśād vāg vadati:* "this very ether was here at the beginning: the same is still here. This ether is Vāc, for Vāc speaks from the ether". Then it is said that Prajāpatī squeezed out Vāc: her sap was the worlds: their sap the deities: their sap the triple Veda: their sap the three vyāhṛtis: and of their sap it is said: *tad etad akṣaraṃ abhavad oṃ iti yad etad /* (8) *sa etad akṣaram abhyapīlayat / tasyābhipīlitasya rasaḥ prāṇedat //* (1, 24, 1) *tad akṣarad eva / yad akṣarad eva tasmād akṣaram /* (2) *yad v evākṣaram nākṣīyata tasmād akṣayam / akṣayaṃ ha vai nāmaitat / tad akṣaram iti parokṣaṃ ācakṣate:* "he squeezed this akṣara; when it had been [**213**] squeezed, sap trickled forth.[21] That flowed, hence it is akṣara. As the akṣara did not perish, therefore, it is imperishable. In fact it is the Imperishable (*akṣayaṃ*): they call it *akṣara* to mystify." We see that in spite of its being "unflowing" further principles do indeed flow out of akṣara. The above account of 1, 23 starts from ākāśa = Vāc, produces from it the worlds, then reverts the order and reduces the Universe, *via* the sacrificial deities, the Vedas, the vyāhṛtis, back to akṣara, which no doubt due to its etymology is here considered an end, but in 1, 1 a beginning. Do we meet here already the first inklings of the later aporion of how to derive from the transcendent Unchangeable the phenomenal changes? For akṣara, being the ultimate juice and essence of things, is therefore their *pratiṣṭhā* "standing-place, foothold, firm basis": JaimUpBr. 1, 10, 10 has: *sthūṇām eva divastambhanīṃ sūryaṃ āhur antarikṣe sūryaḥ pṛthivīpratiṣṭhaḥ / apsu bhūmīś ca śiśyire bhūribhārās satyaṃ mahīr adhitiṣṭhanty āpaḥ //* "They say that the sun is the pillar that supports the heaven; the sun rests on the sky which reposes on the earth; the lands of the earth, which support many things, lie on the waters; and the wide waters are rested on the satyam." Satyam is explained: (11) *om ity etad evākṣaraṃ satyaṃ / tad etad āpo 'dhitiṣṭhanti.*

The inner coherence of all these speculations about akṣara is clear enough. They obviously originate from milieux that were intensely preoccupied with the sacred Word which rules and supports the sacrificial order of the Universe. Searching for that principle from which the established order of ritual equilibrium derives its being, the sacred utterance of ṛc, yajus and sāman which is reflected in and contains all other triads that constitute the world, they arrive at the 'hypostasized' Sacred Word, Mother of creation. But they try to push beyond this ultimate and find a more ultimate basis in the metres that measure the Word, or the feet that measure the metres, or the syllable that measures the foot. It is not yet a particular syllable which is supreme: it is Syllable as such which is the ultimate because it cannot be reduced further. At one stage this Syllable came to be identified with OM, that ubiquitous syllable of consent,[22] in which all recitations have their beginning and end[23] and which from minute to minute is heard resounding at the great sacrifices, **[214]** passed back and forth between the priests of the three Vedas scattered over the sacrificial ground—centre of life and order where these thinkers always returned to find material and inspiration. This akṣara is on the same plane as other terms in which the same quest for the ultimate behind the Order found alternate end-points: *ṛtam, satyam, brahman.*

When we now turn to BĀUp. 3, 8, where Yājñavalkya instructs Gārgī about the akṣara, we notice undoubtedly a more rarefied atmosphere,[24] but there is no reason whatever to separate Yājñavalkya's akṣara from the akṣara we have just studied. Here too the celebrated metaphysician shows his well-known preference for apophasis. To Gārgī's question: what is the frame on which is woven,[25] warp and woof that which is above heaven, below the earth and in between (a formulation that reveals greater philosophic refinement: the obvious heaven, atmosphere and earth are no longer comprehensive enough, but it is clear that the old triad persists) and that which is past, present and future,—Yājñavalkya replies: the *ākāśa*. But Gārgī demands more: what is the frame on which the *ākāśa* itself is woven? The reply is: akṣara, but a completely immaterial akṣara. At its behest do sun and moon, heaven and earth stand supported. But even Yājñavalkya cannot get completely rid of the associations of the Syllable: "at the behest of this syllable do people acclaim generous (yajamānas?), the gods the yajamānas, the deceased ancestors the ladle (with the oblation)".[26]

The MaitrUp. 6, 8 furnishes an ancient commentary on the manner in which Yājñavalkya's akṣara could still be understood: *dve vāva brahmaṇo rūpe mūrtaṃ cāmūrtaṃ ca / atha yan mūrtaṃ tad asatyaṃ yad amūrtaṃ tat satyaṃ tad brahma taj jyotiḥ / yaj jyotir sa ādityaḥ / sa vā eṣa / om ity etad ātmābhavat / sa tredhātmanaṃ vyakuruta / om iti tisro mātrā/ etābhiḥ sarvam idam otaṃ protaṃ caiva / asmīty evaṃ hy āha / etad vā āditya om ity eva dhyāyann*[27] *ātmānaṃ yuñjīteti.* The three mātrās or morae of OM contain all manner of other triads which we have met by the way. The terms clearly refer us to various upaniṣadic passages, and *otaṃ protaṃ caiva* evidently to Yājñavalkya's *ākāśe eva tad otaṃ ca protaṃ ca* etc.

[215] Later, in the later upaniṣads whose authors no longer found their inspiration exclusively in the world of ritual and had the results of their predecessors to start from, akṣara as a 'philosophic' principle has lost most of its associations with the Sacred Word;[28] side by side with the meaning "syllable" in a more strictly grammatical sense and usage, the meaning "Supreme Being", which must derive from the ancient "Great Syllable", goes its separate

way. The term could lend itself readily to the meaning "Supreme Being": it was re-etymologized as the "Imperishable". Less pliant terms like *vāc* itself were doomed,[29] while other terms from the same complex, like *satyam* and *brahman* could again more easily be retained: *satyam* could convey not only "truth, true word" but also "that which is truly so, the true and real and dependable"; *brahman*, whether or not a derivative of *BRH-*,[30] was so etymologized, while it also enjoyed the double advantage of being an archaic word and conceptually but vaguely defined. That the ancient associations could long persist is shown by the history of Indian thought. There can be little doubt that both the *sphoṭavāda* of the grammarians and the *śabdādvaita* of the vedāntins continue with all the philosophical sophistication of later thought the ancient complex of ritualistic speculations in which akṣara belongs. Śaṅkara was still aware himself that the immaterial and transcendent akṣara of Yājñavalkya's instruction was, or could be, interpreted as the "syllable OM"[31] and he went out of his way —according to Bhāskara who refuses to follow him here[32]—to refute this interpretation.

NOTES

1. P. M. Modi, *Akṣara*....(Thesis Kiel 1931; Baroda 1932).

2. Mahābhāṣya *ad* Siddhāntaślokavārttika *post* 1, 1, 8 *aśnoter vā saro 'kṣaram;* cf. Bhāskara, Brahmasūtrabhāṣya 1, 2, 22 *aśnute vyāpnoti svavikārān ity akṣaram.*

3. A. Bergaigne, *Etudes sur le Lexique du Rigveda*, J. As. 1883, pp. 480 ff., s.v. *akṣara;* a more qualified but substantially the same opinion gives H. Oldenberg, *Vedische Untersuchungen* 30, *akṣára, ákṣara im Rigveda* (ZDMG 63, 1909), pp. 293 ff.

4. Cf. my *Studies in Sāṃkhya* 1. *An old text reconstituted*, 2. *Ahaṃkāra*, to be published in JAOS [nos. 6 and 7 in this volume].

5. Ed. by H. Oertel, *The Jāiminīya or Talavakāra Upaniṣad Brāhmaṇa* (JAOS 16, 1894), pp. 49 ff.

6. Oertel renders *pṛthaksalilaṃ kāmadughākṣiti....amṛtaṃ duhānā* with "she that milks immortality possessing individual oceans (?), possessing wish-granting imperishableness;" but analyses *kāmadughā akṣiti*; the *pṛthaksalilam* corresponds to the *salilāni* of RV. 1, 164, 41; *duhānā* "yielding milk"; *akṣiti* here taken adjectivally to *amṛtam*, but probably a corruption of RV. *tákṣatī*, see below.

7. The parallel *sūcyā* in JaimUpBr. where ChUp. has *śaṅkunā* shows that we can accept *śaṅku* here too in the common meaning of "pin, stake", and cancel the meaning "Blattrippe" assumed by Boethlingk (pw, s.v.4) of which this ChUp. is the only occurrence; Hemacandra who gives this mean-

ing "*pattrasirājāla*" (Anekārthasaṃgraha 2, 17) may also have deduced it from the same passage. The expression *sūcyā/śaṅkunā saṃtṛṇṇa-* is parallel to the well-known ones *tantunā/sūtreṇa* etc. *otaṃ/protam* etc., the notion being of one ultimate principle running through, and lying at the root of, all the variety of things.

8. E. Senart (*Bṛhad-āraṇyaka-upaniṣad, traduite et annotée*, Paris 1934), prefers to distinguish *satyam* from *Brahman* and emends: *satyaṃ brahma, [brahma] Prajāpatim.*

9. In this related text *satyam* is distinguished into *sat* and *tyam*, the former representing *brahman's* or *satyam's* embodied, mortal and static aspect, *tyam* its disembodied, immortal and dynamic aspect. The puruṣa is the essence of the latter aspect.

10. *karma vā etat tasya sāmno yad vayaṃ sāmopāsmaha iti* / (8) *atha kim upāssa iti* / *akṣaram iti* / *katamat tad akṣaram iti* / *yat kṣaran nākṣīyateti* / *katamat tat kṣaran nākṣiyateti* / *indra iti* / (9) *katamas sa indra iti*/ *yo 'kṣan ramata iti* / *katamas sa yo' kṣan ramata iti* / *iyaṃ devateti hovāca* / (10) *yo 'yaṃ cakṣusi puruṣa eṣa indra eṣa prajāpatiḥ* / [*sa*] *samaḥ pṛthivyā sama ākāśena samo divā sarveṇa bhūtena* / *eṣa paro divo dīpyate* / *eṣa evedaṃ sarvam ity upāsitavyaḥ*/

11. Cf. *paro divo dīpyate* JaimUpBr. 1, 43, 10 (quoted n. 10), and my remarks in *Studies in Sāṃkhya* 3; Sattva (to be published in JAOS) [no 8 in this volume]

12. The change of the probably original division into one foot or quarter revealed and three unrevealed is interesting. It cannot be accidental that the change coincides with an increasing preoccupation of these thinkers with a more or less *transcendent* Original Being that at creation manifests itself in a *triad*. At the same time it would seem probable that the idea of the three footsteps of Viṣṇu exerted influence: Viṣṇu's connexion with the Puruṣa who is the demiurge definitely belongs in the complex picture. That the four stages of waking, dreaming, dreamless sleep and *turīya* is another application of the same triadic-tetradic scheme is obvious. One wonders if the remarkable notion of three unrevealed or unuttered parts and one revealed or uttered part of Vāc/Puruṣa did not have a basis in sacrificial practice originally, somewhat comparable perhaps to the *aniruktagāna* of the pressing sāmans above. A glance at the development of Vedānta speculation shows how fertile the conception of the partly manifest partly transcendent Demiurge could be.

13. ChUp. reads *sarvā* for *viśvā*.

14. L.c.

15. Cf. his typical statement *ad* 1, 164, 23; "Hier steight zunächst der Dichter von den Höhen der bisherigen Spekulation in die Niederungen der dichterischen Technik und der rituellen Praxis hinab",—in contrast to such stanzas as ib. 20-22 which he admires; in my opinion such an attitude which prefers to assume that agreeable statements as in 20-22 are more important because they are more easily comprehensible imperils a proper understanding of what was important to the authors: personally speaking I would always consider such views as are the outcome of the daily preoccupations of the thinker to be more significant than pleasant but vague parables.

16. Yāska, 11, 41; Sāyaṇa *ad hoc*; Sāyaṇa: "OM" *ad* TaittBr. 2, 4, 6, 12 (Geldner).

17. *prāṇa* (in the context of the speculations we are dealing with mostly singular)∼*ekapadī*; *cakṣuśśrotram*∼*dvipadī*; *vāc*∼*catuṣpadī* because of the "four feet"; *manas* as *aṣṭāpadī* escapes me; *hṛdaya* as *navapadī* possibly on account of its associations with the *navadvāraṃ puram?*

18. The locution remained popular but was no doubt soon understood as "imperishable supreme heaven".

19. Geldner, however, renders: "Im Leibe der Mutter Vater seines Vaters, bei der (heiligen) Rede aufleuchtend, sich in dem Schosz der (Opfer-) Ordnung setzend, Bring uns das kinderreiche Segenswort, das im Himmel leuchtet, du ausgezeichneter Jātavedas Agni."

20. Although, again, we have no reason to doubt the correctness of the traditional etymology, it is curious to note that *KṢAR-* is very rarely used to describe the flowing of recited mantras: we would expect at least some usage of this root which would explain why its negation *a-kṣara* is used specially for "syllable". In the ṚV. *KṢAR-* is used once with *gīr* (1, 181, 7) *ásarji vām sthávirā vedhasā gī́r bāḷhé aśvinā tredhā kṣárantī*, which Geldner renders "es wurde für euch beide, ihr Muster, eine alte Lobrede losgelassen, dreifach in starkem (Strom?) sich ergieszend, ihr Aśvin". We may also cite 8, 49, 6cd *udrī́va vajrinn avatá ná siñcaté kṣárantīndra dhītáyaḥ* "wie ein wasserreicher Brunnen dem, der daraus schöpft, so flieszen (dir) die Gebeten zu, Indra Keulentrager"; and 8, 50, 4, where Geldner renders *dhītáyaḥ* differently: *anehásaṃ vo hávamānam ūtáye mádhvaḥ kṣaranti dhītayáḥ* "zu dem fehlerlosen (Soma), der (ihn) zu eurem Beistand lädt, strömen die süszen Gedanken". Though, as we see *KSAR-* with a word for speech is not altogether unknown, the available instances do not show why the negative *a-kṣara* (which once, 1, 164, 42, flows paradoxically itself) would have come to denote "syllable". Other possibly distinguishable meanings of *akṣára, ákṣara* do not help much because they are too near that of "syllable"—if distinguishable at all: cf. Oldenberg's balanced account l.c.

21. Cf. e.g. ŚatBr. 3, 9, 2, 1.

22. ChUp., 1, 1, 8.

23. Cf. e.g. ChUp. 1, 1, 9, *teneyaṃ trayī vidyā vartate / om ity āśrāvayati / om iti śaṃsati / om ity udgāyati / etasyaivāṣarasyāpacityai mahimnā rasena:* "with it (the Syllable) the triple Veda proceeds: with OṂ the adhvaryu (YV.) calls on (the hotar), with OṂ the hotar (ṚV.) recites the śastra (which ends every mantra with OṂ SavOṂ), with OṂ the udgātar chants the udgītha: (they do so) to honour this Syllable for its greatness, its essence."

24. But we must note that 3, 8 is really a polished sequel to 3, 6 where this rarefied atmosphere is much less in evidence.

25. Cf. Gonda's remarks on the significance of this expression in *Notes on Brahman* (Utrecht 1950), pp. 44 ff.

26. Note that the Brahmasūtrakāra had reason to explain that this *akṣara* is brahman (1, 9, 10): *akṣaram ambarāntadhṛteḥ* "(brahman is) akṣara, because (akṣara) supports (earth) and heaven".

27. Correction of Maryla Falk, *Nāmarūpa and Dharmarūpa* (Calcutta 1943) p. 42, n. 1, misprinted (?) dhyayān (unless we must restore *dhyāyāt*).

28. Though they are not altogether absent in ŚvetUp. 4, 8; 4, 18.

29. Some of her functions were taken over by Sarasvatī, some by Viṣṇu's consort Lakṣmī.

30. Gonda's case for a derivation from *BṚH* seems unanswerable; for a balanced discussion of other views as well, see his *Notes on Brahman.*

31. Bhāṣya *ad* BrS. 1, 3, 10.

32. Bhāṣya *ad* BrS. 1, 3, 10; interesting is that Bhāskara attributes this view to the sphoṭavādins: *kecid* (i.e. Śaṅkara) *akṣaraśabdasya varṇe prasiddhatvād akṣaram oṃkāra iti pūrvapakṣayanti / vaiyākaraṇadarśanaṃ ca sphoṭaḥ śabda īty avatārya gakārādayo varṇā eva śabdā iti sthāpayanti / tad etad adhikaraṇenāsaṃbaddhaṃ.*

6

STUDIES IN SĀṂKHYA (I)

AN OLD TEXT RECONSTITUTED

The importance of the text-group MBh. (Cr. Ed.) 12, 187; 239-40 =(B) 12,194; 247-48; 285=(C) 12, 7066-7128; 8974-9023; 10485-10531 for the early history of Sāṃkhya has long been recognized. Frauwallner in his recent *Geschichte der indischen Philosophie* even describes this text-group as the basic form of Sāṃkhya found in the epic (epische Grundform), constituting the first stage in the formation of Sāṃkhya, still ignorant of the evolution process which is characteristic of the second stage and thenceforth of all Sāṃkhya.[1] Johnston in his monograph *Early Sāṃkhya* attaches great importance to the theory of the *bhāvas* as he finds it in our text and holds that this *bhāva* is probably the oldest name for *guṇa* in the sense of the well-known triad *sattva, rajas and tamas,* and that their function of "psychical, moral qualities" which they have in our text is the original function of the three guṇas.[2] I believe that both Frauwallner and Johnston are wrong and that the very text on which they rest their cases proves them wrong.

It is evident that the two texts of the Critical Edition[3] and the three texts of the Bombay and Calcutta Editions are versions of one text. Belvalkar, the discriminating editor of the Śānti-parvan, has eliminated the third version: it finds its right place in the critical apparatus of 12,187. The second version has rightly been preserved, although the basic MS. $Ś_1$ omits it.

When we read through the two versions we are struck by the fact that the term *bhāva* occurs in two altogether different situations : first in connection with such "sensations, qualities and conditions" as *sukha/prīti, duḥkha/śoka, moha*; *praharṣa* etc., *atuṣṭi* etc., *aviveka* etc.; secondly in connection with a process by which the buddhi modifies itself into manas as its *bhāva*, as in 187, 24ab *atibhāvagatā buddhir bhāve manasi vartate,* 240,

1ab *mano prasṛjate bhāvaṃ buddhir adhyavasāyinī,* and ib. 3ab *yadā vikurute bhāvaṃ tadā bhavati sā manaḥ*. It is clear that we have here two different functions of the term *bhāva.*

We shall isolate the first set of *bhāvas* which is more easily recognizable. Our starting-point is an identical series found in a text which, though no doubt hailing from the same milieu of thinkers, cannot be regarded as still another version of our one text but forms a separate text in its own right: 12, 212 (B. 219) entitled *Pañcaśikhavākya*. We note the following literal agreement in the description of *bhāva* I: 187, (28a)[4]. 30-35=(240, 1d). 239, 20-25=212, (25c).26-31. There is no need to assume interpolation from one text into the other, but we simply conclude that this description of *bhāva* I in 6-7 ślokas was current in a certain milieu in a certain period. Starting from this description we connect all the occurrences of *bhāva/guṇa* where its function is evidently either identical or similar to the *bhāva* of the description. So we connect 187, 21cd-22ab; 25cd; 27; 29; 240, 7; 14.

When we have isolated the passages where *bhāva/guṇa* figures as "sensation, quality or condition," we are left with an odd assortment of stanzas and half-stanzas which have one thing in common: *bhāva* occurs in a function which cannot naturally and evidently be connected with *bhāva* I:

[154] 187 *puruṣādhiṣṭhitā buddhir triṣu bhāveṣu vartate/*21 ab
*evaṃ naraṇāṃ manasi triṣu bhāveṣv avasthitā/*22 cd
seyaṃ bhāvātmikā bhāvāṃs trīn etān nātivartate/
*saritāṃ sāgaro bhartā mahāvelām ivormimān//*23
atibhāvagatā buddhir bhāve manasi vartate/
*pravartamānaṃ hi rajas tad bhāvam anuvartate//*24
*indriyāṇi hi sarvāṇi pradarśayati sā sadā/*25ab
ye ye ca bhāvā loke 'smin sarveṣv eteṣu te triṣu/
*iti buddhigatiḥ sarvā vyākhyātā tava bhārata//*26

240 *mano prasṛjate bhāvaṃ buddhir adhyavasāyinī/* 1 ab
yadā vikurute bhāvaṃ tadā bhavati sā manaḥ/ 3ab
*indriyāṇāṃ pṛthagbhāvād buddhir vikriyate hy aṇu/*4 ab
tiṣṭhatī puruṣe buddhis triṣu bhāveṣu vartate/ 6 cd
seyaṃ bhāvātmikā bhāvāṃs trīn etān ativartate/
saritāṃ sāgaro bhartā mahāvelām ivormimān// 8
avibhāgagatā buddhir bhāve manasi vartate/
pravartamānaṃ tu rajah sattvam apy anuvartate// 10

ye caiva bhāvā vartante sarva eṣv eva te triṣu/
anvarthāḥ saṃpravartante rathanemim arā iva// 14

Now our collection of odd ślokas shows a positive coherence : there is a striking predilection for the root *vṛt* and derivates; an evident preoccupation with creation and modification: *vi-kṛ*; *pra-sṛj*; a series *puruṣa—buddhi—manas—indriyas*; two similes suggestive of cosmology (sea and its waves and current; wheel with three spokes). These points persuade us that our lines have to do with an evolution theory. We read : the *buddhi,* in or under the *puruṣa,* exists actively (*vartate*) in three *bhāvas*; she is like the ocean in that she does, or does not, transcend its *bhāvas*, as the ocean its waves and current; the *buddhi,* beyond *bhāvas* or undivided as it is, exists in a *bhāva manas*; *manas* is a *vikāra* of the *buddhi* : it becomes *manas; rajas* somehow getting active succeeds that *bhāva,* or that *sattvam*; then the *buddhi* enters into some relation with the senses—the text is obscure—but it is clear that it evolves again out of the *bhāva* of every separate sense; all *bhāvas* in the world are somehow comprised under these three, which together roll on along with their objects like the spokes along with the felly.

As far as possible we have followed the order of our texts in this description. A few points have to be settled.

1. 187 *nātivartate* // 240 *ativartate.* Starting from the simile, does or does not the ocean transcend the waves in which it consists (*ūrmimān* // *bhāvātmikā*) and the incoming current of the rivers ? It does : it is the *lord* of the rivers. Besides, it is impossible not to think of the frequent application of the same simile to the transcendent creator who is modified in the *prapañca* as the ocean is modified in its waves, yet transcends the *prapañca* as the ocean transcends its waves which disturb only its surface.[5] Finally, *nātivartate* contradicts *atibhāvagatā/avibhāgagatā*, which both convey the transcendence of the *buddhi.*[6] We will therefore prefer the reading *ativartate.*

2. 187 *atibhāvagatā//* 240 *avibhāgagatā*; both contrast no doubt intentionally with *bhāve manasi vartate*: 'the *buddhi,* originally beyond the *bhāvas* or not yet divided (*vibhāga* ~ *vikāra*: 'not yet evolved'), comes to exist in the *manas* as its *bhāva.*' Neither reading is distinctly preferable to the other.

3. 187, 25: neither the first *hi,*[7] nor *pradarśayati,* nor *sadā*

are contextually significant. The fact that *rajas* gets active and succeeds the aforesaid (*tad*) *bhāva* offers no explication (*hi*) for the fact that the *buddhi* first exists in the manas as its bhāva, *tu* 'Germ. *aber*' is preferable. *pradarśayati..sadā* is not quite nonsense: 'the *buddhi* makes [**155**] the senses always visible,' which conveys some sort of manifestation; but when we find a very well attested variant *pravartayati..tadā* 'the *buddhi* then starts the senses on their career, brings them about, sets them in motion,' the choice is not difficult; besides, we have another derivative of the favorite root *vṛt*.

When we now arrange both versions according to the above description, which presented itself naturally, we obtain a text: 187, 21 ab (~240, 6 cd)—23 (~8)—24 (~10)—25 a (corrected) —240, 4 b — 187, 26 ab (~240, 11 ab) — 240, 11 cd — 187, 26 cd. We have kept to the order in both texts, with one exception: 240, 4 ab. We have not accounted for 240, 3 ab (*yadā vikurute bhāvaṃ tadā bhavati sā manaḥ*) which certainly belongs to our text, and which cannot better be fitted than between 187, 24 ab and cd (240, 10 ab and cd); but since these two half-ślokas are coupled together in both versions and should not be split up arbitrarily, we are inclined to consider 240, 3 ab an additional explication of WHY the *buddhi* exists in the *manas* as its *bhāva*. This view gains in plausibility when we see that there are not less than two doublets of this half śloka: 240, 1 ab and 9 ab; marginal ślokas arbitrarily incorporated in a series of conflated copies? 240, 4 b belongs much more intimately to our text: it explains a stage nowhere else explained: 1. *manas*; 2. senses; 3. evolution out of the senses. We notice that the other ślokas followed one another closely with only an incidental interruption, 290, 406; we wonder if the portion between 240, 4 ab and 6 ab belong to our text. Evidently: they describe how the *buddhi* becomes the senses. This portion corresponds to 187, 18-19 ab, which however differs considerably; still both portions are to be found in corresponding situations. 187, 20 has one more śloka where we find the objects of the senses mentioned; this śloka is split up in 240: 187, 20 cd~240, 5 ab; id. 20, ab~id. 9 ab; this split in itself is proof of the coherence of the two portions before and after 187, 21~240, 6.

After these complicated considerations we are able to constitute the following text:

puruṣādhiṣṭhitā buddhis triṣu bhāveṣu vartate/	A21ab; B6cd
*seyaṃ bhāvātmikā bhāvāṃs trīn etān ativartate//***1**	A23ab;B8ab
saritāṃ sāgaro bhartā mahāvelām ivormimān/	A23cd; B8cd
*atibhāvagatā buddhir bhāve manasi vartate//***2**	A24ab;B10ab
**yadā vikurute bhāvaṃ tadā bhavati sā manaḥ*	B3ab
pravartamānaṃ tu rajas tad bhāvam anuvartate/	A24cd; B10cd
*indriyāṇi hi sarvāṇi pravartayati sā tadā//***3**	A25ab
śṛṇvatī bhavati śrotraṃ spṛśatī sparśa ucyate/	B4cd ~ A18ab
*paśyatī bhavati dṛṣṭī rasatī rasanaṃ bhavet//***4**	B5ab ~ A18cd
jighratī bhavati ghrāṇaṃ buddhir vikriyate pṛthak/	B5cd ~ A19ab
*indriyāṇīti tāny āhus teśv adṛśyādhitiṣṭhati//***5**	B6ab ~ A20cd
adhiṣṭhānāni buddher hi pṛthagarthāni pañcadhā/	A20ab ~ B9ab
*indrıyāṇāṃ pṛthag bhāvād buddhir vikurute hy aṇu//***6**	B4ab
ye caiva bhāvā vartante sarva eṣv eva te triṣu/	B14ab;A26ab
*anvarthāḥ saṃpravartante rathanemim arā iva//***7**	B14cd
†*iti buddhigatiḥ sarvā vyākhyātā tava bhārata//*	A26cd

(A=12, 187; B=12, 240)

1a B *tiṣṭhatī puruṣe* (cf. Cr. Ed. app. on A)—1d A *nātī*—A adds (22 cd) *evaṃ narāṇāṃ manasi triṣu bhāveṣv avasthitā*: doublet of A1 to fill up the śloka after the interruption 21 cd—22 ab—2c B *avibhāgagatā*—* possibly additional (marginal?) śloka explaining 2d; doublets *manaḥ prasṛjate bhāvaṃ buddhir adhyavasāyinī* (240, 1 ab) and *yadā prārthayate* (<*prusṛjate?*) *kiṃcit tadā bhavati sā manaḥ* (ib. 9 ab)—3a A *hi* (cf. Cr. Ed. app. on A)— 3b B *sattvam apy* for *tad bhāvam; sattvam* "attracted" by *rajas? apy* looks like a stop-gap on *rajas* alone see discussion below—3d A *pradarśayati sā sadā* (cf. Cr. Ed. app. on A); B om. 3cd—4-5 acc. to B; A shows traces of B but seems to have been mixed up with a similar series of definitions of senses and names. —4c Belvalkar marks *paśyantī* doubtful; Belvalkar marks *bhavate* doubtful—4d Belvalkar marks *rasatī* doubtful; id. 5a *jighratī*—5cd A *pañcendriyāṇī yāny āhus tāni* (Belvalkar: doubtful) *adṛśyo 'dhitiṣṭhati*—6ab B *adhiṣṭhānānī vai buddhyā* (Belvalkar: doutful) *pṛthagetani saṃsmaret*; sequence 5cd-6ab uncertain but plausible; A om. 6cd; 6d B *vikriyate* (cf. Cr. Ed. app. on B); Belvalkar: *aṇu* doubtful—7a śloka acc. to B; 7ab A reads *ye ye ca bhāvā loke 'smin sarveṣv eteṣu te triṣu*—A om. 7cd— †acc. to A; B om.; no doubt a secondary śloka whereby whole episode is fitted into the "Mahābhārata."

[156] Translation. "1 The *buddhi* controlled by the *puruṣa* exists in three evolved forms of being; characterized as it is by these three forms it goes beyond them, **2** just as the billowy ocean, lord of the rivers, goes beyond the waves of the current. Though really beyond any (evolved) form of being, the *buddhi* comes to exist in the form of being *manas*:* when the *buddhi* modifies its form of being then it becomes the *manas*.* **3** Then however *rajas* gets active and succeeds that form of being: for it is then that the *buddhi* brings about all five senses. **4** Hearing it becomes ear; touching it is called (organ of) touch; looking it becomes eyes; tasting it becomes tongue; **5** smelling it becomes nose: thus the *buddhi* is successively evolved. These (organs) are called senses; the *buddhi* rules in them invisibly. **6** Now these instruments of the *buddhi* have each their own object, five in total: out of each form of being of the senses separately the *buddhi* evolves (the corresponding elemental) atom. **7** All forms of being (things) that exist are comprised under these three forms of being: they unroll themselves each according to its purpose or end, like the spokes roll along with the felly of the cartwheel.

†Thus, O Bhārata, is explained to you the entire course of the *buddhi*."

It should not be necessary to stress that this compact little text with its strong inner coherence is not a purely hypothetical construction, but simply a text legitimately restored on the basis of two incomplete and corrupt versions—comparable to two badly damaged manuscripts—which between them have preserved almost the entire text. It started probably when one palm-leaf, containing on one side st. 1-3 and on the other st. 4-7, was turned upside down and the copyist did not notice. From then on the text was not longer understood and it disintegrated. A short time after the leaf had been copied wrong side up and before disintegration set in, a parallel version came into existence: this explains why 240 has preserved some original readings. It follows that $Ś_1$, though it follows the older text tradition without parallel, has not more authority than the parallel version 240. Probably only B had the explanatory line (*). Our text is probably incomplete, as might be expected: we miss a śloka enumerating the elements. That *aṇu* does indeed stand for "subtle element" is not impossible but not at all likely; still Belvalkar was well advised to accept *aṇu* as the *lectio difficilior*.

I consider this little text very important. It definitely gives the lie to a primitive "Sāṃkhya" without evolution, as Frauwallner construes. There is no mistaking the evolutionary function of *rajas*. Johnston's view that the *guṇas* were originally "moral or psychical qualities of the *buddhi*" is rejected.

The solitary function of *rajas* is curious but not without parallel. MBh. (Cr. Ed.) 12,206 (B 12, 213), 9 cd reads : *rajasy antarhitā mūrtir indriyāṇāṃ sanātanī* "the eternal embodiment of the senses is hidden in *rajas*," and 20 cd *indriyāṇāṃ rajasy eva prabhava-pralayāv ubhau* 'in the *rajas* alone the senses have both their beginning and their end." It is noteworthy that such a function in the process of evolution is here too only ascribed to *rajas*; *sattva* and *tamas* do not figure. We shall have to deal with these passages in greater detail in a study of the *ahaṃkāra*.

There is more epic evidence of *bhāva*[8] in the above sense of "form of being, cosmic phase evolved under the influence of a *guṇa*." Suggestive is 12, 202, 23-24 (B 210, 25-26):

puruṣādhiṣṭhitaṃ bhāvaṃ prakṛtiḥ sūyate sadā/
hetuyuktam ataḥ sarvam jagat saṃparivartate//
dīpād anye yathā dīpāḥ pravartante sahasraśaḥ/

Note the parallelism *puruṣādhiṣṭhitā buddhiḥ* in our text. Incidentally an explication of the well-known term *svabhāva* for *prakṛti* presents itself : "its OWN *bhāva*" as opposed to its three evolved ones. In the sequel of 202 the doctrine of the eight *prakṛtis* follows, but after a series where taste is a product (*guṇa*) of water (*soma*!), smell of earth etc., *manas* of *sattva*, *sattva* is born from *prakṛti* and the possessor of *buddhi* (*buddhimān*) is recognized as the *sarva-bhūtātma-bhūtastha* (cf. Gītā 5, 7; 6, 29/31), *bhāva* returns (34): all these *bhāvas* carry the whole universe, they derive (*śritāḥ*) from the God beyond *rajas* (*virajasam*), whom they call "the highest point" (*paramaṃ padam*). In the next adhyāya, 204 (B 211), the *bhāvas* are described as *svabhāvahetujāḥ* (st. 3) and *avyaktajāḥ*, which are synonyms :

tadvad avyaktajā bhāvāḥ kartuḥ kāraṇalakṣaṇaḥ/
acetanāś cetayituḥ kāraṇād abhisaṃhitaḥ (?)//4//

[157] 'likewise the *bhāvas*, sprung from the *avyakta*, which are known as the causes (evolvents) (in the service) of the agent (=evolving *puruṣa*). Being non-conscient themselves they are conglomerated (?) (starting) from the evolvent conscient one.' In 12-13 it reads :

hetuyuktāḥ prakṛtayo vikṛtayaś ca parasparam/
anyonyam abhivartante puruṣādhiṣṭhitāḥ sadā//
sarajastāmasair bhāvaiś cyuto hetubalānvitaḥ/
kṣetrajñam evānuyāti pāṃsur vāterito yathā//

The stanzas are corrupt, but the meaning of 12 is clear enough, and 13 must mean something like : the fallen *kṣetrajña* is pursued by the *bhāvas rājasa* and *tāmasa*, like dust (~*rajas*) which is raised by the wind. It is clear that the relation between the *bhāvas*, including *svabhāva*, and *puruṣa* is very intimate : they still derive from him. This view is still behind Gītā 7, 12-13 :

ye caiva sāttvikā bhāvā rājasās tāmasāś ca ye/
matta eveti tān viddhi na tv ahaṃ teṣu te mayi//
tribhir guṇamayair bhāvair ebhiḥ sarvam idaṃ jagat/
mohitaṃ nābhijānāti mām ebhyaḥ param avyayam//

To sum up. We find in the older portions of the Mokṣadharma clear evidence that the "*guṇas*"[9] are indirectly responsible by their influence on a higher principle for the evolution of three *bhāvas* "forms of being or becoming (*bhū*), cosmic phases" which in one text which we have reconstituted correspond to *manas*, senses and elements. Almost invariably the relevant passages have suffered badly, a sure indication that already at an early date this function of the triad was no longer understood. It is not the place here to link our evidence up with the upaniṣadic triad of cosmic phases; this may be undertaken in a later study of the most versatile and mysterious *guṇa*, the *sattva*.

NOTES

1. Erich Frauwallner, *Geschichte der indischen Philosophie*, 1. Band (Salzburg, 1953), Chapter 6, pp. 289 ff., esp. 299 ff.

2. E. H. Johnston, *Early Sāṃkhya* (R. A. S. Prize Publication Fund Vol. XV, London, 1937). pp. 31 ff., esp. 34.

3. The edition of the text of the Śāntiparvan, including Mokṣadharma (Fasc. 22-24, with Appendices and Critical Notes; Poona, 1951-53), is complete, except for the important introduction to the whole parvan, which is in the press.

4. The stanzas enclosed in parentheses have *trividhā vedanā* in common: also in my opinion 240, 1d *trividhā karma codanā* (cf. Cr. Ed. App.).

5. Bhavabhūti, *Uttararāmacarita* III, 48; Śaṅkara, BrSBh. 2, 1, 13; Bhāskara, BrSBh. passim; Yāmuna, *Saṃvitsiddhi* (in: Siddhitraya, Chaukhamba Skt. Ser. 10; Benares, 1900), p. 82, st. beginning *jñānādi*, and next one, is closest to the pre-classical Sāṃkhya view of the Puruṣa manifested in his *vibhūti*, a *prakṛti* likened to the ocean.

6. Cf. Belvalkar's critical note (ad 187, 24, p. 2160): "the v. 1. of *atibhāvagatā* .. all denote the transphenomenal state of the Buddhi, when it is not occupied with anything in particular."

7. Unless it be taken as an "expletive particle, marking off successive stages."

8. For some post-epic evidence of the three *bhāvas*, cf. my paper in *Adyar Library Bulletin*, XIX, vol. 1-2 (Adyar, 1955) [no. 3 in this volume].

9. That means: The triad in which *rajas* figures; *guṇa* as the specific term for this triad is relatively late. The question whether the two other evolutionary factors, viz. those behind the evolution of the *buddhi* into the *bhāva* names and into the *bhāva* elements, were indeed known by the terms *sattva* and *tamas* will be discussed in another study on *sattva*.

7

STUDIES IN SĀṂKHYA (II)

AHAṂKĀRA

Ahaṃkāra is one of those deceptive Indian concepts which retain a certain plausibility when translated into our thought and, as a result, are accepted at face value.[1] It arrives comparatively late on the scene of early speculation, if we go by the occurrences of the term in the extant texts. Almost invariably it is associated with terms suggestive or indicative of Sāṃkhya influence. The Sāṃkhya doctrine itself is still too often regarded as a rational system, ever since Garbe[2] described it so. All this has led scholars into believing that *ahaṃkāra* is a typical Sāṃkhya creation, a necessary hypothesis for the consistency of the doctrine, a deliberate rational construction.

Jacobi[3] defines *ahaṃkāra* as the principle "vermöge dessen wir uns für handelnd und leidend usw. halten, während wir selbst, d.h. unsere Seele davon ewig frei bleiben." Garbe[4] adds: "die Funktion des Ahaṃkāra ist also die Hervorbringung von Wahnvorstellungen (*abhimāna*), und zwar derjenigen Wahnvorstellungen, welche die Idee des Ich in rein materielle Dinge und Prozesse hineintragen." Frauwallner[5] writes: "das Ichbewusstsein (*ahaṃkāraḥ*) .. ist eine volkommene Neuschöpfung, zu der er [*sc.* the hypothetical Pañcaśikha] auf folgende Weise kam..Wenn man alle psychischen Vorgänge in das Bereich der Materie verlegte und den psychischen Organen zuschrieb, dann konnte man auch die falschen Vorstellungen von Ich und Mein nicht der Seele lassen..Entweder schrieb man sie einem der bereits gegebenen Organe zu, oder man nahm für sie ein neues Organ an .. Pañcaśikha .. nahm ein eigenes Organ an, das Ichbewusstsein (*ahaṃkāraḥ*)."

All these definitions and descriptions are true enough, as far as they go; but they do not go far enough. None of them really accounts for the most surprising aspect of this "philosophical" concept : its cosmic function of creator of the empirical universe. But why should the spirit's self-projection be equivalent to world creation ? And, an important question, why should the self-projection be erroneous and illusory, but the identical world creation true and real ?

Senart's comments[6] are still to the point: "Les interprètes, même occidentaux, det philosophèmes sāṃkhya prennent volontiers pour monnaie authentique, pour réflexion spontanée, toutes les combinaisons de la doctrine achevée en système." "A traiter les systèmes hindous, ainsi qu'il arrive communément, comme de purs produits de la réflexion raisonnante, pratiquant en parfaite maîtrise l'étude objective des problèmes, à les isoler des inspirations religieuses et des notions courantes qui ont guidé leurs premiers pas, à y supposer une logique serrée et, si j'ose dire, substantielle, dont la pensée hindoue se montre habituellement peu capable, on méconnait les conditions et on fausse les enchaînements de l'histoire."

Research into the genesis of a concept like *ahaṃkāra* is handicapped from the start by the assumption that at the end of the development MUST lie the complete and perfect doctrine.[7] Implicit is an evolutionist a priori. One does not at least reserve the possibility that the classical doctrine really represents a minority doctrine, remaining after the majority views had been dissolved in Vedānta and Pāñcarātra, already moribund when formulated in the Kārikā, dead soon after.[8]

It is this attitude which made Margarethe [16] Steiner's little paper,[9] "Ahaṃkāra in den älteren Upaniṣaden"—to my knowledge the only monograph dealing with the subject—so negative in its results. She set out to find in the upaniṣads the prototypes of the Sāṃkhyan *ahaṃkāra* "erroneous self-projection" before gaining an insight into the whole complex of the concept, and—second limitation—concentrated mainly on the occurrences of the term itself. So she arrived at the conclusion: "der Begriff *ahaṃkāra* ist in den Upaniṣaden derselbe wie bei Īśvarakṛṣṇa in seiner Sāṃkhya-Kārikā."[10] Considering these limitations it is clear that this conclusion cannot be right, that is, completely right.

In our present study we shall depart from the cosmic function of the *ahaṃkāra* in order to find out if the cosmogonical role of the notion allows of a satisfactory explication in the context of early speculations, and how it came to be associated with such ideas as erroneous self-projection of the spirit.

Let us first review the *ahaṃkāra* in the Kārikā. K. 13 declares that it is both a *prakṛti* or evolvent and a *vikṛti* or evolute; 22 that it is an evolute of the *mahān*. In 24-25 it is described as follows :

abhimāno 'haṃkāras tasmād dvividhaḥ pravartate sargaḥ/
ekādaśakaś ca guṇas tanmātraḥ pañcakaś caiva//
sāttvika ekādaśakaḥ pravartate vaikṛtād ahaṃkārāt/
bhūtādes tanmātraḥ sa tāmasas taijasād ubhayam//

'*Ahaṃkāra* is presumption. From it derives a twofold evolution: 1. the set of eleven; 2. the *tanmātra* set of five. The set of eleven, which is *sāttvika,* derives from the *vaikṛta ahaṃkāra*; the *tanmātra* set from the *bhūtādi*; both derive from the *taijasa.*'

What strikes us most in the Kārikā's description of world evolution is that there are two patterns, which we may call "vertical" and "horizontal." Down to the *ahaṃkāra* we have a vertical evolution: the *mahān* descends directly from the *pradhāna*, the *ahaṃkāra* directly from the *mahān*. From the *ahaṃkāra* on this pattern is abandoned: its evolution becomes a ramification. First it divides itself into three secondary *ahaṃkāras* which are all on the same plane; then these three divisions evolve two sets of plural products: the *vaikṛta* evolves the eleven senses, the *bhūtādi* the five *tanmātras*, the *taijasa* is somehow involved in both evolutions. Several points are obscure: What is the relation between the primary *ahaṃkāra* and the secondary ones? What is the chronological order, if any, of the *sāttvika* and *tāmasa* evolution? May we infer from the *sāttvika* and *tāmasa* evolutes congenial evolvents and are we to understand that the *vaikṛta* is the *sāttvika ahaṃkāra*, the *bhūtādi* the *tāmasa* one ? What, then, is the role of *taijasa* and why are there no *taijasa* i.e. *rājasa* evolutes? and how can the *rajas* of the *taijasa* be partly the cause of wholly *sāttvika* and wholly *tāmasa* products? These questions can be reduced to two: why the horizontal pattern and why the guṇas which nowhere else figure in evolution? So much is evident that the function of the *ahaṃkāra* in the evolution process is much more complicated than those of *pradhāna* and *mahān*. By itself it creates the whole phenomenal world, not in successive evolutions, but immediately; it is the father of the world but its ways are mysterious.

No less mysterious is its name. It is currently translated literally as "I-maker" or the like, whereby is obviously meant 'organ which forms the conception of the ego.' But this rendering is not without its difficulties: if this had been the intended meaning when the term was coined, one wonders why the responsible thinker, capable of such conceptual thought, did not express himself more accurately in *ahaṃtā-kāra*. Besides, °*kāra* has as a rule the much more concrete sense of 'fashioning, building, making and doing with one's hands.'

Again, this philosophical concept carries unexpected mythological associations: it is identified with Brahmā and, more frequently, with Brahmā's predecessor Prajāpati in the Mokṣadharma portions of the Mahābhārata.[11] It is true that the sections where this identification is made are comparatively recent; but this holds equally for the introduction of *ahaṃkāra* itself. It must be repeated that the fact of later occurrence is never proof of modernity: the milieux from which these "later" notions hail may have been more conservative and old-fashioned, or less given to broadcasting their views, or simply unlucky in the preservation of their texts. So if similar identifications **[17]** are more frequently made in mythologizing or theistic texts which elaborate supposedly "pure" Sāṃkhya notions in a theistic spirit, this does not mean that *ahaṃkāra* had not carried such associations from ancient times. We may note that especially *ahaṃkāra* carries them, even there where the other principles are not so elaborated. And is there any reason to suppose that Sāṃkhya was originally innocent of theism? Edgerton[12] has shown the contrary. Theistic associations abound from the beginning. MBh. 12, 211, 9 identifies Kapila, the mythical founder of Sāṃkhya, with Prajāpati, reminiscent of ŚvetUp. 5, 2 where Kapila, first engendered (*kapilam.. agre..jāyamānam*) is Hiraṇyagarbha. Arāḍa's Sāṃkhya can hardly be described as theistic; yet it equals Kapila with *buddhi* and Prajāpati with *ahaṃkāra*.[13] It has been remarked that the relation between Pāñcarātra and theistic "elaborations" of Sāṃkhya is close; Pāñcarātra emerges suddenly as a fairly complete system: how long does their relation date back before we have documentary evidence?[14] These considerations have led us straight into the Mokṣadharma; and in this random collection of texts from many different milieux and schools we find that attention is centered, not on the psychological function of ahaṃkāra in the individual spirit, but on its evolutionary function in the process of world creation. It appears that we have grounds enough to concentrate on this latter function and not to exclude from the start the mythological associations as being secondary elaborations.

We have seen that the current translation of *ahaṃkāra* is not without its difficulties. But there is another explanation which so far as been overlooked. Side by side with *ahaṃkāra* we find in later texts *mamakāra*. Explications of *ahaṃkāra* take always the form of a quoted sentence with *iti* : 'I am.. I do..' etc.; of *mamakāra* : 'This is mine' etc. This points to another meaning of °*kāra*, not as in *kumbhakāra* etc., but as in *oṃkāra, vaṣaṭkāra, svāhākāra* etc : 'the cry, uttering or ejaculation : *Aham*!'

I do indeed believe that this interpretation of *ahaṃkāra* explains the creator's part which this principle plays in proto-Sāṃkhyan evolution doctrines. For the 'cry: *Aham*!' as factor of world creation reminds one instantly of the many passages in brāhmaṇas and upaniṣads where an original being, when about to create, cries out: "*Aham*..! *hantāham*..!" Perhaps the clearest instance is found in BĀUp. 1, 4, 1 : *ātmaivedam agra āsīt puruṣavidhaḥ/so 'nuvīkṣya nānyad ātmano 'paśyat/ so 'ham asmīty agre vyāharat/tato ahaṃnāmābhavat*: 'the self was here alone in the beginning in the form of a man. He looked around and saw nothing but himself : and he cried out at the beginning : "Here am *I*." That is how the name *I* came to be.' The creative power of this crying-out, this formulating is shown in MaitrUp. 6, 6 *athāvyahṛtaṃ vā idam āsīt/sa satyaṃ prajāpatis tapas taptvānuvyāharad bhūr bhuvaḥ svar iti/eṣaivasya prajāpateḥ staviṣṭhā tanūr yā lokavatīti* : 'This here was yet unformulated; the real-beyond, Prajāpati, performed *tapas* and then formulated one after the other: "Earth, Sky, Heaven." This is the most solid body of Prajāpati, which consists in the world.' The verb used in both cases is *vyā-hṛ*, used for the ritual, magically powerful cry, or formulation, of the priest. That in our BĀUp. myth the self-formulation, the *ahaṃnāman* : 'Here am I,' is really the beginning, nay the condition of creation becomes clear from the sequel: *so'vet—ahaṃ vāva sṛṣṭir asmy ahaṃ hīdaṃ sarvam asṛkṣīti/tataḥ sṛṣṭir abhavat* : 'He knew : "*I* am creation, for *I* have created all this." That is how creation came to be.' The parallelism of 4, 1 and 4, 5; 6; 7, with the practical applications following the description of Man's exploits, shows their unity to be closer than that of 2-4 which interrupt this parallelism. 4, 5 follows naturally on 4,1; 4, 7 on 4, 5: *tad dhedaṃ tarhy avyākṛtam āsīt/tan nāma-rūpābhyām eva vyākriyate—asau nāma—ayam idaṃrūpa iti/../ sa eṣa iha praviṣṭa ā nakhāgrebhyaḥ*: 'this here was then still unseparated; it was separated as names and forms—"this one is name, he has this form"; he entered into this here down to the nail-tops.' He is the Man *ātmā puruṣavidhaḥ*, whose name is I and whose form is CREATION.

The speculations on creation-by-naming are already old[15] in that period, and in a state of [**18**] transition. An older form is that of TāṇḍyaMBr. 20, 14, 2 which reads: "Prajāpati was here alone. He became Vāc. Vāc became his partner. He wished: 'I will send out this Vāc and it will go and unfold the whole world.' So he sent out Vāc and it went and unfolded all this." A parallel in KāṭhBr. 12, 5 has: "Prajāpati was here. Vāc was his partner. He copulated with her. Thereafter she parted and bore these creatures, then she returned into Prajāpati." Vāc is the self-formulation of Prajāpati, personified in a female partner who brings forth the creatures, that is, formulates them, literally CALLS them into being. Prajāpati may be unformulated (ŚatBr. 1,1,1,13; 1,6,1,20) but is also both formulated and unformulated, measured and unmeasured (ib. 6, 5, 3, 7), as name and as form. In BĀUp. 1, 4, 3—to return to our basic text—we read that the "self as a male" wants to sport but has not partner to sport with; so he desires a partner, and it is said : "He was as big as a man and a woman embracing." This androgynous entity is split into two : they are husband and wife.

It is against this background that we have to view the simple cry: "Here am I." An original being, at first unformulated, formulates himself; this self-formulation is Vāc, from whom creation proceeds further: in other words, this self-formulation is world creation. That the female partner of our version still corresponds to the more ancient Vāc becomes clear from another parallel version. In the creation myth BĀUp. 1, 2, 1 = ŚatBr. 10, 6, 5, 1, an original being Nothing, or Hunger, or Death—one would paraphrase the One-without, the INCOMPLETE one—desires to become himself : *tan mano 'kuruta-ātmanvī syām iti*. Follow several creation stories : one of the primordial waters; one of creation by tripartition; and one where this being desires : "Let there be a second self to me." This second self is a "son."[16] The way in which this "second self" is produced is interesting: *sa manasā vācaṃ mithunaṃ samabhavad aśanāyā mṛtyuḥ* 'by means of his desire[17] he—hunger, death—copulated with Vāc.' The discharge of semen becomes the year:[18] the year is his second self, his "son." He himself bears his offspring for a year, then when it is born, he prepares to eat it, opens his mouth, emits the sound *bhāṇ* while doing so, and so Vāc comes to be. The Vāc with whom he copulated was consequently yet unuttered, still within him. The story continues (2, 5): *sa aikṣata-yadi vā imam abhimaṃsye kanīyo 'nnaṃ kariṣya iti/sa tayā vācā tenātmanedaṃ sarvam asṛjata yad idaṃ kiṃ ca* 'he wished : "If I use my will[19] on him (i.e. the year), I shall make a little food." So by means of Vāc he created with that self all, whatever there is.' The point of the story is that Hunger wants food; hence his offspring is the year which in its three seasons of summer, rains and harvest produces crop. Vāc appears twice, both times unnecessarily it would seem : a relic of her former importance in the process of creation by formulation. If here she is evidently already on the decline, she is even more so in our basic version 1, 4, 1—a mere female partner, anonymous—, and still more in another version (4,10) *brahma vā idam agra āsīt/tad ātmānam evāvet—ahaṃ brahmāsi / tasmāt tat sarvam abhavat* 'the *brahman* was here in the beginning; it knew only itself : "I am *brahman*"; therefrom this all came to be.' Here it is the fact of self-recognition which is the condition of creation. If this last version ignores the female partner, the rudimentary Vāc, by implication, still another version ignores here explicitly: (ChUp. 6, 2) *sad eva somyedam agra āsīd ekam evādvitīyam* 'the *sat* was here in the beginning, alone and WITHOUT A PARTNER.' This sat first produces *tejas*, then the waters, then food. As I have set forth elsewhere,[20] these three "elements" represent the three seasons, summer, rains and harvest; together they constitute the Year, the second self of our version in BĀUp. 1, 2, 1 : hence that after food has been produced the *sat* starts creation : *seyaṃ devataikṣata—hantāham imās tisro devatā anena jīvenātmanānupraviśya nāmarūpe vyākaravāṇīti* 'This deity wished: "Why, I will now enter these three deities (*tejas*, the waters [19] and food) as a living being myself and separate names and forms."' In this creation, too, we can discern the self-creation of *sat* which is completed with its entrance into its three constituent "elements":

the SECOND self above is the LIVING self, the unmanifest becomes the manifest. The unique, self-sufficient *sat* starts creation all by itself. Nevertheless, in spite of the explicit rejection of a partner, there are still traces of the ancient *vāc* in the famous formula *vācārambhaṇaṃ vikāro nāmadheyam*, as I hope to have proved elsewhere.[21]

Is it a far cry from the Sāṃkhyan *ahaṃkāra* to this ancient complex of myths where creation starts from, or even consists in, the self-formulation of an original, unformulated and unformed being ? It may seem so if we concentrate exclusively on the more advanced philosophical aspects of *ahaṃkāra* as the self-projection of the individual spirit; but when we start from the cosmic *ahaṃkāra* it does not. It has been remarked[22] that the cosmic *ahaṃkāra* can only be understood if there is a cosmic personality. There will be no one at present who seriously doubts that Sāṃkhya began by being theistic, in other words, by positing a cosmic person whose self-creation took place in a series of evolutions, one of which—and the most important for world creation—was *ahaṃkāra*.

When we sum up our results we can state our position as follows. We find the beginnings of the concept of *ahaṃkāra* in the older upaniṣads, in this form : at the beginning of creation a primordial being becomes conscious of himself, formulates himself, creates himself; these three distinctions do not really exist : consciousness-formulation-creation is actually one single process. We see that the creation myths where we found this origin of *ahaṃkāra* continue more ancient speculations where the creator's formulation Vāc was projected and personified in a female partner, wife of the creator and progenitrix of creation. This projection is withdrawn and the function of Vāc, who is contained within the creator, taken over by the creator, a process that reaches its climax in the sadvidyā of ChUp. 6. The *ahaṃkāra* is the *ahaṃnāman*, the NAME *I*, by which the creator formulates himself, and to which automatically corresponds a FORM in which the I is embodied. Hence it is said : *Ahaṃ vāva sṛṣṭir asmi* 'I am creation.' The further creation is described in several ways : by copulation with a female partner who is split off by the creator and in whom we recognize a rudimentary Vāc; by tripartition; and/or by separating-out (*vyā-kṛ*/ *vi-kṛ*) names and forms. In several passages the self-creation of the creator is described as his entering into his creation as his body. We started on the interpretation *ahaṃkāra* 'the ejaculation: *Aham*!; self-formulation'; but the difference between formulation and creation, obvious to us, does not really exist in this train of thought: formulation IS formation; name and form are inseparable. As far as we can see, no distinction is made between macrocosmos and microcosmos: the self-formulated being is the cosmos. Nor is there yet evidence of a deprecation of his self-creation.

In this context of speculations we are no longer surprised to meet the term *ahaṃkāra* itself, for the first time, in ChUp. 7, 15. There it is on a par with such universal concepts as *bhūman* 'vastness, infinitude' and *ātman*; it is used to describe the all-comprising totality of things, the universe: *athāto 'haṃkārādeśa eva—ahaṃ evādhastād ahaṃ upariṣṭhād ahaṃ paścād ahaṃ purastād ahaṃ dakṣiṇato 'ham uttarato 'ham evedaṃ sarvam iti* 'so now the doctrine of the *ahaṃkāra*: "I am in the nadir, in the zenith, in the West, in the East, in the South, in the North, I am all that is here."' Miss Steiner discusses this passage and states that in all likelihood it is a later interpolation, because it stands isolated in the train of thought of this upaniṣad.[23] But we may ask: if anyone wanted to interpolate this passage, why should he choose *ahaṃkāra* of all possible notions, which, as Miss Steiner sets out to prove, would have had the same content as in the Kārikā? There is often some confused thinking about interpolations. In cases like this to wish to eliminate interpolations is to wish to eliminate complications. And even there where it can be made plausible, for example by comparing parallel passages, that a certain passage has been interpolated, we have no right to eliminate it, unless we can determine its date accurately and unless we can show definitely that the idea conveyed by it is entirely foreign to the "original" thought. One should rather go to the limit in [20] accepting such passages, both in order not to shut out complications and also because they are evidence. Every concept of early speculations grows more complex with every step in our researches. A genuine interpolation may be an aid to understand it better. In studying upaniṣadic thought we are never dealing with monolithic doctrines. To eliminate later portions is to throw evidence away that has to be explained: what it means, why it was inserted.

In our interpretation we can account perfectly for this *ahaṃkāra : aham evedaṃ sarvam* is *ahaṃ vāva sṛṣṭir asmi*. The universal character of the *ahaṃkāra* is given from the beginning; it cannot be anything but universal for it is the *ahaṃkāra* of the primordial being who creates by it the universe; it is not only the beginning of creation, it is its content.

Miss Steiner's argument that *ahaṃkāra* does not fit, because it would have fitted in 8, 7—where the difference between "false" and "true" *ātman* is set forth—but does not occur there, is hardly conclusive; but it poses the problem of the "reality" of the creation-by-*ahaṃkāra*. We declared that no distinction is made between microcosmos and macrocosmos, and that there is no evidence of any deprecation of creation. Ronald Smith,[24] however, in discussing some of our BĀUp. passages, states: "Any identification of micro- and macrocosm must imply a theory of illusion and projection by the mind, an idealism, and in India as anywhere else, it has to overcome the common sense of the unimaginative. This is usually a matter of time, as their case goes by default in the intellectual world by their [the world's ?] uninterest." I do not quite see how this author arrives at his view: for, to put it also aprioristically, it seems more reasonable to expect that only after the macrocosmos—including the ultimate cause of things—and the microcosmos—including ego and body—have become separated, THEN there is any need for an illusion theory to account, not for their identification, but their separation.

This question has a direct bearing on our topic, for the complex concept of *ahaṃkāra* does not only comprehend the process of cosmic creation but includes the process of erroneous self-projection as well. The illusion of this self-projection does not involve the reality of the creation, only the spirit's identification with it. This point has been enlarged upon in classical Sāṃkhya, that is in an age when a plurality of individual spirits had been assumed and creation no longer started from the spirit but from a non-spiritual matrix. The doctrine is that the spirit, really not involved in the world, becomes involved in it by *abhimāna*, the erroneous presumption that it is the empirical ego in the body and material world. When we transpose this doctrine into the upaniṣadic complex of speculations around the prototype of *ahaṃkāra*, we may describe it as follows: there is no STRICT identity of the original being and his creation. Is there any evidence of a development of the *ahaṃkāra* conception, as we have come to understand it in the older upaniṣads, towards the notion of "degradation" of the original being in his creation?

At the earlier stages there is none: on the contrary, there are suggestions that the original being is originally incomplete and completes himself in creation, as in BĀUp. 1, 4, 17 *ātmaivedam agra āsid eka eva/so 'kāmayata—jāyā me syād atha prajāyeyātha vittaṃ me syād atha karma kurvīyeti/etāvān vai kāmo necchaṃś ca nāto bhūyo vindet..so yāvad apy eteṣām ekaikaṃ na prāpnoty akṛtsna eva tāvan manyate/tasya kṛtsnatā—mana evāsyātmā vāg jāyā* etc. 'the self was here in the beginning, alone; he wished: "I would have a wife, and have children, and be rich, and do work." This is all there is to wish: whatever one desires, there is nothing more to find than that..As long as he has not got them all, one after the other, so long he will feel INCOMPLETE. His completeness: his will (*manas*) is his *ātman*, his wife *vāc* etc.' The story of Hunger, creating to have food, points also at completion through creation.

In the most advanced version of our myth, the sadvidyā ChUp. 6, a change announces itself. In that celebrated śruti it is repeatedly said that the products which evolve (AFTER the *sat* has completed its self-creation by entering into its three constituents and separating names and forms) are *vācārambhaṇaṃ vikāro nāmadheyam.* Although this description has no pejorative value in itself, the sequel shows that primacy is given to *sat*, the *aṇimā* from which all derives and by which all is ensouled, and that a return is conceived which has its end, its AIM, in *sat.* This primacy of the unevolved [21] *sat*, the one before and beyond creation, shows marked affinities with that voiced in another famous śruti, BĀUp. 2, 3, 6 *athāta ādeśo—neti neti/na hy etasmād iti nety anyat param asti/atha nāmadheyaṃ satyasya satyam iti/prāṇā vai satyaṃ teṣām eṣa satyam* 'hence the instruction : "NOT, NOT" : (that means :) there is NOT, repeat NOT, anything higher than he. So (the instruction:) "the true of the true is the Name" (that means): he is more true than the true, *sc.* the *prāṇas*.' The pronoun HE refers to the *puruṣa* whose FORM was described by various comparisons in the preceding lines, and whose NAME is now revealed as "true of the true," i.e. "truest of all." To the *prāṇas*, which, microcosmically, form his *amūrta* 'unsolid' form and are "true" but less true than he is, correspond macrocosmically the "unsolid" wind and sky. But just as the *puruṣa*'s name is truer than the *prānas,* so his form is higher than that *amūrta* form of wind and sky. His form is beyond the sky; hence it is described in terms of bright, i.e. sun-like, objects, like *māhārajanaṃ vāsaḥ, pāṇḍvāvika, indragopa* 'firefly,' *agnyarcis, puṇḍarīka* 'lotus symbolizing the sun.' *sakṛd-vidyutta*; for the sun and the like are beyond the sky. Does it signify anything that the *puruṣa's* FORM is described under his macrocosmic aspect and his NAME under his microcosmic aspect? It implies the identity alike of microcosmos and macrocosmos and of name and form. I do not think with Smith that wind and sky are "an approach to express the immaterial";[25] *amūrta* is not immaterial, but 'unsolid.' That the light-giving objects express it, would seem more probable; but here again it is not the immateriality of light and bright objects which is the *tertium comparationis*, but their transcendence.

It is within this context, I think, that we are to account for the introduction into our creation myth of the notion of the greater, transcendent TRUTH, the greater reality of the UNEVOLVED creator, whose significance is no longer that he creates and completes himself in his creation, his self-creation, but just that he is the One-before, the One-beyond the universe. Therefore, I would be hesitant[26] to quote such passages[27] as BĀUp. 4, 3, 20: *atha yatrainaṃ ghnantīva jinantīva hastīva vicchāyayati gartam iva patati yad eva jāgrad bhayaṃ paśyati tad atrāvidyayā manyate/atha yatra deva iva rājeva—aham evedaṃ sarvo 'smīti manyate so 'sya paramo lokaḥ*, and 4,3,10 *na tatra rathā na rathayogā na panthāno bhavanti/atha rathān rathayogān pathaḥ sṛjate..sa hi kartā* 'when it seems as if they beat him, rob him, as if an elephant threatens him, as if he falls down a well, whatever he considers dangerous when he is awake, all that he imagines in ignorance; when it seems to him that he is a god, a king, or "I am this, I am all," that is his sublime world,' and 'there are no carts, nor bullocks, nor roads: he creates carts and bullocks and roads..for he is the one who makes them.' The context is different from that of our creation myths: these are the fancies of an individual, not the world creation of the supreme One.

Once attention is no longer focused on the original being as the creator, but as the one behind, and before, and beyond creation, he gradually withdraws completely beyond his creation. Creation itself assumes a new autonomy—or, in so far as we recognize in it the female element of progenitrix, we may say it resumes its old autonomy. So ŚvetUp. 4,5, with a deliberate and corrective reference to the sadvidyā ChUp. 6, declares that the unborn male copulates with the unborn female which produces the red, white and black elements—the old view of a partner against which Uddālaka had reacted.

It is always difficult to prove one's case by calling on the upaniṣads as witnesses: they are at once too willing and too evasive. But I hope to have made it abundantly clear that the origin of the creative *ahaṃkāra* must be sought in the ancient upaniṣadic speculations on a self-formulating, self-creating primordial personality. When we follow up the creation myths where such an original person, called Prajāpati, or *ātman*, or *puruṣa*, even *brahman* and *sat*, recognizes, formulates and creates himself, the associations of the texts themselves point the way naturally. In passing we note**[22]** such familiar terms as *ātman, puruṣa, prajāpati, manas, vyākāra, vikāra*, possibly *abhimāna*, creation by tripartition, three constituents—encouraging landmarks—until we arrive at the ŚvetUp. where we find the most modern upaniṣadic affinities with the doctrine of classical Sāṃkhya and where the term *ahaṃkāra* has evidently become already a terminus technicus and occurs in from now on permanent surroundings.

It is difficult to bridge the distance between the age when *ahaṃkāra* was just one other concept in the whole complex of notions surrounding the *puruṣa* creator of the world, and the age when it has become a technical term in a clearly Sāṃkhyan context. That a purposeful thinker got hold of it again, after it had fallen into desuetude is of course not impossible. But considering the fact that when *ahaṃkāra* starts to occur again in the epic it brings along brahmaistic notions and carries mythological or theistic associations, I think it more probable that it had never been lost in circles which developed the upaniṣadic doctrines without broadcasting their views too widely at first.

We shall pass by the younger upaniṣads where the term occurs but the context does not enable us to assess its significance, and return to the Mokṣadharma.[28] We have seen that the classical doctrine of the creative *ahaṃkāra* displays certain obscurities which may be reduced to two problems, that of the "horizontal" evolution pattern and that of the evolutionary function of the guṇas. On studying the texts we find that these two are really one problem.

When we read through the Mokṣadharma we are struck by the

fact that there is hardly any relation between the triad *sattva, rajas* and *tamas*, and *ahaṃkāra*. In a previous study[29] we have shown that there is scanty but conclusive evidence that the triad at one time played a decisive part in the evolution of the world. It is likely that this function is an ancient one: the evidence is found in Mokṣadharma sections which are generally admitted to belong to the oldest stratum; the references and descriptions where the triad has this function are more often than not corrupted and misunderstood; they are limited in number and no progressive unfolding[30] of the theory, which would show its vitality, is evidenced. In fact, at exactly the same moment when we watch the evolutionary, guṇa-influenced *bhāvas* disappear, we see the "psychical" *bhāvas* appear: the members of the triad are here static conditioning factors of the *buddhi's* inner emotional life.

What is the relation between these two sets of *bhāvas*? Our material is limited and does not allow of the smooth explanation that one set attracted the other. We note in the text which we have reconstituted that the *buddhi* of the *puruṣa* is the SOLE principle involved in evolution. It is not a vertical, but a horizontal pattern: not *buddhi* into *manas, manas* into senses etc., but *buddhi* into *manas, buddhi* into senses. And, we may assume, also *buddhi* into elements; this last evolution is not directly given in our text, which shows a lacuna just after saying that the *buddhi* evolves something else out of each of the five senses, but the deduction is legitimate.[30a] From the fact that *rajas* is said to condition the *buddhi* into evolving the senses we may infer that *sattva* and *tamas* also figure, in this way that *sattva* is the factor impelling the *buddhi* to evolve the *manas, tamas* its factor for the elements. In one breath with this evolution effected by the triad is described another function of the triad in conditioning certain sensations of the *buddhi*: the triple *vedanā*: *sāttvika*—pleasure; *rājasa*—misery; *tāmasa*—daze, bewilderment. Under these three heads a number of emotions are grouped (187, 28-35). Although the two sets of *bhāvas*, one of evolutionary phases, one of emotional states, can be distinguished, they should not be separated too sharply from each other. They may quite well complement each other, the first set being states of "external" development of the *buddhi*, the second set states of "internal" development.

Why did the first set gradually disappear? We see that already in the same text (187) the horizontal evolution of the *buddhi* in *bhāvas* is accompanied by a different cosmic inventory of five [23] *bhūtas, manas* the sixth, *buddhi* the seventh, *kṣetrajña* the eighth. The *bhūtas* of this description are primary evolvents: from *ākāśa* spring sound, hearing and the skies. It is clear that this pattern is altogether different. It is still doubtful whether this series of eight evolvents or *prakṛtis* is already conceived as an evolution series. But the same is evident in another series of eight *prakṛtis,* apparently built on the former: *buddhi*→*ahaṃkāra*→*manas*→ *ākāśa*→wind→fire→water→earth; the *kṣetrajña* belongs now in a separate category. It is this vertical pattern which has caught on and replaced the horizontal pattern of the *bhāvas* of the buddhi. We note that the *ahaṃkāra* belongs regularly to this pattern, and that the guṇas do not take any part in the evolution according to this pattern.

There is one exception, and the passage concerned is interesting. Here, in 12,206, *rajas* returns in a role strongly reminiscent of its evolutionary function. In 12 it is said that '*rajas* is cast about in *tamas* and *sattva* rests on *rajas,* and *avyakta,* being the seat of consciousness (*jñānādhiṣṭhānam*) is characterized by *buddhi* and *ahaṃkāra.*' This is probably one of the oldest epic mentions of *ahaṃkāra.* Then 15 reads:

karmaṇā bījabhūtena codyate yad yad indriyam/
jāyate tad ahaṃkārād rāgayuktena cetasā//

'each sense successively, being impelled by *karman* which is the seed, originates from *ahaṃkāra* under influence of the *cetas* which is coupled with *rāga.*'

The meaning of *rāga* becomes clear from 9:

rajasy antarhitā mūrtir indriyāṇāṃ sanātanī/

'the eternal embodiment (=manifestation) of the senses is concealed in (has its origin and end in) the *rajas*'; and from 20

indriyāṇāṃ rajasy eva prabhavapralayāv ubhau/

'the senses have in the *rajas* alone their origin and dissolution.' It is evident that *rāga* in 15 represents *rajas* of 9 and 20; but it must be noted that *rajas/rāga* is in 15 an emotional state of the *buddhi.* This shows us how very close the two sets of *bhāvas* are: occasionally they might coincide. When we compare the function of the *rajas* in the evolution of *buddhi* into senses, we cannot doubt that here the same evolution is alluded to, that *rajas* is consequently a factor in evolution and works through the *rāgayukta cetas,* i.e.

the *buddhi* influenced by *rajas* and in a state of passionate activity. But there is an important variation: the *buddhi* does not evolve the senses directly but out of *ahaṃkāra.*

In this only, isolated instance where *ahaṃkāra* is associated with *rajas* as a factor of evolution we observe that at the basis is a primary connexion of *rajas* with the *buddhi*; in other words, fundamental is our other "horizontal" evolution pattern into which *ahaṃkāra* has been fitted. As we said, regularly *ahaṃkāra* belongs in the "vertical" one. On the little evidence we have we must conclude that the introduction of *ahaṃkāra* here is secondary, and vice versa that the introduction of the triad *sattva*, *rajas* and *tamas* into the pattern represented by *ahaṃkāra* is likewise secondary. In this instance both patterns coalesce partially.

Not only do we infer that the association between the evolving factors, the guṇas, and the evolvent *ahaṃkāra* is secondary, but there is also evidence to show that their SYSTEMATIC association, as we find it in the Kārikā, is comparatively late.

In the system of the Kārikā the hierarchy of the products of *ahaṃkāra* is: first senses and *manas*, which are *sāttvika*, and second the *tanmātra* which comprises the *bhūtas* and is *tāmasa*. But the more original doctrine reverses these positions: the senses are products of the *bhūtas*. Rāmānuja sums up the situation accurately when he states that in the Mahābhārata the senses are *bhautika.*[31] In fact, I believe that the terminology of the Kārikā itself bears traces of this older order: *bhūtas*→senses. The three aspects under which the *ahaṃkāra* evolves the two sets of eleven senses and five tanmātras have special names of apparent antiquity: *vaikṛta*, *taijasa* and *bhūtādi*, in the order of the Kārikā. *Bhūtādi* is the most transparent term: it is clearly a synonym or an epithet of the *ahaṃkāra* as the originator of the *bhūtas.*[32] *Vaikṛta*, also *vaikārika*, and *taijasa* are more difficult.

Strauss[33] argues that *vaikṛta* means the *ahaṃkāra* **[24]** as the *vikṛti* of the *buddhi* which itself is a *vikṛti* of the *pradhāna*. This would make the term another epithet; but it is not just the *ahaṃkāra* by itself which is called *vaikṛta*, but the *ahaṃkāra* AS THE ORIGINATOR OF THE SENSES: the senses specify the *ahaṃkāra* as *vaikṛta*. We may compare MBh. 12,291,23 (B. 300, 24), a relatively recent text, where *vaikṛta* occurs after the evolution has been described of *brahmā*→*mahān* (=Hiraṇyagarbha=*buddhi*)→*ahaṃkāra* (=Prajāpati *ahaṃkṛta*); this typically "vertical" evolution continues:

bhūtasargam ahaṃkārāt tṛtīyaṃ viddhi pārthiva/
ahaṃkāreṣu sarveṣu caturthaṃ viddhi vaikṛtam//

'the third evolution is that of the *bhūtas* from the *ahaṃkāra*; the fourth evolution, the *vaikṛta*, takes place within all these products of the *ahaṃkāra* (i.e. the *bhūtas*).' From the sequel it may be gathered that the *ahaṃkāra*-born *bhūtas* are the *mahābhūtas* and that the *vaikṛta* evolution is that of the correlated objects or *viśeṣas*, sound, colour etc.: AT THE SAME TIME originate the ten senses. In other words, the senses go with the *viśeṣas* of the elements and constitute together the *vaikṛta* evolution, deriving from the elements which are the *vikṛti* of the *ahaṃkāra*: senses and *viśeṣas* form the secondary evolution of the *ahaṃkāra*. Not without interest is another text, MBh. 12,337, 63-73. Here three classes of human beings are described: the first is *sāttvika*, the second *vyāmiśra*, i.e. *rājasa* and *tāmasa* with a redeeming admixture of *sattva*, the third *vaikārika* 'twice degraded,' *rājasa* and *tāmasa* without any *sattva*. This special use of *vaikārika* opens our eyes to the unexpectedness of the equation *sāttvika ahaṃkāra* = *vaikārika ahaṃkāra*.

If we are, therefore, right in accepting *vaikṛta* as "product of the *vikṛti* (*bhūtas*) of the *ahaṃkāra*," consequently as a term for the fourth creation, the senses,[34] it follows that the Kārikā reflects in its terminology an order or hierarchy contrary to its professed one: *ahaṃkāra* = *bhūtādi*→*bhūtas* (*vikṛti* of *ahaṃkāra*)→senses (*vikṛti* of a *vikṛti*:) *vaikṛta*, a typically vertical pattern which has become horizontal: *ahaṃkāra* = *sāttvika*/*vaikṛta*→senses; = *tāmasa*/ *bhūtādi*→*tanmātra* (elements/*viśeṣas*). By the introduction of guṇa qualifications three changes have been effected: the vertical pattern has become horizontal; the order objects—senses has been reversed; a tripartition of *sāttvika, rājasa* and *tāmasa* replaces the evolution in two degrees: *vikṛti*→*vaikṛta*.

We can account in several ways for the introduction of the guṇa qualifications, which as far as I can see is peculiar to the Kārikā. It may be a result of systematization: after the example of *pradhāna* and *buddhi* the *ahaṃkāra* also got its three guṇas. But there may yet be lingering memories of the old triad as factors of evolution, which worked in what is the *ahaṃkāra*'s privileged field.[35] Still more ancient associations may be present: the *ahaṃkāra*, or its upaniṣadic prototype, occasionally started creation by tripartition.

The most difficult term to explain is *taijasa*. The old interpretation was built on the relation *taijasa*=*rājasa ahaṃkāra*, so that *taijasa* was rendered as 'energetic principle.' Now that we have seen that the relation of *ahaṃkāra* with the *guṇas* is secondary, a result of the coalescence of two evolution doctrines, we can no longer explain *taijasa* by *rājasa*. Besides, *taijasa* does not convey the meaning 'energetic like *rajas*'; it is a derivate of *tejas* 'light and its power of heating and glowing,' a concept that is very high up in the hierarchy of Indian notions; if we are to connect it with a *guṇa*, we would connect it with *sattva* rather than *rajas*.

The only *tejas* from which we can derive our *taijasa* is the first of the three constituents of sat in the sadvidyā ChUp. 6. This is of course highly conjectural. Still it may be argued that the guṇas of Sāṃkhya derive from such triads as that of the three forms (*rūpāṇi*), *tejas*, water and food, of just this upaniṣadic evolution myth.[36] Then there is the ancient evolution in which *sattva* would correspond to *manas, rajas* to the senses, and *tamas* (or its predecessor) to the elements. Could this *sāttvika manas* ever have been described as *taijasa*? And might not the term have bgen hanging around the whole complex of creation myths and evolution doctrines as one of the loose ends which all Indian thinkers are loath to cut off? It is a loose end in the Kārikā.

[25] Vijñānabhikṣu[37] knew, and preferred, an older doctrine which he tried to integrate in the Kārikā scheme: the *sāttvika* product is *manas*, the *rājasa* (*taijasa*) the senses, the *tāmasa* the *tanmātras*. In support he quotes an interesting smṛti:

vaikārikas taijasaś ca tāmasaś cety ahaṃ tridhā/
ahaṃtattvād vikurvāṇān mano vaikārikād abhūt//
vaikārikāś ca ye devā arthābhivyañjanaṃ yataḥ/
taijasād indriyāṇy eva jñānakarmamayāni ca//
tāmaso bhūtasūkṣmādir yataḥ khaṃ liṅgam ātmanaḥ/

'the ego is of three kinds, *vaikārika, taijasa and tāmasa*; the *manas* evolves from the *vaikārika,* i.e. the ego principle that is being modified (*vikurvāṇa-*); *vaikārika* are also the (superintending) deities (of the senses), from whom (arises) the manifestation of the objects. The senses themselves, both the sensorial and motorial, derive from the *taijasa*. The subtle cause of the elements is *tāmasa*, from which aether the subtle body of the *ātman*.' Though this is clearly an attempt to give a more satisfactory function to *taijasa*, yet it is clear that the explanation is somewhat forced. In order to retain the patently original *vaikārika* character of the senses (and the *manas* with which they are inseparably connected) and, at the same time, arrange them anew under *taijasa*, the senses are by way of compromise divided into the superintending deities and senses proper. The explanation of *vaikārika* as *vikurvāṇa* is unconvincing: it is obvious a product of *vikṛta* or *vikāra*.

A similar passage in Viṣṇu Purāṇa 1,2,46 f. reads:

bhūtatanmātrasargo 'yam ahaṃkārāt tu tāmasāt/
taijasānīndriyāṇy āhur devā vaikārikā daśa//
ekādaśaṃ manaś cātra devā vaikārikāḥ smṛtāḥ/

'the *tanmātras* and elements evolve from the *tāmasa ahaṃkāra*. The senses are said to be *taijasa*, their ten superintending deities being *vaikārika*; in that (division) the deities and the eleventh, the *manas*, are known as *vaikārika*.' Rāmānuja, discussing the passage in Vedārthasaṃgraha §57, and followed by Viṣṇucitta in his VP. commentary, explains *deva* as 'sense' and renders: 'some contended that the senses are *taijasa*, but I hold that the ten senses are *vaikārika*, etc.'; the other commentators explain as above. But elsewhere the same purāṇa preserves the memory of another,—and in view of our above remarks undoubtedly older—, order in 1,15,19f.:

prathamo mahataḥ sargo vijñeyo brahmaṇas tu saḥ//
tanmātrāṇāṃ dvitīyaś ca bhūtasargo hi sa smṛtaḥ/
vaikārikas tṛtīyas tu sarga aindriyakaḥ smṛtaḥ//

'it should be known that the first evolution is that of the *mahat*; this evolution proceeds from Brahmā. The second evolution is that of the *tanmātras*; this one is known as the creation of the elements. The third evolution is that of the senses; this one is the *vaikārika*.' This is certainly an ancient order of evolution: *brahmā* →*mahat*→*bhūtas*→senses, which clearly corresponds to that of MBh. 12,291 without *ahaṃkāra*.

NOTES

1. Mbh. quotations are from the critical edition of Mokṣadharma in Śāntiparvan, ed. S. K. Belvalkar, fascc. 22-24 (Poona, 1951-53).

2. Richard Garbe, *Die Sāṃkhya-Philosophie: Eine Darstellung des indischen Rationalismus* (Leipzig, 1927).

3. H. Jacobi, *Philosophische Monatshefte*, XIII, p. 420, quoted by Garbe, o. c., p. 311.

4. Garbe, o.c., p. 311, after Kārikā 24; Sūtra 1, 72; 2, 16.

5. Erich Frauwallner, *Geschichte der indischen Philosophie*. Band I (Salzburg, 1953), ch. 6, pp. 309-10.

6. Emile Senart, "Rajas et la théorie indienne des trois guṇas," *J. As.*, 11me série, tome VI (1915), pp. 153; 164.

7. Cf. Franklin Edgerton, "The Meaning of Sāṃkhya and Yoga," *AJP*, XLV (1924), p. 6.

8. Cf. Frauwallner, o.c., p. 475.

9. In *Festgabe Garbe, Aus Indiens Kultur* (Erlangen, 1927), pp. 109 ff.

10. *O. c.*, p. 114.

11. MBh. 12, 175, 16; 291, 20; 299, 7; 300, 12.

12. *O. c.*, pp. 7 ff.

13. Aśvaghoṣa, Buddhacarita I ed. (Calcutta, 1933), II trsl. (ib., 1936), by E. H. Johnston; reference is to 12, 21 and the translator's note.

14. For *ahaṃkāra* in "systematic" Pañcarātra, see F. O. Schrader, *Introduction to the Pāñcarātra* (Adyar, 1916), pp. 75 ff.

15. For a rather apodictical but thought-provoking discussion see Maryla Falk, *Nāmarūpa and Dharmarūpa* (Calcutta, 1947), esp. ch. 1; her important *Il mito psicologico nell' India antica* was not accessible to me.

16. In the sense that it is the product of Hunger; but the very expression "second self" shows that it is intended as a self-creation, a self-manifestation.

17. In these creation myths *manas* has regularly the sense of 'will,' rather than of 'mind' (always a make-shift); cf. above *mano 'kuruta=akāmayata=aikṣata.*

18. *tad yad reta āsīt sa saṃvatsaro 'bhavat*; undoubtedly a direct symbolism of seminal fluid and rains is intended.

19. That the only occurrence of *abhi-man* in the older upaniṣads is in just this context is certainly significant.

20. In *Rāmānuja's Vedārthasaṃgraha* (Poona, 1956), Intr., ch. I.

21. In "Vācārambhaṇam," *Suniti Kumar Chatterji Jubilee Volume=Indian Linguistics*, XVI (Poona, 1955), pp. 157 ff. [no. 2 in this volume].

22. A. B. Keith, *The Sāṃkhya System* (London, no date), p. 80.

23. *O.c.*, p. 111.

24. Ronald M. Smith, "Birth of Thought II: Bṛhadāraṇyaka Upaniṣad," —*ABORI* XXXIV (1953; Poona, 1954), p. 57.

25. *O. c.*, p. 61.

26. I do not deny, in fact consider it very likely, that the same tendency that has found expression in the quoted and similar passages is responsible for the gradual devaluation of the universe as the creator's body and the exultation of the creator as transcending the universe; but the identity of macrocosmos and microcosmos in the creator's person requires that the effects of this tendency be directly shown in the context of creation.

27. As cited by Miss Steiner, *o.c.*, p. 110, as the upaniṣadic prototype of *ahaṃkāra* in her exclusive sense of 'erroneous self-projection of the individual.'

28. The term *ahaṃkāra* in the younger upaniṣads and its general position in the Mokṣadharma have been discussed ably by E. H. Johnston, *Early Sāṃkhya* (London, 1937), to which I refer the reader.

29. *JAOS*, LXXVI (1956), pp. 153 ff. [no. 6 in this volume].

30. If we except 12,206 discussed below.

30a. On second thought I am inclined to be more positive about *aṇu* in the line *indriyāṇāṃ pṛthagbhāvād buddhir vikurute hy aṇu*, *JAOS*, LXXVI (1956), p. 155, śloka 6; one is reminded of the elemental atoms in Vaiśeṣika.

31. My ed. *Rāmānuja's Vedārthasaṃgraha* 57; cf. also Frauwallner, "Untersuchungen zum Mokṣadharma I: Die nichtsāṃkhyistischen Texte," *JAOS*, XLIV (1925), pp. 63 ff.

32. Otto Strauss, "Zur Geschichte des Sāṃkhya," *WZKM*, XXVII (1913), pp. 260 f., but in this function the *ahaṃkāra* may have succeeded another principle, e.g. *ākāśa*.

33. *O. c.*, p. 260.

34. Which in purāṇic Sāṃkhya are regularly called *vaikārika* themselves.

35. From a historical point of view both explanations amount to the same thing, since the *ahaṃkāra* has "succeeded" the *buddhi* in its function of creator.

36. Senart, *o. c.*, p. 151; I intend to return to this point in a further study on *sattva*.

37. Sāṃkhyapravacanabhāṣya ad Sāṃkhyasūtra 2, 18.

8

STUDIES IN SĀṂKHYA (III)

SATTVA

Among the classical guṇas, *sattva*, *rajas* and *tamas*, the first, though in many respects the most mysterious one, has most readily been taken for granted in its classical function. Senart has shown the cosmologic origin of *rajas*;[1] and, although the same has never been done for *tamas*, this concept has always been understood in a much more "total" sense than that of 'spiritual insensibility.' *Sattva*, on the contrary, with its seeming transparency of meaning and lack of Vedic background, was easily accepted as a more advanced abstraction conveying the concept of all that is good in the spirit and the world, with no other cosmological content than was lent to it by its original "psychological" or "moral" function.

At first sight there seems to be little doubt that the three terms of the triad belong together intimately. This does not prevent that occasionally we meet them in pairs: *rajas* and *tamas*, *sattva* and *tamas*, but not, as far as I can see, *sattva* and *rajas*; there is also another pair, *tapas* and *tamas*. Sometimes *rajas* occurs alone. *Tamas* forms also part of a different set of four: *viparyaya*, *aśakti*, *tuṣṭi* and *siddhi*, the first of which, *viparyaya* or "ignorance," comprises the five subdivisions *tamas*, *moha*, *mahāmoha*, *tāmisra* and *andhatāmisra*.[2] Likewise *sattva* occurs alone, in a great variety of meanings: in an older period it was more or less synonymous with *buddhi*, and there are occasions where *sattva* even represents the "material" and is directly opposed to *kṣetrajña*. These meanings of *sattva* occur in contexts which evidently are part of proto-Sāṃkhyan doctrines; nonetheless they are usually sharply distinguished from *sattva* 'first guṇa' without an attempt to justify this distinction historically. Other functions of *sattva* seem to be still further removed: 'excellence,' 'being, creature, thing,' 'character,' such usages as in *bodhisattva* etc.

Often, and especially by those who are prone to rationalize the Sāṃkhya, stress is laid on the abstract nature of *sattva*, which in their view compares favorably with more primitive terms like *rajas* and *tamas*. Indeed, -*tva* is an abstracting and conceptualizing suffix, and *sat* itself is not infrequently regarded as one of the most admirably abstract concepts of early Indian thought—although *sattva* is only rarely derived from this *sat* 'the being One, Being,' but more usually from a *sat* rendered "good" (which is however more accurately "strictly observing, meticulously exact, punctilious"), and accordingly *sattva* is translated as "goodness."

I believe that in dealing with *sattva* scholars have started from the wrong end of the development, as they have done in the case of *ahaṃkāra*. Without considering how far the classical Sāṃkhya of the Kārikā was representative of contemporaneous Sāṃkhya doctrines, let alone of the many theories the Kārikā presupposes, they were ready to accept the concepts of the later system as their criteria; as in the case of *ahaṃkāra* they may have been misled by the comparatively late appearance of *sattva* as the first guṇa and the fixed sense which it has as this guṇa from the early occurrences onwards. One result of this classicism was the acceptance of *sattva* and the other guṇas as factors only conditioning the individual soul's *buddhi*, their cosmological function being looked upon either as secondary or as superseded.[3] Senart, in his study of *rajas*, reacted against this aprioristic view, but as far as the cosmic origin of *sattva* was concerned confined himself to a tentative suggestion, while against his entire argument grave objections can be raised. Przyluski started where Senart had left off, but he confused the issue with his hazardous speculations.

In the two preceding studies which have appeared [89] in this Journal,[4] the writer has tried to show that the proto-Sāṃkhyan texts have preserved vestigial evidence of the ancient evolutionary function of the guṇas, memories of which where perpetuated in the syncretistic *ahaṃkārā* doctrine of the Kārikā. We mentioned in passing[5] that we understood by "guṇas" a triad in which *rajas* was a term, which later came to be called three guṇas, and which did not NECESSARILY comprise at its origin the other two guṇas *sattva* and *tamas*. We saw that the evidence has been preserved in the oldest stratum of the Mokṣadharma and was there soon misunderstood and corrupted, and we concluded that these evolutionary "guṇas" must have been ancient; finally we suggested that their final disappearance was caused by the greater appeal of the cosmic theory which inventorized, and later evolved, the world by five elements, *ākāśa*, wind, fire, water and earth.

We shall start our inquiry into the origins of *sattva* with an inquiry into the origins of the evolutionary triad called "guṇas." We have found that this evolutionary triad is called "*bhāvas*" in the oldest portions of the Mokṣadharma in a creation account where the *buddhi,* under the influence of or with the assistance of the guṇas, evolves into three successive phases of being or becoming, *bhāvas*, viz. *manas*, senses and elements.[6] If we should try to go beyond the epic evidence to search for corresponding doctrines or accounts, we should have to turn to the upaniṣads; when we do so, we find we are not entirely without suggestive clues, but it is immediately clear that we shall have to reorient ourselves to some extent.

This reorientation when we pass from the earliest post-Vedic evidence to the upaniṣads is always necessary and always difficult. Seldom do we find the concepts of the "epic age" in the same form in the "Vedic age," or rather should we substitute "milieu" for age, for chronological priority of Vedic to post-Vedic notions is not necessarily a fact. On the other hand, there are so many points of contact that some sort of continuity cannot be denied; still in many cases it is hazardous or even impossible to derive "later" concepts from the upaniṣads, i.e. those upaniṣads that are strictly speaking Vedic. Rather, we should look for certain basic patterns which underlie doctrines of both milieux and not concentrate too much on the literal contents of these patterns, in the sense that every term should have its direct counterpart, or the correspondence of the entire triad must collapse. In many cases it may be presumed fruitfully that the philosophoumena of the epic do not derive directly from those of the Vedic upaniṣads and the preceding Vedic literature, but that in both we have developments, parallel or divergent, of a more original set of patterns that have been elaborated upon in different milieux according to the demands and the mentality of each. This does not have to mean that the history of certain concepts or groups of concepts escapes all reconstruction, nor that this reconstruction should be wholly conjectural. But we shall have to guard against too simple explanations and too glib generalizations: for, although there is a distinct tendency in Indian thought to proceed from the simple to the elaborate, there is also a tendency from the comprehensive to the specialized. There is a multivalency in more ancient thought which, without ever being wholly lost, gives way to more precise thought constructions, and to emphasize a posteriori certain definite valencies in earlier thought is therefore not always justifiable.

Since Oltramare[7] and Oldenberg[8] we look for the prototypes of the guṇas in the upaniṣads of the Śvetāśvataras and of the Chandogas. A well-known passage in ŚvetUp. 4,5 describes an "unborn male" who copulates with an "unborn female" and produces red, white and black creatures. This is clearly a reference—in my opinion a corrective one—to similarly colored products described in the creation account of ChUp. 6, where an original being called *sat* produces *tejas*, *āpas* and *annam* which are the red, white and black forms (*rūpāṇi*) of the world to be. It must however be noted that Indian commentatorial tradition is not of the same opinion. Śaṅkara[9] and Rāmānuja[10] [90] both explain these three "elements" of ChUp. 6 to be used *pradarśanārtham*, representing the entire series of the five elements, if not the other principles from *Mahat* down as well. But important is at least that Sāṃkhyan connections are being recognized. To my knowledge there is only one epic passage where the identity of the three forms of ChUp. 6 and the three guṇas of Sāṃkhya is explicitly stated. MBh. 12,291,45 after a description of the guṇas continues:

śuklalohitakṛṣṇāni rūpāṇy etāni trīṇi tu/
sarvāṇy etāni rūpāṇi jānīhi prākṛtāni vai//

Several points are worth noting: the use of *rūpāṇi* proves that the reference is indeed to ChUp. 6; the emphasis on their *prākṛta* nature is curious but significant; and finally the reversion of the order red-white, not a transposition for metrical reasons,[11] is of some importance.

Starting from these correspondences—for whatever they are worth—between the triad of the guṇas and the triad of *rūpas*, Senart tried to demonstrate that the original function of the guṇas was cosmic, and that these guṇas originally referred to the three worlds. To the first view I subscribe, with the added support of the epical *bhāva* doctrine, but with the reservation that the three guṇas as a triad had this cosmic origin and not necessarily the three guṇas *sattva, rajas* and *tamas* by themselves. On the second view that the guṇas or *rūpas* of the ChUp. account represent the three worlds a few remarks must be made.

Although there is no doubt that from Vedic times on the three worlds, heaven, atmosphere and earth played their part in cosmogony, there is also clear evidence of a creation myth where world creation was not effected in space but in time. This creation in time was described concretely as the succession of the three seasons, summer, rains and harvest, in the course of which crop is produced to sustain creation. This is the significance of the equivalence: *sa eṣa saṃvatsaraḥ prajāpatiḥ* 'the Creator is the Year.'[12] We have touched on the meaning of BĀUp. 1,2 in another context,[13] and we must return to it now to enlarge on the myth of hunger and food. In this cosmogonic myth several accounts are brought together which we must distinguish before we can discern what holds them together.

This cosmogony begins: "Nothing at all was here at first. This world was enveloped by death alone, that is by hunger. For death is starvation. He conceived the desire: 'I may be myself'. " The formula with which the cosmogony begins is stereotyped. The "nothing-at-all" is, very concretely, death, and this death is specified as starvation, so that death is not an end but a beginning, the nothing-at-all not a nothing-MORE but a nothing-YET. His creation starts with a desire, a *manas,*[14] and the nothing-yet becomes someone, an *ātmanvin* or 'a being with a self to it', on the strength of his desire. Thereafter creation is related in three different accounts.

Account I reads: "He went about chanting. Of his chanting the waters came to be. (He exclaimed:) 'When I just chanted *kam* came to be.' This is the mysterious meaning of *arka*: *kam* befalls him who knows this mysterious meaning of *arka*. *Arka* equals the waters. That which was the reed of the waters, that conglomerated and became the earth. On it he exhausted himself. Of his exhausting himself, heating up himself, the essence *tejas* came forth, that is fire." Whatever may be the truth in his other remarks, Ruben is right in pointing out that "chanting is what the rainmakers and brahmins did."[15] But Ruben does not bring out the force of this point. For Starvation is really up to making rain and from his charms the rains did come. The charms work and become rain, are therefore rain: *āpo vā arkaḥ*. These rains swell the rivers and the flotsam of reed borne down-stream forms the earth floating on the water. On this earth the Creator exhausts himself and secretes fire; the sexual symbolism is thinly disguised [91]: from the heat of exhaustion the *rasa* of *tejas* (both words for the semen virile) pours forth. We remark that creation here is effected in three seasonal phases: starvation personified conjures up rain; earth conglomerates and takes shape; fire originates. That the waters are the rains is evident from the floating reed which covers monsoon torrents. The rains swell the rivers. Without rain, which makes new life possible, there is famine and starvation; hence starvation must start creation by making rain, to produce crop and sustain life.

Account II starts from this tripartite creation and inventorizes the world under three aspects. The Creator splits himself in three: himself, sun and wind. The same tripartition is also expressed in "this *prāṇa* is made triple," where an equivalence *ātman* = *prāṇa* "that which makes one a living being" is implicit. A different creation myth, that of the Cosmic Person who constitutes the world in different parts of his body,[16] is forced into the pattern of tripartition, but not very successfully. At the end there is a return to the theme of I: *sa eṣo 'psu pratiṣṭhitaḥ* 'he is based firmly upon the waters.'

Account III departs from the original desire: "I may be myself," and continues: "He desired: "There be a second self to myself." Through this desire he copulated with Vāc, and that which was his semen became the year: for before then there had been no year. He bore it for as long as a year; after that long a time he delivered it. When it was born he opened his mouth to it: he emitted the sound *bhāṇ* and that sound became Vāc. He thought: "If I use my will upon it, I shall make a little food." So he created with this self of himself by Vāc all this, whatever there is, the hymns of *ṛk*, *yajuḥ* and *sāman*, *chandas*, the sacrifices, men and animals. Whatever he created he started to swallow." This "swallowing" is no doubt a variation of what elsewhere is called "entering into it,"[17] whereby the self-creation of the original being is completed, and is directly comparable to *sat*'s entering into the three *rūpas* as a living being when food has been produced. The Creator, so to speak, takes food and thereby starts the life of creation, which is himself.

What holds these three accounts together so that they could be incorporated in this series of mystic instructions on and about the *aśvamedha*? It is just this creation of food by a process in three phases, stages or parts, which is the theme of account I where the esoteric significance of *arka* was explained by exploiting the homonymy of *arka* 'charm' and *arka* 'fire' and a mystic meaning of *kam* 'water' but also 'bliss'. This multivalent *arka* is the sacrificial fire which is mysteriously equivalent to the *aśvamedha* by being the death of the sacrificial horse—but a death to end all death, for he who knows this equivalence is safe from double-death.[18]

For anyone who lives in India the coming of the rains is the turning-point of the year. After the elemental force of summer, sapping the resources of man and nature, transforming the plains into bleak wasteland, the onset of the monsoon is the dawn of life and creation. In the nothingness of the sky white clouds appear, in the dry beds of almost forgotten rivers torrents come down with a vital force that is at once frightening and reassuring. Whatever the more remote associations of the primordial waters one hears about—the embryonic water in which the child is born, or the surface of the unconsciousness from which consciousness emerges—in India at least the waters of creation should represent principally the rains and the swelling rivers. The negation of existence before the rains come, real starvation, gives way to a new vitality in man and nature; fodder is plentiful, the plains are green, the crop is harvested. Life starts anew. Clearly the thinkers behind this starvation and creation myth are not simply worshippers of hunger, as Ruben calls them.[19] Their myth is, as so often, a realistic account of the realities of their life. And one may wonder if the annual miracle of creation through seasonal change was not the main inspiration of the creation myths where an original being creates the world in three stages, from the fierce promise of summer through the fecundating waters to the abundance of harvest whose regions are sky, atmosphere and land. For when we now return to the creation account of ChUp. 6, we see that the tripartition of *tejas*, *āpas* and *annam* tallies exactly [92] with the yearly succession of seasons. The evolution which takes place in time can be understood much more easily in the terms of successive seasonal changes than in terms of the three cosmic layers in which no priority is so immediately given as in the succession of summer, rains and harvest. The term *annam* in Uddālaka's account is not just *pṛthivīlakṣaṇam*, as Śaṅkara has it[20]—who, as we saw, equates these three phases with the classical five elements—, but just what it means: crop, rice, FOOD. The text leaves us in no doubt: *tasmād yatra kva ca varṣati tad eva bhūyiṣṭham annaṃ bhavati/adbhya eva tad adhy annādyaṃ jāyate.*[21] And just as Starvation, after creating the Year, starts to create with it "his second self," that is the world, his self-creation, so *sat* starts to create the world (separating out names-and-forms) after it has entered into *tejas*, the waters and food.[22]

We wondered if the evolution theories did not start from a vision of creation as SEASONAL creation, in three stages which corresponded to the seasons or their functions and effects and through them with the regions where they are supposed to operate. It is intriguing that in the earliest portions of the Mokṣadharma the rival creation doctrine of the five elements is not yet an evolution theory.

It was necessary to discourse on the ideas behind the three *rūpas* of the creation account in ChUp. 6 in order to appreciate Senart's view that *tejas*, *āpas* and *annam* represent the three worlds and are prototypes of the three guṇas *sattva*, *rajas* and *tamas*. The eminent French scholar has collected materials to show that *rajas* has the meaning 'atmosphere' rather than 'dust, dirt', but his results might now have to be reconsidered in the light of Burrow's recent study on the etymology of *rajas.*[23] Burrow, dissatisfied with the traditional etymology of *rajas* which presupposes a meaning "dark space", proposes, with a wealth of arguments ,two new derivations for two homonyms *rajas*, one in the sense of "space, expanse, intermediate space, sky", from *raj-* 'to stretch, extend', and one in the sense of "dust, dirt" from *raj-/lag-* 'to cling to.' But he subscribes to the view that the guṇa *rajas* is to be explained from the latter sense "dirt, etc." Probably this view is founded on his opinion that *rajas* '(intermediate) space' ceases to occur after Ṛg- and Atharvaveda; but this point is debatable. Granting even that in some cases it is difficult to decide whether *rajas* means "atmosphere" or "dust whirling in the sky", there are a number of passages where the first meaning is clearly the right one. For instance BĀUp. 5, 14,3 *athāsyā etad eva turīyaṃ darśataṃ padaṃ parorajā ya eṣa tapati..parorajā iti sarvam u hy evaiṣa raja upary upari tapati*; when we consider that the first three padas are, inter alia, represented by *bhūmir antarikṣaṃ dyauḥ* (14, 1), the interpretation of *parorajas* 'beyond cosmic space' is clearly indicated. In BĀUp. 6,3,6 a meditation on *bhargo devasya dhīmahi* reads: *madhu naktam utoṣasaḥ/madhumat pārthivaṃ rajaḥ/madhu dyaur astu naḥ pitā/bhuvaḥ svāhā,* where *pārthivaṃ rajas* means either "the region of earth", or "above the earth". Similarly *rajas* in MāhānārUp. 5, 8 and 12:

yat pṛthivyā rajaḥ svam antarikṣe virodasī/
imās tad āpo varuṇaḥ puṇātv aghamarṣaṇaḥ//
rajo bhūmis tvamām rodayasva pravadanti dhīrāḥ/

Such expressions cannot be separated from e.g. ṚV. 7, 100, 5d *kṣayantam asya rajasaḥ parāke* and similar formulae. The same explanation of *rajas* is often more appropriate in such compounds as *virajas-* etc. than the usual renderings are; e.g. MBh. 12, 203, 34

ete bhāvā jagat sarvaṃ bhavanti sacarācaram/
śritā virajasaṃ devaṃ yam āhuḥ paramaṃ padam//

"These forms of being comprise the entire world of mobile and immobile beings; they rest on the god who is transcendent, whom they call the highest point."[24]

I have found no evidence for the assumption that the guṇa *rajas* derives from *rajas* "dirt" with a shift of meaning "dirt"→"moral defilement",→cosmic principle as Burrow assumes: "this rajas in the sense of spiritual defilement forms one of the guṇas of the Sāṃkhya system, at [93] first a purely psychological division, later elevated to the status of cosmogonical principles."[25] To be sure, there is ample evidence that *rajas* was given a psychological function and thus interpreted as *rāga,* from *raj-*, "passionate attachment', which in its turn was linked up with another *rāga,* from another raj-, "red color", but the psychological function developed out of the cosmological one. In this respect the epic *bhāva* doctrine is instructive: we see that the evolutionary "guṇas" effect external changes of the *buddhi,* into *manas,* senses and elements; the internal changes of sensations and emotions follow. When abiding in the manas, the *buddhi* enjoys happiness; when abiding in the senses, the buddhi is subject to the conflicting emotions of sensual life. Another distinction of *nivṛtti* and *pravṛtti* is related to the *mano-* and *indriyabhāva.*[26]

It is true that in the *bhāva* doctrine the thinkers have already gone a long way towards an individualization of cosmic creation processes; but that such processes lie at the root of the epic *bhāva* cosmogony cannot be denied. We concede that the direct evidence for the evolutionary and, by extension, cosmogonic origin of the guṇas is slender; but the evidence for an original psychological function and a later elevation "to the status of cosmogonical principles" is non-existent.

To sum up: Burrow's new views on *rajas*, for all the clarity they have brought to other uses of the term, do not invalidate Senart's view that *rajas*, as guṇa, originally had the meaning "atmosphere". The fact that this older *rajas* fell into desuetude—though we may differ about the "date"—certainly contributed to the reinterpretation of this guṇa as "dust, dirt, defilement", though other factors, the devaluation of created life and the forces that sustain it, played a more important role.

Although the correspondence *rajas* ~ *āpas*, proposed by Senart, is not necessarily disproved if the other correspondences, *tejas* ~ *sattva* and *annam* ~ *tamas* are shown to be untenable, yet the cumulative evidence of all three correspondences would surely carry more conviction; unfortunately, these correspondences are far from clear. Certainly an equivalence or correspondence of *rajas* and *āpas* has much to commend itself: both occupy the same place in their triads; *rajas* 'intermediate space, sky, atmosphere' is the region of the "waters," i.e., the clouds which rain and swell the rivers; the color white (*śukla-*, but one can also think of the "resplendent waters") ascribed to the waters would fit the clouds of *rajas* very well.

A similar correspondence *tamas—annam* is much less commendable. *Annam* is called black, and though we can think of the dark wet soil at the time of sowing, it is quite possible that the black color has nothing to do with *annam* as such but is simply the third in a triad of colors existing independently as a classification scheme which has been brought into connection with the triad of *rūpas* because to some extent they tallied: *tejas* red, *āpas* white, and therefore *annam* black. But this does not have to mean that therefore *annam* stands for *tamas*. It seems to me that too much has been made of these colors in the reconstruction of the history of the guṇas. The fact that later on we find the guṇas likened to the white, red and black threads (in this order) woven into a piece of cloth does not mean that these colors derive directly from ChUp. 6. For all we know red-white-black may have been a popular color scheme in clothes[27] and the colors of the strands or threads (*guṇas*) may have stuck to the threads when these came to be used as a symbol of the universe into which three constituents are woven. The supposed connection of white with *rajas* was at any rate soon dropped and, probably under the pressure of the reinterpretation of *rajas* as *rāga* 'passion' combined with the supposedly identical *rāga* 'red color', red was henceforth the color of *rajas*, while the higher guṇa, no longer connected with the concrete fire of sun, etc. but with light and brightness generally, came to be described as white. For other uses to which this triad of colors was put we may compare the teaching of Aruṇa, the father of the Uddālaka of ChUp. 6, who discerned five *rūpas* in the sun itself: red, white, black, ultra-black and the throbbing in the centre of the sun:[28] evidently this pentad is built on the triad, and it shows that the triad was not at all fixed in its connection. Besides there are other series of colors in which also *harita* and *piṅgala* appear.[29]

[94] It is difficult, further, to show the cosmic origin of *tamas*.[30] The ancient *tamas*, which is the primeval night of nothingness from which creation appears, cannot really be quoted, because there is a vast difference in the creative roles of both notions of *tamas*. To be sure, MaitrUp. 5,2 makes an attempt[31] to combine the guṇa *tamas* with the primeval *tamas*, but the combination is very forced indeed. Moreover, the fact that in the systematized guṇa doctrine *rajas* and *tamas* belong together and the hypothesis that granted the equivalence of *rajas* and *āpas*, *tamas* and *annam* must therefore also be equivalent, do not really follow, as Senart maintains. *Sattva*, *rajas* and *tamas* are really disparate terms, and an hypothesis based on their original coherence begs the question.

Neither *sattva* nor *rajas* in their central senses—even if one takes *rajas* 'dirt'—form a contrast with *tamas* 'darkness.' But there is evidence of a *tamas* in a more easily understandable opposition to *tapas*, darkness—light ~ ignorance—knowledge. MBh. 12, 209 (B.216), 16 reads:

evaṃ hi tapasā yuktam arkavat tamasaḥ param/
trailokyaprakṛtir dehī tapasā taṃ maheśvaram//
tapo hy adhiṣṭhitaṃ devais tapoghnam asurair tamaḥ//
etad devāsurair guptaṃ tad āhur jñānalakṣaṇam//

The first śloka, relatively lucid in the vulgate,[32] is obscure in the critical edition, but clearly the transcendence of the soul (which is here the underlying cause of the universe) over this universe is compared with that of *tapas*, represented by the sun, over *tamas*; the cause of the soul's transcendence is *tapas* "for *tapas* is ruled by the gods, whereas *tamas*, which destroys *tapas*, is ruled by the asuras; that which is preserved by gods and asuras alike—

apparently something higher than *tapas*—is called knowledge." This last knowledge is also called *tapas* in 210 (B.217),

trailokyaṃ tapasā vyāptam antarbhūtena bhāsvatā/
sūryaś ca candramāś caiva bhāsatas tapasā divi//
pratāpas tapaso jñānaṃ loke saṃśabditaṃ tapaḥ/
rajastamoghnaṃ yat karma tapasas tat svalakṣaṇam//

"the universe is pervaded by *tapas* which shines from within; sun and moon in the sky borrow their light from *tapas*. The light of *tapas* is knowledge which is therefore known in the world as '*tapas*'. The function of destroying *rajas* and *tamas* is typical of *tapas*." It is clear from the choice of words that both passages somehow belong together. The introduction of *rajas* in the last line is quite unexpected, but in this passage as above in 209 the pair *tapas*—*tamas* is simply equated with the triad *sattva*, *rajas* and *tamas* with which both texts are mainly concerned: on 209,17 quoted above follows in similar terms:

sattvaṃ rajas tamaś ceti devāsuraguṇān viduḥ/
sattvaṃ devaguṇaṃ vidyād itarāv āsurau guṇau//

If *tapas*, or rather the *pratāpa* of *tapas*, may have claims to an absolute character by being the redemptive knowledge in ch. 210, its connection with the guṇas brings it down to a lower level; so in 209, 19 it is said that there is something higher than *sattva-rajas-tamas* = *tapas-tamas*:

brahma tat paramaṃ vedyam amṛtaṃ jyotir akṣaram/
ye vidur bhāvitātmānas te yānti paramāṃ gatim//

Generally, it would seem to me, *tapas* is higher up in the hierarchy of notions that the *sattva* with which it is juxtaposed here. Surely the pair *tapas-tamas* intrudes somewhat in our context, but it is clear that we here have another attempt to amalgamate more or less parallel series.

These incidental correspondences between *tapas* and *sattva* hardly provides a basis for an equivalence *tapas* = *sattva*, apart from the fact that it would entail an equivalence *tamas* = *rajas-tamas*, for which however much more can be said.[33] Even less of a foundation has the equivalance *sattva* = *tejas* which Senart suggests tentatively.[34] The symmetry and synonymy of the triads of the guṇas and the triad of the *rūpas* in ChUp. 6 are indeed far from being "perfectly established". A correspondence [95] *rajas* ~ *tapas* is possible, certainly; a correspondence *tamas* ~ *annam* has no other ground than the black color which suits *tamas* but is attributed to *annam*; now to assume an equivalance *sattva*=*tejas* because of the "perfect symmetry and synonymy" of the other terms is really taking too much for granted.

The equivalence of *sattva* and *tejas*, which Senart suggests only tentatively, is taken for proved by Przyluski. This scholar accepts[35] without question the identity of the three guṇas with the three cosmic worlds of sky, atmosphere and earth as deduced by Senart from the supposed symmetry of guṇas and *rūpas*. He then compares ChUp. 2,23,3-4 where Prajāpati, by using his creative power of *tapas* on the worlds, produces the three Vedas, and by using his *tapas* on the Vedas produces the sounds *bhūḥ*, *bhuvaḥ* and *svaḥ*. This of course is a variant of the story where Prajāpati creates the worlds by articulating these three sounds, with the addition of the well-known *tapas* of other creation accounts. But Przyluski, operating with the principle of "symmetry" which by now has become a law, concludes from this ChUp. 2 text to a series *tapas*+three worlds; then since there is a series *sat*+three *rūpas* and a series of three guṇas, he substitutes everything for everything else and arrives at a series *tapas—tejas—rajas—tamas*, the only virtue of which seems to be that now we have four neuters in *-as*. Departing from the "guṇas" *tejas*, etc. but failing to find a clear line of development from these "cosmic guṇas" to the classical guṇas, he turns for an explanation to the Iranian Ohrmazd, Mithra and Ahriman, to explain which he turns to the Babylonian cosmology of heaven, earth and sea. These remote analogies occasion an etymology of *guṇa*~Aw. *gaona* " 'poil' et par extension 'couleur de poil, couleur' ". Such methods of course fail to carry any conviction.

With this criticism of the attempts by two eminent scholars to reconstruct the early history of the guṇas we do not mean to convey that the *rūpas* of ChUp. 6 and the guṇas have nothing to do with each other,[36] but that we should be very careful when we discover corresponding triadic patterns to insist that each and every term has its correspondent. Better results might be had when we study the guṇas themselves, while constantly keeping in mind the triadic pattern to which they belong at one stage and to which they need not have belonged originally. The multivalency particularly of *sattva* even in Sāṃkhyan contexts leads us to expect that the study of this concept, covering a wider field and so providing more evidence, may help us to clarify at least part of the problem more satisfactorily.

In dealing with the many meanings of *sattva* we shall confine ourselves mainly to those which the term has in proto-Sāṃkhyan contexts. As far as I am able to judge these meanings are 1. *sattva* as the material counterpart of the *kṣetrajña*; 2. as the *buddhi*; 3. as a *bhāva* of the *buddhi*; 4. as a state of well-being amounting to release; 5. as the first of the three guṇas.

It is a curious fact that in one Mokṣadharma text no less than three of the above meanings of *sattva* occur, the first three. The text is 12, 187=239-240, according to Frauwallner[37] the *epische Grundform* of Sāṃkhya, though I would hesitate to subscribe to this scholar's view that our text is *klar und folgerichtig*.

Sattva as counterpart of *kṣetrajña* and sum-total of world creation occurs in the following stanzas:

sattvakṣetrajñayor etad antaraṃ paśya sūkṣmayoḥ/
sṛjate tu guṇān eka eko na sṛjate guṇān// 187, 37

"understand that *sattva* and *kṣetrajña*, which are both subtle principles, differ in this that the former creates the elements and the latter does not."

na guṇā vidur ātmānaṃ sa guṇān vetti sarvaśaḥ/
paridraṣṭā guṇānāṃ ca saṃsraṣṭā manyate sadā// 40

"the elements do not know the *ātman*, but he knows the elements always; he is the observer of the elements, but always imagines that he is their creator."

sṛjate hi guṇān sattvaṃ kṣetrajñaḥ paripaśyati/
saṃprayogas[38] *tayor eṣa sattvakṣetrajñayor dhruvaḥ//* 42

[96] "for the *sattva* creates the elements whereas the *kṣetrajña* looks on: this is the invariable relationship between *sattva* and *kṣetrajña*."

āśrayo nāsti sattvasya kṣetrajñasya ca kaścana/
sattvaṃ manaḥ saṃsṛjati na guṇān vai kadācana// 43

"there is no further cause of either *sattva* or *kṣetrajña*;[39] *sattva* creates the *manas*.."[40]

Compare also 228, 31cd:

sattvaṃ kṣetrajña ity etad dvayam apy anudarśitam/

A similar meaning of *sattva* as comprising the whole of creation is found in the Sāṃkhya of Arāḍa as described by Aśvaghoṣa in his Buddhacarita[41] 12, 17:

prakṛtiś ca vikāraś ca janma mṛtyur jaraiva ca/
tat tāvat sattvam ity uktam sthirasattva parehitat//

"evolvent and evolute, birth, old age and death sum up *sattva*: so it is taught; go beyond it, O constant One."[42]

The following stanzas 18-19 describe *prakṛti* and *vikāra*, whereupon 20 continues:

asya kṣetrasya vijñānāt kṣetrajña iti saṃjñi ca/

where *asya kṣetrasya* evidently resumes *sattva*. The term recurs in 23:

ajñānaṃ karma tṛṣṇā ca jñeyāḥ saṃsārahetavaḥ/
sthito 'smin tritaye jantus tat sattvaṃ nātivartate//

"ignorance, act and desire are known as the causes of continued existence; so long as man takes his stand on these three he will not overcome the above *sattva*."

The same *sattva* we recognize in Carakasaṃhitā,[43] śarīrasthāna 1,47:

bhāvās teṣāṃ samudayo nirīśaḥ sattvasaṃjñakaḥ/
kartā bhoktā na sa pumān iti kecid vyavasthitāḥ//

"one school maintains these principles and their origination, without a divine creator, which is called *sattva*; as well as a *puruṣa* who is neither agent nor recipient." This can only mean that *sattva* is the cause of the elements and as such opposed to the *kṣetrajña* who is not really involved in creation and its effects.

Another meaning of *sattva* lies near that of *buddhi*. It is already announced in KaṭhUp. 6 (=2,3),7:

indriyebhyaḥ paraṃ mano manasaḥ sattvam uttamam
sattvād adhi mahān ātmā mahato 'vyaktam uttamam//

"beyond the senses is the *manas*, beyond the *manas* the *sattva*, beyond the *sattva* the great *ātman*, beyond the great one the unevolved." One is instantly reminded of BhG. 3,42 where the hierarchy reads: senses—*manas*—*buddhi*—*ātman*, and of the *bhāva* doctrine where the *puruṣādhiṣṭhitā buddhiḥ* evolves *manas* and senses, as well as of in the same chapter (187, 37 quoted above) the statement that *sattva* creates the *manas*. The same correspondence, if not actually equivalence, of *sattva* and *buddhi* is evident in MBh. 12, 203, 33

manaḥ sattvaguṇaṃ prāhuḥ sattvam avyaktajaṃ tathā/

"*manaḥ* is a product of the *sattva*, the *sattva* derives from the *avyakta*."

How are we to account for these different functions of *sattva* (1) as creator and creation, (2) as the *buddhi*? They are not really different: primary is the function of *buddhi* which is the evolvent of the "psychical" organs *manas* and senses and the material elements, which together constitute world creation. In these early forms of Sāṃkhya creation does not necessarily start from a higher principle than the *buddhi*,[44] e.g., *avyakta*, [97] *pradhāna* or *prakṛti*, but from the *buddhi* itself; nor has the *ahaṃkāra* yet taken over the evolutionary functions of the *buddhi*. As the *buddhisattva* is indeed creation and thus the 'material' counterpart of the unaffected *kṣetrajña*. It is just this creatorship of the *buddhi* which is the theme of the entire chapter 187, not only in the *bhāva* doctrine or in the ślokas on *sattva* quoted above, but also in odd ślokas as 16-17:

guṇān nenīyate buddhir buddhir evendriyāṇy api/
manaḥṣaṣṭhāni sarvāṇi buddhyabhāve kuto guṇāḥ//

iti tanmayam evaitat sarvaṃ sthāvarajaṅgamam/
pralīyate codbhavati tasmān nirdiśyate tathā//

"the *buddhi* precedes the evolutes[45] completely: the *buddhi* alone precedes all five senses with the sixth sense *manas*: how could there be evolution if the *buddhi* did not exist? Therefore this entire universe with mobile and immobile creatures is made of the *buddhi* (in which) it has its origin and its end; therefore it is thus described."

The approximation of *buddhi* and *sattva* is the result of the coalescence of parallel doctrines which listed these entities high up in their hierarchies of evolution, sometimes starting evolution from it, sometimes not. In one context this coalescence may have been more complete than in others. Interesting is the usage of a cumulative term in the Yogasūtrabhāṣya pointed out by Johnson:[46] *buddhisattva* in the sense of *buddhi*: this strikes us as a comprehensive formula summarizing the identical functions of both terms. Elsewhere however both principles stand side by side as in the late MBh. 12, 308, 103-4:

dvādaśas tv aparas tatra buddhir nāma guṇaḥ smṛtaḥ/
yena saṃśayapūrveṣu boddhavyeṣu vyavasyati//
atha dvādaśake tasmin sattvaṃ nāmāparo guṇaḥ/
mahāsattvo 'lpasattvo vā jantur yenānumīyate//

"then there is a further element known, the twelfth one (sc. after 10 senses and 11th *manas*), called *buddhi*, by which the person decides about things to be known which could not be resolved by the preceding means of knowledge. Beyond this twelfth one there is a further element called *sattva*, by which a person is judged to be *mahāsattva* or *alpasattva.*" We shall discuss the suggested relation between °*sattva* and *sattva* as the element later on; our chief interest here is that the element *sattva* is listed between *buddhi* and *ahaṃkāra* and that it can only continue the above *sattva.*

In this connection Carakasaṃhitā, sūtrasthāna 1,46 deserves mention:

sattvam ātmā śarīraṃ ca trayam etat tridaṇḍavat/
lokas tiṣṭhati saṃyogāt tatra sarvaṃ pratiṣṭhitam//

sa pumān cetanaṃ tac ca tac cādhikaraṇaṃ smṛtam/
vedasyāsya tadarthaṃ hi vedo 'yaṃ saṃprakāśitaḥ//

"*sattva,* the *ātman* and the body are a triad like a trident, by their combination the world exists: the universe is based upon it; it constitutes the *puruṣa*, which is the knowing principle: and that is the qualification for the Veda, for the Veda has been revealed for his sake." The commentator equates *sattvam* here with *manas* in a general sense, and Johnston suggests *cetanā* or *buddhi.*[47]

The MaitrUp. knows two *sattvas* besides the first guṇa which also occurs, and both are quoted in apparently ancient ślokas. MaitrUp. 6,38 reads: *agnihotraṃ juhvano lobhujālaṃ bhinatty ataḥ sammohaṃ chittvā na krodhān stunvānaḥ kāmam abhidhyāyamānas tataś caturjālaṃ brahmakośaṃ bhindad ataḥ paramākāśam atra hi saurasaumyāgneyasāttvikāni maṇḍalāni bhittvā tataḥ śuddhaḥ sattvāntarastham acalam acyutaṃ dhruvaṃ viṣṇusaṃjñitaṃ sarvāparaṃ dhāma satyakāmasarvajñatvasaṃyuktaṃ svatantraṃ caitanyaṃ sve mahimni tiṣṭhamānaṃ paśyati/atrodāharanti—*

ravimadhye sthitaḥ somaḥ somamadhye hutāśanaḥ/
tejomadhye sthitaṃ sattvaṃ sattvamadhye sthito 'cyutaḥ//

"while offering the *agnihotra*, he breaks through the net of greed; having torn through perplexity, [98] not praising the forms of anger and concentrating on desire, he then pierces the fourfold whorl of *brahman* and thence into supreme space; in that whorl he breaks through (these four) concentric layers formed by sun, moon, fire and *sattva*, and then, being purified, beholds the one within *sattva*, immovable, indestructible, called Viṣṇu, all-highest splendor, the isolated spirit endowed with the power of having all his desires realized and with the power of omniscience, and abiding in his own transcendence.[48] On this they cite: "within the sun is moon, within the moon is fire, within the fire is *sattva*, within the *sattva* the Indestructible." Evidently a yoga process is described here. In *lobha*, *saṃmoha*, *krodha* and perhaps *kāma* we recognize functions of *rajas* and *tamas*. The *brahmakośa* is the flower-cup of the mystic lotus in the centre of which is a space surrounded by a whorl of four concentric layers of leaves; these four *maṇḍalas* are connected with sun etc. in a light symbolism that is typical of the speculations about the mystic lotus. *Sattva*, we note, is a higher principle than *tejas*, it is the last screen or the first covering, and when this innermost layer is pierced the highest spirit—who is a person—within the inner space is beheld in mystic contemplation.

MaitrUp. 4,3 describes the *pratividhir bhūtātmanaḥ* "the rule by which to counter the *bhūtātman*"[49] and quotes:

tapasā prāpyate sattvaṃ sattvāt saṃprāpyate manaḥ/
manasaḥ prāpyate hy ātmā yam āptvā na nivartate//

"by the performance of *tapas* one reaches *sattva*, from *sattva* the *manas*, from *manas* the *ātman*, having attained which one does not return." This is apparently a different *sattva* which we can connect with the *sattva* of ChUp. 7,26,2: *āhāraśuddhau sattvaśuddhiḥ sattvaśuddhau dhruvā smṛtiḥ smṛtilambhe sarvagranthīnāṃ vipramokṣaḥ/ tasmai mṛditakaṣāyāya tamasaḥ pāraṃ darśayati bhagavān sanatkumāraḥ* "when the taking of food has been purified, the *sattva* becomes pure; when *sattva* has been purified, the recollection is secure; when the recollection has been secured, all bonds will be loosened. Thus did the venerable Sanatkumāra show Nārada, cleansed of all impurity, the end of *tamas*." The *āhāraśuddhi* is surely the result of a special regulation in taking food, a *tapas*, and *smṛti* corresponds to *manas*. Interesting is the opposition of *tamas*, the darkness of ignorance and impurity. At a later point we shall try to narrow down the meaning which *sattva* has here; at this point it suffice to note the yogic association of the term.

Leaving aside for the moment the third meaning of *sattva* we distinguished, *sattva* as the first *bhāva*—the *manobhāva*—of the *buddhi,* and concentrating now on the fourth, *sattva* as a state of well-being tantamount to release, we will consider the following evidence. In the closest relation to the functions described above we meet the term in this meaning in such texts as MBh. 12,245,3:

pratirūpaṃ yathaivāpsu tāpaḥ sūryasya lakṣyate/
sattvavāṃs tu tathā sattvaṃ pratirūpaṃ prapaśyati//

"just as the light of the sun is seen reflected in water, so the one who is possessed of *sattva* sees the *sattva* reflected"; and 4:

tāni sūkṣmāni sattvasthā vimuktāni śarīrataḥ/
svena (tattvena) tattvajñāḥ paśyanti niyatendriyāḥ//

"those who are first in *sattva* and know the *tattvas* see these subtle *tattvas* released from the body by virtue of their own (*tattva* or *sattva*) when they have subdued the senses." The *sattva* here appears as that subtle stuff of which release is made; it is transcendent and must be attained by a process of yoga. Important is the reflection of *sattva* which may be compared with the reflection of the soul in matter, the *abhimāna* strictly speaking; there is a plurality of *tattvas* which can exist apart from the body and apparently constitute the *sattva.*[50] But it is not the same as the soul, it is [99] the soul's state of release; nor yet is it the *buddhi,* but beyond it (cf. 8). But in a comparable passage *sattva* does to some extent correspond to the *buddhi*: 12, 238, 9-10:

hitvā tu sarvasaṃkalpān sattve cittaṃ niveśayet/
sattve cittaṃ samāveśya tataḥ kālaṃjaro bhavet//

cittaprasādena yatir jahāti hi śubhāśubham/
prasannātmātmani sthitvā sukham ānantyam aśnute//

"having given up all desires (a function of the *manas*) the yogin must bring the spirit in *sattva*; having brought the spirit in *sattva* he will become a *kālaṃjara* ascetic.[51] By virtue of the serenity of his spirit the yogin gives up both good and evil *karman,* and, with complete tranquillity abiding in the *ātman,* he attains bliss and infinitude." One may hesitate to equate *citta* with *manas* or with *buddhi,* but *buddhi* seems definitely preferable, for serenity is a quality of the *buddhi* rather than of the *manas*: *sattva* thus becomes the serenity itself, free from all disturbances. Similarly 205, 29:

tasmād ātmavatā varjyaṃ rajaś ca tama eva ca/
rajastamobhyāṃ nirmuktaṃ sattvaṃ nirmalatām iyāt//

"therefore the yogin must give up both *rajas* and *tamas,* so that his *sattva,* freed from *rajas* and *tamas,* becomes spotless."

In some of the above instances we may hesitate in deciding whether *sattva* is indeed the released state of the soul or the condition for release. Yet when we compare the unequivocal statements of later date that all three guṇas must be overcome if release is ever to be achieved, it is clear that the above instances convey a different position: emphasis is on the purification of *sattva,* not on the subduing of it. One thing becomes increasingly clear from the evidence marshalled above: the *sattva* which at certain times and in certain contexts shows distinct correspondences with the *buddhi* cannot be separated from the *sattva* which becomes associated with the guṇas *rajas* and *tamas.* Nor is this *sattva* an entirely "material" entity. An important consequence is that *sattva* on the one hand and *rajas* and *tamas* on the other hand do not belong to the same category altogether. Instructive is the quoted MaitrUp. 6, 38 where functions, later (or elsewhere) ascribed to *rajas* and *tamas* (*lobha, saṃmoha,* etc.) appear as obstacles in a yogic process of integration in which the last and decisive step is to overcome *sattva*: but between these *rājasa* and *tāmasa* obstacles and *sattva* many other principles intervene. Interesting is also MBh. 12,246, 9ff. where the body is compared to a town in which the *buddhi* holds sway; the *manas* is the executive (*arthacintaka*), the senses are the people. In this town rage two virulent diseases, *rajas* and *tamas,* which undermine authority and drag *buddhi* and *manas* down to the level of the senses. *Sattva* is absent here, but it is undoubtedly represented by the *buddhi* as the transcendent authority. Similarly 217, 10-11:

ye tv evaṃ nābhijānanti rajomohaparāyaṇāḥ/
te kṛcchram prāpya sīdanti buddhir † yeṣāṃ praṇaśyati//
buddhilābhe hi puruṣaḥ sarvaṃ nudati kilbiṣam/
vipāpmā labhate sattvaṃ sattvasthaḥ saṃprasīdati//

"those who do not know this, being absorbed in *rajas* and *tamas* (=*moha*), find misery and decline, (for) their *buddhi* decays.[52] When a person has gained the *buddhi,* he wipes off all impurity:

being free from evil he gains *sattva* and as a *sattvastha* he is in a state of perfect serenity." Here again we notice how close *buddhi* and *sattva* are: *sattva* is the unaffected state of the *buddhi*, free from *rajas* and *tamas*. Similarly *rajas* and *tamas* appear in 206, 1:

> **tamasā sādhyate moho* **rajasā ca nararṣabha|*
> *krodhalobhau bhayaṃ darpa eteṣāṃ* †*sādhanāc chuciḥ||*

"*moha* results from *tamas*, and wrath and greed, fear and conceit from *rajas*;[53] by subduing them[54] one becomes pure." And if *sattva* is described in 12 as *tamasi saṃsthitam*, just as *rajas* is *tamasi paryastam*, this does not put all of them in the same class, for *tamas* may be so opposed to both *sattva* and *rajas*. Elsewhere we have brought out [**100**] the significance of the fact that in this adhyāya *rajas* is connected with the senses: this connection might on the part of *sattva* imply a similar connection with *buddhi* or *cetas*, which after the foregoing discussions has nothing remarkable.

Frequently one gets the impression that *rajas* and *tamas* form really ONE collective concept comprising between them all obstacles to release and so form together an antihesis to *sattva*. Helpful is a comparison with Arāḍa's Sāṃkhya. Some scholars have made a problem out of the fact that Aśvaghoṣa does not include the "guṇas" in his description, that means: the guṇas in the number, nomenclature, meaning and function they have in the Kārikā and in other "official" Sāṃkhya texts. But if we are to suspect Aśvaghoṣa of unfair dealing, so we should suspect the many authors of the Mokṣadharma who omit these guṇas. The guṇas in their classical functions obviously were not an invariable feature of a unitary Sāṃkhya "system". We have shown that the relation between *ahaṃkāra* and guṇas is secondary; *avyakta*, often the vehicle of the guṇas is mentioned in passing by Arāḍa and then forgotten: in fact its role in epical Sāṃkhya is far from universal. Besides, the introduction of the role of the guṇas as universal constituents is comparatively late. This does not mean that it was a late invention: we believe, and we have shown arguments, that the doctrine of the three guṇas as cosmic magnitudes—from which function they derive their character constituents—and the doctrine of the prakṛtis originally were competing theories, and only in our oldest texts do we see them side by side, to be followed by the almost exclusive presence of the prakṛtis in various stages of development. Arāḍa, we note, adheres to the eight prakṛtis. Therefore the only situation where the absence of the guṇas might legitimately cause surprise and even suspicion would be with and around the *buddhi*, for just with the *buddhi* do the guṇas, in any function, have the most persistent connections. And there is it precisely that we find them. *Sattva*, we saw, appears as the sum-total of body and psyche, in other words as the *buddhi* and its creation, and includes the obstacles to release: *avidyā, karma,* desire (st. 23). But in the same stanza the punning vocative *sthirasattva* (cf. *mahāsattva, alpasattva* MBh. 12, 308, 104) shows that the author was aware of *sattva* in a sense related to the transcendent aspect of the *buddhi*.[55] These obstacles and opposites to the "transcendent", that is released, *buddhi* are further on summarized under *avidyā*, which is described in st. 33:

ity avidyāṃ hi vidvān ca pañcaparvāṃ samīhate/
tamo mohaṃ mahāmohaṃ tāmisradvayam eva ca//

"the expert claims that ignorance is fivefold, viz. *tamas, moha, mahāmoha, tāmisra* and *andhatāmisra*." These are the same five divisions that are enumerated in the Kārikā under *viparyaya* 'ignorance.' We note that all five are synonyms or near-synonyms of *tamas*: *moha* replaces *tamas* regularly. BhāgPur. 3,20,18 uses *mahātamas* for *mahāmoha*.[56] But we note also that in the subsequent description of these terms not only *tāmasa* qualities are summed up, but also typically *rājasa* ones, i.e., qualities etc. which in the doctrine of the three guṇas are classified not under *tamas* but under *rajas*.[57] In other words, side by side with the dual division of *rajas* and *tamas* we find one comprehensive complex of *tamas* which itself is again subdivided into five classes indicated by variations on the word *tamas*.

What, then, is the relation between *rajas/tamas* and the five-fold *tamas*? If we accept Senart's view, corroborated by epical evidence for such a function, that *rajas* started its career as a cosmological entity, and explain the later oblivion of that function partly from the early obsolence of *rajas* 'space, atmosphere' as Burrow has shown and its simultaneous reinterpretation as *rajas* 'dirt' combined with *rāga* 'passion,' it is easy to see how this *rajas*, which was from of old associated with the *buddhi*, came to be identified with some of the qualities so far listed under *tamas*, viz., *kāma, lobha, rāga* and *krodha, dveṣa.* Under this hypothesis we are able to account for all the different functions of *rajas* we have encountered. We may state the entire hypothesis as follows.

Rajas originally was a cosmic entity, "sky, atmosphere", between earth and sun/sky as the second in a triad of earth, atmosphere and heaven. These three worlds at one point came to be regarded [**101**] as stages in a process of world creation, probably under the influence of speculations which described creation as a succession of seasons with sun/summer, atmosphere/clouds-rains, earth/harvest and also under the influence of the creation-by-formulation of the names and things *bhūḥ bhuvaḥ svaḥ*.[58] In circles which we may associate with the names Sāṃkhya and Yoga, where the principal interest was centered on the way to release which is implicit in any evolution theory of creation, the old conception of a cosmic person who creates the world as his body (a conception that also underlies the more "naturalistic" creation accounts as the self-creation of some original being) was developed according to the same triadic pattern, but with a more advanced and above all pronouncedly MICROCOSMIC aspect: this *puruṣa* created the world from his *buddhi* in three direct evolutions, *manas*, senses and elements. But more or less contemporaneously, perhaps a little later, the process of creation came to be described differently: the world had been inventoried under 7 or 8 principles, and this inventory itself became an evolution theory, though of a different pattern: the horizontal pattern of one being or cause which becomes three effects successively—the old triadic scheme—gave way to a vertical pattern where the first effects the second, the second the third, etc. This pattern replaced the horizontal pattern almost completely: the reason was undoubtedly the greater flexibility of the vertical pattern which allowed the addition of new principles for which a need was felt. Here and there, especially around the creation of *manas*, senses and elements, the old triadic scheme persisted and upset the vertical order of descent in the doctrines of those who attempted to synthetize various theories, e.g., the author of the Kārikā; but the *buddhi* lost his function of sole creator though it retained the three "moods" that were the reflections of its three creations on its at first pure and unaffected self. Elsewhere in milieux, one may presume, where the vertical pattern of the seven or eight principles had first been developed, these affections of the *buddhi* (if that was how they called the same principle) were described in an entirely different manner: they distinguished a pure state of enlightenment, sometimes called *tapas*, which was in fact a state of release or from the point of view of creation a transcendent state, and three stages of increasing deterioration, *tuṣṭi*, *aśakti* and *viparyaya* or *avidyā*, of which the last stage, the complete opposite of enlightenment, was subdivided into five categories with names which are variations of the *tamas* that is occasionally met as the antithesis of *tapas* and *sattva*. The three "moods" of the *buddhi* in the more old-fashioned doctrine, once their basis in a tripartite creation had been given up, assimilated themselves to these four stages. The second term in their triad, *rajas*, which gradually must have been reinterpreted as "dirt, defilement, passion" when not only its old meaning "intermediate space" but also its function of cosmic factor of creation became obsolete, attracted those qualities, etc. among the *tamas* complex which accorded well with its supposed passionate character: *rāga* etc. and its opposite *krodha* etc. To the third term, "*tamas*" oı whatever they called the entity which once as "earth" corresponded to *rajas* 'atmosphere', were left those qualities of "inaction, insensibility, stupefaction, unconsciousness" which accorded with its character of inanimate nature. Thus the *tamas* complex was reformed into a dual *rajas-tamas* complex in those milieux where memories of a triadic *buddhi* lingered; other circles, as that of Arāḍa, which remained untouched by the renovations of those who had just abandoned a position they had given up long before, continued with a single *tamas* complex.

This hypothesis may appear quite circumstantial but does not assume more than what, in different phases of our inquiry, we had fair to excellent reasons to accept. As far as I can see, it accounts for the known facts about *rajas*: its old function "atmosphere" which Senart has shown to be connected with the guṇa *rajas* and which must have had its place in a triad sky/atmosphere/earth, or summer/rains/harvest; the recurring connection of *rajas* with the senses and no such recorded connection of *tamas* with the senses; the function of *tamas* in the single *tamas* complex where it comprises typically *rājasa* elements; and the transition of *rajas* "atmosphere" to *rajas/rāga*. To be sure, the historical picture has become more and more complex, but this was only to be expected: if all the facts were known, our explanation would certainly be found to err on the side of simplicity rather than complexity. There must have existed **[102]** scores and scores of more or less isolated little centres where parallel doctrines were being evolved out of a common source. Occasional meetings at pilgrimages and festivals, reports from other and remote *āśramas* brought by wandering ascetics, polemic encounters with other preachers must have resulted in a laborious process of partial renovation and conservation, more precise definitions of doctrines and eclecticism, readjustments of terminology, etc. At this stage to credit these little centers with the name "schools" is to do them too much, or too little, honor. Among those who recognized one another's doctrines as related, normalization prevailed with all the inconsistencies and syncretism of which the final doctrines show traces. We had a glimpse of them when we discussed the Kārikā doctrine of *ahaṃkāra*. Most of the process must elude us necessarily, but we stand a better chance of recovering the little that is left by allowing for the greatest diversity, rather than the greatest uniformity of doctrine.

If we now return to *sattva*, we realize that the great diversity of its functions and meanings will also be due to a long process of doctrinal and terminological readjustments and maladjustments. Only in part can we account for them as stages of historical development of the concept. A concept so vaguely defined by the literal meaning of its name is likely to be used in increasingly different contexts. To force its functions into one line of evolution would be to simplify ureasonably. But we may attempt to show why just this *sattva* could acquire at times quite antithetical meanings.

We have suggested more than once that the evolution doctrine of the *buddhi* with the three "guṇas" and that of the *buddhi* with the *prakṛtis* were to some extent competing theories which after a probably long drawn process of amalgamation finally coalesced, though not invariably. Interesting is in this connection the description of a Sāṃkhya doctrine in MBh. 12, 290, 14 ff. Here a number of principles are enumerated as follows: *sattva* with ten guṇas (*daśaguṇaka*), *rajas* 9, *tamas* 8, *buddhi* 7, *manas* 6, *ether* 5, *buddhi* 4, *tamas* 3, *rajas* 2, *sattva* 1. It is not clear what is meant by *daśaguṇaka*, etc., probably "ten-fold" somehow understood as "tenth" and implying the preceding nine and itself. But we find in this enumeration three clear series: 1. *sattva*, *rajas* and *tamas*; 2. *buddhi*, *manas*, ether; 3. *buddhi*, *tamas*, *rajas*, *sattva*. In other words, the *buddhi* heads two series: that of the *prakṛtis*, *buddhi*, *manas*, ether and the other elements, and that of the guṇa triad, while this triad also occurs by itself. In the sequel we find a rather desperate attempt to include as many series as were known to the author: sight-color: nose-smell: ear-sound: tongue-taste: body-touch: wind: ether: *moha*: *tamas*; *lobha*: riches; this series is not difficult to follow, with its side-by-side enumeration of the elements, the senses and the *viśeṣas*, which are followed significantly by *rajas* (represented by *lobha*) and *tamas* as the guṇas associated with senses and elements. But then follows confusion: strides: Viṣnu; *bala;* Śakra; belly*:* fire (sc. *vaiśvānara*); goddess (= earth): waters: *tejas*: wind: ether: *mahat*: *buddhi*: *tamas*: *rajas*: *sattva*: *ātman*: *īśa*: Nārāyaṇa: *mokṣa*, which is syncretism at its worst. Then follow the lines:

jñātvā sattvayutaṃ dehaṃ vṛtaṃ ṣoḍaśabhir guṇaiḥ/
svabhāvaṃ cetanāṃ caiva jñātvā vai deham āśrite//

madhyastham ekam ātmānaṃ pāpaṃ yasmin na vidyate/
dvitīyaṃ karma vijñāya nṛpate viṣayaiṣiṇām//

"knowing that the body is possessed of *sattva* and enveloped by 16 guṇas, and that both *svabhāva* (prakṛti) and *cetanā* (buddhi) rest on the body, and that inside the body there is the one *ātman* in which no evil is found, and knowing secondly the *karman* of those who strive after the sense-objects, O lord.." To bring order here seems hopeless, but conspicuous are the uncertainty of the position of the triad vis-à-vis the 7 *prakṛtis* and the importance in the quoted ślokas of *sattva* which seems to sum up the 16 guṇas and is therefore the body as a whole—including *prakṛti* and *cetanā*—and that within which the one *ātman* resides untouched. Apparently the author or authors are at a loss how to combine the triad with the *prakṛtis* and probably also the last *sattva* with the guṇa *sattva*; it is tempting to seek the cause of the confusion in the fact that they knew the triad in a function also assumed by the *prakṛtis*, and *sattva* as the sum-total of creation and as the "*buddhi*", very much in the sense in which we met it in MaitrUp. 6, 38.[59] The whole passage is a striking example **[103]** of the encounter of different doctrines and the failure of synthesis.

We passed by the third function of "*sattva*" as the first evolved *bhāva* of the *buddhi*, corresponding to *manas*. We have no unequivocal evidence that this *bhāva* is indeed equal to, or conditioned by a factor called *sattva*. We assumed it from the parallelism of what we have termed the external *bhāvas* (the second of which is *rajas*, the factor of the senses) and the internal *bhāvas*, *sattva-rajas-tamas*. Version B reads *sattva* where we would expect it: but since a copyist may have been struck by the same parallelism, I should cautiously prefer the non-committal variant *bhāvam* of Version A. That there is a triad of evolvent factors behind the three external *bhāvas* would seem to be beyond doubt, and the probabilities are that the first is *sattva*.

Having exhausted the meanings of *sattva* in texts suggestive of Sāṃkhya in the Mokṣadharma section of the epic, we may ask ourselves: can we find an "original" *sattva* from which the later functions of this concept can be naturally derived? A few considerations should precede our inquiry. First be it repeated that the evidence about *sattva*, as well as the facts about the relation between *rajas* and *tamas* for which we have tried to account in the above hypothesis, should warn us not to assume beforehand that, since *sattva* is principally known as the first of the three guṇas, it therefore has always been in a triad and we are to look for an ancient triad to fit it in. Actually we are reasonably sure only that *rajas* always belonged in a triad; *tamas* did not. Secondly the fact stands out that *sattva* especially when it occurs by itself mostly occurs in evolution doctrines which describe an individuation rather than a cosmogony. But having made this observation we are to remind ourselves immediately that the distinction, though useful, is far from being sharp. World creation was described as the individuation process of a cosmic being. This is probably the most significant fact on which we ought to test our ability to follow the associations from one set of myths about creation to another set of more sophisticated theories of evolution. Though we may glibly talk about macrocosmic and microcosmic aspects, this equivalence of the world at large and the world that is the person is difficult to understand; and even more difficult to operate with, for it is clear that just in the epoch with which we are dealing macrocosm and microcosm become separated somehow, but not so completely that many concepts do not remain ambivalent for a long time. In *rajas* we have a clear case where a macrocosmic entity loses its macrocosmic content almost entirely;[60] but not in all cases the distinctions are so clear-cut. Therefore if we say that *sattva* figures often in speculations where attention is not so much focused on cosmogony as on individuation, we cannot be sure we have made a meaningful statement; but more meaning may we gather from the fact that *sattva*, in the variety of its functions, frequently occurs there where the upward progress of return to the original state of person or original being is described rather than where the downward progress of creation is the sole topic.

These observations may clear the way before we attempt an etymology of *sattva*. To render the term with "goodness" is to start from its moral function as the first of the guṇas which, as universal constituents, by their interplay and relative preponderance determine the phenomena of the world and the character of man. But we have seen that this *sattva* is historically the same as the *sattva* in other meanings, and this rendering of the term[61] would hardly account for such meanings as "sum-total of body and creation", which is a much wider notion. Moreover, as we pointed out in passing, this meaning of *sat* 'good' is not very satisfactory: it conveys "morally good" insofar as it denotes "strict and punctilious in doing one's duty, esp. in ritual detail." An abstraction of this *sat* would hardly be expected to figure prominently in the hierarchy of doctrines in circles which were definitely not characterized by their undue preoccupation with ritualistic exactitude. We should **[104]** look for another *sat* which figures as an elevated principle in a creation or evolution account where the upward progress of yogic return is expressed or implied.

This *sat* is, I think, to be found in such texts as the celebrated Sadvidyā of Uddālaka, ChUp. 6,[62] where an original being called *sat*, by a process of tripartition, creates the phenomenal world which again returns to its source and is reabsorbed in it; this reabsorption means the release of the individual soul.[63] The Vedāntins, esp. the advaitins, have interpreted this *sat* as *sattāmātram* and many a translator has followed them; but it is clear that *sat* is an original creator with an *ātman*[64] to it, and that *sat* here means "the being which exists (here and now)."

We have seen that *sattva* can denote the body-complex, the aggregate of elements and psyche, of the *puruṣa* or *kṣetrajña*, "the embodied soul." In such contexts the totality of the body—which is creation at large—can be understood as the *sat-tva* of this soul, as the condition which makes this soul a *sat*, "an entity which exists concretely."[65] We may adduce here another meaning of *sattva*, not considered so far, which is very common: "living being, a being generally, but animate rather than inanimate."[66] Such concrete meanings of an "abstract" noun in *-tva* should warn us against interpreting *sattva* too abstractly. Renderings like "a being," or "*Wesen*" which runs like a scarlet thread through the many meanings distinguished by Böhtlingk-Roth, are deceptive: they presuppose an abstract "being, *Sein*", whereas *sattva* presupposes a concrete "existing thing". The habit of translating this *sat* itself as "Being", already in ṚV. 10,129 is at best an error of anachronism.

Elsewhere the present writer has discussed this *sat* in some detail[67] and here his remarks will be confined to the following. In such hymns as ṚV. 10, 129, etc. *sat* is the product of *asat*, which might be rendered: "that which is not yet a *sat*", but not just "non-existent", let alone "Non-being". The emergence of *sat* out of *asat*, one might say, the reification of *asat,* takes place under the general supervision of a personal creator, though there is a tendency to dispense with his services. This emergence of *sat* out of *asat*, *asat*'s becoming a *sat,* remains the current view till Uddālaka disposes of *asat* and has creation start with *sat* alone. But *sat* remains a being that fulfills itself in creation, and already in ṚV. 10, 129 we can talk of the *sattva* of *asat*. Uddālaka, while doing away with *asat.* is quite aware of his originality as his justification shows.[68] The problem, as I see it, was the anbivalence of *asat*: Uddālaka finds it impossible to derive from *asat* "non-existent" and *asatya* "not as it is and always has been and ought to be", "not fixed, permanent and true", a *sat* that is not only the all-comprehensive existent and persistent Original Being but also the *satya*[69] with all its associations. But *sat* and *asat* also formed another contrast. Instructive is a passage in BĀUp. 2, 3 where the *brahman* is said to have two forms, a solid and an unsolid one (*mūrta* and *amūrta*), which are *sat* "existing here, palpably" and *tyad* "the yon, existing beyond *sat*," compared in this text with the sun and the person within it. This *tyad*, or unsolid or transcending aspect of brahman is *satya*; where *sat* is the mortal, *tyad* [105] is the immortal. This unsolid, transcending entity is also called *asat*, which one would like to render with "unreified" rather than "unreal." The *sattva* of the *sat* here is just that it is an obviously existing, tangible, solid thing.

It is this *asat* which in a number of texts, and by Uddālaka's adversaries, was regarded as the first "cause." Faced with the problem how to derive from an *asat* 'non-existent and untrue' a *sat* creation, Uddālaka resolved it by simply doing away with *asat*. The authors of TaittUp. 2, faced with the same ambiguity of *asat*, solved it by equating it with *sat* in terms reminiscent both of ChUp. 6 and BĀUp. 2, 3. TaittUp. 2, 6-7 reads:

asann eva sa bhavati asad brahmeti veda cet|
asti brahmeti ced veda santam enaṃ tato viduḥ||

...so 'kāmayata | bahu syāṃ prajāyeyeti | sa tapo 'tapyata | sa tapas taptvā | idaṃ sarvam asṛjata | yad idaṃ kiṃ ca | tat sṛṣṭvā | tad evānuprāviśat | tad anupraviśya | sac ca tyac cābhavat | niruktaṃ cāniruktaṃ ca | nilayanaṃ cānilayanaṃ ca | satyaṃ cānṛtaṃ ca| satyam abhavat | yad idaṃ kiṃ ca | tat satyam ity ācakṣate | tad apy eṣa śloko bhavati|

asad vā idam agra āsīt tato vai sad ajāyata|
tad ātmānam svayam akuruta tasmāt tat sukṛtam ucyate||

...yadā hy evaiṣa etasminn adṛśye 'nātmye 'nirukte 'nilayane 'bhayaṃ pratiṣṭhāṃ vindate | atha so 'bhayaṃ gato bhavati: "Non-existent shall one become, when one knows *brahman* for 'non-existent'. When one knows that *brahman* exists, then they know that one is existing."..."He wished: I will be many, I will beget. He heated himself up;[70] after having heated up himself, he discharged[71] all this, whatever there is. Having discharged it, he entered into it. Having entered into it, it became *sat* and *tyad*, formulated and unformulated, conscious and unconscious, solid and unsolid, real and unreal: it was real, whatever there is. That is why they say: "it is real."[72] On this there is this śloka: "The *asat* was here at first; from it arose the *sat*: it made itself a person; therefore it is said to be well-done."[73]...When one finds oneself security, a firm foothold on this invisible,[74] unpersonified, unformulated, unsolidified (*asat*), then indeed one will have reached complete security." Here we have the two meanings of *asat*: "non-existent", the opposite of *asti*, in the first śloka, and "unreified" in the second śloka. In the creation account of the prose commentary the masculine *saḥ* refers to *ātman* or *prajāpati*, and the same original being is referred to as a neuter in *sac ca tyac cābhavat*, etc. *Tyad, aniruktam, avijñānam, anilayanam* and *anṛtam* (*asatyam*)[75] explain the *asat* of the following śloka. The created world is something real, reified, *satya*. Here again we see how the creator becomes a *sat* when he has entered into his creation, i.e., reified himself. In the śloka the same view is repeated: from the *asat* the *sat*

originated, it (*asat*) personified himself; for *asat* is *anātmya* "not (yet) a being with an *ātman* to it, not personified."

In the earliest occurrences of the term *sat* appears as a more or less technical term for the manifest creation that emerges from the unmanifest under the aegis of a personal creator who is really the *asat* reifying himself. *Sat* thus is the first created product, it is the whole of creation; but it is also the prime cause of creation for it is the being that has reified itself in creation. But very early already we see that the "personal creator" is separated from this *asat* becoming *sat*, though not everywhere. It would seem that where the notion of an original creator behind *sat* persisted, *sat* was the created, creation; there where the personality vanishes, a process that starts in ṚV. 10, 129 and is completed in ChUp. 6, *sat* was the self-created creator. It would seem that *sattva*, undoubtedly a notion that was elaborated in circles where the idea of a personality —with increasingly microcosmic features—persisted, reflects in its functions the aspect of *sat* as the **[106]** reified and created. As such it could easily become linked up with tripartite creation, for as we have seen the triadic pattern was very frequently used in creation accounts: *sat* of ChUp. 6 itself creates itself in the three stages of *tejas*, *āpas* and *annam* and then personifies itself by entering into these three entities as a living being.[76] But *sat* was not necessarily involved in triads, and we see *sattva* exist outside such groupings. As the first created creature *sat* was here and there approximated to the *buddhi*, which originally was the self-recognition of the original being as a person, an *ātmanvin*, and *sattva*, the "createdness" of this being, could become the state of this self-recognition or *buddhi*. *Sattva* thus lost some of its autonomy to *buddhi*, but preserved it in other circles where it could still sum up the entire creation or, microcosmically, the *puruṣa's* body. *Sattva* not only had its own ambivalence from *sat* which was both creator and created, but when linked up with *buddhi* came to share a corresponding ambivalence of this "self-recognition": the FINAL liberating self-recognition on the one hand, and on the other hand the INITIAL creative self-recognition, which gradually, with the increasing primacy of the transcendent and unmanifest as the unalterable "truth," became a mistaking oneself for creation, a misconception;[77] this function, with the function of creator at the bottom of it, was also transferred to another originally equivalent[78] entity called *ahaṃkāra*. So *sattva* could be either tantamount to release, the *buddhi's* self-revelatory insight, or the first step out of and the last step before a state of release. In the latter function it could describe a person's CAPACITY OF RELEASE, as I think, we find it in *sthirasattva, mahāsattva, alpasattva* etc. It would seem probable that *bodhisattva* belongs to this *sattva*: it describes a personality that has reached the last step before reaching the redeeming knowledge and can have this knowledge at will. Probably also the *sattva* of ChUp. 7,26,2 and Maitr Up. 4,3, where this capacity of release, purified by *tapas*, precedes *smṛti* or *manas*, in which we may very well have synonyms of *buddhi*.

It is not clear how *sattva* came to be associated just with *rajas* and *tamas*. Probably it succeeded to a principle like *tapas* or *jyotis*, which acquired the connotation of "light of knowledge" and had its opposite in "darkness' and "obscuration". It is very likely that *rajas* 'atmosphere' brought the triadic pattern along; where *rajas* does not occur we find no clear triads, though both *sattva* and *tamas* have definite potentialities to be involved in groupings of three. However that may be, once the three were united in a triad they were all but inseparable, and no more than hints survive of independent functions of *sattva* and *tamas*.[79] They were so united at an early date; there is no reason to doubt that the three guṇas of AthV. 10,8,43 refer to the precursors of *sattva*, *rajas* and *tamas*;[80] and the speculations about the mystic [107] lotus—with which *sattva* was also associated—show that the date of this passage cannot be removed too far from comparable speculations in the earliest upaniṣads.[81]

NOTES

1. Emile Senart, "Rajas et la théorie indienne des trois guṇas," *JAs.* 11me série, tome VI (1915).
2. Sāṃkhyakārikā 47.
3. Cf. e.g. E. H. Johnston, *Early Sāṃkhya* (London, 1937), p. 38.
4. "Studies in Sāṃkhya (I), An Old Text Reconstituted," *JAOS*, LXXVI (1956), pp.153 ff.; and "do., II, Ahaṃkāra," *JAOS*, LXXVII (1957), pp. 15 ff. [nos. 6 and 7 in this volume].
5. *JAOS*, LXXVI, p. 157[9] [no. 6, note 9].
6. MBh. 12,187 etc. as reconstructed *JAOS*, LXXVI (1956), pp. 153 ff.
7. Paul Oltramare, *L'histoire des idées théosophiques dans l'Inde*, Vol. I (Paris, 1906), p. 240.
8. Hermann Oldenberg, *Die Lehre der Upaniṣaden und die Anfänge des Buddhismus* (Göttingen, 1923[2]), p. 186.

9. ChUpBhāṣya 6, 2, 3; Sūtrabhāṣya 2, 3, 10 (Poona ed., p. 272) beginning *nanv itarāpi śrutir.*

10. Śrībhāṣya 2, 3, 1-14; cf. also my note in *Rāmānuja's Vedārthasaṃgraha* (Poona, 1956), translation 17.

11. One might, however, mention the rule that in a compound the longer word follows the shorter one; but we shall see that there are excellent reasons why the)second term of the triad, *rajas*, acquired the red color.

12. E.g. ŚatBr. 10, 2, 4, 1; 2, 6, 1; 4,2, 1; 11, 1, 1; PraśnUp. 1, 9; MaitrUp. 6, 15 *sa kālaḥ sakalaḥ/sakalasya* (sc. *brahmaṇo*) *vā etad rūpaṃ yat saṃvatsaraḥ/ saṃvatsarāt khalv imāḥ prajaḥ prajāyante..saṃvatsaro vai prajāpatiḥ / kālo' nnaṃ brahmanīḍam ātmā cety.*

13. *JAOS, LXXVII* (1957), p. 18 [no. 7, p. 58].

14. So already ṚV. 10, 129, 4

15. Walter Ruben, *Die Philosophen der Upaniṣaden* (Bern, 1947), p. 123: "...sang Hymnen (wie die primitiven Regenmacher und die Brahmanen taten) und schuf damit die Wasser."

16. ṚV. 10, 90 etc.

17. ChUp. 6, 3, 2-3; TaittUp. 2, 6; see below.

18. BĀUp. 1, 2, 7 *apa punarmṛtyuṃ jayati nainaṃ mṛtyur āpnoti*: *mṛtyur asyātmā bhavati devatānām eko bhavati.*

19. *Philosophen*, p. 123 "Verehrer des Hungers."

20. To whom Senart refers; the passage is ChUp. 6, 2, 4 *tā* (sc. *āpas*) *annam asṛjanta pṛthivīlakṣaṇam/pārthivaṃ hy annam.*

21. ChUp. 6, 2, 6.

22. On the self-creation of *sat* see below.

23. T. Burrow, "Sanskrit *rájas*", *BSOAS*, XII, p. 645.

24. Cf. also MuṇḍUp. 2, 2, 9 *hiraṇmaye pare kośe virajaṃ brahma niṣkalam.*

25. O. c., p. 469.

26. The same adhyāya, MBh. 12, 187, 50.

27. Ruben, *Philosophen*, p. 164, "gerade diese drei Farben aber sind in alter Technik der Keramik and Webekunst üblich und in primitiven Mythologien belegt."

28. ChUp. 3, 1-5.

29. E.g. ChUp. 8, 6, 1; BĀUp. 4, 3, 20.

30. I.e. *tamas* as the third guṇa.

31. *Tamo vā idam agra āsīt* etc.

32. This reads in d. *tamaso 'nte maheśvaraḥ*, so that the translation runs: "for the (*manas* of st. 15), when possessed of *tapas*, shines forth like the sun beyond *tamas*: the embodied soul, whose prakṛti is constituted by the universe, is the supreme lord when the *tamas* has been passed"; for the "end of *tamas*," cf. ChUp. 7, 26, 2 quoted below.

33. See below.

34. Emile Senart, "La théorie des guṇas et la Chāndogya Upaniṣad," in *Etudes asiatiques* (=jubilee volume of *BEFEO*; Paris, 1925), p. 287.

35. J. Przyluski, "La théorie des guṇa," *BSOAS*, VI (1931), pp. 25ff.; and "La loi de symétrie dans la Chāndogya-Upaniṣad," *BSOAS*, V, esp. pp. 491 ff.

36. The sequel will show how near our own studies will lead us to Senart's conclusions.

37. Erich Frauwallner, *Geschichte der indischen Philosophie*, Band I (Salzburg, 1953), ch. 6, p. 292.

38. A well-attested variant reads *viprayogaḥ* 'difference.'

39. I would prefer this rendering to that of Deussen-Strauss, *Vier philosophische Texte des Mahābhāratam* (Leipzig, 1906), in B. 194, 44; p. 184: "das Sattvam und der Kṣetrajña haben keine gemeinschaftliche Basis."

40. The fourth pāda is obviously corrupt; we expect: "*sattva* creates the *manas* and the further evolutes," as in 37; cf. Belvalkar's note on 187, 43.

41. Edited and translated by E. H. Johnston, 2 vols. (Calcutta, 1933-36).

42. On *sthirasattva*, see below.

43. Ed. V.K. Datar (Bombay, 1922).

44. I do not propose to enter here into a discussion of *buddhi/manas* etc., which deserve a separate monograph; but on the whole it is clear that both terms reflect the original "self-recognition" and "desire" to become a person or sat of the unreified creator who (which) was *asat* or *avyakta*; for a few remarks on this point see below.

45. Note this meaning of guṇa; renderings like "product, element, evolute, constituent" are approximations: guṇa denotes all at once; the term deserves further study, cf. also Senart, "Rajas et la théorie indienne des trois guṇas"; Johnston, *Early Sāṃkhya*, p. 30.

46. O.c., p. 50.

47. O.c., p. 51.

48. Cf. texts like ChUp. 8, 1, 1 *atha yad idam asmin brahmapure daharaṃ puṇḍarīkaṃ veśma daharo 'sminn antar ākāśaḥ/tasmin yad antas tad anveṣṭavyaṃ tad vāva vijijñāsitavyam...5 etat satyaṃ brahmapuram* ["this fortess of brahman (=body creation) is real": cf. note 72 below on *tat satyam*] *asmin kāmāḥ samāhitāḥ/eṣa ātmā..satyakāmaḥ satyasaṃkalpaḥ.*

49. "The embodied, elemental *ātman*," the material world.

50. The subtle elements (*tattvāni*) may be compared both to the *sūkṣmaśarīra* and to such elements as *tejas* etc. in which the sat of ChUp. 6 primarily subsists. I should prefer to read *sattvena* for *tattvena*, though the distinction is very slight as the above remark shows.

51. Deussen-Strauss translate: "wird man [unerschütterlich wie] der Berg Kālañjara werden," but it seems preferable to read here a reference to theory and practice of yogins associated with this mountain or region.

52. Belvalkar marks *yeṣām* doubtful; at any rate *teṣām* seems preferable.

53. The editions, including Cr. Ed., read *rajasā...tamasā* which should be transposed.

54. Belvalkar marks *sādhanāc* doubtful; I translate *sādanāc* from the variants.

55. See below.

56. In Viṣṇu Pur 1, 6, 41 *tāmisra* and *andhatāmisra* are names of hells.

57. Viz. in 12, 34 *mahāmohas tv asaṃmoha kāma ity eva gamyatām*, and 36 *tāmisram iti cākrodha krodham evādhikurvate.*

58. In the Kālāgnirudra Up. however *rajas* appears in a series with *bhūrloka*, *sattva* with *antarikṣa*, *tamas* with *dyaurloka*!

59. The one *ātman*, which is in the middle of the body possessed of *sattva* and in which there is no evil, is the *apahatapāpātman ātman* in the mystic lotus in the *brahmapura* of ChUp. 8, 1, 1 and this MaitrUp. text.

60. It exists on as "universal constituent" of *pradhāna*, which is not more than a rudiment of its original function.

61. Nearest perhaps is sat in such passages as Tāṇḍya MBr. 15, 12, 2 *sad vai vāmadevyaṃ sāmnāṃ sad virāṭ chandasāṃ sat trayastriṃśaḥ stomānāṃ satām antān saṃdhyāyottiṣṭhanty api ha putrasya putrah sattvam aśnute*, where *sat* means "excellent" (Sāyaṇa: *utkṛṣṭa*), and *sattva* "excellence"; Bohtlingk-Roth render *sattva* here by "Wesen, Character," which is not so appropriate.

62. Senart was, as far as I know, the only one who ever suggested such a connection; his suggestion was tentative and mainly inspired by his attempt to connect the guṇa *sattva* with the *tejas* of ChUp. 6.

63. ChUp. 6, 8. 6.

64. See below.

65. It is tempting to explain *sattva* in Gopatha Br. 2, 4, 12 similarly: *prajāpatir etebhyaḥ prāṇebhyo 'nyān devān sasrje/yad u cedaṃ kiṃ ca pāṅktaṃ tat sṛṣṭvā vyājvalayat / te hocur devā—mlāno 'yaṃ pitāmaho 'bhūt* (e.c. Gaastra) / *punar imaṃ samīryotthāpayāmeti / sa ha sattvam ākhyāyābhyupatiṣṭhate/yadi hi vā api nirṇiktasyaiva kulasya saṃdhyukṣeṇa yajate sattvam ākhyābhyupatiṣṭhate* "Prajāpati created the other gods out of these prāṇas; having created all these five he set them afire (sacrificed them); the old father had become exhausted (i.e. the fire had died down) [I transpose]; then the gods said: 'let us shake him up and revive him'. Having called on his *sattva* he rose again up to them. (Similarly) if someone sacrifices by kindling (*saṃdhukṣeṇa*?) a pile which is extinguished as (water) was sprinkled over it, (the fire) rises up again by calling on its *sattva*." The passage is far from clear nor its readings certain; but it would appear that *sattva* here represents the inner life-giving substance of *prajāpati*/sacrificail fire (identical: *yo vai prajāpatiḥ sa yajñaḥ*).

66. *Sattva* 'thing' is attested very rarely.

67. *Rāmānuja's Vedārthasaṃgraha*, Intr. I.

68. ChUp. 6, 2, 1-2 *tad dhaika āhuḥ—asad evedam agra āsīd ekam evādvitīyam / tasmād asataḥ sad ajāyateti / kutas tu khalu somyaivaṃ syād iti katham asataḥ saj jāyeta.*

69. Cf. 6, 8, 6 *sa ātmā tat satyam.*

70. This *tapas* corresponds to the *tejas* of ChUp. 6 and the *tapas* of BĀUp. 1, 2 discussed above.

71. *Sṛj-*.

72. E.g. Uddālaka ChUp. 6.8.6 *sa ātmā tat satyam*, where *ātman* and *satya* both denote the reified original being.

73. *Sukṛtam*; one could render "well-finished, completed."

74. Cf. the invisible person (*tyad*) in the visible sun (*sat*) in BĀUp. 2, 3.

75. Another description is *avyaktam* which, originally synonymous with *asat*, came to denote on the one hand the transcendent *ātman*, on the other hand the primordial matter, *pradhāna*, to which the creator's function of the *ātman* were delegated.

76. It is clear that *ātman* in. . *anupraviśya jīvenātmanā* is the *sat* now personified; cf. my remarks in *Rāmānuja's Vedārthasaṃgraha*, Intr. I.

77. *Abhimāna*, which originally is presumably the same as the *abhimāna* of BĀUp. 1, 2, 4: *sa aikṣata—yadi vā imam abhimaṃsye kanīyo 'nnaṃ kariṣya iti*, where *imam* is the original being's "second self," i.e. personification.

78. Self-recognition and self-formulation being the same process.

79. For all the attention we have here given these autonomous functions of *sattva* and *tamas*, it is plain that they are in a very small minority as compared with their function as members of the guṇa triad.

80. There is no evidence to show that they were really called *sattva, rajas* and *tamas*. Personally I should be inclined to think that *sattva* came to occupy the first place in a triad of which *rajas* was the second term and succeeded there to a first term *jyotis* or *tapas* or *tejas*. We see for instance *jyotis* appear in a triad in statu nascendi with *rajas* and *tamas*, AthV. 8, 2, 1-2 *á rabhasvemām amṛtasya śnúṣṭim ácchidyamānā jarádaṣṭir astu te / ásuṃ ta ā́yuḥ púnar á bharāmi rájas támo mópa gā mā́ prá meṣṭhāḥ // jī́vatāṃ jyótir abhy ehi arvā́ṅ ā́ tvā́ harāmi śatáśaradāya / avamuñcáś mṛtyupāśā́n áśastiṃ drā́ghīyo ā́yuḥ pratarā́ṃ te dadāmi*. Whitney-Lanman translate: "take thou hold of this bundle (?) of immortality; unsevered length of time be thine; I bring back thy life, thy life-time; go not to the welkin (*rájas*), the darkness. Come hitherward unto the light of the living; I take thou in order to live for a hundred autumns; loosening down the fetters of death, imprecation, I set for thee further a longer life-time." As the translators remark: "it is indeed a little startling to find the two names (sc. *rajas* and *tamas*) here side by side." Whether *rajas* has the meaning of "welkin" or "blackness of dirt" etc., the triad is still a dyad and the whole situation is neatly comparable to *tapas/sattva→tamas/-rajas-tamas* of MBh. 12,209, 10, supra. In the opposition *jyotis←→rajas-tamas* is doubtless also reflected that of the two paths of light and darkness (ChUp. 5, 10, 1; BhG. 8, 26) which here find a worldly application.

81. In an Appendix to her II *mito psicologico nell' India antica* (Memorie della Reale Accademia Nazionale dei Lincei, 1939, serie vi, volume viii, fascicolo v), Maryla Falk has discussed the origins of the guṇas ("Genesi della dottrina dei tre guṇa," appendice II, p. 415/703ff.) particularly in relation to AthV. 10, 8, 43 etc. and ChUp. 6. Her views on the origin of the triad as a triad are too closely connected with her general hypothesis on the origin of the yogic puruṣa doctrine, which she traces back to the oldest texts, to be easily made intelligible out of context. In Ath V. and ChUp. texts the three guṇas which surround the *puṇḍarīka* are "il luminoso fluido dello hṛdākāśā con i suoi tre colori principali (corrispondenti alle tre sedi del cuore), entre cui, secondo la concezione spesso documentata nelle Upaniṣad, è contenuto potenzialmente l'ātman." With the last remark I agree to the extent that the Creator, as we have seen, reifies and personifies himself in three cosmic stages—worlds/seasons—which, with the increasing "microcosmification" of the creation process, with all its soteric implications, come to lend their pattern to different forms of psychological life. I cannot enter here into a discussion of her arguments which are in part answered in this and former studies and in part outside the scope of the present study which, apart from describing the general background of cosmogonic triads, concerned itself mainly with the individual histories of the three terms. Miss Falk's book, stimulating for all the opposition it evokes, was not available to me in India where this article was written and could not be given the consideration which it has rarely found but richly deserves.

9

DHARMA AND MOKṢA

This paper is meant to provide some historical background on the question of the distinction between *dharma* values and *mokṣa* values in Indian thought. The Indian context requires that we view "moral values"—I shall hereafter avoid the term—first in relation to different eschatologies. Very roughly, we may distinguish two.

First, the conception of an "after-life" which, though interrupted by intervals of heaven and hell, remains on the same level as the present life, and, although its varying degrees of "spirituality" (*caitanya* and related terms) encompass the entire range from worm to Brahmā, cannot be regarded as essentially different from human life. This is *saṃsāra*, "transmigration," usually involving the doctrine that a certain "soul" continues from life to life in an embodied existence, the facts of his body and his life being largely dependent on what acts the individual has performed in former such lives, yet affording limited scope for gradual self-perfection—but on the same level—by meritorious acts.

Second, the assumption of *mokṣa*, "release," from the above "bondage" (*bandha*) to continued embodied existence. Taken by and large, all Indian systems acknowledge that a supreme effort of consciousness, a total isolation of a person's awareness of his "soul," representing a "supreme soul," from all that is non-soul is the means to achieve this release. Buddhism does not positively start from a concept of soul, but negatively from that which is non-soul, preferring to describe the self-recognition of the soul as *nirvāṇa*, the extinction of the flame of life-thirst, and the indescribable that remains after the extinction as being void of all worldly description.

When we inquire into the history of these conceptions, much, of course, must remain obscure; still, there is sufficient evidence to justify certain conclusions.

Examining the oldest texts, we find, instead of transmigration, a hopeful prospect of heavenly joys in an after-life. Access to this abode is afforded by the performance of ritual acts, which are not infrequently discouraging in complexity and expenditure. But it soon becomes clear that the obtaining of heaven is far from the overriding concern of sacerdotal circles, that, in fact, their prime concern is to control and maintain the universe as it is. Such control and maintenance are sought and found in the perfect knowledge and [**34**]impeccable application of rites which may be said both to constitute and to produce the *dharma* of the universe, which means approximately the maintenance of the proper equilibrium of the cosmos. In the sacrificial area the forces that control the world are generated, are brought into interplay, and are guided by priests who profess to full mastery by virtue of their knowledge. There is an undeniable magnificence in the certainty of purpose and the elaboration of its achievement which forces us to recall that roughly in the same age Āryan supremacy was carried from Sindh to the Western sea and from the foothills of the Himālayas to the Vindhya range.

But in the most ancient age we already have intimations of different outlooks and practices. From the *Ṛg Veda* onward we meet personalities who were evidently outside brahministic sacerdotalism. These figures, long-haired, given to self-induced states of "ecstasy" and intoxication, apparently sought after other states of well-being which involved principally themselves and through themselves possibly others to whom they extended medicine-man services. We recognize remote precursors of the *yogins,* and among them precursors of a Gautama and a Mahāvīra.

In later portions of the Brāhmaṇas, the Āraṇyakas, and the early Upaniṣads, we find a growing preoccupation on the part of officiating priests, who continue to think in ritualistic terms, with the ultimate basis of the ritually poised cosmos. This ultimate is identified both with certain ritualistic constants, most generally either Word or Fire, or a diunity of them, and with a divine creator. This creator (the *yajñapuruṣa*, the "sacrifice-person"[1]) certainly was believed in as a personal deity in other circles, but among officiating priests ever more closely approximated to the creative principles of ritual.[2] A certain hierarchic organization was imposed on the cosmos, frequently a triad, and this hierarchy was conceived of as stages of creation in a creation process originating from the ultimate cause. Basically this creation process was a self-creation, a self-manifestation of the original One, an individuation which ended with his or its becoming a person (*ātman*).[3] Increasing significance was being attached to his or its original state, before the self-creation—represented as a ritual event—took place and speculations arose about the reversion of the self-creation. Probably under some influence from [35] protoyogic circles, there was a tendency to enact ritually and produce such a reversion, which amounts to complete transcension over man's created, i.e., embodied, condition.

At one stage of this complex of speculations there entered the idea of transmigration, which first appears, not as rebirth, but as redeath. This redeath was said to be conquered by certain rituals accompanied by knowledge of the great cosmic connections enacted in the sacrifice and involving the creation process.[4] It is of importance to note that before transmigration was introduced into these speculations the ritual practicability of ascension and transcension had already been articulated and that the idea later called *mokṣa* did not come into being as a corollary of bondage in *saṃsāra*. Transmigration was absorbed into a system that afforded room for it, but was not itself basically altered. We may further stress a point usually ignored in discussions of *karman*: transmigration could solve a very real problem of applied ritualistics. If performed properly by a qualified person, a rite has an inherent efficacy in producing its result. There is no God dispensing services as he sees fit; results are automatically forthcoming. But what happens, it is asked, if the fruit fails to be realized, if the son fails to be born or rain fails to fall? The casuistry involved is known only from a later date, but for the problem to be mentioned then must imply its previous actuality.[5] We find a factor distinguished, called *apūrva,* which is the latent power of the act to bring about its fruit. This potency may continue and be actualized in a later life if adverse circumstances—early death of the beneficiary, etc.—prohibit its immediate realization. It is of interest to note this point, since it is exactly this latent power of man's acts which is carried forward in successive lives of his transmigrating "soul". The doctrine of *karman* and *phala,* act and fruit, is less a product of man's sense of justice, that one shall be punished and rewarded for what one has done, than a necessary consequence of the doctrine of the inherent efficacy of the acts. By "act" (*karman*) we have always first to understand the ritual act; by ignoring this plain fact such disciplines as the *karmayoga* of the *Bhagavadgītā* become unintelligible.[6]

Dharma is the observance of the necessary acts that keep the world intact. *Dharmas,* as the forces that are active in maintaining this world, efficacious [36] potencies set loose for constructive purposes, are known in early Buddhism (*dhammas*) as *Daseinsmächte* of a comparable kind. It is necessary to keep in mind these functions of a term that can be rendered only very freely and loosely by "virtue".

Dharma retains much of this total sense of the cosmic status quo and the specific acts of all manner of beings which enforce it. *Dharma,* in Hinduism, is the cosmically or "religiously" determined activity of all existing beings to maintain the normal order in the world. Therefore it can be rendered "norm," a meaning particularly known from Buddhism. Yet, we should not think of *dharma* as both the act and its result, as something static, but as a balance which is constantly being struck. It retains the connotation of powerful activity operating in the universe and even constituting this universe. These activities called *dharma* are imposed as a kind of natural law on all existent beings in the universe; and a being's initiating of such activity is not a moral act contingent on his disposition, but an innate characteristic,[7] that which makes a being what it is, assigning the part it is to play in concert. It is the *dharma* of the sun to shine, of the pole to be fixed, of the rivers to flow, of the cow to yield milk, of the *brahmin* to officiate, of the *kṣatriya* to rule, of the *vaiśya* to farm.

It is as difficult to define *dharma* in terms of Western thought as it is to define "culture" in Sanskrit, and for the same reason: both are all-comprising terms including institutions, a way of thinking and living, accomplishments characteristic of people. Even modern usages of the term show the all-inclusive scope of the concept of *dharma*: one speaks of Hindu *Dharma,* Christ *Dharma,* where the term denotes far more than a certain creed.

These remarks may warn against a natural overestimation of the significance of the *trivarga* (*dharma, artha,* and *kāma*) as classifying different sets of practices. In principle, all three are *dharma.* It is not less important for man to seek *artha*, achievement in his occupation in the largest sense of the word, or to gratify those desires that maintain the population of the earth, than to follow the precepts of religion and observe the canons of law. One cannot choose the rule of *dharma* if that implies that one can also refuse to do so, even less than in our society we can choose to live on a level where law is not applied and yet form part of the society.

In other words, *dharma* is all that activity that a man, if he is to live fittingly, is required to contribute to the fixed order of things, to the norm of the universe, which is good and should not be altered. *Adharma* is the exact opposite: acts contrary to the established order in the widest sense of the [37] word. The acts performed by man exist, once performed, forever, carrying their latent potential to a new scene where they will materialize in new circumstances for man to live in.

Mokṣa, "release," is release from the entire realm which is governed by *dharma,* that is, in the picturesque phrase, the Egg of Brahmā. It stands, therefore, in opposition to *dharma,* but the opposition is of another kind than that of *adharma* to *dharma. Dharma* upholds the established order, while *adharma* threatens it; *adharma* is sheer lawlessness. *Mokṣa*, however, is the abandonment of the established order, not in favor of anarchy, but in favor of a self-realization which is precluded in the realm of *dharma.* Occasionally, especially in the *Bhagavadgītā*, we find sentiments to such extent in favor of the established order that aspirants are discouraged from abandoning it openly, but this is the exception rather than the rule. Fundamental to Indian thought is the idea that the world and phenomena, being transitory, can never be an ultimately valid goal, that there is a lesser trueness in the creation than in that principle or person from whom creation originated, who is eternal, constant, reliable, free from changes and transformation, unalterable, and therefore truly real. Consequently, there is universal agreement that to seek communion with that ultimate is a higher purpose than to perpetuate one's existence in the world order. Let the world be, if you can do better.

As said above, more or less distinct developments contributed to the articulation of the ideal of *mokṣa,* though there can be no doubt that there was a great deal of interaction and exchange between these developments. The originating milieu of a certain conception of *mokṣa* remained largely decisive as to the methods pursued to achieve it.

For our present purposes we may distinguish three different disciplines, the *upaniṣadic*, the *yogic* and the *bhakti.*

The upaniṣadic *mokṣa* was developed out of the ritualistic world-view. The later parts of some Brāhmaṇas, the Āraṇyakas, and the Upaniṣads show the efforts of the priest to exhaust totally the signification of the ritual as a cosmic reproductive event. In the course of a general evolution in which the original gods and powers, propitiated for certain purposes by certain rites, had gradually to give way to an ever more total interpretation of the rite as a perpetuating reproduction of cosmic becoming and being which involved the gods as much as officiants and utensils, as parts of a whole much vaster than they were, this "whole," manifested in ritual, gave rise to speculations as to the "whole entity", of which the ritual and the ritually perpetuated cosmos were the manifestations. The knowledge of the One behind the ritual is increasingly important, to the extent that eventually it was felt to be useless [38] to perform rites without this knowledge. With this knowledge the priest enacted in his rite, and even in himself, the self-manifestation of the One beyond; and in so far as man himself was the self-manifestation—for it is reflected on different levels, *adhilokam, adhibhūtam, adhiyajñam, adhyātmam*[8]—man could by virtue of his knowledge of the rite transcend himself through the rite and return to the state before manifestation. Knowledge was the principal means, the rite its application.

The origins of *yoga* are largely obscure. It seems probable that primitive inducement of trance states is at the root; Yoga itself has never got rid of it. Though there is a superstructure of Sāṃkhya-inspired rationalization, the physical manipulations, breath control, deliberate exhausting of the wakefulness center by pin-pointed concentration, by hypnotic repetitions of formulae, and, in heretical and perhaps more original forms, by intoxication, etc., self-hypnotization into a trance sleep or cataleptic states, where every consciousness ceases, sufficiently testify to the archaic practices of shaman and medicine-man.[9] Sāṃkhya cosmogony was superimposed on the practices, and the *yogin* was thought to repeat in the gradual slackening and ceasing of supposedly hierarchically ordered functions in reverse order the self-creation process of the ultimate in himself and to return through a sequence of self-dissolution to the original state of non-manifestation.

The theistic *bhakti* discipline is probably most related to what is called mysticism in the West. Inspired by an illimitable love for God, the yearning soul by a process of ever more absorbed contemplation reaches an ecstasy of yearning which transports him to the most perfect union possible with God. Frequently, since the deity remains distinct from the soul that seeks him, though the soul itself may lose all individuality in the absorption of his contemplation, the idea of a heavenly abode returns—Vaikuṇṭha.

We have left out of consideration here a *mukti* discipline which, after Yoga, is probably best known outside India, the *karmayoga* of the *Bhagavadgītā*. Though far from being so important or central in Indian soteriology as is often erroneously supposed, it is indeed a most interesting doctrine, a hybridic construction attempting to achieve a compromise between two incompatibles.

Dharma, as we saw, is the norm of action for the world as it is: its realm is *saṃsāra.* It involves the observance of a great number of precepts, all aimed at upholding the given order of things, from procreation and occupational success to law, religious worship, and pilgrimage, and thus the performances [39] of acts, ritual acts, which achieve this purpose. *Mokṣa,* on the contrary, starts with a deliberate rejection of this order, a refusal to submit to its demands, a total severance of all ties with family and society and all laws and customs regulating it, with the universe at large and the rites which contribute to its stability. A *brahmin* choosing *saṃnyāsa* renounces caste. What possible relation can there be between *dharma* and *mokṣa*?

This question has occupied the best minds in Indian thought. In Vedānta, the discussions center around the meaning of the first words of the *Vedānta Sūtra*: "Subsequently, therefore, arises the desire to know *Brahman.*" (*Athāto brahma-jijñāsā*). Can this mean that this desire for *mokṣa* through knowledge is conditioned by something that precedes it? The question is hotly disputed. The original Vedānta view was indeed *jñānakarmasamuccaya,* i.e., the combination of both knowledge and act; but acts necessarily involve results, and the results bind the performer. Śaṃkarācārya, to quote the most explicit rejector, is obliged to state that ultimately there can be no direct relation between any part of *saṃsāra* and the knowledge of *Brahman*, which is synonymous with release. "The knowledge of *Brahman* puts an end to any activity," he states,[10] and in the *Upadeśasāhasrī*[11] he repeats emphatically the necessity of *saṃnyāsa*, the absolute relinquishment of all worldly ties.

Other thinkers continued the *jñānakarmasamuccaya* doctrine

but not without important modifications. Rāmānuja, for instance, as in other cases adhering to a more traditional view and simultaneously modifying it, puts it thus, that acts if performed not for their results, that is, as factors contributing to the established order, but solely as propitiation and worship of God, are indeed an indispensable propaedeusis to *bhakti* and, through *bhakti*, to release. We note that, hardly less than in Śaṃkarācārya's case, for Rāmānuja, too, the acts have lost their own significance; it is not the result that matters, but the intention. Rāmānuja was undoubtedly inspired by the *Bhagavadgītā*, on which, however, he imposed a stricter order than the original authors did.

The *Bhagavadgītā* is interesting for its documentation of a fundamental conflict between the *jñānayogin*, who is, largely, the *yogin* of the second category distinguished above, with a Sāṃkhya or proto-Sāṃkhya rationale, and the brahministic upholders of *karman* and *dharma,* between the asocial *saṃnyasins* and the mainstays of society. Release had already become the supreme goal of human aspirations: but where did that leave those whose sacred duty it was to maintain the cosmic order through the rites which only they were qualified to perform? And if they were to renounce their duty and step out to work for their own salvation, where would that leave the [40] world? The world obviously must go on, if only because the demands on the capacity and effort of the aspirant to release are too high to be met by the ordinary person. The compromise that is achieved is extremely interesting: continue to perform the necessary acts, but abjure their results. So, by changing one's intention, namely, not to enjoy the good fruits resultant on the performance of good deeds, one can prevent those fruits from being realized. But that means also that the efficacy of an act is no longer automatic, and if thought through consistently this proposed change of doctrine could reform the entire doctrine of *karman.*[12] But it remains a makeshift solution which the authors are quite hesitant about, sometimes preferring it to *jñānayoga*, sometimes subordinating it to *jñānayoga;* only when stated as part of *bhaktiyoga* does it become meaningful.

NOTES

1. Cf. the Puruṣa Sūkta, *Ṛg-Veda* X. 90; the ritual basis is provided by the immolation of a human victim symbolically represented in, for instance, the concluding rites of the *pravargya*, the recitation of the Śunaḥśepa legend at the *rājasūya*. See J. Heesterman, *The Ancient Indian Royal Consecration*

(The Hague : Morton & Co., 1957), and the late Agnicayana rituals (the rituals of the building of the fire).

2. Hence the personality of Brahmā, the Creator whose four mouths (also representing the *ākāśa*, "ether") pronounce the four Vedas at the beginning of creation; he is a popular personification of *Brahman* in the older function of the ritually creative sacred Word.

3. I refer to my papers : "Studies in Sāṃkhya (II) : Ahaṃkāra," *Journal of the American Oriental Society*, 77, No. 1 (March 15, 1957), 15ff., and "Studies in Sāṃkhya (III): Sattva", *ibid.*, No. 2 (June 15, 1957, 88ff. [nos. 7 and 8 in this volume].

4. BĀUp 1,2.

5. We find it in Pūrvamīmāṃsā discussions on the immorality of the soul (which, to the Mīmāṃsaka, is naturally the performing agent's soul). Thus the Mīmāṃsaka is able to account for the *jñānakāṇḍa* portions (portions containing esoteric knowledge) of the Veda (Āraṇyaka and Upaniṣad), which, to him, are subordinated to the *karmakāṇḍa* portions in so far as they provide the evidence for the eternality of the *ātman*, which the ritual requires.

6. It is particularly those ritual acts which presuppose in the performer a desire for a certain fruit (type : *svargakāmo jyotiṣṭomena yajeta*, "one desirous of heaven should sacrifice with the Jyotiṣṭoma") that binds the performer to the enjoyment of the automatically forthcoming fruit, and only secondarily other acts.

7. Hence *dharma* could assume the meaning of "essential property; property," among the logicians.

8. "With reference to, or as applied to, the (three) worlds, the constituent elements, the ritual, the performer's person."

9. Cf. Mircea Eliade, *Schamanismus und Archaische Ekstasetechnik* (Zurich : Rascher Verlag, 1957).

10. BĀUp 1,4 7.

11. Especially in the *gadya* (prose) portion.

12. If it is possible to "wish away" the *karmaphala* (fruit of the act) while doing the act, this means that the act is deprived of its finality, and its performer of his motivation, so that other motivations have to be discovered for the agent, e.g., as the *Gītā* proposes, a sense of social responsibility. Rāmānuja, keenly realizing that the *Gītā's* doctrine of the renunciation of the rewards of the acts always envisages ritual acts, explains, in his *Gītābhāṣya*, that among the three categories of acts (*nitya*, "daily recurring,"; *naimittika*, "occasional"; and *kāmya*, "inspired by desire") the last category alone must be given up. This follows naturally from the Mīmāṃsā theory, since in the *kāmya* acts (type *svargakāmo jyotiṣṭomena yajeta*) the performer's desire-for-heaven is his qualification (*adhikāra*), and unless he desires the *phala* (e.g., heaven) he cannot even perform the act; the *nitya* acts, on the other hand, have no *phala*.

10

VĀCĀRAMBHAṆAM RECONSIDERED

In his recent contribution to this journal[1] Professor Kuiper has clarified the linguistic issues involved in the interpretation of the crucial *vācārambhaṇam* of ChUp. 6.1 and 6.4. The distinguished scholar discusses lucidly the derivation of *ārambhaṇa* from a root *rambh*, its connection with *ā-rabh, ā-labh, ā-lamb*, and he decides himself in favor of a reference of our term to RV. 10.81.2 which I had proposed in an earlier paper.[2] Reviewing my suggestions he remains uncertain about my precise analysis of *vācārambhaṇam*.[3] As a result both of Kuiper's fresh inquiry and of a personal correspondence with Professor Edgerton who declared himself unconvinced by my general interpretations as given in my brief and here and there ambiguous[4] paper, I have studied the phrase anew. The conclusions to which I was led were unexpected but, I believe, rewarding. It may be opportune, now that the matter is fresh in the reader's memory, to submit them to his judgment.

Kuiper at the outset rejects summarily the possibility that *vācārambhaṇam* is anything but a compound[5] with as first member an *ā*-stem *vācā* built on *vāc* f. This is certainly defensible, though one should like to see more adstructive material for the assumption of *vācā* or a similar *ā*-stem that is preferred to *vāc*, etc. in composito. Yet, since *vācā ārambhaṇam* is also defensible I would be inclined to postpone the assumption of an exceptional *vācā* f. until a perfect understanding of the entire phrase had shown that the more obvious instrumental of *vāc* f. really makes no sense. **[296]** This brings us back to the meaning of the whole phrase.

Beside our expression the phrase contains two more problems: the precise function of *nāmadheyam,* and the positively extraordinary use of *satyam* in *mṛttikety eva satyam.* However one prefers to read the phrase, it is equally clear that it consists of two abbreviated sentences and that *vikāra* is the logical subject of the first.[6] Yet *nāmadheyam* seems to be the grammatical subject. And no usage of *satyam* in the older upaniṣads quite prepares us for a *satyam* that describes any cause of any *vikāra*; and, although unconcerned with the explanation of *vikāra*, etc. in the first sentence which seems to remain unconnected with his evolution account,[7] the author is at pains to identify the *satyam* in all seven occurrences of the phrase.

Let us consider all seven. The first three are in ChUp. 6.1, introductory to the instruction proper which posits an original *sat* evolving three *rūpas*, reanimating these *rūpas* by entering into them,[8] and thereupon embarking upon a process of *vikāra*,[9] or the creation of names and forms. After this the principal instruction is set forth in 6.4. In 6.1 Uddālaka had questioned Śvetaketu: "Did you ask to hear the *ādeśa* in what manner the whole is known through one?" And in 6.4 the ancients are said to exclaim: "Now no one can quote us anything that we cannot classify according to these three *rūpas*: if we know something red, we know it for the *rohita rūpa* of *tejas*, etc."

What occasions this exclamation which plainly marks the conclusion of the instruction Uddālaka had promised in 6.1? The preceding lines read: *yad agne rohitaṃ rūpaṃ tejasas tad rūpam/ yac chuklaṃ tad apām / yat kṛṣṇaṃ tad annasya / apāgād agner agnitvam / vācārambhaṇaṃ vikāro nāmadheyaṃ trīṇi rūpāṇīti satyam.* Curiously all translators felt so sure about the meaning of the disputed phrase that they interpreted the preceding *apāgād agner agnitvam* in a sense which derives from their (i.e. Śaṅkara's) interpretation of the phrase but is obviously wrong: "That **[297]** which makes fire what it is—the 'phenomenal entity' fire—disappears from fire, (for) the effect is but a verbal handle, a mere name: what is real are the three *rūpas*." Thereupon the ancients exclaim that now they can classify all things. Let us distantiate ourselves for a moment from an admittedly prejudiced exegesis dating from a later millennium and agree that this makes no sense.

What the text really says is this: "The red in fire is the red of *tejas*, the white that of *āpas*, the black that of *annam*. Issues (from these three *rūpas*) that which makes fire fire." *apāgāt* at the beginning of the sentence conveys the immediate connection of the action with what precedes. *agner agnitvam* cannot be separated from the well-known brāhmaṇa usage: Rudra's Rudratvam consists in this that... (*rudrasya rudratvam*). What makes *agni agni*?

The three *rūpas*. There is positively no justification for denying the "reality" of *agni*; the fact that these three *rūpas* are described as *satyam* does not mean that their effects are "unreal".[10] *apāgāt* is not "disappears", but "issues, goes forth, arises"; what the three *rūpas* "let off" (*apa-sṛj*), "goes off" (*apa-gā*). Without pronouncing on their ontological reality the author wants to emphasize that such high-ranking principles as fire, sun, moon, lightning —sometimes themselves considered the supreme—are in fact produced by the supreme, i.e., the three *rūpas*. Having completely made this point he adds the disputed phrase. The significance of *satyam* in it had already been illustrated by three different examples (6.1): the three *rūpas* are the "cause" of such effects as *agni*, etc. just as clay, copper, iron are the cause of clay, etc. products. Just as all clay products are recognized through clay as being of clay, so all red entities are recognized through redness as being of the red *rūpa tejas*. As clay, so each of the three *rūpas* and all *rūpas* mixed. Śvetaketu has been presented with a viable scheme of world classification and the ancients declare themselves satisfied with it.

When we now consider the phrase we remark 1. that it summarizes a point already completely made and fully illustrated; 2. that consequently it could be missed entirely without leaving a gap in the exposition; yet it is three times adduced illustratively and four times applied in the doctrine proper; 3. that the first part remains unconnected with the author's account and goes unexplained, but *satyam* is 7 times explicitly identified. All this makes for one conclusion which we can also reach in a different manner.

Uddālaka wonders if his son has asked for a certain *ādeśa* such that all **[298]** is known through one. He has not and now asks his father. The latter thereupon gives a worldly example of how one thing of a kind makes for knowledge of all things of that kind. This is obviously *not* the *ādeśa* itself,[11] but an illustration. Then the word denoting the kind itself, resp. clay, copper, iron, is fitted into a severely abbreviated phrase, reduced to its bare nouns, and fitted thus that *satyam* in it is made to describe this clay, copper and iron. Uddālaka immediately after that phrase concludes: "Such is the *ādeśa*, my son." There can be no doubt that the phrase *vācārambhaṇam...satyam* is the *ādeśa*, that it is an *ādeśa*.

The translators have ignored that *ādeśa* is not just "teaching, instruction" generally, but something more precise. It is a doctrine in a nutshell, a briefly indicated conception which requires further interpretation for the pupil but for the initiated contains a world of meaning. They generally take the form of severely abbreviated sentences describing equivalencies and identifications (so two words, subject and predicate usually suffice), which, if the upaniṣadic commentary does not happen to survive, sometimes remain obscure: *tad vanam,*[12] *ā3 ā3,*[13] *taj jalān,*[14] *kapyāsaṃ puṇḍarīkam.*[15] to quote a few. Others are explained, *āditya brahma.*[16] Others [299] are quoted more than once and apparently allow of different interpretations: *neti neti* is a famous example.[17]

ChUp. 3.5.1 ff. gives a clear idea of their significance. In a metaphor of bees and flowers, *ṛcaḥ, yajūṃṣi, sāmāni, atharvāṅgirasaḥ* are respectively bees to the flowers Ṛgveda, Yajurveda, Sāmaveda and *itihāsa-purāṇam.* Together these four (or five) comprise the sacred lore. Then follows: *guhyā evādeśā madhukṛto brahmaiva puṣpam*: brahman "sacred lore" has as principle the secret *ādeśas*; they are higher than the brahman, which itself is higher than the Vedic texts.[18] The *ādeśa* is the brief *signalement,* as Renou excellently renders, both of the supreme and of the conception of the supreme, of that which the pupil then must *upāsitum.* Thus *ādeśa* and *upāsanā/upaniṣad* are very nearly synonymous.[19] ŚatBr. 10.4.5 (*agnirahasya*) describes as *upaniṣadām ādeśaḥ* a series of *upāsanās*: agni is vāyu, agni is āditya, agni is year, altar is vāc, vāc is sun, altar is death, etc. etc.

An *ādeśa* therefore is the indication in a few words of an esoteric thesis about a great cosmic connection. Their origins may be remote and the phrases allow of different reinterpretations. *tad vanam* "the wood is that (brahman)" must refer to brahman as cause and is likely to be an *ādeśa* built on TaittBr. 2.8.9.6,[20] but is reinterpreted (or also interpreted) as having to do with desire (*vāñch-*). *tajjalān* for *taj jalāni*[21] must be a similar equation of brahman with the primeval waters (Śaṅkara: *tajjalān = tajja, talla* and *tadana*), *ā3 ā3* very probably refers to the initial *a* sound in *OM,* itself an *ādeśa* of incredible fecundity. Frequently they exploit the words beyond their actual meaning to convey esoteric depth: *OM3* is *ud-gī-tham,* [300] brahman is *gāyatrī,*[22] the supreme's name is *sat-tyam, sat-ti-yam, sati-yam.*[23]

Although by discovering that our phrase is an *ādeśa* in the precise meaning of the term we may have aggravated our problem, at least we have now identified it. That Uddālaka quotes the *ādeśa* (for an *ādeśa* is almost by definition a current key-phrase[24] interpreted for himself by every thinker, all of them together constituting an amorphous collection of, comparatively speaking, protosūtras of which the upaniṣads embody the various commentaries), that Uddālaka therefore probably QUOTES this *ādeśa* must have a particular significance; and this significance must have lain in the second part, that about *satyam*. For the author is at pains to identify this *satyam* with the three *rūpas*, illustrating his meaning in the introduction in terms which sound tantalizingly new to the initiated Śvetaketu whose teachers did not know of this application of the *ādeśa*. And in fact, Uddālaka presents his own doctrine of *satyam* as something different, something new.

In ChUp. 6.2 we have what is I believe the first attempt of an Indian theologian to use logic in reforming a doctrine. "*Sat* was here alone originally, nothing else. There are those who say that *asat* was here originally and that *sat* arose from *asat*: but how is it possible that something which EXISTS arises from something that EXISTS NOT? No, *sat* was here alone." Uddālaka here challenges the current doctrine of *satyam*. This old doctrine, as old as the Ṛgveda, states the primacy of *asat* from which *sat* came forth. This at one point became formulated in the *ādeśa* of the supreme's name "*satyam*". *satyam* describes the supreme which is both *sat* and *tyad/tyam*, i.e., *asat*, *sat* being the "embodied", *asat* the "disembodied".

The speculations about this *ādeṣa* "brahman's or satyam's name is *satyam*", are, with those on *OM* and *ātman*, the most numerous of all upaniṣadic commentaries on single ādeśas. ChUp. 8.3.4 *tasya ha vā etasya brahmaṇo nāma sat-ti-yam iti, sat* is *amṛtam, ti* is *martyam, yam* what connects both. BĀUp. 2.1.20 *tasya* (*brahmaṇa*) *upaniṣat satyasya satyam iti.* Ib. 2.3.6 *atha nāmadheyaṃ satyasya satyam iti.* 4.1.4 *satyam ity etad* (*brahma*) *upāsīta.* 4.5.1 *te devāḥ satyam evopāsate / tad etat tryakṣaraṃ sa-ti-yam iti.* Taitt Up. 2.6.1 where the creator (corresponding **[301]** to *asat* as appears from 2.7.1) has created the world by tripartition *satyam abhavad yad idaṃ kiṃ ca / tat satyam ity ācakṣate*. There are more instances, but these will suffice.

Let us now return to a previous point. In the first sentence of our phrase *vikāraḥ* must be the logical subject. Can it also be the grammatical subject, and be so in the proper place, that is *following* the predicate? There is not the slightest doubt in my mind that it can be and is. There is absolutely no authority[25] for the traditional punctuation which by placing a comma after *nāmadheyam* makes it the grammatical subject, instead of the logical *vikāraḥ*. And after our demonstration that the phrase is an *ādeśa*, our recognition of Uddālaka's preoccupation with *sat* and *satyam*, and our quotations from other texts on the name of the *satyam* that Uddālaka declares to change, there will be no one who does not feel the immediate *rightness* of the sentence in the ādeśa: *nāmadheyam..satyam*. We have now identified at least one *ādeśa*, happily a most popular one, and simultaneously rephrased more satisfactorily the other one. The whole phrase now reads: *vācārambhaṇaṃ vikāraḥ / nāmadheyaṃ trīṇi rūpāṇīty eva satyam*. Uddālaka has something new to say about *satyam*, and as so many others he uses the well-known *ādeśa* to say it with.

Several stages can be discerned in the interpretation of the "Name is Satyam" *ādeśa* before him. First, *sat-tyam/tyad*~*sat-asat*. This *asat* first becomes *sat*, then (or thus) evolves creation.[26] Thus essentially TaittUp. 2.6.1, but already uncertain about the meaning of *asat*.[27] Second, *sat-tyam*, *sat* being the solidly, palpably existent, *mūrtam, martyam; tyam* "yon" replacing *asat*, particularly continuing the primacy, transcendence, subtlety of *asat*, not tangible (atmosphere, *prāṇa*), *amūrtam amṛtam*. [302] Brahman is both at once: *dve rūpe*. Thus ChUp. 8.3.4 f.,[28] BĀUp. 4.5.1; basically[29] BĀUp. 2.3.6). Third, *sat* and *tyam* in the second formulation do no longer constitute the entire brahman (or this brahman is not the highest): there is an order above it, the flaming puruṣa in sun and eye (BĀUp. 2.1.20; 2.3.6); so brahman (or the "more supreme" puruṣa) is *satyasya* (*sat-tyasya*) *satyam*. Note that in all three stages a triadic pattern underneath is given and maintained.

Upon this Uddālaka presents a new interpretation of *satyam*, of which Śvetaketu's teachers had never heard. He does away with the two brahmans, keeps the triad, but bolder even than the third interpretation, lifts *sat* above the triad. This is one way of looking at it. Another way[30] is that he returns to the very oldest view, substitutes *sat* for *asat* which starts creation by self-tripartition, this creation being *asat's sattva, ātman* or *puruṣa*: for Uddālaka's *sat*, too, really only becomes a creator when he has entered the *three* rūpas *jīvenātmanā*. The translation of the sentence NĀMADHEYAM TRĪṆI RUPĀṆĪTY EVA SATYAM therefore is; "THE NAME (of the supreme) IS SATYAM, I.E. (as analysed in three syllables sa-ti-yam) THE THREE RŪPAS."[31]

On *vācārambhaṇaṃ vikāraḥ* a little remains to be said. Since *ārambhaṇam* must be a noun predicative of *vikāraḥ* the disputed expression can, if Kuiper is right and the word is a compound, only be a tatpuruṣa. It is an *ādeśa* not so far met with. *vikāra*[32] must principally refer to the creation by *sat* or *satyam*, that is the great creation,[33] not the effectuation of any [303] product, and evidently *vāc* plays a leading role in the eventuation of creation. But Uddālaka's doctrine with regard to *vāc*, as far as we have it at least, remains undeveloped; yet its very inclusion and repetion must point at the great significance the author attached to *vāc*.

This significance is still recoverable from the further chapters. Vāc, according to 6.5 is the very subtlest product of the very subtlest rūpa, *tejas*, of *sat*. The order of creation is therefore Sat→ three rūpas constituting sat→*vāc*. ChUp. 6.5 suggests the following order in creation: 1. *sat—tejas, āpas, annam;* 2. *tejas—vāc, manaḥ,* bone; 3. *āpas—prāṇa,* blood, urine; 4. *annam—manaḥ*, flesh, faeces. This order is curious but we can now reconstruct its basis. We have basically four reflections of the third stage of *satyam* speculations. Structured in those terms we have three orders :

1. *tejas* — *vāc–(manaḥ)*
2. *āpas* — *prāṇa*
3. *annam* —bone/blood/flesh/urine/faeces.

The second order is the *tyad/tyam* order, *āpas* cosmically corresponding to *antarikṣa* "atmosphere" and *prāṇa* as *tyam* constituting the *amūrtam, amṛtam.* The third corresponds with *sat*, the very obviously *mūrtam,* "embodied", and mortal. On the highest order remain *tejas*, representing heaven and sun, abode of the flaming puruṣa, and *vāc*.[34] *Manas* certainly belongs there too,[35] but is significantly put after *vāc* in one series. When we therefore take the second stage of tripartitions as simple triads moved down, which they certainly were in the speculations that furnished the basis for 6.5, the fact stands out that *vāc* was first as the first creature.

This is sound old doctrine. It remains recoverable from the jumble of second-stage tripartitions (which we now stress with particular significance occur in a text *following after* Uddālaka's first promised instruction 6.1–6.4 was concluded) and is moreover expounded seven times in Uddālaka's first teaching in *vācārambhaṇaṃ vikāraḥ*. Assuredly we have in the teaching ascribed to Uddālaka son of Aruṇa and father of Śvetaketu only a digest of a more circumstantial exposition, which may, or may not, have originated from Uddālaka. It is for instance inconceivable that the real Uddālaka, an udgātar of note, could possibly have so systematically avoided references to ritualistic trains of thought as the present text represents it. It is entirely credible that further explanations of *vāc* have been digested out in later times when we see the ancient notions of *vāc* as the creator's self-expression, as the progenitrix of creation, become obsolete, [304] leaving surviving terms, notably *ahaṃkāra*, to be reinterpreted in a context of more newly developed notions. But as so often, just below the surface we find here too uncovered the ancient doctrines. From the context of associations of the Name of the supreme cannot be excluded the speculations about a brahman that becomes creation by recognizing itself for an ātman and naming itself *Aham.*[36] This near relationship between the supreme's creation and the supreme's self-articulation may quite well have furnished the link between the two *ādeśas* in our phrase, of which the parallelism is striking.

If we now attempt a translation of the first sentence we must preface that the exigencies of translating into another language necessitate a definiteness at variance with the comprehensiveness of the original; from among all the connotations of *ārambhaṇa* we must make a choice which does not pretend to include all that is included in it. Still, since we have to settle on some translation this will do: VĀCĀRAMBHAṆAM VIKĀRAḤ "(the Supreme's) CREATION IS (his) TAKING HOLD OF VĀC." Several others can be suggested: "creation is the Supreme's basis on Vāc," "creation is the taking hold by Vāc." *ārambhaṇam* is no doubt a reference to RV 10.81.2, where it is juxtaposed with *adhiṣṭhānam*; but I believe that Kuiper is too cautious when he wishes to exclude different connotations of *ārambhaṇam* from the connotations the term has here.[37] The "basis" is also the beginning; for juxtaposed with RV. 10.81.2 is in stanza 4 also the *vanam* and the [305] *vṛkṣaḥ* which underlies as an *adhiṣṭhāna* the worlds; and wood and tree are obviously the materials of which the creator took hold to fashion the world. As must have become clear, etymological exactitude was hardly a prime concern of these thinkers who in their *ādeśas* or *upaniṣads* summed up as many connections as the terms themselves could possibly provide in their sounds and their meanings. If one insists on a grammatically satisfying explanation of *vācā*, Kuiper's suggestion of a *vācā* f., in composito, may be considered; one may also think simply of an irregular sandhi of *vācas* before *ā*°, *vāca ā*° becoming *vācā*°. But the instrumental *vācā* thus suggested could, though 'erroneous', undoubtedly be excellently accounted for as Vāc's instrumentality in creation by these masters of the mystifying Word whose unsurpassed capacity of envisioning a whole and expressing it totally is singularly well illustrated by the great variety of meanings that later exegetes have discovered from our famous phrase.

CORRECTION

In my article "Vācārambhaṇam reconsidered" (*IIJ*, II/4, 295ff.) I was misled, quoting from notes, into attributing to the phrase *apāgād agner agnitvam* a meaning which it cannot have (297.7–17). It is clear from the parallel passages ChUp. 6.4.2 and 3 that *agneḥ* is an ablative, and that the correct translation therefore is "fireness goes forth from fire". The slip, inexcusable though it is, does not invalidate the central argument. The portion 6.4 asserts that everything is reducible to the three rūpas and can thus be known and recognized through them, in the same way as clay pots can be recognized through clay (*etad dha sma vai tad vidvāṃsa āhuḥ..na no 'dya kaścanāśrutam amatam avijñātam udāhariṣyatīti hy ebhyo* (*rūpebhyo*) *vidāṃ cakruḥ* 6.4.5). From the point of view of the rūpas, fire, sun, moon and lightning are themselves reducible to the three rūpas because they consist of them; hence they cannot be regarded as final entities (they merge in the three rūpas), but they do not by that token lose their reality.

NOTES

1. "*Vācārambhaṇam*", *IIJ*, I (1957), 155ff.
2. "*Vācārambhaṇam*", *Indian Linguistics*, 16 (Festschrift Chatterji, 1955), 157ff. [no. 2 in this volume].
3. It never occurred to me that *vācār*° was a compound and I took *vācā* as instrumental to the action of *ārambhaṇa*; but since I allowed other connotations of *ārambhaṇa* to be implied in the phrase the precise relationship had to remain vague.

declares that *brahman* cannot be *asat*, but *asti brahmeti*: clearly the same problem as Uddālaka faced, and disposed of, in 6.2.1-2, the old asat being no longer understood and now regarded as just "non-existent." But in the creation account immediately following in 2.7, a "personal" creator is introduced (*brahman/ātman*) who creates himself as creation: *idaṃ sṛṣṭvā tad evānuprāviśat/ tad anupraviśya sac ca tyac cābhavat...satyaṃ cānṛtaṃ ca / sat-tyam abhavat yad idaṃ kiṃ ca / tat sat-tyam ācakṣate / tad apy eṣa śloko bhavati*—(2.7) *asad vā idam agra āsīt tato vai sad ajāyat / tad ātmānaṃ svayam akuruta tasmāt tat sukṛtam ucyata iti*, which is the old view again.

28. In spite of the fact that there are only two orders, *amṛtam* and *martyam*, the triadic pattern was so influential that *satyam* still was analysed into three; *sat-ti-yam;* here *ti*, the dispensable svarabhakti syllable, is the *martyam, sat* the *amṛtam*; comparably in TaittUp. 2.6 *satyam* seems to correspond with *sat, anṛtaṃ* to *tyad/tyam.*

29. This text retains the two orders of brahman, *sat* and *tyam*, but adds a higher order of puruṣa (thus also restoring the triad); hence *satyam* (=brahman) has for this puruṣa to be extended to *satyasya* (*sat-tyasya*) *satyam.*

30. And this is what Uddālaka himself says: the supreme is not represented by one syllable, as in the second stage, nor as a third order beyond *sat-tyam* as in the third stage, but as all three orders which, as *satyam* (*sa-ti-yam*) constitute *sat.*

31. Paraphrased: the supreme's name is indeed Satyam, since the three orders summed up in *sa-ti-yam* are the three orders that constitute *sat* the creator.

32. The use for "product generally" is late, only after the Sāṃkhyakārikās where *vikāra/vikṛti* is "evolute in a creation process."

33. In the early prose upaniṣads, including the original MaitrUp., *vi-kṛ/ vyā-kṛ* occurs only to describe the primary world creation of the supreme (*vi*-BĀUp. 1.2.3; MaitrUp. 6.3; *vyā*—ChUp. 6.3.2., 6.3.3—our context—, BĀUp. 1.4.7). One Aitareya Up. (6.1) passage is quite relevant: *kataraḥ sa ātmā, yena vā rūpaṃ paśyati yena vā śabdaṃ śṛṇoti yena vā gandhān ājighrati yena vā vācaṃ vyākaroti yena vā svādu cāsvādu ca vijānāti;* on the relation between *vyā-hṛ* and *vyā-kṛ* see some remarks in my *Ahaṃkāra.* Considering the general use of *vi/vyā-kṛ* it is wholly unjustified to assume for our *vikāra* another meaning than its own context concerned with evolution suggests.

34. I may dispense with quoting on the relation between *vāc* and *ākāśa.*

35. Though the view of the *prāṇamayaṃ manaḥ* may have occasioned *manas*'s degradation when *prāṇa* was demoted.

36. See my *Ahaṃkāra* [no. 7 in this volume].

37. I doubt if *ārambhaṇam* of KāṭhS. 7.15 quoted by Kuiper as meaning "point of support" is really only that (o.c. 157). In GopBr. 1.2.15 the same quotation occurs in the following context: *aditir vai prajākāmaudanaṃ apacat / tata ucchiṣṭam āśnāt / sā garbham adhatta / tata ādityā ajāyanta / ya eṣa odanaḥ pacyata ārambhaṇam evaitat kriyata ākramaṇam eva.* The significance of the *odana* being an *ārambhaṇa* can hardly be separated from the *odana*'s instrumentality in the procreation described. [But now cf. p. 309, (of *IIJ*) where Professor Kuiper stresses the explicit parallelism between *ārambhaṇa* and *ākramaṇa* and the absence of indications that the word connotes also some-

thing else. I felt that the very justification of the odana's being an *ārambhaṇa* lay in the fact that Aditi uses it to produce the Ādityas. Whether one wishes to consider this a connotation or a denotation (but where, one could ask also Thieme, stops one and begins the other?), the fact remains that the initiating role ascribed to "basis", and particularly *ārambhaṇa*, caused the word to be treated as a form of *ā-rabh*, and that this "connotation" caused a change in "denotation". The occurrences of *ārambhaṇa* where it is at once a "basis" and a "starting-point for producing or initiating activities" should in my opinion not too exclusively be identified with a meaning "basis" but rather noted as stages to a final meaning of initiating, getting a hold on, etc., which certainly partly resulted from the existence of a closely resembling *ā-rabh*, but only partly : unless the meanings were sufficiently close, mere formal resemblance would not necessarily affect semantic changes, as the existence of homonyms demonstrates. Kuiper's view and mine are not fundamentally at variance, but reflect at most a difference in degree of emphasis, discernible only in border-cases.]

11

THE INDIAN HERO AS VIDYĀDHARA

To a large extent it is true that we are better informed about the religious doctrines and practices, moral ideals, and metaphysical speculations of pre-Muslim India than about any other aspect of the Indian civilization. The authors whose works have come down to us, whether Hindu or Buddhist, largely belonged to a class which was preoccupied with its sacerdotal prerogatives, its pedagogic duties and its functions as the guardian of a sacred tradition. But, although we must recognize the great significance of their articulate eschatology in our valuation of the Indian Weltanschauung, the mere mass of evidence for one set of values should not tempt us to overlook the actual importance of different outlooks. While the increasingly prevailing note of quietistic world despair may have set the key, other notes were sounded. Nor should we forget that the Indian looked upon anything that fell short of a conceivable ideal state of being as an occasion for sorrow, and that accordinly the intention of the very notion of sorrow was inflated. In spite of an undeniable plaintiveness about life in general, the Indian's attitude was essentially melioristic; and though the moralists in unison complain about the misery of man's fate to live, there are few indications that the average person's life was more than ordinarily unpleasant. To a point, sorrow was a theological presupposition, comparable to original sin, and one cannot help feeling that it was more dogma than reality. Meanwhile, the stereotype of the miserable life has passed into the cultural history, and now, corrobarated by some distressing facts of contemporary Indian economics, has become the most widely known item about the Indian civilization—the teeming millions of suffering humanity.

If one reads those texts least afflicted by moralists—the poetry, especially lyrical poetry, and the vast literature of tales and romances—one gets a different picture of civilized Indian life. There was a delight in living, an artistic sensitiveness, a cool headed drive to make good in the world, and an air of cultured sophistication in the enjoyment of the rewards of prosperity, as far removed from the stern disenchantment of the sages as is the spirit of a rustic Brahman freehold from the urban wit of the ocean-port Tāmraliptī.

Yet, if one comes down to essentials, the ideals and aspiration —the "daydreams"—which find expression in the stories and romances, remain, in spite of vast difference in temper and spirit, close to those that have guided higher Indian thought. Or perhaps we must change the order; for it is an enduring characteristic of Indian thinking, even of the highest order, that it never loses contact with popular conceptions and beliefs, but returns time and time again to find new inspiration in the immediate experiences of everyday life. When we inquire into the salient features with which the people who enjoyed stories have endowed the character of their heroes, we find the same features **[306]** that characterize the Indian culture ideal of the saint. Even a cold blooded adventurer like Apahāravarman of the *Tales of the Ten Princes* has more of the virtues that go into the making of a saint than his cynical behavior would make us suspect. It is the purposes to which he applies his virtues, and not his qualities themselves, which distinguish him.

The ideal type of man in the stories, the composite of many heroes who display the same characteristics in varying degrees, is endowed with a particular quality of spirit which we can perhaps best paraphrase as presence of mind. He is consistent and persevering in his endeavors,, dedicated to his goal, and more often than not he is so because he has given his word for it. Although his actions are primarily self-centered, this very constancy in the pursuit of his purposes renders him dependable for others when his self-interest happens to coincide with theirs. If he is in a subordinate position, which of course does not happen often, this makes for an unstraying loyalty. The latter is also the function of the last basic characteristic, the capacity for relinquishing anything that is his or due to him, a capacity that is only imperfectly rendered as generosity, but when actuated by compassion, a quality often adorning his character, is close to it.

The quality which we paraphrase as presence of mind is not

so much a function of worldly wit or cleverness, as its condition. It is the articulation of a constant cagy awareness of what is going on, the refusal to permit oneself to be distracted momentarily, the preparedness and collectedness of one's faculty of discrimination and decision. It is what the philosophic psychology calls *buddhi*, which comprises both this wide-awake vigilance and the capacity for immediately acting upon what comes within its purview. This faculty is the hero's principal weapon in the struggle for survival. When Gomukha, one of the most appealingly human personalities of Indian literature, finds himself unexpectedly in the presence of a very beautiful girl and is caught unawares, his first exasperated thought is, when he has collected his senses, "Damned be my presence of mind and my voice which were surprised off guard and praised be my hands which went through the motions of greeting! I am nothing but my hands—mind and tongue have perished on me. For only the vigilant live, and he who is found off guard is already dead!" Seldom does the hero allow his mind to be distracted; when he does, and danger, always lurking, assails him, it is his own distraction he blames, not the forces that beset him. Apahāravarman, the master burglar, has been drinking with his wife, and in his drunkenness decides to empty the city of its wealth and fill his wife's house with the loot. "I burst loose, like a rutting elephant from his chain, and with no other weapon than my sword, set out in a fury of violence. When I fell in with a patrol of the town-guard I fought them without thinking: crying 'thief', they attacked, but hardly angry, playful rather, I killed off two or three of them before the sword slipped from my drunken hand and I collapsed with rolling bloodshot eyes. The emergency sobered me up and my head cleared at once. In a moment I collected my senses and thought: 'Aho! I am in dire trouble, and only because of my own lunacy!' " The heightened awareness, the undistracted concentration on what is going on which characterizes the hero, is exactly the same faculty the aspirant to release employs in the pursuit of man's highest purpose. It is this same mental discipline which does not allow a moment of distraction, the same concentration which, intensified to the apogee of consciousness that changes its essence, breaks through to the beyond.

A corollary of the hero's supreme presence of mind and resolution is his ruthlessness **[307]** in taking advantage of his adversary's lack of control. The hero is one of the perils perpetually lying in wait for anyone who lowers his defences. Apahārvarman mercilessly ruins the wealthy and greedy merchant Arthapati; but the moral is not primarily that the merchant should have been less greedy but that he should have been better prepared. In a world where only the vigilant survive, he had the misfortune to be a short-sighted fool.

The hero's perseverance, sometimes against heavy odds, is the quality by which he is able not only to bring out the latent potential of his personal destiny, but even to overcome its limitations and progress farther on his road to perfection. The story of the gambler Śaktideva, who finds and eventually possesses the City of Gold, is an excellent case in point. The perseverance which the hero exhibits in his exploits is frequently forced upon him by his word, for to be true to his word, as Somadeva says somewhere, is the true greatness of the great. In the Śaktideva story it is the gambler's promise, made in a moment of frustrated anger, that is his main motivation to continue in his apparently vain pursuits to find the City of Gold. Thus a hero's given word may become his destiny. And it is not necessarily his own word which is binding. Budhasvāmin's version of the Bṛhatkathā includes an interesting dispute between a disillusioned mendicant and an eager Brahman student about the relative importance of fate and a person's own agency. The mendicant, upholding the automatic fulfilment of destiny, tells the story of a young man of whom it is predicted that he will marry an evil wife just before the woman is actually born. The man flees from Sindh to the Doāb, unknowingly marries there the girl who had been evacuated by her parents from Sindh, flees again to Indonesia, and on his return to the mainland, meets her again in Banaras. In his tale of the blind workings of fate there is no clear indication whether it was the fate predicted by the seer which pursued him, or rather that the prediction itself had become fate. But in the counter-tale of the student, describing a solemnly sworn alliance between two merchants who predestine the marriage of their yet unborn children, it is perfectly clear that it was their word which was the actual fate, circumvented only with the greatest of efforts. It is, obviously, the old idea of the inherent efficacy of the solemnly or ritually uttered word; though in a gradually lesser degree, the man who has given his word has subjected himself to the power of his word, which, once spoken, is irrevocable because it is no longer within his control, just as the discomfited sage who has too rashly cursed an offender must confess himself unable to change the autonomous operation of the power thus let loose, though by a new word he may be able to decree how this power will be spent and the curse terminated. This notion of the inherent efficacy of the solemn word, however unfamiliar to us (in spite of the invariably quoted, and misquoted, passage *John* I: 1), is of fundamental importance at the beginning of Indian philosophy.

Perseverence and constancy have as their function dependability. The word is *dhīra*, describing the poise and mental equilibrium which is the condition of constancy and reliability, frequently likened to the repose of the ocean deeps which, in spite of minor disturbances at the surface, remain largely unperturbed. Thus it is synonymous with wisdom as expressed in action, and the qualification of *gambhīra* 'deep' denotes less the penetration of a man's intelligence than the profundity of his imperturbability.

This profundity is also articulated as the hero's capacity of relinquishment. This renunciation is celebrated in many stories. It may be a brigand's relinquishment of a **[308]** stray girl (lost property which, when found, will not be claimed by the owner) as in one of the Vampire's Tales and in Apahāravarman's story; it may also be the ultimate relinquishment of the Bodhisattva who renounces the Buddhahood, which is within his grasp, to do good to his fellow beings by acts of great sacrifice. Compassion is not a momentary emotion aroused by incidental encounters. It is the corollary of the saint's own sense of relinquishment and not rarely it has an admixture of contempt for the beneficiaries of his renunciation. In one of the Vampire's Tales a little boy sacrifices himself for the king of his country; for the author and his audience the nobility of the gesture does not lie in the other-directed emotions that inspire it, but in the self-directed merit of the action: it is primarily to add this merit to the balance that is carried forward from life to life, and the boy is quite explicit in his contempt for the motivations of those who are involved in his self-sacrifice. To the maniacal self-renunciation of the great sages of the epic, Buddhism may have added an element of compassion, but one feels that it is this renunciation itself as the means to a person's higher purposes which is fundamental, not the benefit of others.

As sketched, the hero's character seems designed for purposeful action; naturally, one would say, for a story lives by its action. Still in the Indian hero there is an instinct deliberation and a pin-pointed concentration of purpose not easily matched by the stories of other cultures. Moreover, the range of his action is unlimited. And it is in the infinite capacity of the persevering man that we find the most characteristic theme both of Indian thought on its highest levels and of the Indian tale on a more worldly plane. What I should like to note as the most characteristically Indian type of tales of the Indian culture is the Vidyādhara story. This is not just a subjective selection from a wide choice of story types which the literature offers; it is proved to be characteristically, and therefore inalienably, Indian by its peculiar failure to migrate. A stupendous amount of work and erudition has been bestowed by scholars on the study of tales migrating from India to other cultures, but rarely, if at all, has the question been raised why certain tales, popular and widely distributed in the homeland, either were not exported or failed to make good elsewhere. The Vidyādhara tale tried to migrate, we have evidence for that, into Muslim territory, but failed signally. And it is clear why.

The Vidyādhara is one of the most interesting of the twenty-odd different kinds of supernatural beings that occur in the story literature. For unlike any other god, deity, vampire or hobgoblin, the Vidyādhara is originally a man. Though his affinity with other celestial beings, like the Gandharvas, has occasioned a similar mythology of a race of Vidyādharas created by Śiva, with a king in control, definitely localized cities, etc., there can be no real doubt that the Vidyādhara represents man become superman by virtue of his knowledge. By his own efforts and through the proper science man can become a Vidyādhara, not through the usual promotion from life to life through which an occasional human soul may aspire to become a god for a while, but instantaneously, during this very life.

The word means 'possessor of science', science being virtually synonymous with magic. For the science that makes a man a superman is the knowledge of the appropriate formulae and spells that give him entire control over his destiny and allow him to transcend his human limitations. There is no doubt that the figure of the Vidyādhara has been patterned on the aspirant to liberation; for the common man in any case and, we may presume, for many practitioners, the main requirement to gain entrance to that yonder world of liberation which, transcending the old heaven, immediately assumed [309] the attributes of the old heaven in the popular mind, was the mere knowledge of the secret formulae upon which the Brahmans of old had based their ascendancy over world and afterworld. It is related as much to the mysticism of a higher order, yoga in its different applications (which itself has many magical trappings), as to the black arts of the necromancer. In the Vampire's Tales an aspirant to the state of Vidyādhara arranged an elaborate black *pūjā* and ritual offering terminating in a human sacrifice meant to gain control of the corpse-spirit Vetāla. Elsewhere the preliminaries involve the ripping out of an unborn child. The character of the Vidyādhara shares the dual characteristics of its origination: it is a benevolent, artistic and amorous spirit, but also a boon companion of demons and goblins and a bogy with which small children are frightened.

The Vidyādhara as the apotheosis of the ideal hero is largely confined to the popular domain where a complete literature has sprung up around him which has been styled bourgeois. His great vehicle is the famous Bṛhatkathā, the "Great Storybook," a dialectic composition from the first half of the first millennium A.D., ascribed to a Guṇāḍhya, now lost in the original but surviving in several Sanskrit reproductions from which Lacôte[1] in an excellent study has authoritatively attempted to describe and, to some extent, reconstruct the original. Later literature shows that this book was considered the book of the Vidyādhara par excellence, but there were many other Vidyādhara tales which were incorporated in the Kaśmīrian recension of the Bṛhatkathā, best known from Somadeva's eleventh century work *Kathāsaritsāgara,* the 'Ocean of Story.'

Man's attaining the position of a Vidyādhara is, in most tales, the reward of great and persistent efforts. The idea very evidently is that man can work himself up to that celestial status, though it remains reserved for the very few, just as the attainment of release, by its severe demands upon capacity and effort, remains closed to the many. The pleasures of his high status are hardly novel and reflect disarmingly the common ambitions of the average person: an infinite capacity of gratifying an amorous nature; the ability to escape gloriously and take to the air as an aerial spirit, fast as thought, snatching occasionally an unsuspecting princess; a regal residence in vast terraced palaces with golden and gem studded walls where hosts of attendants wait on the hero, recumbent on a gem encrusted couch, with the choicest banquets; a talent for music and song; and lastly a celestial bride of unsurpassed beauty and accomplishments.

The very human aspirations of which the Vidyādhara is the incarnate fulfilment should, however, not make us forget that the man who has attained this position has transcended his human limitations in a very real sense; and it is this very same belief in man's capacity to overcome his human condition which is at the foundation of Indian thinking, however the pleasures attendant upon the transcension may be described. The extent to which this type of tale, of a human being passing to a higher superhuman state of being through his own efforts, is culturally determined is illustrated by the reception it found in Islamic culture.

In the Kathāsaritsāgara we find a small cycle of Vidyādhara stories built around the narrative of Śaktideva and the City of Gold. The story is that a certain princess announces that she will marry only a man (Brahman or nobleman, adds the class conscious compiler) who has seen or visited the City of Gold. Proclamations are made but nobody puts forward his claim, until a bankrupt gambler, who has nothing to lose, Śaktideva, tries to risk it and claims falsely that he knows the city. His ignorance is exposed and the hero vows that he will prove his word and find the city. He sets [310] out on a veritable odyssey which leads him from hermitage to remote hermitage, those traditional clearing houses of travellers' reports, and is directed to the ocean. He sets sail with a merchant, but the ship founders, and the hero is swallowed by a fish which is caught off a distant island, and set free. The king promises his help and takes him in a small craft to a festival where pilgrims from all corners of the archipelago assemble: someone may know the city. In the middle of the ocean the hero sees a divine tree rise from the surface and the craft is pulled to a maelstrom at the foot of the tree. While ship and skipper are dragged to the Mare's Head fire at the bottom of the maelstrom, the hero saves himself in the tree. A swarm of giant birds comes home to roost, and when one of them announces that it will fly to the City of Gold on the next day, the hero hides between its feathers and is thus transported to his goal. He is welcomed and entertained by a Vidyādhara girl with whom he lives in anticipated wedlock, until the girl tells him that she will be absent for a short while and warns him not to enter the middle storey of the palace. Curious, the hero cannot help himself and entering the middle storey finds in a room the dead body of the princess of his home town. In adjacent rooms two more bodies of beautiful damsels are found. Wonderingly, the hero walks out to the balcony, and looks down on a pond in a garden where a riderless saddled horse stands waiting. The hero descends to mount the horse but is kicked into the pond from which he emerges in his home town. He makes good his claim to the princess that he knows the City of Gold, only to see the girl drop dead after a reassuring promise of eventual reunion. The hero starts once more and finally, after many adventures, reaches the City of Gold, marries the princess and the other girl as well as the meanwhile revivified bodies, and at last is transformed into a Vidyādhara.

There are other stories which clearly derive from a common basis. The seventh Vampire's Tale has a hero who, sailing to Ceylon, sees a flagpole rise from the surface of the ocean. His ship founders but he dives after the sinking flagpole to find himself in a temple of the goddess in a submarine city. He meets a celestial girl who, while pretending to welcome him, has him bathe in a pond from which he emerges in his home town. The king, indebted to him, lends his assistance and together they repeat the journey to the submarine city and the girl, where the hero finally marries her.

In the twelfth Vampire's Tale, a king's councillor, on his way to Sumatra, sees a celestial tree rise from the surface of the ocean. A beautiful girl in the tree sings a song of fate. Back home the councillor tells the king his adventure and the king falls in love with the idea of the girl, repeats the same journey, dives after the sinking tree, finds and marries the girl. Then his bride tells him that she must go away for a few days and warns him not to enter the Crystal Pavilion, where is a magic pond which transports a man back to his homeland. The king embraces his bride, jumps in the pond with her, to emerge in his kingdom. The woman, really a Vidyādharī, appears now to have lost her knowledge, and remains.

It is clear that the last story is built on (the originals of) the other two, of which the principal characteristic is that a man finds a celestial woman in an only magically accessible city, loses her through a horse and/or a magic pond, but returns, and on his return becomes a Vidyādhara, wedding the girl and reigning in her city. This story, with numerous elements that are unmistakably identical both in content and sequence with those in the Indian stories, has migrated to Muslim territory. We find it in at least three related forms, twice in the *Arabian Nights*, that is, in the Third Qalander's Tale (16th night) and the fourteenth tale of the Sindibādnāma (588th–591st nights),[2] and once in a Persian tale, the first story of the Three Dervishes.[3]

[311] The third Qalander, 'Ajīb ibn Khasīb, after many other adventures, arrives at a palace with curious residents: an old *shaikh* and ten youths all blind in one eye. At a set hour the youths cover their heads with ashes and begin mourning. 'Ajīb is urged not to inquire into their curious behavior, but at last he persuades them to tell him. Reluctantly they sew him in a ram's skin, the lump is snatched up by a giant bird who leaves him on a mountain near a beautiful palace where forty damsels welcome him. He lives there for a year in great joy, but at the end of the year the girls announce that they have to absent themselves for forty days. He is urged to make himself at home in the meantime, to enter forty doors that open on entertaining scenes, but under no condition to open one golden door. He cannot help himself, and enters the forbidden chamber where he finds a black horse with a golden saddle. He mounts the horse, but it does not stir until he kicks it with his heel and finally strikes it with a dagger. Then the horse opens its wings, soars up in the skies and finally alights on the roof of another palace. When the hero dismounts, the horse flicks its tail and strikes out his eye. Tumbling into the palace 'Ajīb finds the *shaikh* and the ten one-eyed youths, who expel him. He spends his life mourning.

The other Arabian story has a similar unhappy ending, and so has the Persian one. In the latter, a jeweler's son, who sings entrancingly on his roof, is kidnapped by a giant bird who brings him to a palace inhabited by birds. At a set hour the birds are transformed into a fairy princess and her attendants. The hero falls in love, but after having been entertained for several days, receives on a certain day a resounding blow from his beloved, which transports him back to the roof of his dwelling.

It is clear what has happened to the original from which the three related Muslim stories have descended. Crossing from one culture granting the ability of man to rise from the limitations of his manhood to a higher condition described in the secular stories as semi-divine, into another culture with a religion whose first article of faith is that there is no other god than God, that human beings can never transcend their humanity, and are able to reach salvation not through their own efforts but only by destiny, the original tale was so adjusted to the new environment in which it ventured so as to lose its entire point. The point of the Indian story is that after an initial failure which sets the hero back to his starting point, because as yet he has not earned the position that would permit his success, the hero once again sets out on the same journey and now succeeds by transforming himself, or earning an automatic transformation, into a being of higher order. At the exact point where the Indian story describes the return of the hero Islam made a cut.[4] There is no god but God, and the Muslim hero who never tires of extolling the deity spends his life mourning over a lost paradise which he is forbidden to regain.

NOTES

1. Félix Lacôte, *Essai sur Guṇāḍhya et la Bṛhatkathā* (Paris, 1908).
2. "Alf Laila wa Laila" in the Macnaghten edition.
3. Reuben Levy, *The Three Dervishes* (Oxford, 1923).
4. We must add that in Kathāsaritsāgara 108, 52-56, elements of the Śaktideva story are used in a story of a hero who lives some time with a witch and loses her through the kick of a horse in a forbidden "middle storey." There is no return, the hero attaining *siddhi* in a different manner. However, it is out of the question that it was this abbreviated and incomplete episode which originated the Muslim versions.

12

KAPYĀSAṂ PUṆḌARĪKAM

One of the most touching stories of Indian hagiography is the one that describes the rupture of the Vaiṣṇava saint and philosoper Rāmānuja with his teacher Yādavaprakāśa. This Yādavaprakāśa —not to be confused with his namesake the 'bhedābheda-vādin'—was a follower of Śaṅkara, for whom the all-powerful and all-merciful God of religion was but an unreal projection of the impersonal brahman. Differences had already been many, but the final rupture came at last on the day when the teacher was explaining *ChUp*. 1,6.6-7 to his pupils: "Verily, that Golden Person who is beheld within the orb of the sun, with golden beard and golden locks, all golden even unto the tips of his fingers: his eyes are like the lotus resembling a monkey's posteriors." Thereupon the young Rāmānuja shed a tear and the tear rolled down his cheek, dropped and burnt into the thigh of his teacher.[1]

Yādavaprakāśa followed here Śaṅkara's interpretation[2] of this śruti *tasya yathā kapyāsaṃ puṇḍarīkam evam akṣinī*, which reads: *tasya yathā kaper markaṭasyāsaḥ kapyāsaḥ | āser upaveśanārthasya karaṇe ghañ*[3] *| kapipṛṣṭhānto yenopaviśati | kapyāsa iva puṇḍarīkam atyantatejasvy evam asya devasya*[4] *akṣiṇī*. Roth has adopted this meaning and registers in pw s.v. *āsa* the meaning "Gesäss" for the last term of the compound *kapy-āsa*. Boehtlingk[5] rejects this and adopts a variant *kapilāsa* "with reddish pollen" which, however, is a *lectio facilior* not borne out by the oldest testimonies at our disposal. Deussen, as always followed by Hume,[6] treats *kapyāsa* as a name for a lotus of a certain kind. Senart[7] does not [337] want to commit himself on the term but leans towards Deussen's explanation. Radhakrishnan[8] follows Śaṅkara as usual, but renders the compound tactfully by "red". Excepting Boehtlingk, no one has tried to improve really upon Śaṅkara's etymology which nevertheless they are loth to accept.

The term is worth considering. In spite of its seeming transparency it appears that the compound was, long before, Saṅkara, explained in not less than six different ways—a sure sign that the originally intended meaning of the term was no longer known. All six are found in the oldest known gloss on the *Chāndogya Upaniṣad* by a Vākyakāra known under the names of Brahmanandin Ṭaṅka Ātreya. This Vākya has been commented on by Dramiḍa and has since been transmitted with this Bhāṣya, which seems to have carried great authority in pre-Śaṅkara Vedānta.[9] If we are to believe Ānandagiri, Śaṅkara knew and consulted the Dramiḍabhāṣya when he composed his Upaniṣadbhāṣya. Both Ṭaṅka's Vākya and Dramiḍa's Bhāṣya are now lost but for a few fragments; but Sudarśanasūri, commenting on Rāmānuja's Vedārthasaṃgraha, quotes one of Ṭaṅka's six explanations literally and describes the other five.

Not only does Ṭaṅka's antiquity justify a reconsideration of the term, but also is Śaṅkara's interpretation far from convincing. His *āsa*—in the sense of "seat of the body" is, as far as I know, not attested elsewhere. The comparison raises difficulties: there are two *upamās*: "Just as the lotus is *kapyāsa*, so are the eyes of the God." Śaṅkara ignores the gender when he paraphrases: "Just as the lotus is like a *kapyāsa*, i.e., very flashy, so are the God's eyes." Besides, is "flashiness" really the *tertium comparationis*? The *puṇḍarīka* is generally the white lotus, which may be described as brilliant, no doubt, but is hardly comparable either to a monkey's seat or to a person's eyes. Deussen's solution of a generic name is facile and solves nothing.

It is easier to reject previous explanations than to offer a better one. Moreover, we may wonder whether we are supposed to understand the word: there are other instances where upaniṣadic thinkers used cryptic words whose occult meanings could be understood only by the initiated. But a few observations may be made which shed light on the choice of the term for the context to which it belongs.

In the order to discover, not necessarily the "real meaning" of the word, but its associations which may be more significant, we must consider the context where a sun-like divine personality is described who is all golden—and golden means in this age "reddish" rather than "yellowish"—and whose eyes, themselves the microcosmic correspondents of the sun, are also reddish. The puṇḍarīkākṣa among [338] the gods is Viṣṇu *alias* Hari, whose connexions with the ancient Puruṣa are intimate. The term *puṇḍarīka* is not an indifferent word for lotus: it is the word for "mystic lotus "*par excellence*. Indeed, almost every word of the context is charged with mystical association and *sousentendus,* so much so that we should be over-cautious in taking the sense of such a bizarre word as *kapyāsa* for granted.

Of the eyes which are *kapyāsa* it is said later: *atha ya eṣo 'ntar akṣaṇi puruṣo dṛśyate..tasyaitasya tad eva rūpaṃ yad amuṣya rūpaṃ yan nāma tan nāma*: "that person who is beheld within the eye, his form is the form of that one (in the sun).. the name of one is the name of the other" (1,7,5). This total identity, expressed by means of the two fundamental principles of individuality, name and form, of the macrocosmic Person in the sun and the microcosmic Person in the eye—the latter again likened to a lotus which is "reddish"—gives a peculiar significance to our term. For this Person is not only sun and eye or within it, but also *puṇḍarīka* or within it. BĀUp. 2,3,6. has: *tasya haitasya puruṣasya rūpaṃ..yathā puṇḍarīkam.* The lotus figured from of old as a symbol of the puruṣa; and, insofar as this puruṣa is also symbolized[10] in the the sun—is indeed the solar creator or his descendant and heir—the lotus represents the sun. There is a suggestive parallelism between lotus and the sun: the immaculate splendour of the lotus arising from water and mud, untouched and transcendent on its stalk, has always struck the Indian poets and the artists have made the most of this symbolism of sun and lotus.[11] There is more to it: the ancient creation myths of the world arising from the waters and the old associations of *agni apāṃ napāt* form also part of the whole complex of macrocosmic and microcosmic interrelations of sun, lotus and personal demiurge. The divine lotus[12] from which Brahmā mahātejāḥ, the universal creator, emerges on the navel of Nārāyaṇa floating on the primaeval waters is undoubtedly the same lotus.

For there was a great mystery concealed in the cup of the lotus: *atha yad idam asmin brahmapure daharaṃ puṇḍarīkaṃ veśma daharo 'sminn antar ākāśaḥ / tasmin yad antas tad anveṣṭavyaṃ tad vāva vijijñāsitavyam* (*ChUp*. 8,1,1); and the uninitiated, who do not understand how the inside of a lotus can conceal a mystery, are told: *yāvān vā ayaṃ ākāśas tāvān eṣo 'ntar hṛdaya ākāśaḥ.. sarvaṃ tad asmin samāhitam* (ib. 8, 1,3). Aruṇa, whose name shows his preoccupation with the sun, described and elaborated the same image as follows: *asau vā āditye devamadhu...ṛgveda eva puṣpaṃ tā amṛtā āpaḥ......etaṃ ṛgvedam abhyatapan| tasyābhitaptasya yaśas teja indriyaṃ vīryaṃ annādyaṃ raso 'jāyata| tad vyakṣarat tad ādityam abhito 'śrayat | tad vā etad ādityasya rohitaṃ rūpam* (*ChUp.* 3, 1, 5): every time it is this flower [339] which, as ṛc, yajuḥ, sāman, (atharvāṅgirasa) itihāsapurāṇa and as bráhman, is the object of the creative power of tapas and so produces the red, white, black and ultra-black, and the colourless throbbing in the centre of the sun: the five aspects under which the existent beings and things are grouped. And every time after the mention of the *puṣpa* follows: *tā amṛtā āpaḥ* "there are the eternal Waters," wholly outside the laboured flower-honey metaphor, which can be understood only as the primaeval Waters from which this flower arises.

Not less intimate than here is the association of the lotus with the sun in *AthV.* 10, 2, 31-32.

aṣṭā́cakrā návadvārā devā́nām pū́r ayodhyā́ |
tásyāṃ hiraṇyáyaḥ kóśaḥ svargó jyótiṣā́vṛtaḥ ||
tásmin hiraṇyáye kóśe tryáre trípratiṣṭhite |
tásmin yád yakṣam ātmanvát tád vai brahmavído vídụḥ ||

Here the metaphors are deliberately mixed and microcosmic and macrocosmic imagery intermingled to convey the all-comprehensiveness of the mystery within that golden flower-cup. Likewise *AthV.* 10, 8, 43:

puṇḍárīkaṃ návadvāraṃ tribhír guṇébhir ā́vṛtam |
tásmin yád yakṣám ātmanvát tád vai brahmavído viduḥ ||

The wondrous person within that golden flower-cup, the golden seedvessel of sun and lotus, is also Hiraṇyagarbha "the Golden Seed," of whom the *Ṛgveda* relates:

hiraṇyagarbháḥ sám avartatā́gre bhūtásya jātáḥ pátir éka āsīt | "in the beginning the Golden Seed came to be, and when he was born he became the one lord of creation" (10, 121,1). This Golden Seed is borne by the waters (ib. 7), like Viśvakarman who is the father of the eye,[13] the all-seeing one:[14]

tám íd gárbhaṃ prathamám dadhra ā́po
yátra devā́ḥ samágacchanta viśve |

ajásya nā́bhāv ádhy ékam árpitam
yásmin víśvāni bhū́vanāni tasthúḥ //

This Golden Seed was also conceived of as an egg. The primaeval waters, desiring to bring forth, produce tapas which becomes a golden egg (*ŚatBr*. 11, 1, 6, 1). Elsewhere Prajāpati produces this egg from the waters by tapas (*ib*. 6, 1, 1, 10), just as later on Brahmā the Hiraṇyagarbha, who is born from the lotus that arises in the navel of the one God of the Waters Nārāyaṇa, creates the egg of the world: [340] a telling example of how all these images exist on in an age which feels no longer their coherence.

Was this Seed already in *ṚV*. 10, 27, 16 described as *kapila*? The text gives no clue. But we can follow the traces of the golden seed, who is also the solar puruṣa, the first creator and first creature, down through the upaniṣads until we find him described as *kapila*. In *hiraṇmayaḥ puruṣa ekahaṃsaḥ* (*BĀUp*. 4, 3, 11) another aquatic image joins the others. In *BĀUp*. 5, 15, 1. (*IśUp*. 15) the solar imagery prevails, but this poetic evocation begins:

hiraṇmayena pātreṇa satyasyāpihitaṃ mukham /
tat tvam Pūṣan apāvṛṇu satyadharmāya dṛṣṭaye //

"the face of the true one is covered by a golden vessel : open it, O sun, so that He of the true conduct may be seen!"[15] In *Muṇḍ Up*. 2, 2, 9 we find a conscious reminiscence of[16]—as well as a reply to—*AthV*. 10, 2, 31-32 quoted above:

hiraṇmaye pare kośe virajaṃ brahma niṣkalam /
tac chubhraṃ jyotiṣāṃ jyotis tad yad ātmavido viduḥ //

and 3, 1, 3 reads:

yadā paśyaḥ paśyati rukmavarṇaṃ kartāram āśam puruṣam brahmayonim/

In Śvet *Up*. 4, 12 the person who is the Golden Seed of creation returns:

yo devānāṃ prabhavaś codbhavaś ca viśvādhipo rudro maharṣiḥ/
hiraṇyagarbhaṃ paśyata jāyamānaṃ sa no buddhyā śubhayā saṃyunaktu //

and this great *rudra* ṛṣi is described in 5, 2

yo yoniṃ yonim adhitiṣṭhaty eko
viśvāni rūpāṇi yonīś ca sarvāḥ /
ṛṣiṃ prasūtaṃ kapilaṃ yas tam agre
jñānair bibharti jāyamānaṃ ca paśyet //

It is customary to leave *rudra* and *kapila* here untranslated, as if they were proper names. But *rudra* need not have lost its adjectival value[17]; it qualifies the *hiraṇyagarbha* who is not equated with Rudra (on the contrary Rudra's incidental claims to sovereignty[18] may have resulted partly from juxtapositions as we have here) but described as "reddish" just as he is described as *kapila, hiraṇmaya* **[341]** etc.

All these qualifications, whether applied to sun, lotus, *kośa, pātra*, etc. are applied to the Golden Person concealed under these forms. That the sun, called *rohita* in a well-known passage,[19] is so described is no doubt partially due to the fact that it represents fire, tejas, tapas. The *puṇḍarīka* "white lotus" is called golden or reddish-yellow because of its yellow stamina; *kāñcana* is listed as a word for the *bījakośa* "seed-vessel" of the lotus.[20] The same applies to the *puṣkara* "blue lotus" which in *Harivaṃśa* 3, 12, (299), 2 is called *hiraṇmaya*—cf. 15-16. Though Gonda rightly points out that gold is "also a token of an incorruptible nature,"[21] it would seem to me that the golden colour of the seed-vessel which becomes visible when the sun rises and the lotus opens is the primary association. And though the lotus with its form of receptacle may be looked upon as a specifically female symbol,[22] sexual connotations are largely absent; it is the aspect of *matrix* which clearly predominates, the calyx in which lies embedded the golden seed of creation.

Other contents of *kapila* should be understood from its frequent connexions with the sun and the deities associated with it, like *agni* and *hari*. Likewise the well-known myth of the 60,000 sons of Sagara who were burnt to ashes by the sage Kapila Bhagīratha and revived by the floods of the Ganges is likely to have its origin in the evaporation of "the innumerable laughter of the sea," the thousands of rivers and rivulets which vanish in the summer and are replenished by the floods of the rainy season. Interesting is the case of the sage Kapila, the mythical founder of the Sāṃkhya system, who started his career as an epithet of such beings as Hiraṇyagarbha. Keith[23] is certainly right in seeking his origin in passages like ŚvetUp. 5, 2. Hiraṇyagarbha, first creature born of the primaeval universal creator, played an important part in the creation myths which were the prototypes of Sāṃkhyan cosmogony. That a mythological personality ranking high in a hierarchy is later regarded as the founder of a system that has been developed from it is not uncommon: Nārāyaṇa is the founder of Pāñcarātra. Kapila, already firmly established in the Mahābhārata as the founder of Sāṃkhya, is still identified with Hiraṇyagarbha in some passages.[24] As the first creature Hiraṇyagarbha could represent the buddhi,[25] which itself originally was a cosmic creative potency; so we find *kapila* used as a term for the Sāṃkhyan buddhi.[26] In this context the frequent identifications of Kapila with Prajāpati, Viṣṇu, Kṛṣṇa and Vāsudeva become intelligible.[27]

[342] The word *kapi*, from which *kapila* is supposed to derive, is occasionally found listed in the meaning of "sun",[28] no doubt because the sun is "red and ruddy": *kapila*. This meaning gave rise to a pseudo-etymology *kapi* "sun"<*kaṃ pibati*, in which at least the relation of sun with water is interesting. Viṣṇu, who is *hari*—an epithet also used for a monkey—, is found described as *kapi.*[29] Has Arjuna's epithet *kapidhvaja* any particular significance in this connexion? That this inseparable companion of Kṛṣṇa Vāsudeva might have been associated originally with the brightness of day, dawn and lightning[30] is far from impossible.

It is my contention that the term *kapyāsa*, whatever its exact sense, is to be understood within this entire context of associations which we have sketched. It is obviously preferable to the sense of "monkey's posteriors." We are not justified in putting forth the aesthetic argument that this sense offends our taste as long as we know nothing of contemporary aesthetics—though the descriptions of the Golden Person and his "symbols" surprise by their singular poetic beauty. Of course we cannot disprove that *kapyāsa* may have been a name for lotus by way of *Volkswitz,* though it is difficult to imagine this for other ones than the red lotus; but even then the adoption of the term by the author of our *ChUp.* passage would lend it a significance far beyond the original joke. The fact remains that *āsa* in the postulated sense is further unknown and that *kapyāsa* is never found among the scores of Sanskrit words for lotus.[31]

More to the point is the fact that the *ChUp.* section in which the term occurs indulges generally in linguistic occultism. As we have shown elsewhere the text belongs to the context of *akṣara* speculations.[32] The cryptic *tajjalān,* explained as a compound of *tad—,—ja,—la* and*—an,* may put us on our guard. In our present text the word *udgītha* is taken apart with little pretension to scientific explication. Possibly we have become a little too linguistically minded to understand such fantastic explanations and declare ourselves too easily satisfied with *kapyāsa* in the above meaning because at least it follows the book.

If we now turn to Ṭaṅka's interpretations we should keep in mind that he was, in time and in spirit, nearer to this stage of speculation than Śaṅkara, and his doubtless fantastic explanations should not be summarily condemned : this author too indulged in fantastic explanations. The occasion of Sudarśanasūri's introduction, in his *Tātparyadīpikā* on the *Vedārthasaṃgraha,* of Ṭaṅka's commentaries is Rāmānuja's poetic paraphrasis of this Chāndogya śruti, which begins: *yo 'sāv ādityamaṇḍalāntarvartī taptakārtasvaragirivaraprabhaḥ sahasrāśatasahasrakiraṇāṃśu* [343] *gambhīrāmbhaḥsamudbhūta–sumṛṣṭanāla–ravikaravikasita–puṇḍarīkāmalāyatekṣaṇaḥ...puruṣavaro darīdṛśyate.* On the compound *gambīrāmbhaḥ*, etc. Sudarśana explains that the Vākyakāra had given six meanings, three rejected and three accepted, on which latter three Rāmānuja bases his paraphrasis. The rejected three are 1. *kapyāsa*<*kapi* "sun"+*āsa* "orb"; 2. <*kapi* "monkey"+*āsa* "back"; 3. "slightly opened" (*īṣad vikasitam*).[33] The accepted three are 1. <*kapi* "sun"+*āsa* (*tenāsyate kṣipyate vikāsyate*), on which Ṭaṅka is directly quoted: *ādityakṣiptaṃ vā, śrīmattvāt*" or: "thrown (open) by the sun, on account of its brilliance;" this corresponds to Rāmānuja's *ravikaravikasita*—; 2. <*kapi* "stalk" (<*kaṁ pibati*)+*āsa* "seat, place where one is seated", corresponding to Rāmānuja's *sumṛṣṭanāla*—; 3. <*ka* "water"+preposition *api* (which may lose its *a*[34])+ "to be," corresponding to Rāmānuja's *gambhīrāmbhaḥsamudbhūta*—.

To sum up, we have grounds for rejecting Ś.'s etymology which was endorsed by Roth. Boehtlingk's adoption of the variant *kapilāsa* is, in view of Śaṅkara's and Ṭaṅka's testimony, not justified. Deussen's device of explaining the word as a class-name shelves the difficulty. Ṭaṅka's six explanations, including Śaṅkara's, are from a modern scientific point of view curiosities but not therefore devoid of significance: folk etymologies often help us to understand the associations that went with certain terms in certain ages and milieux. Even if we disregard the 'meaning' "sun" for *kapi*, we have to recognize that there were close connexions between *kapi, kapila* and the sun or the solar puruṣa, either because of the reddish colour comparable to *hiraṇya*, etc. or because of more ancient, possibly non-Aryan relations between monkey, or rather *kapi*, and sun. That *kapila* is known as a word for lotus does not mean that the compound *kapyāsa* only refers to the colour of the flower: to the author the associations of sun, lotus eye and puruṣa were obvious as the context shows. The last member of the compound is obscure: Boehtlingk's suggestion of "pollen" it tempting, in view of the special significance of the seed-vessel of the lotus in this complex, but unfortunately this meaning is not attested. Personally I would consider it a mystical description of the kind *tajjalān*, etc. which went with the mystic lotus *puṇḍarīka*. We may compare the "eight-wheeled nine-gated invincible fort of the gods" of *AthV*. 10, 2, 31-32, in which there is a "seed-vessel surrounded by brilliance," or "the town of the brahman" of *ChUp* 8, 1, 1: the lotus was primarily the receptacle, the *abode* of the mysterious being, so we might explain *āsa* as "seat, abode." We should not try to be too definite about the meaning, but attempt to understand the word within the sketched context of associations in which it was coined, or at least applied. Even then it is not precluded that Ś.'s profane meaning was recognized and exploited to conceal its mystic content, the mysterious person within.

NOTES

1. *Śrī Rāmānuja Campū by Rāmānujācārya*, ed. by P.P. Subrahmanya Sastriyar (Madras 1942), p. 37 f.
2. *Chāndogyōpaniṣadbhāṣya* 1, 6, 7.
3. On the authority of Pāṇini 3, 3, 19 *akartari ca kārake saṃjñāyām* "(nouns formed with suffix—a to vṛddhied root occur not only in the meaning of the root (as per 3, 3, 18 *bhāve*), but also) in the sense of any kāraka, except agent, provided it be a technical term"; Siddānta-kaumudī cites, inter alia, *prāsa* "missile."
4. Note that in his *Brahmasūtrabhāṣya* 1, 1, 21 Śaṅkara explains this deity as merely a glorified individual soul, not even the Paramapuruṣa, which view Rāmānuja counters in *Śrībhāṣya* 1, 1, 21.
5. Otto Boehtlingk, *Khándogjopanishad*, kritisch herausgegeben und übersetzt (Leipsic 1889); he translates "mit röthlichem Blütenstaube" and notes in his *Anmerkungen* : "*Kapyāsa* soll nach S. ein Affengesäss bezeichnen. Ein schönes Beiwort der Lötusblüte.' *āsa* Asche, Staub kōnnte wohl, wie Roth annimt, auch den Blütenstaub bezeichnen." The fact remains that not only Ś reads *kapyāsa*, but also Ṭaṅka, as is clear from the interpretations given below. If the lectio *kapilāsa* had had any currency it would no doubt have been eagerly utilized by the commentators.
6. Paul Deussen, *Sechzig Upanishad's des Veda* (Leipsic 1921); R.E. Hume, *The Thirteen Principal Upanishads* (Oxford 1934[2]).
7. E. Senart, *Chāndogya Upaniṣad* (Paris 1930) p. 9, n. 1.

8. S. Radhakrishnan, *The Principal Upanishads* (London, 1953), p. 348.

9. For the sake of brevity I refer to my *Rāmānuja's Vedārthasaṃgraha* (Poona 1956), Introduction II, where these matters are discussed, and Appendix where the extant fragments are shown against the *ChUp.* passages, and translated.

10. Gonda, discussing the lotus as Viṣṇu's emblem (J. Gonda *Aspects of early Viṣṇuism* (Utrecht 1954), p. 104, n. 52) warns : "This term symbolism of the lotus, is not correct, because the ancient Indians, like other peoples in their circumstances and of their cultural niveau, did not look on a lotus-flower as a mere outward sign of a principle or a divine 'concept'; for them it was a visible representation, the very embodiment of the divine itself."

11. *Cf.* J.N. Banerjee, *IA*, 54, p. 161.

12. *Cf.* e.g. *MBh.* 12, (Crit. Ed.) 175 (=B 182).

13. *ṚV.* 10, 82, 1.

14. *ṚV.* 10, 81, 2; for Viśvakarman's solar connexion, cf. 10, 170, 4.

15. *satyadharmāya*, resuming *satyasya*, is the object with 'case-attraction' of *dṛṣṭaye*; Deussen, Senart etc. make it the logical subject.

16. as there is another reminiscence in 2, 2, 6.

17. whether "red" or "celestial," *Cf.* Pischel, *Vedische Studien* 1 (1888), p. 56, and the recent dicussion of Mayrhofer, Der Gottesname Rudra *ZDMG* 103, p. 140 ff. (*rudras rodas* "himlisch") and Pisani, Dennoch Rudra "der Rote," *ZDMG* 104, p. 137 ff.

18. *Cf. Atharvaśikh Up.*

19. *AthV.* 13, 1, 6ff.; *Cf.* 13, 2, 25 where *tapas* is *rohita's* creative power.

20. R. Schmidt, Flora Sanscritica : Der Lotus in der Sanskrit Literatur, *ZDMG* 67, p. 462ff.

21. Gonda, *o.c.* p. 104, n. 52.

22. S. Hummel, *Geheimniss tibetischer Malereien* (Leipsic 1949), p. 5, quoted by Gonda, l.c.

23. A.B. Keith, *The Sāṃkhya System* (London. no date), p. 9.

24. e.g. *MBh.* 12, 296,39; cf. Deussen--Strauss, *Vier philosophische Texte des Mahābhāratam* (Leipsic 1906) *ad hoc* (=310, 40), p. 637.

25. *MBh.* 12, 291, 17; Māṭharavṛtti *ad* Sāṃkhya Kārikā 22.

26. Aśvaghoṣa, *Buddhacarita*, ed. and trsl. by E.H. Johnston (2 vols., Calcutta 1933-36) 12, 31, with translator's note.

27. I refer to Sorensen's *Index to the Mahābhārata*, s.v. Kapila.

28. pw.s.v. *kapi*.

29. pw.s.v. *hari*; *Viṣṇusahasranāma* has *kapi*, *kapila* and *kapīndra*; *Medinīkośa* (pāntavarga 2) *kapiḥ..madhusūdane*; *Kalpadrukośa* (p. 322, 46) *hariḥ.. kapiḥ*; the latter kośa has also (p. 436, 6) *puṣkaraḥ..kapiḥ*.

30. *ṚV.* 6, 9, 1; 1, 49, 3.

31. Schmidt, *o.c.*

32. I refer to my paper *Notes on akṣara* (Deccan College Bulletin Vol. XVII, No. 3, Dec. 1955, pp. 204 [no. 5 in this volume].

33. No etymologies given.

34. According to the well-known rule *vaṣṭi bhāgurir allopam avāpyor upasargayor* "Bhāguri approves the elision of *a* in the prepositions *ava* and *api*."

13

*AKṢARA**

A few years ago two distinguished indianists, Gonda[1] and Renou,[2] simultaneously expressed their dissatisfaction with the more or less accepted view on the semantic development of the term *bráhman,* from "sacred formula, hymn, etc." to "supreme principle." Both concurred in the opinion that the most ancient meaning—most ancient insofar as it happens to be attested in the most ancient document, the Ṛgveda—is really too narrow to allow for the use of the term in *āraṇyaka* and *upaniṣad,* and must reflect the specialized usage in sacerdotal milieux of a more comprehensive significance. For Gonda the notion behind *bráhman* is that of a vast but not unspecific power of support and foundation which in the speech of the Vedic priest-poets was especially articulated as "ritual, sacred or magical utterance," the bearer of that power. For Renou the term signifies that powerful activity which by way of a putative original meaning "riddle, enigma" came to denote the very object of those riddles that sought to encompass the great cosmic coherence.

Reviewing their suggestions, a third vedicist, Thieme,[3] disagreed with both. Rejecting both the original meanings and etymologies proposed, he put forward a novel etymology of *bráhman* on the basis of an original meaning more construed from the meaning of supposed non-Sanskrit cognates than elicited from the unmistakable meaning of the Sanskrit texts. As Thieme himself to some extent recognizes, no one of the three attestations he quotes for this original meaning "formation, either of an embryo or of a poem" (RV. 10.61.7; 10.65.11; AitBr. 5.15.5) is really convincing. In fact, they are not very suggestive, and one may suspect that a meaning "formation" would not occur to someone who, while looking for still another etymology of *bráhman,* had not at once certain German uses of the verb "to form"[4] and the mere possibilities of Gr. *bréph-os* in mind from the outset. As this original meaning must be denied, the etymology based upon it (IE *mrégu̯h-men-; *mre/ogu̯h- > *bréph-os, morph-é*, bráh-man) lacks urgency.

Committed to a methodological view-point which allows him to pronounce on the general meaning without exploring too far the actual denotations (etymology in one case, exegesis in the other, both sharply to be distinguished), Thieme is content to note for the upaniṣadic *bráhman* the meaning (*Bedeutung*) "die durch das Wort *bráhman* [**177**] bezeichnete Kraft" and the denotation (*Sinn*) "das letzte Prinzip",[5] and thereby must remain fundamentally at cross-purposes with Gonda and Renou who attempted to find in this denotation a criterion to establish more precisely the meaning of *bráhman*. Yet their question is etymologically relevant: does in the functions of *brahman* as a universal principle survive a specific meaning which enabled just this word among several near synonyms to acquire those functions? By denying for the older texts the meanings they propose, Thieme has not really answered their question, and we must conclude that the question, and the answers suggested, still stand.

Renou raises the question: if *bráhman* as a word for sacred, etc., utterance could develop a meaning of "supreme principle," why had words with similar meanings, like *dhī, vāc, mantra, uktha, stoma* such a different fate?[6] More meaningfully the question could be restated: is *brahman* the only word that underwent these semantic changes, and if so, why just *brahman*? We must immediately remark that of the five words enumerated, the first two may claim attention as parallels. *Vāc* as Prajāpati's consort and progenitrix of the world sometimes reaches an eminence entirely comparable to that of *brahman*. *Dhī* becomes identified with *buddhi*, the creator's self-recognition, and will, as the first product of creation, be the highest in the hierarchy of creative principles, like *brahman*. At another occasion[7] I have tried to demonstrate that in *ahaṃkāra*, too, we have a term which, originally denoting an utterance, consequently assumed a role in world creation and the cosmology and psychology based on the creation process. Examples, therefore, seem not to be wanting. Still it may be said that *brahman* is a principle of a different kind: but is it? Do we have in the case of *brahman* really a word of a different meaning, different from the meaning generally prevailing in the texts of the same milieux which later elevate it to its high status? After all that has been written about this word, it requires some temerity to produce another opinion and more presumption to believe oneself right. But there may be some heuristic value in approaching the question of *brahman* obliquely, not dealing with this term alone but with other terms which undoubtedly denoted an "utterance" and yet became a name for "the absolute." One of these terms, which in every phase of the ancient text occurs side by side with *brahman*, which seems to have had even less of a significant—philosophically significant—content than *brahman*, yet acquired even more rapidly than *brahman* itself this philosophical significance, appears to be especially relevant: not only because it proves that a word denoting some kind of an utterance could indeed denote God, but also because in its case, as well as in *brahman*'s, secondary connotations confirmed and continued its position when the original speculations about word and sound became obsolete. This term is *akṣara* "syllable."

Already in the Ṛgveda Saṃhitā *akṣára*[8] claims the position of a supreme principle, without however for a moment ceasing to mean "syllable". So 1.164.41-42: *gaurī́r mimāya salilā́ni tákṣaty ékapadī dvipádī sā́ cátuṣpadī / aṣṭā́padī návapadī babhūvúṣī sahásrākṣarā paramé vyòman // tásyāḥ samudrā́ ádhi ví kṣaranti téna jīvanti pradíśaś cátasraḥ / tátaḥ kṣaraty akṣáraṃ tád víśvam úpa jīvati //* "the Buffalo-Cow has lowed, building lakes, having become one-footed, two-footed, four-footed, eight-footed, nine-footed, of a thousand syllables in the supreme heaven; on the rivers that flow out from her live the four quarters of space; therefrom flows the Syllable: on it lives all the world."

Even here a different rendering of *akṣára* has been proposed. Geldner[9] prefers to interpret the *akṣára* on which all the world lives as "imperishable"[178]—*a-kṣara*, a view against which Bergaigne had already protested.[10] Geldner, however, suffers from a preconception about supreme beings:[11] not wishing to believe that a syllable could, as SYLLABLE, be a source of creation, he prefers a generally descriptive sense, without asking what to these thinkers was the imperishable, and why. But not only does the same term *akṣára* occur twice in the same context as syllable (39; 42 in *sahásrākṣarā*), but the earliest commentaries on this passage leave no possible doubt that the disputed *akṣára* was firmly conceived of as "syllable," namely TaittS. 5.1.9.1 and JaimUpBr. 1.10.1, which we shall discuss presently.

The Cow of this mantra is unmistakably *Vāc*, the life-giving sacral Word, here represented as the roaring thunderstorm which announces the rainy season; just as the monsoon storms—like the cow—pour down their revivifying showers, building lakes which inundate the soil and sustain creation, so the Word manifests itself in the sacred formulae which, over the sacred fire in the sacrifice, bring about the rains. But the ultimate measure of the Word is the Syllable from which all formulae start and to which their power can be reduced. Without the knowledge of this first and ultimate. what use are the hymns? So ib. 39: *ṛcó akṣáre paramé vyòman yásmin devā́ ádhi viśve niṣedúḥ / yás tán ná véda kím ṛcā́ kariṣyati yá ít tád vidús tá imé sám āsate//* "what can he bring about with the hymn who does not know the Syllable in the Supreme heaven in which the gods are seated? Only those who do know it are here sitting together in discussion."

Since the syllable is the smallest bit of speech that can be spoken and the first that must be spoken, it is conceived at once as the matrix and as the embryo of speech and all that can be effected by it. But for speech, that is the ritually powerful utterance, to be effective at all, it must be spoken in conjunction with the ritually powerful fire of the sacrifice. But this fire, too, is effective only in conjunction with the appropriate formulae. Together they originate, inseparable, in the womb of the true order.[12] Thus RV. 6.16.35-36: *gárbhe mātúḥ pitúṣpitā́ vidídyutānó akṣáre / sī́dann ṛtásya yṓnim ā́ // bráhma prajā́vad ā́ bhara jā́tavedo vícarṣaṇe / ágne yád dīdáyat dìví //* "As Jātavedas, most excellent Fire, sparkling in the Syllable which is thy mother's womb, as thy father's father seated in the womb of the true order, deliver the child-bearing *bráhman* which radiates in heaven".

The interdependence, the biunity, of Word and Fire could hardly be expressed more completely. Fire is contained in the germ of Speech, which is the Syllable; and the Syllable itself is the embryo which becomes the fully delivered *brahman*; but Fire is also wedded to Word, for without Fire the Word cannot even conceive the Syllable which is the germ of the ritually potent Formula, hence Fire is also the father of the Syllable which in its turn begets the powerful Fire of the sacrifice. The birth of Word and Fire is a cosmic event which is reproduced in the sacrificial area but happened primordially, at the beginning of creation, in heaven. But once reproduced in the sacrificial area, this area itself becomes the matrix of the cosmic order: it is the source from which the *bráhman,* the ritually powerful utterance, is born to beget offspring again,[13] the source therefore of the everlasting continuity of the true order which, after its first initiation in heaven, is perpetuated ever since. Every single term at some time will become the epitome of this total conception: *etaj jyotir etad akṣaram etat satyam etad brahma*—it is almost a refrain in the upaniṣads.

Cosmically this event is summed up in the incomparable line, 3.55.1 ab: *uṣásaḥ pū́rvā ádha yád vyūṣúr mahád vi jajñe akṣáraṃ padé goḥ* "when the ancient dawns first dawned the Great Syllable was born in the footstep of the Cow." The life-granting [179] Voice calls the world into being by CALLING it; in the first foot—for the voice speaks poetry—arises the first syllable from which everything else will follow. The significant relation between Syllable and Sun will occupy us later.

Unless we understand the significance of the ritually effective Word for a class of priests for whom the cosmic order was predicated upon the ritual order, and the significance of the actual manifestation of that Word in the embryonic Syllable which grows into the fully potent *bráhman,* we shall misunderstand the more advanced speculations which are inspired by this central ritual event. If we render *akṣára* as "imperishable," why is what imperishable? The source of all continuity is Word and Fire; whatever is imperishable is imperishable just by virtue of this pair. *Akṣára* is imperishable just because it is the Syllable, the principle of continuity to which everything can be reduced and from which everything can be derived.

In an interesting text of the Sāmaveda tradition, the JaimUpBr. 1.1, we read an account of how the creator squeezed out the classes of creation whose juice or sap, i.e., their first principle, became a higher class. He continues to squeeze until he arrives at the very last principle of all classes of creation, the *akṣara—athaitasyākṣarasya rasaṃ nāśaknod ādātum / om ity etasyaiva seyaṃ vāg abhavat / om eva nāmaiṣā / tasyā u prāṇa eva rasaḥ* "he could not take the juice of this *akṣara*; of this *akṣara, OM,* the Word came to be, for the Word is indeed *OM.* The juice of Word is Breath, etc." Thus having found the ultimate, the irreducible, the creator starts creation; *akṣara,* that, through which the Word exists, can of course be nothing but "syllable." Here the syllable is identified: it is the syllable *OM.*

Elsewhere creation is said to start from ether, which is not only the region of the sun but also the medium of sound and thus the natural substratum of the couple Fire and Word. This ether as prime principle evidently continues the *paramáṃ vyòman,* with which the Ṛgvedic *akṣára, bráhman* and even the *brahmán*[14] are so closely associated. JaimUpBr. 1.23.1 reads: *ayam evedam agra āsīt / sa u evāpy etarhi /* (2) *sa yas sa ākāśo vāg eva sā / tasmād ākāśād vāg vadati* "this (ether) was here at first. It is the same ether which is still here. This ether is Word, for the Word speaks from the ether."

The term *akṣara* goes through an interesting evolution. On the one hand it exists on as a word for syllable in the grammatical sense of the word, on the other hand it retains the significance of first and last principle of the cosmic order and so its creator, a significance which it originally acquired just by meaning "syllable." In one milieu it persists as a name for the absolute, however conceived of, is gradually, when the *Vāc* speculations become obsolescent (but rather later than we expect) reinterpreted as "imperishable" in order to rationalize its function as a supreme entity, and eventually (but later than the early metrical upaniṣads), it becomes an adjective. In another milieu, probably that of the Sāmaveda, *akṣara* was specifically identified with the syllable *OM*, which then takes over the role of being a name for the Supreme, until it becomes a symbol for Hinduism in very much the same way as the cross is a symbol for Christianity.

That *akṣara* is indeed imperishable inasmuch as it is "syllable" is clear from such passages as JaimUpBr. 1.23.3ff. The Word that speaks from ether is squeezed out: its juice is the three-world universe, whose juice is the gods, whose juice is the triple Veda. The juice of the Veda is the three *vyāhṛtis*; of their juice it is said: *tad etad akṣaram abhavad OM iti yad etad* "that became the *akṣara*, namely *OM*." The text continues (8) *sa etad akṣaram abhyapīlayat / tasyābhipīlitasya rasaḥ prāṇedat /* (1.24.1) *tad akṣarad eva / yad akṣarad eva tasmād akṣaram /* (2) *yad evākṣaraṃ nākṣīyata tasmād akṣayam / akṣayaṃ ha vai nāmaitat / tad akṣaram iti parokṣam ācakṣate* "he squeezed this *akṣara*; when it was squeezed juice trickled forth. That flowed, hence it is *akṣara*. As the *akṣara* did not perish, therefore it is *akṣaya*. In fact, *akṣara* is really *akṣaya*; they call it *akṣara* to mystify."[15] As the syllable *OM*, *akṣara* is still **[180]** "syllable"; yet *OM* has already usurped so much of *akṣara's* supremacy that there are attempts to reinterpret the term as "that which flowed into the world," and "that which does not perish." So *akṣara* has a tendency to become an attribute to *OM,* instead of *OM* a specification of "syllable." Generally, however, it remains one expression: *OM ity etad akṣaram.*

The relation between *akṣara* as *OM* and the three *vyāhṛtis* is interesting. These utterances, *bhūḥ bhuvaḥ svaḥ,* represent the three worlds, in fact there are accounts[16] that the three worlds arose through their formulation. But all three are contained in *OM*3. So ChUp. 2.23.3-4 *prajāpatir lokān abhyatapat / tebhyo 'bhitaptebhyas trayī vidyā saṃprāsravat/ tām abhyatapat / tasyā abhitaptāyā etāny akṣarāṇi saṃprāsravanta bhūḥ bhuvaḥ svar iti / tāny abhyatapat / tebhyo 'bhitaptebhya oṃkāraḥ saṃprāsravat / tad yathā śaṅkunā*[17] *sarvāṇi parṇāni saṃtṛṇṇāny evam oṃkāreṇa sarvā vāk saṃtṛṇṇā / oṃkāra evedaṃ sarvam.*

The same speculation occurs in JaimUpBr. 1.10.1-2 where it forms part of an exegesis of RV 1.164.41-42: *sā pṛthak salilaṃ kāmadughā *takṣatī*[18] *prāṇasaṃhitaṃ cakṣuśśrotaṃ manasā vyāptaṃ hṛdayāgram...sahasrākṣaram ayutadhāram...amṛtaṃ duhānā sarvān imān lokān abhi vikṣaratīti* "She, milch-cow of desires, yielding (as her milk) the elixir of immortality, building (?) separate lakes, composed with breath, possessed of sight and hearing, rich in speech, pervaded by mind, culminating from the heart[19] ...with a thousand syllables, ten thousand streams,[20] flows out into all these worlds." Incidentally such passages raise the question whether the popular notion of the *kāmadhuk* does not ultimately derive from the representation of *Vāc* as a cow. ChUp. 1.3.5 in an entirely comparable context has: *dugdhe 'smai vāg dohaṃ yo vāco doho 'nnavān annādo bhavati ya etāny evaṃ vidvān udgīthākṣarāṇy upāsta ud-gī-tha iti.*

That the connection between *akṣara* "syllable" and the syllable *OM* was first laid in Sāmavedic circles cannot be proved. But we note that this explicit connection remains confined in the older, texts to the Sāmaveda, notably the JaimUpBr. and the closely related ChUp.; implicitly the same connection is found also elsewhere, as we shall see. In any case, the Sāmavedic interest must reflect a sacerdotal preoccupation which was conspicuously articulated in the *agniṣṭoma* ritual itself. Noteworthy in the ChUp. is the special relation between *OM* and *udgītha,* which, as far as I can see, does not occur before. Why specially the *udgītha*? The *udgītha* may begin with *OM, but the prastāva* ends with it, and generally the cry *OM*! is the commonest sound heard at the sacrifice, as the present writer, who once attended every minute of one of the more elaborate derivates of the *agniṣṭoma,* can testify. There must be a special relevance in the equation *OM* = *udgītha.*

There is. At the three climaxes of the *agniṣṭoma* ceremonial, the three soma pressings, the *udgītha* is chanted in a most curious way. In the sāmans proper to these stages, the *pavamānastotras,* the *udgītha* is chanted with *aniruktagāna.* This "chanting without actually pronouncing" is done by substituting the sound *O* for every syllable, so that for example the first *udgītha* of the *bahiṣpavamānastotra*, which reads *pávamānāyéndave abhi* **[181]** *devam iya* (ṚV. 9.11.1—SV 651; 763) is actually sounded as

$$\text{OM-O}\bar{2}\text{-O}\bar{2}\text{-}\overset{1r}{\dot{\text{O}}}\text{-}\overset{r}{\text{O}}\text{-}\overset{r}{\text{O}}\text{-O-O}\bar{2}\text{-O-}\overset{1}{\dot{\text{O}}}\text{-}\overset{r}{\text{O}}\text{-}\overset{r}{\text{O}}\text{-O-}\overset{2}{\dot{\text{O}}}\text{1212.}$$

When one hears it chanted, it sounds like the repetition of the initial *OM* with which the *udgītha* begins. And that is what it must have been: LāṭŚS. 7.10.20 prescribes here: *śeṣam udgātā manasā tu svabhaktim oṃkāraṃ tathā svaraṃ vācā gāyet* "the udgātā must chant the remaining portion (i.e., after the *prastāva*); his actual part, however, he must chant in thought, (having the words themselves in mind), and just the *Oṃkāra* and also (its) vowel with the voice." Caland[21] quotes a *prayoga* which explains: *oṃkāreṇākṣarāṇi cchādayan vācā gāyet* "he (the udgātā) must chant (the udgītha) aloud with his voice while concealing the actual syllables with *OM.*"

This practice itself, which can be dated with the ChUp., must have originated from esoteric speculations about the Syllable, esp. the syllable *OM*, and the actual *brahman,*[22] of the mantra. The function of the sāman, stepchild of Vedic and ritual research, in the sacrifice is really most important. Perhaps one must have heard it chanted at a sacrifice to appreciate this point. It is the fullest manifestation of the sound of the mantra, the very generator of the power of the sacral word which is drawn upon at certain stages in the ceremonial. Just at the climaxes of the ritual the actual words do not even seem enough; their very principle, the ultimate Word is enunciated, instead of the manifest words that from it derive their efficacy.

The identification of *akṣara* with a definite syllable, *OM,* marks another stage in the development of the term. *Akṣara* is no longer the syllable as such, which derives its importance from the fact that it measures ritual utterances, metres, etc.,[23] but a certain syllable, or rather sound, which is the hypostasized *brahman* and from which the Veda and hence the world originates. That just *OM* became the *akṣara*, par excellence, allows, at least partially, of explanation. It is striking that in various passages, where this superemacy of *OM* is speculated upon, the triadic cosmological patterns that gain in importance through *brāhmaṇa* and *āraṇyaka* are elaborated. In *OM* = *udgītha, ud-gī-tha* sums up in its three syllables whatever triads the author may care to think of. Likewise, in the speculations about *OM bhūḥ bhuvaḥ svaḥ,* where the three *vyāhṛtis* are thought to manifest the three *mātrās* of *OM*3. There is little doubt that the *pluta* pronunciation of *OM*, which already in the *śikṣopaniṣad* of the Taittirīyas is elaborated,[24] further contributed to the selection by these esoteric phoneticians of this syllable of consent as the syllable that epitomizes the universal pervasiveness of the ritual word.

As could be expected, the same development of *akṣára* is found in milieux which did not necessarily connect the Syllable with *OM*. In TaittS. 5.1.9.1, evidently inspired by ṚV. 1.164.42, it is both a metrical unit (as in ṚV. 1.164.24) and the source of creation: *ṣaḍbhir dīkṣayati ṣaḍ vā ṛtava ṛtubhir evainaṃ dīkṣayati / saptabhir dīkṣayati sapta chandāṃsi chandobhir viśvo devasya netur ity anuṣṭubhottamayā juhoti / vāg vā anuṣṭup tasmāt prāṇānāṃ vāg uttamā / ekasmād akṣarād anāptaṃ padaṃ tasmād yad vāco 'nāptaṃ taṃ manuṣyā upa jīvanti / pūrṇayā juhoti / pūrṇa iva hi prajāpatiḥ prajāpater āptyai / nyūnayā juhoti / nyūnād dhi prajāpatiḥ prajā asṛjanta / prajānāṃ sṛṣṭyai* "he consecrates him with six (verses): the seasons are six, so he consecrates with the seasons; he consecrates with seven (verses): the metres are seven, so he consecrates with the metres. He pours the oblation with the last anuṣṭubh, *viśvo,* etc.; the anuṣṭubh is Word, hence Word is the best of the Breaths. The pāda is incomplete by one syllable; therefore men live on that which is the incomplete part of the Word. He pours with the complete Word,—for Prajāpati is, so to say, complete,—in order to have Prajāpati complete. He pours with the incomplete Word,—for from the deficient **[182]** part of the Word did Prajāpati create the creatures,—in order to create the creatures."

In this brief but very pregnant piece of exegesis several notions are blended. There is first the Syllable on which all the world lives. But this idea is combined with another, the division of the Word in a higher and a lower part, the complete and the incomplete Word; cf. RV. 1.164.45 where the incomplete part of Vāc is spoken by men (*turīyaṃ vāco manuṣyā vadanti*). This idea is of course the same as that which underlies the division of the Puruṣa (RV. 10.90.3). All these ideas are interrelated in the conception of the uttered/unuttered Vāc ~ created/uncreated Prajāpati. The unuttered, uncreated and hence still incomplete Creator formulates and completes himself in self-creation out of the unuttered Word which is the Syllable.

Here, as in the JaimUpBr., as in fact already in the Ṛgveda, *akṣara* "syllable" transcends uttered speech: it is the subtle, germinal principle of the Word, the unborn embryo which when born will be the Word that is creation. This is expressed in a later text, MuṇḍUp. 1.1.4-5 as follows: *dve vidye veditavye iti ha sma yad brahmavido vadanti parā cāparā ca / tatrāparā ṛgvedo yajurvedaḥ sāmavedaḥ śīkṣā kalpaḥ vyākaraṇaṃ niruktaṃ chando jyotiṣam iti / atha parā yayā tad akṣaram adhigamyate* "the experts in Vedic lore say that there are two sciences to learn, a higher and a lower one; the lower one consists in the three Vedas and the Vedāṅgas; the higher science is that through which the *akṣara* is learnt." Ib. 7 continues: *tathākṣarāt saṃbhavatīha viśvam* "from the *akṣara* all in this world originates," and, ib. 1.2.13, *tasmai sa vidvān...yenākṣaraṃ puruṣaṃ veda satyaṃ provāca tāṃ tattvato brahmavidyām* "he who possessed the science taught the other that which is truly the brahman-science, so that he would know the *akṣara,* the *puruṣa*, the *satya*". The knowledge of the *akṣara*, or the *brahmavidyā* 'proper' (*tattvataḥ*), evidently concerns the esoteric connotations of the Syllable, which is the hypostasized, the higher *brahman,* in contrast to the lower *brahman* "Vedic lore." Similarly MāṇḍUp. 1 *Om ity etad akṣaram idaṃ sarvam / tasyopavyākhyānam—bhūtaṃ bhavad bhaviṣyad iti sarvam oṃkāra eva / yac cānyat trikālātītaṃ tad apy oṃkāra eva / sarvaṃ hy etad brahmāyam ātmā brahma so 'yam ātmā catuṣpāt* "all this is the syllable *OM*. The explanation of this: *OM* is everything in past, present and future; *OM* is also that which is beyond the three times. For this *brahman* is indeed all; *brahman* is this *ātman,* and this *ātman* consists of four quarters."[25] Here we meet the same equation *akṣara OM = brahman = ātman,* but *akṣara/brahman* include the lower science of the lower creation.

In the last quotations we have passed the line beyond which all translators derive the word *akṣara,* not from the old "syllable" of immediately preceding texts, but from another *akṣara-*, mfn. "imperishable." But is there really any valid reason to assume that the *akṣara* of the later *upaniṣads,* Mokṣadharma literature and the Bhagavadgītā is genetically a different concept from "syllable as the ultimate measure of ritually potent speech—source of creation—unuttered transcendent principle of speech—*OM* as the subtle germ of the *Veda*—syllable as the womb and embryo of the *bráhman,*" which we have met so far? This is not to quibble about translations (in fact, we ought to leave *akṣara* at one stage untranslated because it has become a kind of proper name), for evidently *akṣara* no longer means just "syllable." But neither does it mean just "imperishable"; it is not synonymous with descriptive words like *akṣayya, nitya, dhruva,* and the like, for in later texts *akṣara* still carries along the connotations and associations that went with *akṣara* "syllable."

Before we enlarge on the interesting implications of the usage of *akṣara* in the metrical upaniṣads, we have to deal with Yājña-valkya's well-known discourse[26] on *akṣara,* which is the first occurrence of the so-called "new" *akṣara,* "Imperishable Being." The famous adhvaryu is questioned by his wife Gārgī about the first principles of the cosmos: What is the frame on which are woven that which is above heaven, that which is below the earth, and that which is in between? (The formulation itself is quite interesting: there is an attempt to sum up a vaster universe than the old universe of the three worlds, but even this vaster universe can only be viewed from the triadic pattern set by those three worlds.) Yājñavalkya's reply is *ākāśa*: ether, region of the sun, medium of the word, is from of old a very high and therefore a very original entity. But Gārgī insists: on what is *ākāśa* woven? In another, less digested, version[27] Yājñvalkya tells her to hold her tongue : **[183]** "Don't ask too much, Gārgī, lest your head fly apart!" But here the adhvaryu goes on: *ākāśa* is woven on *akṣara.* The statement lacks surprise after the Jaim-UpBr. speculations about the primacy of *akṣara* side by side with the primacy of *ākāśa* which is *vāc,* or even after the RV. passages where *akṣara* was closely associated with the *paramáṃ vyòma.*

Yājñavalkya's important contribution here is that *akṣara* is described as a completely transcendent entity; and the tendency which we followed through the Syllable's equivalencies with *OM* and its narrow connections with the unformulated, uncreated, still incomplete creator, has now reached its climax: *tad akṣaraṃ Gārgi brāhmaṇā abhivadanty asthūlam anaṇv ahrasvam alohitam asneham acchāyam atamo 'vāyv anākāśam asaṅgam arasam agandham acakṣuskam aśrotram avāg amano 'tejaskam aprāṇam amukham amātram anantarabāhyaṃ na tad aśnāti kiṃcana na tad aśnāti kaścana.* Still, however rarified[28] this *akṣara,* this completely transcendent entity has now become, the old associations of the Syllable cannot help persisting: at the behest of the *Akṣara* exists the true order of the world: sun and moon, heaven and earth, year and its divisions, eastward and westward rivers behave as they should; and this cosmic order is, as indeed we would expect from the celebrated adhvaryu whose name perpetuates his brilliance at sacrifices, firmly based in the ritual order: "at[29] the behest of this *Akṣara,* O Gārgī, people praise the generous (so praise) the gods the (generous) yajamāna and so do the deceased ancestors who depend on the oblation." And again he echoes the Ṛgvedic poet ("what use are the hymns if one does not know the syllable?") in the immediate sequel:[30] "if one does not know this *Akṣara*, then one's oblations, sacrifices and austerities for many thousands of years in this world will come to an end; and when one departs from this world without knowing the *Akṣara,* one is miserable."

Though it be true that Yājñavalkya's *Akṣara* is highly abstract (but this qualification is objectionable), in fact more so than in many occurrences in the chronologically later metrical upaniṣads, we have no reason to assume that this *akṣara* is genetically different from *akṣara* "syllable, etc." The predominantly transcendental connotations are the last phase of a tendency that we see start long before, when the term still clearly reveals its original meaning. Increasingly, *akṣara* loses its more ancient functions as "syllable" but retains the connotations "first and fundamental principle of the cosmic order," which it acquired by meaning "syllable."

When we now turn to the later vicissitudes of the word, we must keep in mind that, however absolute some statements may sound about the primacy and supermacy of Word and Syllable—whether *vāc, akṣara, brahman, ahaṃkāra*—, in the background hovers the one who spoke it. In the older upaniṣads there is a persistent effort to do away with this dualism, which continues, or repeats in other terms, that of the male and female progenitors of the mythopoeic age. But this may be more appearance than reality; for, though in the supremes of the upaniṣads the "male" Fire as against the "female" Word are completely blended, yet the one entity thus obtained retains dual features. Vāc, as Prajāpati's partner, may do entirely without him in appearance, but Vāc's most significant expressions, *akṣara* and *brahman,* effortlessly take on "male" or "personal" functions. This rudimentary dualism becomes virtually indistinguishable from another dualism: the self-creating creator is represented in different phases, that of the still UNCREATED, unmanifested creator, and that of the CREATED creator. The created creator, *puruṣa, ātman,* etc., then assumes the functions which we describe as "male." Yet, since this self-creation is often a self-formulation, the relation may be inverted and the second phase is then the "female". We do well to keep these two dualistic patterns distinct, for through them we can in part account for the bewildering variety of conceptions about the Supreme which the older and later upaniṣads evidence.

It is in this complex pattern that we find terms like *akṣara* and *brahman* used in the later upaniṣads, which reflect the opinions of a greater variety of thinkers and schools than the older, more brahmanistic ones. We find that key-terms have lost many of their sacerdotal relevancies and exist on **[184]** as names of high-ranking principles, whose position in creation hierarchies was not fixed. If in one text we find *akṣara* and *brahman* described as a transcendent supreme being divorced from creation, and in another as almost female sources of creation, or even as the lower (i.e., actual) creation itself, we do not have shifts in the meaning of the terms so used, but a varying treatment of the problem of creation. A term not 'mean' *prakṛti* here and inactive male person there, but the term is used as a name for a creative agent or agency who or which may be divided in different stages, phases or aspects, to anyone of which the name, from among a wide selection of names, may get attached. Anyone of the associations that went with the originally more comprehensive, less analytically distinguished conception, may emerge as a henceforth fixed principle and the name of a more comprehensive entity out of that more comprehensive complex may continue as the name of a more specialized principle.

Akṣara illustrates neatly all these possibilities. Take for example the special use of *akṣara* with *puruṣa* which will end with the noun becoming an adjective to *puruṣa*, parallelled by *brahman* becoming *Brahmā*. The association of Syllable and Person starts long before. We saw our term, unmistakably "syllable," figure in a creation context with Prajāpati who created the creatures from the incomplete Word, the unuttered Syllable. In JaimUpBr. 1.43 *akṣara* is identified with the *puruṣa*, for "etymologic" reasons first with the person in the eye, who is then equated with Prajāpati: (8-10) *katamat tad akṣaram iti / yat kṣaran nākṣīyateti / katamat tat kṣaran nākṣīyateti / indra iti / katamas sa indra iti / yo 'kṣan ramata iti / katamas sa yo 'kṣan ramata iti iyaṃ devateti / so 'yaṃ cakṣusi puruṣa eṣa indra eṣa prajāpatiḥ / sa samaḥ pṛthivyā sama ākāśena samo divā sarveṇa bhūtena / eṣa paro divo dīpyate / eṣa evedaṃ sarvam ity upāsitavyaḥ.*

This equation of *akṣara* and *puruṣa* is also implicit in ChUp. 8.3.5; here *satyam* is syllabicized as *sat-ti-yam* to support a triadic inventory of the cosmos entirely comparable to that of *ud-gī-tha* in ChUp. 1, which is *akṣara*. To the three syllables correspond *bhūḥ bhuvaḥ svaḥ*, which are not only the universe, but the "spoken" universe; in other words, the three *vyāhṛtis* stand to the creator as the creation stands to *akṣara*. This SPOKEN universe or creation is equal to the CREATED creator, the *puruṣa*, whose highest phase is represented cosmically in the sun, microcosmically in the eye. Not only are the connections between the *vyāhṛtis* and *OM* very close—the complete formula has *OM* either preceding or following —, *OM* being their source and subtle container, but also are the parallel relations of *OM*—*vyāhṛtis* and *puruṣa*—creation (as is already implicit in 8.3.5), really the same relation: *puruṣa*—*udgītha* (ChUp. 1.6.6-8) or *OM*—*udgītha* (ChUp. 1.1).

The same is stated in the old MaitrUp. 6.3 *dve vāva brahmaṇo rūpe mūrtaṃ cāmūrtaṃ ca / atha yan mūrtaṃ tad asatyam / yad amūrtaṃ tat satyaṃ tad brahma taj jyotiḥ / yaj jyotiḥ sa ādityaḥ / sa vā eṣa om iti / etad ātmābhavat / sa tredhātmānaṃ vyaguruta / om iti tisro mātrāḥ / etābhiḥ sarvam idam otaṃ protaṃ caivāsminn iti.* In Yājñavalkya's account, which the last line recalls, this same *akṣara*, at whose behest (*praśāsana*) the cosmic order is maintained, has similar personal features in spite of its thorough-going depersonalization. The personalization of *akṣara* continues and seems to increase in popularity, just as the personalization of *bráhman* as *Brahmā*.[31] This process was assisted by the more ancient connections between Word and Fire, which are interdependent in their cosmic significance; the ritual fire is more consciously identified with the sun (and, on the *adhyātma* level, with the digestive fire, the *prāṇa* and the eye) and this identification is enacted ritually in *agnicayana* and *agnyādhāna*.[32] But already in RV. 3.55.1 the Great Syllable is born in the footstep of the cow at the first appearance of DAWN.

The solar *puruṣa*, the one beyond the sky, who in JaimUpBr. and ChUp. is equated with the *akṣara*, *OM*, is also the creator; and inasmuch as the creator himself is a person, *OM* is *ātman* and *puruṣa*. All these notions are present in such lines as Praśn Up. 5.5 *yaḥ punar etaṃ trimātreṇom ity etenaivākṣareṇa paraṃ puruṣam abhidhyāyīta sa tejasi sūrye saṃpannaḥ*.[33] This *akṣara*, *OM*, is equated with *brahman* (5.1) *etad vai satyakāma paraṃ cāparaṃ ca brahma yad oṃkāraḥ | tasmād vidvān etenaivāyatanenaikataram anveti*, and from 5.7 we learn that this syllable, *OM*, gives access to [185] the highest world: *ṛgbhir etaṃ yajurbhir antarikṣaṃ sāmabhir yat tat kavayo vedayante | tam oṃkāreṇaivāyatanenānveti vidvān yat tac chāntam ajaram amṛtam abhayaṃ paraṃ ceti.* The world to which the knowledge of the Sāmaveda gives access is certainly the heaven, from among the three worlds summed up in the person of the created creator earth, atmosphere, heaven. The knowledge of all three Vedas together is the *aparaṃ brahma*, the lower Word as in MuṇḍUp. 1.1.4-5; whereas the transcendent Veda, the *akṣara* or higher *brahman*, leads one to the very highest point, the beginning and therefore the end. *Akṣara* and *Brahman* are two names of the same supreme: KaṭhUp. 2.16 *etad dhy evākṣaraṃ brahmaitad dhy evākṣaraṃ param | etad dhy evākṣaraṃ jñātvā yo yad icchati tasya tat.*

In texts like the PraśnUp., where *akṣara* is a neuter noun in all other occurrences, there is no reason to treat it as an adjective in 4.9, however deceptive the context: *eṣa hi draṣṭā spraṣṭā śrotā ghrātā rasayitā mantā boddhā kartā vijñānātmā puruṣaḥ | sa pare 'kṣare ātmani saṃpratiṣṭhati* "this puruṣa who is. . the *vijñānātmā*,[34] is based upon the supreme, the *akṣara*, the *ātman*," Cf. 4.10 *vijñānātmā saha devaiś ca sarvaiḥ prāṇā bhūtāni saṃpratiṣṭhanti yatra | tad akṣaraṃ vedayate yas tu somya sa sarvajñaḥ sarvam āviveśeti,* where *akṣaram*, n., is equated with, but not adjectival to, the omniscient, all-pervading *ātman*.

But, as we pointed out, *akṣara* may continue as some kind of "female"[35] principle of creation, subordinated to an aloof person. So MuṇḍUp. 2.1.1-3 reads *tathākṣarād vividhāḥ somya bhāvāḥ prajāyante tatra caivāpiyanti / divyo hy amūrtaḥ puruṣaḥ..akṣarāt parataḥ / etasmāj jāyate prāṇo manaḥ sarvendriyāṇi ca,* where this person is indeed higher than *Akṣara*, and is the *para* because he is before and beyond creation. But how mobile these hierarchies still are is shown by ib. 2.2.2-3 *tad arcimad yad aṇubhyo 'ṇu ca yasmin lokā nihitā lokinaś ca / tad etad akṣaraṃ brahma sa prāṇas tad u vāṅ manaḥ / tad etat satyaṃ tad amṛtaṃ tad veddhavyaṃ somya viddhi ..tad evākṣaraṃ somya viddhi.*

Just as there is a higher and a lower *brahman*, so we find a higher and a lower *akṣara*. ŚvetUp. 1.7 *udgītam etat paramaṃ tu brahma tasmiṃs trayaṃ supratiṣṭhākṣaraṃ ca / atrāntaraṃ brahmavido viditvā līnā brahmaṇi tatparā yonimuktāḥ* "this is explained to be the supreme brahman: in it are the triad and their firm basis, the *Akṣara*.." This *Akṣara* is the higher one, on which the triad, e.g. *bhūr bhuvaḥ svaḥ,* or a successor triad like the guṇas[36] is based. The lower *akṣara* is the *kṣaram* which is related to the *akṣaram* as *vyaktam* is to *avyaktam* (ŚvetUp. 1.8; 1.10). This *avyakta* is not yet entirely the primordial matter of Sāṃkhya, but still rather the creator's state before creation, just as *akṣara* was the unuttered Word from which Prajāpati created the creatures. And just as *Brahman* may comprise both its higher and lower phases, so occasionally *Akṣara*: BhG. 11.18 *tvaṃ akṣaraṃ paramaṃ veditavyam* "thou art to be known as the *Akṣara*, the supreme," is followed in 11.37 by *tvam akṣaraṃ sad asat tatparaṃ yat*: "thou art the *Akṣara*: the reified, the unreified and that which lies beyond them," which recalls BĀUp. 2.3. where the lower *rūpa of brahman* is *sat* "reified," almost "solidified," the higher form *asat* "unreified," beyond which is yet another stage, the *satyasya satyam,*[37] the Puruṣa. But the author, or one of the authors, of the Gītā still remembers the Vedic and sacerdotal significance of the name. After having declared that he is supreme, as the Sāmaveda is supreme among the Vedas (10.22), Kṛṣṇa says *girām asmy ekam akṣaram* "I am supreme as the One Syllable is supreme among words."[38] In 3.15 *Akṣara* is a higher principle than *Brahman*: *karma brahmodbhavaṃ viddhi brahmākṣarasamudbhavam / tasmāt sarvagataṃ brahma nityaṃ yajñe pratiṣṭhitam* "ritual action derives from the *brahman,* and the *brahman* from the *akṣara*; therefore the all-pervading *brahman* is based eternally upon ritual worship." Edgerton[39] notes here that this "*brahman* clearly equals *prakṛti*"; but the whole passage (3.9-15) is devoted to ritual, and *brahman* in this context can scarcely be anything but the old *brahman* "Vedas and Vedāṅgas," higher than which is the "science that is brahman-science proper," **[186]** the *akṣara* (MuṇḍUp. 1.2.13). But ultimately Edgerton is right again in that this *brahman* is a lower BRAHMAN, the actually manifested *brahman*, which indeed corresponds with the manifest creation.

Gradually we see that *Akṣara*, and so, it would seem, *Brahman*, too, are so exclusively viewed under the aspect of their creativeness, their power to bring things about, even creation as a whole, that original functions of "syllable," "ritually effective utterance," of which functions this creativeness was the most important aspect, themselves become obsolescent. Thus the 'evolution' of the functions in which the terms are used is really the evolution of the creation doctrines with which they were linked up inseparably. Several terms are levelled, *puruṣa, ātman, akṣara, brahman, avyakta, sattva,* etc.; as supreme creative principles, as names of the "first cause," they may be regarded either as the "uncaused cause, uncreated creator," i.e., the original being before and aloof from creation, or as the "creating and created creator." In these functions they may be opposed to any other term, but also to themselves: higher and lower *brahman*, *avyakta* and *vyakta*, *akṣara* and *kṣara, ātman* and *puruṣa, puruṣa* and *kṣetrajña,* etc.[40]

* * *

When we now survey the career of *akṣara*, perhaps the most striking fact about it is that between the meanings "syllable" and "name of the first cause" there is much less of a gap than we, with our conceptions, would be inclined to think. In "syllable *OM*" it even exists on in the meaning of "syllable" long after it has come to name the absolute. When we try hereunder to describe successive stages in the development of the uses of the term, we must keep in mind that we are not talking about a semantic development of a certain word, but are concerned with the evolution of the concept "first cause, source of creation," one of whose names was *akṣara*.

Originally *akṣara* meant "syllable." This syllable was not a grammatical artifice of analysis, but a very concrete tool for priest-poets who measured their metrical utterances by syllables. From the beginning we are concerned with *akṣara* as syllable of metrically arranged words in an utterance which is believed to possess an inherent efficacy for these purposes to which it is applied under—the proper ritual conditions. As the measure of such an utterance, the syllable not only has its full share of the power attributed to the utterance, but inasmuch as it rules the complete metrical shape of the utterance and is therefore prior to it, and inasmuch as it is the first and smallest pronounceable unit of speech, it is the true repository of all the power of the formula. This power is tremendous. The ritually spoken Word is the foundation of the cosmic order which is represented and reproduced in the sacrificial area. Anything can be effected with it, for all that has name falls within its realm. This total ritual efficacy is contained in the syllable; hence the syllable is the prime expression of the Word on which all the world lives. Not only is the syllable the smallest pronounceable unit to which all formulae can be reduced, it is necessarily the very first imaginable one, it is the absolutely original manifestation of Word at the dawn of creation. But for the formula to be effective, it must be spoken over and with the ritual fire. This necessary concomitance is always given, and it is given from the start. Since the name is a feature of the thing it names, to name the feature is to create the thing, that is under the proper ritual conditions. So the syllable is not only the embryo, it is the WOMB of creation. The universe as a whole has been called into being by a creator; the syllable, the yet unuttered, the yet unborn Word, is the "nothing" from which the formulated was called to be. As the hypostasis of Word, and of all that can be effected by Word, this Syllable (if we still care to render it so), was itself given a name: it was identified with a particular syllable, *OM*, which, apparently meaningless—a mere affirmative interjection—manifests its extraordinary power in the recitations it introduces, nay PRODUCES. As womb of the world—the fire being its begetter, husband and offspring,—it might be supposed to create by itself, to be really identical with the creator who is the fire, the solar *puruṣa*. For not only is the creator a creator solely by virtue of his Word, he, the unuttered, unformed, incomplete, is made complete, is made himself, by the Word. When thereupon the original unuttered creator—the three feet of Vāc, the three quarters of the *puruṣa*—is considered the true beginning, the ultimate behind and beyond creation, then *akṣara* may either be this original state itself, or the actual manifestation of creation. **[187]** So invariable, finally, is in certain circles the concomitance of creator/*puruṣa*/*ātman* with *akṣara* felt to be, that their continuous juxtaposition with *akṣaram,* n., (which in all cases—inevitably singular cases—except the first has the same endings), leads to its adopting masculine gender, a change materially assisted by the possible and later on increasingly exploited meaning of "imperishable," so that it becomes descriptive of the *puruṣa* or *ātman.*

We have repeatedly rejected the translation "imperishable." This was not because that would be wrong—in fact it is right and at a certain stage it is no longer justified to render it "syllable"—, but because that might imply that the imperishable *akṣara,* from Yājñavalkya onward, is genetically a different term. Now that it has become clear that it cannot be a different term, that it does indeed continue the ancient Syllable, we must add immediately that the possibility of deriving *akṣara* from KṢAR and privative *a-* "unflowing, constant, imperishable" probably saved the term as a name for the first cause from oblivion. When the term is taken up in philosophizing circles that were apparently no longer close to the ancient ritual and started their speculations from teachings no longer strictly confined to officiating priesthood, the connotations of syllable are not yet quite obsolete but begin to be replaced by that of "imperishable."

Is it possible to maintain a parallel development in the functions of the term *brahman*? From the beginning *akṣara* and *brahman* have strikingly parallel careers, at every stage meeting each other in comparable functions, so that for *brahman,* too there seems reason to conclude that it really as a word for "ritually effective utterance" rose to name the first cause. In other words, whatever the original meaning of the term, its average Ṛgvedic meaning on which Gonda, Renou and Thieme alike agree, was the decisive factor in its evolution. But—and here Gonda's researches prove of very great importance—other connotations, now not of the concept, but of the word itself, must have contributed significantly to its chances of survival. After Gonda's massive array of material it seems certain that these connotations came from the root BṚH- and its derivatives. For the development of the functions attributed to the term *brahman* it is not essential that *brahman* be a derivate of this root; the highly relevant point is that from early times onward its users THOUGHT it was. If *brahman* is indeed from BṚH-, it may still be its specialized usage of "ritually powerful and effective priestly utterance" which led the way to "first cause." If *brahman* was only mistakenly connected with BṚH- by its users, these associations helped it on its way and kept it there. Much less than one would gather from Thieme's review is Gonda concerned with the etymology of the word for its own sake; his important contribution is in the phenomenology of the concept, and he has shown overwhelmingly in how rich a variety of ways the power of *brahman* was believed to be active and how persistently this power draws upon the capacities conveyed by BṚH-. Whether one believes with Gonda that the specific powers conveyed by this root and its derivates were at the basis of the vocal power expression which *brahman* denotes in the older texts, or that *brahman* as the ritually prepared and pronounced utterance became the vehicle of powers connoted by terms not necessarily etymologically related to the word, the merit of his contribution stands unaffected: that *brahman* in its functions was so close to the meanings expressed by the root BṚH- that even if etymological relationship is untenable (which remains to be seen), one may now safely say that these very close associations contributed significantly to just *brahman's* rise to supremacy. We have seen that the same holds for *akṣara*: when the more ancient speculations about the power of formulation gave way to more advanced classification attempts which continued to operate with the terms that previous thought had produced for first and universal principles, the old term for syllable survives by virtue of what are evidently secondary connotations.

NOTES

*This paper is partly based on a brief note which appeared in the *Bulletin of the Deccan College Research Institute*, 17 (1955-56), 204ff., under the title "Notes on Akṣara" [no. 5 in this volume].

1. J. Gonda, *Notes on brahman* (Utrecht 1950).
2. Louis Renou, "Sur la notion de 'bráhman,' " *JAs.* (1949), 7ff.
3. Paul Thieme, "Bráhman," *ZDMG*, 102 (1952), 91 ff.
4. Cf. his characteristic remark, oc., p. 113 : "Wenn *bráhman* im RV die (dichterische) Formulierung, also eine sprachliche Formung, bezeichnet, werden wir *ohne weiteres* [italics mine] vermuten, dass es ursprünglich "Formung" überhaupt bedeutete.."
5. O. c., 121 f.
6. O.c., 7ff. "entre la valeur de 'principe universel' (ou de quelque manière qu'on voudra l'appeler) qui est acquise dans les brāhmaṇa et déjà solidement

fixée dans l'Atharvaveda, et la valeur de 'hymne' ou de 'formule' qu'atteste le Rigveda dans son ensemble, il y a un fossé difficile de franchir. Sans doute, l'intense spéculation qui dès l'origine a marqué tout ce qui touche à la 'parole' pouvait acheminer ce mot vers une pareille surrection d'emploi. Mais pourquoi ce vocable plutôt que tel autre, plutôt que des termes génériques comme *dhīḥ*, *vāk* ou *mántraḥ*, ou des termes déjà spécialisés comme *ukthám* ou *stómam*?" Thieme agrees (o.c., 101) : "Es ist schwer glaublich, dass ein Wort von der Bedeutung 'Formel, Hymnus' die Rolle übernehmen konnte, die *bráhman* später als Name des 'Absoluten' spielt....So weit stimme ich Renou völlig bei."

7. "Studies in Sāṃkhya (II), Ahaṃkāra," *JAOS*, 77 (1957), 15ff. [no. 7 in this volume].

8. I shall not enter into a discussion of *akṣára* as against *akṣará*, but follow here H. Oldenberg's opinion in "Vedische Untersuchungen 30, *akṣára, akṣará* im Rigveda," *ZDMG*, 63 (1909), 203 ff.

9. K.F. Geldner, *Der Rig-Veda* I (Cambridge Mass., 1951), *ad loc.*

10. A. Bergaigne, "Etudes sur le Lexique du Rigveda," *JAs* (1883), 480 ff.

11. And appropriate statements about them, cf. his note ad 1, 164, 23 "hier steigt zunächst der Dichter von der Höhen der bisherigen Spekulation (i.e., the metaphors of 20-22) in die Niederungen der dichterischen Technik und rituellen Praxis hinab" : but it is just through this technique and practice that most discussions about the supreme, even in the upaniṣads, become intelligible.

12. This is dramatized, for instance, at the *agnimanthana* ceremony. While the yajamāna drills the fire and the sāmaveda priests in the background chant the strengthening sāmans, the hotar holds himself ready to start reciting the appropriate mantras at the first wisp of smoke that will rise from the lower drilling block. When the drilling fails and the smoke disappears, the mantra, too, ceases; to start again when the smoke appears again. One can say that the mantra bears the fire, or that the fire begets the mantra. Cf. also RV 10.90.5 where Puruṣa begets Virāj and is himself borne by Virāj.

13. In the expression *bráhma prajā́vad* we see the beginnings of Prajāpati and Brahmā the creator.

14. E.g., RV. 1.164.35. The natural medium of speech, and therefore the element where speech 'originates,' is ether, hence the equation of *paramám vyòman* and *brahmán* who is the medium of the sacred utterence is obvious. As Thieme rightly observes, "sein Dichten ist nur die Wiederholung der Urschöpfung der Wahrheitsformulierung *en miniature*." (o.c., p. 112). Cf. also RV. 10.90.12 where the Puruṣa's mouth becomes the Brahmin.

15. The popular etymology *yad akṣarad eva tasmād akṣaram* raises the question of the etymology of the word, which was apparently a problem for these thinkers. On the one hand it does not "flow" any more, being the irreducible source (JaimUpBr. 1.1), yet it "flows out" into creation (RV. 1.164.42; JaimUpBr. 1.24.1). It is interesting to note that another etymology has been proposed just for *akṣara* "syllable." *aśnoter vā saro 'kṣaram*, i.e., *aś—sara→ akṣara* (Mahābhāṣya *ad* Siddhāntaślokavārttikā *post* 1.1.8), which Bhāskara also exploits for *akṣara* "Supreme Being" : *aśnoti vyāpnoti svavikārān ity akṣaram* (Brahmasūtrabhāṣya 1.2.22, which deals with Yājñavalkya's Akṣara,

below). The root *KṢAR-* is used for the "flowing" of speech (RV. 1.181.7; 8.46.6; 8.50.4); is in akṣara "non-flowing" just this irreducible ultimate of metrical speech understood from the beginning?

16. E.g., MaitrUp. 6,3.

17. We can do away with the meaning *śaṅku* "Blattrippe" (pw s.v. 4), based on Hemacandra, *Anekārthasaṃgraha* 2.17 "*pattrasirājāla*" (which was probably also deduced from the same passage); in the parallel JaimUpBr. 1.10.2 we have *sūcī* for *śaṅku* : *yathā sūcyā palaśāni saṃtṛṇṇāni syur evam etenākṣareṇeme lokās saṃtṛṇṇāḥ.* The idea is certainly that of herb-leaves stuck on a stake to dry.

18. Oertel's text (*JAOS*, 16 [1894], 49ff.) reads *kāmadughākṣiti*, which makes no sense. Oertel renders "she that milks immortality possessing individual oceans (?)," thereby also taking medial *duhānā* in an active sense. I take *akṣiti* as a corruption of *takṣatī* from the RV passage which it paraphrases.

19. RV *ékapadī* explained as *prāṇa-saṃhitam*, where *prāṇa* must be regarded as the first manifestation, the first creation; *dvipádī* as *cakṣuḥ* and *śrotra*; *cátuṣpadī* as *vāc*, which is of course four-footed; *aṣṭā́padī* as *manas* is beyond me; *návapadī* as *hṛdaya*, possibly on account of the *navadvāraṃ puram*? The translation of *hṛdayāgram* is uncertain.

20. *ayutadhāram* is obviously inspired by *sahásrā́kṣaram*, which the author apparently associated with an *akṣara* somehow understood as "flow".

21. Caland-Henri, *L'Agniṣṭoma* (Paris, 1906-07), p. 180, ff134, n. 38. In the Vājapeya ritual which I attended all three pavamanastotras were executed this way. In the final *udgītha* the *O* was replaced by an *A*, which is an even subtler evocation of the ultimate, inspired, if I am right, by the *A* of AUM into which *OM* is eventually analyzed. This analysis is, however, comparatively late and does not seem to start before the later upaniṣad stratum; the triad understood in *OM3* is at first that of *bhūḥ bhuvaḥ svaḥ*, with which the syllable is so closely connected; and only when this triadic *OM* was thus established, the esoteric *AUM* speculations began.

22. The fully articulated formula.

23. As, e.g., RV. 1.164.24.

24. TaittUp. 1.5-6; cf. also MaitrUp. 6.3 and 6.5, which, as I hope to show in a forthcoming study *The Maitri and Maitrāyanīya upaniṣads* are concerned with the *agnyādhāna and agnihotra* speculations of the Maitrāyaṇīyas.

25. That is to say, the COMPLETE ātman.

26. BĀUp. 3.8.

27. BĀUp. 3.6.

28. In PraśnUp. 4.9 the *vijñānātman* that is the CREATED Akṣara is described as the positive counterpart of this negative uncreated Akṣara.

29. *etasya vā akṣarasya praśāsane Gārgi dadato manuṣyāḥ praśaṃsanti yajamānaṃ devā darvīṃ pitaro 'nvāyattāḥ.*

30. *yo vā etad akṣaraṃ Gārgy aviditvāsmiṃl loke juhoti yajati tapas tapyate bahūni varṣasahasrāṇi antavad evāsya tad bhavati yo vā etad akṣaraṃ Gārgy aviditvāsmāl lokāt praiti sa kṛpaṇaḥ.*

31. On the relation of Brahma to *bráhman* from a different viewpoint, see Gonda, o.c. 62 ff.

32. I must refer the reader to the study announced in note 24.

33. "He who will represent the supreme person with this triadic syllable *OM* will find perfection in *tejas*, in the sun."

34. The *vijñānātman* is the created puruṣa, which relates to the uncreated *Akṣara* as the *vijñānamaya ātman* of TaittUp. 2 to the *ānandamaya ātman*, the *buddhi* of the old Sāṃkhya to the *puruṣa*, etc. etc.

35. For *brahman*, cf. such usages as *brahmayoni*, ŚvetUp. 5.6; MuṇḍUp. 3.1.3; BhG. 14.3-4.

36. Cf. my remarks in "Studies in Sāṃkhya III; *Sattva*," *JAOS*, 77 (1957), 88 ff. [no. 8 in this volume].

37. I refer to my observations in "Vācārambhaṇam reconsidered," *IIJ*, 2 (1958), 4 [no. 10 in this volume].

38. And *gīr* is esp. the solemn utterance.

39. Franklin Edgerton, *The Bhagavad-Gītā* (Cambridge, Mass., 1946), *ad loc.*

40. And this duality is most concisely stated in the *ādeśa* of the Name *Satyam*, which is *sat*, the lower, and *tyad*, the higher.

14

THE GAJĀSURASAṂHĀRAMŪRTI IN MEGHADŪTA 36

Of the 111 stanzas adopted in Hultzsch's edition of the Meghadūta no less than three are devoted to a poetical evocation of the Mahākāla temple of Ujjayinī. In the first of these stanzas (34) the Cloud is invited to act as a sacrificial drum at the dawn offering to Śiva, in the next one to soothe with fresh raindrops the nail-marks on weary temple girls, while in stanza 36 the Protean cloud is told to "attach" itself to the god in a particular fashion so as to remove his desire for a fresh elephant skin.

This verse has created occasional difficulties, due in part to one of the commentators. On closer investigation the correct interpretation suggests a few interesting questions which may be worth discussing.

Stanza 36 reads[1] as follows:

paścād uccairbhujataruvanaṃ maṇḍalenābhilīnaḥ
sāṃdhyaṃ tejaḥ pratinavajapāpuṣparaktaṃ dadhānaḥ |
nṛttārambhe hara paśupater ārdranāgājinecchāṃ
śāntodvegastimitanayanaṃ dṛṣṭabhaktir bhavānyā ||

The mythological reference here is clear enough: the verse must refer to Śiva's dance with the elephant skin. Zimmer-Campbell[2] refer in *The Art of Indian Asia* to a myth according to which Śiva killed a demon Gaja by challenging him to a dancing duel and dancing him to death; the god flayed the animal and "wrapped in this dripping trophy, performed at dusk a horrendous solo before his divine consort, the Goddess."

Whatever problem concerning the precise interpretation of the stanza has arisen relates to the first pāda. First there is an incomplete *śleṣa*: "Clinging later on in a circle to the arms of the god, as you cling in a circle to the forest of trees in the western sky," *paścāt* to be taken alternatively as "later on" and "in the west," the forest of trees as the many arms of the god or as a real forest. It is clear that the red contours of the cloud appearing behind and above the trees on the western horizon have inspired the image. The trees resemble the arms of the dancing god, the red cloud the bloody elephant skin he is holding up.

[65] Vallabhadeva[3] has misunderstood this image, for reasons we shall presently discuss. He renders *maṇḍalena* by *tiryak* "horizontally", suggesting that the cloud hovers horizontally over the god. In this the most recent translator Assier de Pompignan[4] has followed him: "alors, quand Paśupati commencera sa danse, étends-toi horizontal au-dessus le la haute forêt de ses bras dressés." Now *maṇḍalena* cannot really mean "horizontally"; it must mean "by way of a circle, in the form of a circle." Somehow combining both the idea of horizontal and of circular, Paranjpe[5] in his notes thinks of a spiral movement by which the cloud seeks to withdraw from entanglement in the god's arms; but since the third *pāda* states that the cloud must thus remove the god's desire for an elephant skin, it is clear that the cloud must allow itself to be seized.

The technical use of *maṇḍalena* is elucidated by the actual images of Śiva doing this dance.[6] They show the god dancing with one foot on the elephant's head, with at least 4, or 8 or even 16 arms (a veritable forest) turned upward, and his consort on a smaller scale below him watching.[7] This aspect is known as the *gajāsurasaṃhāramūrti* or *gajahāmūrti*, descriptions of which are found in the Suprabheda, the Aṃśumadbhedāgama and the Śilparatna. The last two include the following direction:[8] *prabhāmaṇḍalavac cheṣaṃ gajacarma prakalpayet:* "he should fashion the remaining part of the skin so as to form a *prabhāmaṇḍala*."

Prabhāmaṇḍala is a technical term for the aureole or nimbus surrounding an image, perhaps most clearly illustrated by the well-known *naṭarājas*. This word is quite well-known to Kālidāsa who uses it frequently for the radiant nimbus surrounding the body of holy personages. He uses it in Ragh. 15.82 and 17.23, Kum. 6.4 and 7.38; *sphuratprabhāmaṇḍala* occurs in Ragh. 3.60, 5.51 and 14.14; Kum. 1.24; a variation *chāyāmaṇḍala* occurs in Ragh. 4.5. In the *maṇḍala* of Megh. 36 we have a use of the same word, only apparently abbreviated: *prabhā-*, *sphuratprabhā-* and *chāyāmaṇḍala* are here more fully qualified as *maṇḍalena . . . sāṃdhyaṁ tejas . . . dadhānaḥ*.

The use of this word in the description of a stance of the god well-known from iconography corroborates the *a priori* probability that the poet visualized an actual image of the god in the *gajāsurasaṃhāramūrti*. This raises the question whether the description of just this form of the god here, in a description of the Mahākāla temple of Ujjayinī, can be a mere coincidence or whether Kālidāsa, who as scholars agree, knew Ujjayinī very well, actually evokes in a poetical image a real image found there.

It is noteworthy that the Mahākāla temple, old center of the **[66]** Pāśupatas (and hence probably Kālidāsa's use of Paśupati here), was particularly famous because of its liṅga. The poet himself elsewhere refers to this liṅga as *jyotirliṅga*.[9] Is it again accident that Kālidāsa in his fullest description of the temple omits mention of this celebrated liṅga or may it be suggested that the *jyotirliṅga* implies the *gajāsurasaṃhāramūrti*?

The Kūrma Purāṇa's description of a temple in Benares, dedicated to Śiva as Kṛttivāseśvara, is suggestive here. In 1.32. 16-18[10] the text adds the following myth:

asmin sthāne purā daityo hastī bhūtvā Bhavāntikam |
brāhmaṇān hantum āyāto ye'tra nityam upāsate||
teṣāṃ liṅgān mahādevaḥ prādur āsīt trilocanaḥ |
rakṣaṇārthaṃ dvijaśreṣṭhā bhaktānāṃ bhaktavatsalaḥ ||
hatvā gajākṛtim daityaṃ śūlenāvajñayā Haraḥ |
vāsas tasyākarot kṛttiṃ Kṛttivāseśvaras tataḥ ||

"In this place a demon formerly became an elephant and came to (the image of) Bhava to kill the Brahmins who constantly were worshipping there. The three-eyed Great God appeared from the Liṅga, O most eminent of Brahmins, in order to protect his votaries, as he loves his devotees. Having contemptuously killed the elephant-shaped demon with his trident, Hara made a garment out of his skin, hence he is the Lord of the Skin Garment."

The "myths" of the killing of the elephant demon are even more than usually inconsistent, and suggest that in fact the icon had a greater distribution than the myth that went with it and that myths were reanalysed from the icon. From the spare account in the Kūrma it seems more likely that the myth is inspired by the actually present image.[11] It is worth remarking that there is a close relation here between the Liṅga and this *gajahāmūrti*: may the statement that Śiva emerged from his Liṅga to kill the elephant demon and do his triumphant dance robed in his skin be taken to indicate that the image was composed of a Liṅga with in front of it, perhaps in relief, the *gajahāmūrti*? I have not been abie to find a *gajahāmūrti* as part of a Liṅga, though other representations of Śiva in the Liṅga are of course quite well-known. There is evidence that Śiva in this mūrti is represented as emerging from a pillar,[12] which is but a slight variation from the Liṅga. Kālidāsa's use of the word *jyotirliṅga* in the Raghuvaṃśa may be significant; it is best analysed as a karmadhāraya: "the Liṅga which is light" where *jyotiḥ* may well represent the *prabhāmaṇḍala* of Meghadūta 36.

The evidence at my disposal seems to indicate that the *gajahāmūrti* image is most widely distributed in the South, where the **[67]** *Tāṇḍava* still forms part of the ritual; the village Vaḻuvūr in Tanjore district, where a bronze image of this form is found, is held to be the original scene of the dance. In the North it seems to have fallen in disuse, if it were ever popular there, in spite of the connexion that Kālidāsa makes of it with the Mahākāla temple in Ujjayinī and the existence of a temple dedicated to this form (and therefore almost certain to have contained an image of it) in that microcosm of Hinduism, Benares.

Vallabhadeva, who hailed from Kashmir, clearly did not know the myth, nor the image: hence his *maṇḍalena* = *tiryak* and hence also his misinterpretation of *śāntodvegastimitanayanam*, which he paraphrases: *vidyudunmeṣābhāvāc chāntodvegāni..nayanāni*, as though the Goddess had been terrified by the Cloud's lightning. Whether Mallinātha, who renders *maṇḍalena* by *maṇḍalākāreṇa*, actually understood the meaning is open to question: he gives the myth as follows: *gajāsuramardanānantaraṃ bhagavān Mahādevas tadīyaṃ ārdrājinaṃ bhujamaṇḍalena bibhrat tāṇḍavaṃ cakāreti prasiddhiḥ*: "It is common knowledge that the Lord Mahādeva, immediately upon crushing Gajāsura, performed Tāṇḍava while holding his bloody skin in the circle of his hands:" the images have normally only one hand holding the skin, the other hands holding a variety of emblems, among which the *śūla*.[13] held in a hand stretched out in front of the god, is the most prominent; besides it is the skin/cloud which forms a (*prabhā-*) *maṇḍala*, not the arms or hands. Here again the iconographic association seems to have been absent from Mallinātha's mind.

The word *uccair-* should be taken in compound with *bhujataruvanam*, and not with Vallabhadeva,[14] adverbially to *abhilīnaḥ*.

The word is well taken: the many arms, or at least the hands, point upward, and this upward direction is emphasized by the emblems held by them.

The translation of Kālidāsa's verse then should read as follows: "Later on, clinging like the nimbus to the God's forest of arms as in the western sky you cling like an aureole to the forest of trees, bearing the radiance of dusk, blood-red like the flowers of the China rose, you must kill Paśupati's desire for a dripping-fresh elephant skin, while this act of devotion is witnessed by Bhavānī with eyes that have become calm now that their terror has been appeased."

NOTES

1. The variants are unimportant for the discussion.
2. Heinrich Zimmer, *The Art of Indian Asia, its Mythology and Transformations*, completed and edited by Joseph Campbell, Bollingen Series XXXIX, New York 1955, vol. I, 359f.
3. Quoted from the Hultzch edition.
4. *Meghadūta*, traduit et annoté par R.H. Assier de Pompignan, Collection Emile Senart, Paris 1938, p. 14.
5. *Kālidāsīyaṃ Meghadūtam*, edited with English translation and notes by V.G. Paranjape, Poona 1935, p. 110, quoted from de Pompignan, loc. cit.
6. Compare, Zimmer-Campbell, vol. II, plates 408 and 445b; J.N. Banerjea, *The Development of Hindu Iconography*, Calcutta 1956, pp. 486 f., plate XXXIII, 2; T.A. Gopinath Rao, *Elements of Hindu Iconography*, vol. II, part 1, pp. 150 ff., plates XXX-XXXIII.
7. Gopinath Rao, op. cit. p. 151.
8. See appendices B, p. 76 ff. to Gopinath Rao, o.c. Vol. II, 2.
9. Raghuvaṃśa 6.34.
10. Bibliotheca Indica, Calcutta 1886.
11. Banerjea, op. laud. 487 : "It may be incidentally suggested here that the mythology underlying Gajāsurasamhāramūrti might have developed out of the epithet kṛttivāsa, i.e., '(a god) who has the hide of an animal (elephant here, Śiva may also use tigerskin as his apparel) for his garment,'—one of the hundred such epithets given to Rudra in the Śatarudriya." The Varāha Purāṇa account noted by Gopinath Rao, op. laud, I, p. 379 would point in a similar direction.
12. Zimmer-Campbell, o.c. p. 360.
13. Note that in 34 Kālidāsa refers to Śiva as Śūlin.
14. Followed by de Pompignan, who while printing *uccair* in compound renders: "étends-toi horizontal au-dessus de la.."

15

THE RELATIVE DATES OF ŚAṂKARA AND BHĀSKARA

Next to nothing is certain concerning the age of that most neglected of Vedāntins, Bhāskara, except that he must have flourished after Śaṃkara. This fact is abundantly testified by almost every page of his *Śārīrakamīmāṃsābhāṣya,* which might well be styled an anticommentary. His great adversary throughout his *bhāṣya* is Śaṃkara, and he misses no opportunity to attack him in bitter arguments. It is also certain that Bhāskara wrote before Vācaspati who discusses Bhāskara's views on the relation between Brahman and the phenomenal world in his *Bhāmatī* on ŚBh., I. 1.4.

Perhaps it will never be possible to date Bhāskara more precisely. But it may be worthwhile, since data are so scarce, to point out a curious correspondence between Śaṃkara and Bhāskara which, on the face of it, would tend to show that not only did Bhāskara know Śaṃkara but Śaṃkara also knew Bhāskara.

Of Bhāskara's works only two are so far known: the commentary on the *Brahmasūtras* and the one on the *Bhagavadgītā.*[1] There is, however, evidence **[269]** to show that Bhāskara also commented on the *Chāndogya Upaniṣad.* We have his own declaration to this effect; discussing BrS. III. 1.8 *kṛtasyātyaye 'nuśayavān*...he states: *chāndogye cāyam evārtho 'smābhiḥ pradarśitaḥ*—'In the *Chāndogya* we have illustrated this precise meaning'. This can only be understood as an explicit statement that Bhāskara in fact commented on the *Chāndogya Upaniṣad.*

In this fact, however interesting for the bibliography of Bhāskara, there is nothing remarkable; the *Chāndogya* was definitely popular in the old Vedānta, as is evidenced by the attention the Brahmasūtrakāra gave it, and by the old *vākya* of Ṭaṅka (also known as Brahmanandin and Ātreya) and the *bhāṣya* on this *vākya* by Dramiḍa. On several occasions Bhāskara himself quotes from these old predecessors.[2] But most remarkable is the rest of

Bhāskara's sentence. He declares that he has illustrated this precise meaning 'by adducing an illustrative instance'—*dṛṣṭāntopanyāsena.* The curious problem is that Śaṃkara knows this same instance and refutes it in his own comment on BrS. III. 1.8.

Bhāskara's *dṛṣṭānta* reads as follows: *yathā kaścit sevako rājakulaṃ praviṣṭaś cirāvasthānād upakṣīṇopakaraṇaś chattrapādukādimātraparicchadaḥ sthātum aśaknuvan nivartate*[3]—'just as some attendant who has entered the **[270]** royal palace for service and whose accoutrements have dwindled after his long stay there, returns because he is unable to continue to stay there when his paraphernalia are reduced to an umbrella, sandals and the like.' Bhāskara's statement *chāndogya cāyam evārtho 'smābhiḥ pradarśito yathā..iti dṛṣṭāntopanyāsena* must be understood to mean that he himself adduced this *dṛṣṭānta.*

Śaṃkara discusses it: *nanu* (Ś. identifies himself with this objection) *niravaśeṣakarmaphalopabhogāya candramaṇḍalam ārūḍhaḥ* / (reply) *bāḍham / tathāpi svalpakarmāvaśeṣamātreṇa tatrāvasthātuṃ na labhyate / yathā kila kaścit sevakaḥ sakalaiḥ sevopakaraṇai rājakulam upasṛptaś cirapravāsāt parikṣīṇabahūpakaraṇaś chattrapādukādimātrāvaśeṣo na rājakule 'vasthātuṃ śaknoti*: 'However, he has ascended to the moon[4] in order to consume the fruits of his acts without any remainder.'—'Certainly. Nevertheless it would be impossible to remain there with only a very little *karman* left, just as, for example, some attendant, who has approached the royal palace with all accoutrements for royal service,[5] is unable to remain there at the palace when his many accoutrements have been used up completely and he has only his umbrella, sandals and the like left. Likewise, he is unable to remain on the moon with only a remnant of *karman* left.'

Śaṃkara quotes this *dṛṣṭānta* in a discussion of some view[6] held by others (*kecit tāvad āhuḥ*); he rejects it—*na* **[271]** *caitad yuktam iva* 'the comparison does not hold.'[7] He points out that the impoverished attendant *does* have some of the paraphernalia for service left, while the transmigrating soul must have used up all the *karman* that accrued from those sacrifices that conducted him to heaven: *tathā sevakasyopakaraṇaleśānuvṛttiś ca dṛśyate.* On the other hand, Bhāskara is not only explicit that he himself adduced the *dṛṣṭānta*, but also sticks to it: *na hy asau hastādiṣūpabhukteṣu tatputrādiṣu vā nivartate / kiṃ tarhi / chattrādinā vyatiriktena*—'he does not return only when his hands have been used up or his sons, etc. What then? With his umbrella, etc. remaining.' The text is not quite in order. All the MSS. available for this part of the text have *hastādiṣūpayukteṣu tatputrādivan nivartate.* °*upayukteṣu* is certainly to be emended °*upabhukteṣu*, and *tatputrādiṣu vā* seems best for *tatputrādivan.*[8] But in spite of this uncertainty it is quite obvious that Bhāskara sticks to his *dṛṣṭānta: kiṃ tarhi / chattrādinā vyatiriktena.*

Bhāskara's point here is that these few remaining pieces are more in the class of personal apparel—without which he would not be suffered at court—than accoutrements disposable by the king; hence he uses different terms, *paricchada* and *upakaraṇa*,[9] these pieces of apparel remain, nor does he go so far as to sacrifice his own body or his son, etc. Likewise the sojourn on [272] the moon does not use up all the Karmic resources of the transmigrating soul: *evam atra karmasamudāyāpekṣayopabhuktāt karmaṇaḥ karmāntaraṃ śeṣaśabdavācyam iti*—'likewise in this case too: what the word *śeṣa*[10] denotes is *karman* OTHER than the *karman* used up, with regard to the whole mass of a person's *karman.*' This is also the precise meaning which he illustrated in the *Chāndogya: yāvad āmuṣmikaphalaṃ karma tat sarvaṃ tatraiva kṣayayitvāvaśiṣṭenaihikaphalena japahomadānādināvarohantīti.*

Assuming that Bhāskara correctly ascribes the *dṛṣṭānta* to himself these conclusions follow *prima facie*: 1. Bhāskara wrote a commentary on the *Chāndogya* in which he used the *dṛṣṭānta*; 2. Śaṃkara knew this *dṛṣṭānta* from this commentary and set out to refute it; 3. Bhāskara, who without the slightest doubt knew Śaṃkara's *bhāṣya,* knew Śaṃkara's refutation of his own *dṛṣṭānta* and now returned to it to clarify it.

These are far-reaching conclusions to be drawn from this one correspondence. We may get away from them, not very satisfactorily, by assuming that Bhāskara himself quoted the *dṛṣṭānta* from another source which was independently known to Śaṃkara. This is not very satisfactory because (given the fact that Bhāskara's *BrSBhāṣya* is later than Śaṃkara's and therefore than probably his *Chāndogyabhāṣya* too) we must then also accept (1) that Bhāskara, despite Śaṃkara's earlier refutation of it and despite the fact that Bhāskara's view of *anuśaya* is really the same as Śaṃkara's, for no [273] discernible reason resurrected the refuted *dṛṣṭānta* in his *Chāndogyabhāṣya*, and (2) once more returned to it in his later *Brahmasūtrabhāṣya* in a manner strongly suggesting a defence against Śaṃkara's misunderstanding of it. Was this *dṛṣṭānta* so sacred that it had to be revived twice against Śaṃkara's reasonable objections?

In itself a possible contemporaneity of Śaṃkara and Bhāskara, which I do not propose but raise as a question, is not implausible. Paul Hacker in his valuable monograph on Vivarta[11] has pointed out with some emphasis that Bhāskara understood Śaṃkara 'better', that is to say, more clearly in Śaṃkara's own terms, than the great Advaitin's immediate pupils. This would by itself justify any attempt to approximate Bhāskara's date to Śaṃkara's. That even great thinkers are not born in a historical vacuum but presuppose an intellectual ambience and a milieu of fellow-philosophers who by their polemics and even antagonism contribute materially to the making of a new thinker, Indian legend has recognized in the tradition of the famous relationship of Śaṃkara and Maṇḍana. Is it possible that Bhāskara, whose bitter tone sometimes almost seems to suggest a personal relationship, also belonged to this milieu?

NOTES

1. A critical edition and annotated translation of the *sūtrabhāṣya* by the present writer will soon be published in the Harvard Oriental Series; the first edition and translation of the fragmentary *Gītābhāṣya* by Daniel H.H. Ingalls and Dr. Subhadra Jha are also due to appear there.
2. I may refer to my discussion in *Rāmānuja's Vedārthasaṃgraha*, Poona, 1956, pp. 24-30, and Appendix §2.
3. Readings differing from Dvivedin's (Bhāskara's *Brahmaśūtrabhāṣya*, Chowkhamba Sanskrit Series, 70, 185, 209, Benares, 1915) are based on manuscript materials.
4. The discussion concerns the *pañcāgnividyā*, esp. ChU, V. 10. 4-5.
5. Bhāmatī : *hāstikāśvīyapadātivrātaparivṛtaḥ*.
6. *svargārthasya karmaṇo bhuktaphalasyāvaśeṣaḥ kaścid anuśayo nāma*, a view definitely not supported by Bhāskara, see infra.
7. Differently Bhāmatī: *evakāre prayoktavye ivakāro guḍajihvikayā prayuktaḥ*.
8. I cannot construe *tatputrādivat* meaningfully.
9. Śaṃkara however speaks only of *upakaraṇa*.
10. In the quoted Smṛti : *tataḥ śeṣeṇa viśiṣṭadeśajātikularūpāyuḥśrutavṛttavittasukhamedhaso janma pratipadyante*.
11. Paul Hacker, *Vivarta : Studien zur Geschichte der illusionistischen Kosmologie und Erkenntnisstheorie der Inder* (Ak. Wiss. u. Lit., Mainz, Abh. G.u. S-w. Kl. 1953, 5; Wiesbaden 1953).

16

THE NAME "PAÑCARĀTRA"

The followers of the so-called Pañcarātra sect have invented numerous explanations for the word *pañcarātra*, which has become the general name of that class of Āgama texts from which the sect derives its ritual traditions. These interpretations invariably start from the element *pañca*, "five," and the implications which a set of *five* may have for the system: the five is connected with sets of five doctrines, or to the organization of the subject matter in the texts, which may be divided into five chapters; and they ignore the element °*rātra*- which so mysteriously forms part of the name. When some kind of pentad has been selected, °*rātra*- is interpreted in a fanciful way to agree with that pentad. For instance, the Nāradīya Saṃhitā gives *rātri* the sense of "knowledge," and five kinds of knowledge are then supposed to be represented by *pañcarātra*.[1] Not much greater interest should be attached to the fact that the Mahāsanatkumāra Saṃhitā is divided into five parts called "Nights";[2] for although Schrader leaves open the possibility that *rātri* may have acquired a sectarian meaning of a "cardinal doctrine as well as the chapter or work dealing with that doctrine," it is clear that any such "meaning" of *rātri* must be secondary: it presupposes "Pañcarātra" as the name of the system, for [292] *rātri* is not known anywhere else in such meaning as "tantra" or "saṃhitā."

Schrader himself[3] is inclined to believe that the original use of the word *pañcarātra*, which literally means "[something] lasting five nights [and days]," is connected only with the conception of the quintuple god, who is manifested as *para, vyūha, vibhava, antaryāmin* and *arcā,* and that this original use can be discovered from the *pañcarātraṃ sattram* of Śatapatha Brāhmaṇa 13.6.1.1. This interesting passage links Nārāyaṇa with a five-day sacrifice. It reads: "puruṣo ha nārāyaṇa 'kāmayata/atitiṣṭheyaṃ sarvāṇi bhūtāni aham evedaṃ sarvaṃ syām iti sa etaṃ puruṣamedhaṃ pañcarātraṃ yajñakratum apaśyat tam āharat tenāyajata teneṣṭvātyatiṣṭhat sarvāṇi bhūtānīdaṃ sarvam abhavat ("This *puruṣa*, Nārāyaṇa, desired: 'May I surpass all these beings, may I be all this world.' He found the *puruṣamedha,* a five-day sacrifice, took it, sacrificed with it. Having sacrificed with it, he surpassed all beings and became all this world").

Without any doubt this passage must be connected with the famous Puruṣa Hymn (Ṛgveda 10.90), and it is inspired either directly by this hymn or by the same myth which underlies the hymn. While in Ṛgveda 10.90 the *puruṣa* is not identified by name, in our passage he is identified as Nārāyaṇa; but this deity is mentioned as the seer who first saw the hymn Ṛgveda 10.90. As in 10.93.3, the *puruṣa* in the Śatapatha Brāhmaṇa passage both exceeds creation and constitutes it; creation likewise proceeds by means of, or in fact consists in, a *puruṣamedha*, the sacrifice of a man, of which the *puruṣa* is here the agent, there the victim. This *puruṣamedha* is qualified as *pañcarātra,* "lasting five days"; that it is a five-day rite is not inexplicable. To me it seems that this pentad must be associated with the role of the number five in many *agnicayana* speculations on the world, its creation and inventory, where, for example, the five layers of bricks are made to represent the five layers of creation and the five stages in which creation is effected. Likewise Nārāyaṇa becomes "all this" in five days.

Although this Śatapatha Brāhmaṇa passage cannot be said to be irrelevant to the development of Nārāyaṇa's divinity and creator's function, still the possibility that it has suggested the use of *pañcarātra* as the name of a system associated with Nārāyaṇa must be judged to be very remote. The connection of *pañcarātra* and Nārāyaṇa in the passage is incidental and, as we saw, part of a completely different context. Besides, one casts about in vain in early Pañcarātra for a characteristic pentad which could have invited the association with **[293]** the *pañca* in the name. Even if we agree with Schrader that the epical Nārāyaṇīya, in which all but one of the explicit references to Pañcarātra in the Mahābhārata are to be found, is a second-hand account, it is evidence enough, along with the Saṃhitās, that the theory of this system was not at all typified by any pentad, but by a tetrad: the quaternity of the godhead, namely, Nara, Nārāyaṇa, Hari and Kṛṣṇa, who are overshadowed by the Kṛṣṇaite quaternity of Vāsudeva, Saṃkarṣaṇa, Pradyumna and Aniruddha.

It would therefore seem to me that an entirely different approach to the problem of the name is indicated. Of what precisely does "Pañcarātra" consist? The Saṃhitās present us with a highly disproportionate dual division of the contents of the system: on the one hand, an ever more atrophied "philosophy," which serves as a superstructure, and, on the other, an exuberantly growing ritual part, which is really the principal content. In the old Pādma Tantra the proportion is one to ten.[4] In the important Pārameśvara Saṃhitā, the ritual manual of the old "pañcarātric" service in the Raṅganātha temple of Śrīraṅgam, the *jñānakāṇḍa* is almost wholly lost—if it was ever there.[5] It is very hard to make out what kind of ritual observances went with epical Pañcarātra,[6] but it seems safe to assume that the development of Pañcarātra took place mostly in its ritual component to the detriment of the superstructure of philosophy, to such an extent that, except for a characteristic doctrine or two, "Pañcarātra" was tantamount to this ritual.

It was principally ritual in the view of the earliest apologist of Pañcarātra of whose views we are informed. Yāmuna, in his Āgamaprāmāṇya,[7] does not accent the philosophical component at all, beyond a defense of the Vyūha doctrine against the attacks of Śaṅkara and Bhāskara in their commentaries on Brahmasūtras 2.2.42-45. First of all he understands Pañcarātra as a tradition of ritual worship. For him it signifies certain typical sacraments like the *dīkṣā*, or "consecration", *ārādhana*, or "propitiation", and other aspects of a ritual surrounding an iconic God; *pūjā*, the devotion to the *arcā* or "image", function and use of *nirmālya* and *naivedya*; rites like the *pañcakālikā*. Pañcarātra conveys a very similar significance to the Vedāntadeśika in the Śrīpañcarātrarakṣā.

[294] Whatever its ritual epiphemomena, the Pañcarātra as described in the Nārāyaṇīya was of a very different kind. It was a religious philosophy and discipline, comparable to Sāṃkhya, Yoga and Pāśupata, with which it is repeatedly enumerated.[8] The theory centers on a set of four principles, which present a pattern that is closely related to that of some schools in epical Sāṃkhya, but are conspicuous insofar as they are consistently identified with mythical personalities.

The Supreme Being is said to have a fourfold nature. Two series of names describe these four natures or "aspects". One is of minor importance, the other of major and enduring importance. It is related[9] that the eternal Nārāyaṇa was born the son of Dharma in four forms in the Kṛta age during the Svāyaṃbhuva manvantara as Nara, Nārāyaṇa, Hari and Kṛṣṇa Svāyaṃbhuva. The devotion to Nārāyaṇa, which is the general concern of the Nārāyaṇīya—a devotion also called Sātvatamata and supposed to have been proclaimed by the sun[10]—is particularly associated with the people of Śvetadvīpa to the north of the Milk Sea. Although thus there was a definite identification of both doctrine and devotion with the personality of Nārāyaṇa, the most common description of the quaternity of God is in Kṛṣṇaite terms: Vāsudeva, Saṃkarṣaṇa (or Baladeva), Pradyumna, and Aniruddha. In the terms of this relationship, which is, above all, a kinship relationship, is also captured the relation between God, soul and body.

The Supreme Being, the soul of all beings, is Vāsudeva, who, from a more "philosophical" point of view, is also the Puruṣa in his transcendent state. This *puruṣa* enters the five elements which together constitute the body.[11] The context conveys that from this contact between *puruṣa* and body the *jīva* appears, that is, the embodied soul, or the *puruṣa* in an embodied state. This *jīva* is occasionally called Śeṣa[12]—a name related to Nārāyaṇa—but much more frequently Saṃkarṣaṇa,[13] the name of Kṛṣṇa Vāsudeva's half-brother. Saṃkarṣaṇa produces the *manas,*[14] or mind, which is also described [295] as an incarnation of Sanatkumāra,[15] but most frequently identified with Kṛṣṇa's son by Rukminī,[16] Pradyumna. From this *manas* called Pradyumna originates the one who is "agent, cause and instrument, from whom the universe of moving and unmoving entities derives, the God manifest in all action,"[17] the ego-organ Ahaṃkāra, named Aniruddha after Pradyumna's son.

This doctrine apparently enjoyed considerable currency and in many places in the epic, also outside the Mokṣadharma section, references to it may be found. The best way to describe it is: Kṛṣṇa devotion gone philosophical. The philosophical basis is easily recognizable; it is that of the so-called eight evolving natures or *prakṛtis* (*jīva, manas, ahaṃkāra,* and the five elements). The first three seem to deviate from the more usual set of the *buddhi,*[18] *ahaṃkāra* and *manas*; and there is occasion to wonder if the series is not in fact a variation of the more ancient, seven-*prakṛti* series, in which the *jīva* heads the series of seven evolvents. Noteworthy is the "personalization". By personalizing these principles an attempt is made to describe what relation, evolutionary or otherwise, exists between them. The fact that God is called Vāsudeva and the embodied soul Saṃkarṣaṇa proves that an independent coexistence of God and the individual soul was admitted: for Saṃkarṣaṇa is Kṛṣṇa's half-brother, not his son. Besides, the fact that the embodied soul, the *jīva*, is identified with Saṃkarṣaṇa may go to show that the relation between *jīva* and *manas* was at one stage not viewed as a cause-effect relation (Saṃkarṣaṇa is not Pradyumna's father), which would bring us farther into antiquity when there was not yet an evolutionary relationship between the *prakṛtis*.

It is not clear what relation obtains between the Kṛṣṇaite series and that of Nara, Nārāyaṇa, Hari and Kṛṣṇa Svāyaṃbhuva. After the latter series has been described as the manifestation of the four-fold God,[19] only the former Kṛṣṇaite series is enlarged upon, when an account is given of Nārada's visit to Śvetadvīpa.[20] And on Nārada's [296] return to the Bādari hermitage, only Nara and Nārāyaṇa are brought back on the scene.[21] Perhaps we here have to do with regional variations in philosophically developing Vaiṣṇavism, variations that are destined to be absorbed into a "Pañcarātra" system.

The tradition in which the cosmology and individuation theory of *puruṣa, jīva, manas* and *ahaṃkāra* was formulated with Kṛṣṇaite nomenclature, and which surely also involved a Kṛṣṇa devotion, is described as Sātvata, Bhāgavata and Pañcarātra. But in the context of this tradition the literal meaning of the last name, "that of the five nights", does not admit of interpretation. It is remarkable that the Nārāyaṇīya itself makes an attempt to reinterpret the term *pañcarātra*. In the Nārāyaṇa litany 12.338 (325).4 Nārāyaṇa is called *pañcayajña pañcakālakartṛpate pāñcarātrika*: "[Homage to] Thee of the five offerings, lord of those who perform the *pañcakāla* ritual, Thee of the Pañcarātra." Unless I am mistaken, this points to an interpretation of *pāñcarātrika* as relating to that tradition which observes pentads of rituals; here, then, for the first time, an attempt at interpretation based exclusively on the number five.

An explicit reference to the Pañcakāla is to be found in 12.336 (323).51:

tair iṣṭaḥ pañcakālajñair harir ekāntibhir naraiḥ /
bhaktyā paramayā yuktair manovākkarmabhis tadā //

("Hari [Viṣṇu] is worshiped by those men, seeking exclusiveness, who know the Pañcakāla, who have supreme devotion in thought, speech and action").

If my suggestion that the Nārāyaṇīya connects the name *pañcarātra* with *pañcayajña/pañcakāla* is right, we still must regard this as a reinterpretation; for *pañcarātra*, a span of five nights and days, cannot originally have signified a ritual taking place five times a day.

More than for the aid it gives in discovering the etymology of Pañcarātra as the name of a tradition, the epical evidence is helpful for the understanding of the tradition's milieu. The juxtaposition of it with Sāṃkhya, Yoga, and Pāśupata,[22] the references to the esoteric nature of the doctrine, and the intimations concerning the ascetic life of its adherents, suggest strongly that the Pañcarātra way of life was typically that of those seekers after wisdom and enlightenment whose beliefs and practices were somewhat outside the pale of Vedic ritualist sacerdotalism. Like so many wandering sages, recluses and pilgrims who from the sixth century B.C. (and doubtless before) went about preaching, or settled down in semi-retirement from active life to a life of contemplation, the Pāñcarātrikas, whose doctrine later on also [297] remains linked with the innovators rather than the conservatives, seem also to have been part of that eremitical movement which largely reformed the Vedic tradition in the last millennium B.C. These seekers were not necessarily organized in definite groupings—although the very fact of the early emergence of "monastic" orders in Buddhism and Jainism indicates that many of them adapted to an existing pattern and observed similar or comparable regulations and vows, which could become a basis for a monastic rule. The commonest and most decisive of such vows were homelessness and its corollary, religious mendicancy. Pilgrimage, both for the blessing of the sacred places and for the liberality of the crowds sure to be there, gave direction to their vagrancy.

If we then find that non-doctrinaire literature mentions people styling themselves Pāñcarātrikas who have no clear creedal affiliations but fall neatly in the pattern of the wandering saint, we are not particularly surprised; for in Pañcarātra as the name of a certain system we may well have the specialized usage of a term that once had a wider scope and denoted a characteristic of a group of people among whom a significant number—if only in one region—became so representative that henceforth the name was attached to them and their doctrine.

The oldest extant version of the Bṛhatkathā, Budhasvāmin's Bṛhatkathāślokasaṃgraha,[23] which gives an excellent picture of life on what we may call the middle-class level, attaches the name of Pāñcarātrika to a certain householder. This householder (in this text this term is generally used for a *vaiśya*) is a prosperous farmer who, when getting old, decides to give up his old way of life and to look for salvation. It may be a result of the condensation of the text that he is already called a *parivrāṭ pāñcarātrikaḥ*[24] before he has effectively given up home and possessions. In 26.63 he complains: "dhyānādhyāyapradhānaṃ ca vihitaṃ bhikṣukarma yat / vaiśyakarmābhiyuktasya tasya nāmāpi nāsti me// ("To act as a mendicant in the way it is enjoined, with principal devotion to meditation and study, is not for me, as I am engaged in the duties of a vaiśya").[25] Turned *pāñcarātrika* he is but a minor sādhu—though later he proves to possess the faculty of prevision—and he is rather fuzzy on theory: "The sages of old have prescribed that those who have chosen to establish a household should [298] go on a pilgrimage to the holy places, when with advancing age they become lax in the performance of their duties. The Vedānta school holds that one should be guided by Brahman the Ferryman. Thus if one aspires to liberation, he must not omit Avimukta near Benares from his itinerary. Therefore, I have decided to depart for Benares tomorrow, for the religion of the Buddha has a reputation for efficiency."

The passage gives and amusing picture of the probably general confusion in the minds of minor mendicants. Pilgrimages make him think of sacred fords (*tīrthas*), which remind him of *Tāraka*, both as a name of Brahman and a feryyman, which reminds him of the ferry to the Avimukta, the most sacred quarter of Benares, and of Tārā, the Buddhist goddess. Clearly, also, his *pāñcarātrika* character implies no special allegiance to any special doctrine; the word merely qualifies *parivrāj* "a wanderer of the five nights".

What do these five nights mean? The same text tells us precisely.

The occasion is a conversation between a (disguised) Pāśupata wanderer and his young Brahmin friend. The wanderer remarks to the youth that his affection for him has caused him to overstay his time in Rājagṛha and that he is now obliged to depart. For even householders have to obey certain observances for their own good, let alone those who seek after the highest good. He continues: "You know this life-rule of the wanderers: 'ekarātraṃ vased grāme pañcarātraṃ muniḥ pure' ("the sage must live one night in a village, five nights in town").[26]

This "life-rule" does not apply to Pāśupatas alone: the householder of the other narrative was not a Pāśupata. But it seems unquestionable that what made this householder a "wanderer of the five nights" was precisely the observance of this life-rule of the wanderers. What both have in common in the stories is that the life-rule keeps them on the road, and that the road leads them to places of pilgrimage. In this context a *pāñcarātrika* is a follower of the five-nights rule, a minor and not particularly respectable wanderer,[27] whose wanderings lead him to places of religious interest. The choice of his *tīrtha* is naturally dictated by his general religious orientation, by the *iṣṭadevatā*, one may say, of the pilgrim, though many will be common to all denominations.

The rule to which the Pāśupata refers with such evident confidence[28] [299] that it is a matter of common knowledge is in fact also found elsewhere. Vijñāneśvara,[29] commenting in his Mitākṣarā on Yājñavalkyasmṛti 3.58 and dealing in general with a saṃnyāsī's residence, adds this śloka, quoted from Kaṇva:

ekarātraṃ vased grāme nagare rātripañcakam |
varṣābhyo 'nyatra varṣāsu māsāṃs tu caturo vaset ||

It would seem to me that this sense of *pāñcarātrika* is likely to be original. Originally it referred to an itinerant religious recluse, who followed the characteristic five-nights rule, by which he was bound to move out of town after every five nights to stay a night in a village. There were also other rules, of which the best known is the one that orders one to move daily.[30] Such wanderers need not belong to any particular school or system, though they would as pilgrims, be guided by special devotions to deities. But devotional religion often went philosophical, and it then acquired a set of doctrines which more and more identified the wanderers in a culture where the desire for clear group identification is paramount.

We may assume that in certain regions, especially those of the great Vaiṣṇava centers, the *pāñcarātrika* was known as a devotee of Nārāyaṇa or Kṛṣṇa. The name may have stuck to him when, on the one hand, Kṛṣṇaism was systematized by the adaptation of Kṛṣṇa legend to general philosophical principles, with certain ritual observances, etc. and, on the other hand, the *pañcarātra* rule itself fell into desuetude. The name *pāñcarātrika* was then re-analysed as "follower of the Pañcarātra system", and a name Pañcarātra derived from *pāñcarātrika* as the name of that system which *pāñcarātrikas* followed.

NOTES

1. F.O. Schrader, *Introduction to the Pāñcarātra and the Ahirbudhnya Saṃhitā* (Adyar, 1916), p. 24.
2. *Ibid*.
3. *Ibid*., p. 25.
4. If we take the parts dealing with *jñāna* and *yoga* together (cf. Schrader, *op. cit*., p. 22).
5. Govindācārya, *Śrī Pārameśvara Saṃhitā* (Śrīrangam, 1953); only the first adhyāya constitutes the "jñānakāṇḍa", and most of that chapter is devoted to praise of Pañcarātra and the text itself.
6. The *pañcakāla* ritual is mentioned regularly; see below.
7. I refer here to a study of this text to be published soon.
8. For example, MBh. 12. (Bombay) 339.111 (cr. ed. 326.100); 349 (337).1; 64 (62-63).
9. 12.334 (321).8-9.
10. For example, 12.335 (322). 19; 24.
11. 12.339 (326).33-34 : "tad [sc. *śarīram*, constituted of the five elements, st. 32] āviśati brahman na dṛśyo laghuvikramaḥ / utpanna eva bhavati śarīraṃ ceṣṭayan prabhuḥ // na vinā dhātusaṃghātaṃ śarīraṃ bhavati kvacit / na ca jīvaṃ vinā brahman vāyavaś ceṣṭayanty uta."
12. 12.339 (326).35.
13. 12.339 (326).35; cf. also MBh. 5.67: *saṃkarṣaṇam agrajaṃ sarva-bhūtānām*, and created by Kṛṣṇa; thus 12.207 (200).10; 344 (332).16.
14. 12.339 (326).37-38.
15. Cf. MBh. 1.67: Pradyumna is an incarnation of Sanatkumāra; in 10.12 S. is the name of Kṛṣṇa's son by Rukminī.
16. Cf. also MBh. 6.65, where Kṛṣṇa creates himself out of himself as Pradyumna, and evolves Aniruddha from Pradyumna; in 13.159 Pradyumna is Kṛṣṇa's third form; these and similar texts deserve more study, particularly from the point of view whether the identification of Kṛṣṇa, etc. with evolutionary principles has influenced their relations.
17. 12.339 (326).38.
18. But *manas* may take the place of *buddhi*; cf. my "Studies in Sāṃkhya (III) : Sattva" (JAOS 77.1957) [no. 8 in this volume].

19. 12.334 (321).9.
20. 12.336 (323).27 ff.
21. 12.339 (326).110-11.
22. Also with Sāṃkhya, Yoga, and Vedāraṇyaka: 12.349 (337).1.
23. Edited and translated by Félix Lacôte (translation continued by Louis Renou), Paris, 1908-29.
24. BKŚS. 21.59.
25. This is probably the correct translation; otherwise Lacôte, *op. cit.*, whom I followed in *Tales of Ancient India* (Chicago, 1959), p. 131.
26. BKŚS. 22.220.
27. One is reminded of the disrespect in which, according to Yāmuna, *op. cit.*, systematized Pañcaratra was held; it may be relevant that MBh. 3.189.9-10 states that Nārāyaṇa was worshipped by kṣatriyas and vaiśyas.
28. But the Brahmin youth was an expert on *dharma.*
29. I am indebted for this reference to J.D.M. Derrett in a personal communication; he also points to Gautama quoted by Lakṣmīdhara, *Kṛtyakalpataru*, Mokṣakāṇḍa (ed. K.V.R. Aiyangar, Baroda, 1945), p. 49, which is referred to by Medhātithi on Manu 6.43.
30. The five-night rule may be considered a relaxation of rigidity, well in keeping with the somewhat lowly character of its followers; Derrett also refers me to K.V.R. Aiyangar, *Aspects of the Social and Political System of the Manusmṛti* (Lucknow, 1949), pp. 140-41, where a three-night rule seems to be implied.

17

THE ELEPHANT SCENE OF MṚCCHAKAṬIKA, ACT TWO

The exhaustive comparison by Georg Morgenstierne[1] of the texts of the *Cārudatta* ascribed to Bhāsa and the *Mṛcchakaṭika* ascribed to king Śudraka demonstrates sufficiently that, whatever the precise relationship between the two plays,[2] the latter as a rule expands and enlarges upon the *Cārudatta*. In many cases it is impossible to make out whether the expansion in *M* is original to *M* or reflects a similar greater wealth of detail in the original *Cārudatta*, of which the presently available text might well be itself an abbreviation; but there are some instances where it can be argued reasonably that the exemplar of *M* has been deliberately embroidered upon and added to by the author hiding behind the name Śūdraka. The most striking instance is, of course, the introduction in *M* of the political plot involving the Pretender Āryaka, son of Gopāla, to which no reference at all can be found in *C*, whereas there is a passage in *M* which suggests that the author consciously took a cue in one phase of the new political plot from the *Pratijñāyaugandharāyaṇa* of Bhāsa.[3]

It may be found worthwhile to discuss here another instance where Śūdraka has embroidered at least to a certain extent, but where his expansion [27] would also indicate that the original *Cārudatta* was more elaborate than would appear from its present version.

In both *C* and *M* there appears a comical character who had been a retainer of Cārudatta in his rich days as his personal masseur; this masseur has incurred a gambling debt and seeks refuge in Vasantasenā's house. At first sight *C* appears to treat the Masseur as a minor character, intended only to remind Vasantasenā of Cārudatta and to bring out the generosity of the courtesan in having her pay off the Masseur's debt. Śūdraka, however, involves the Masseur in a farcical brawl before he appears at

Vasantasenā's door, expands the Masseur's desire to take up the life of a *saṃnyāsin* into his conversion to Buddhism, makes him (according to the commentator) the victim of Vasantasenā's mad elephant, and introduces him later in the play as the savior of Vasantasenā. In *C*, on the other hand, the Masseur goes off, as soon as the debt is paid, and, one might think, for good. A closer study of *C* in comparison with *M* shows, however, that *M*'s exemplar must have been more detailed about the Masseur.

The present text of *C* does not explicitly state that the Masseur in fact becomes a *saṃnyāsin,* but there is interesting evidence that he does. In *C*, Vasantasenā dismisses the Masseur with: "Now go, sir, and restore your good temper by seeing your friends!" whereupon the Masseur replies: *ajja eva kadāi ṇivvedeṇa pavvajeam / jai iaṃ pariaṇe sankantā kalā bhave tado ayyite aṇuggahido bhaveam*—"sometime this very day[4] I will become a mendicant out of disgust with this world. I shall consider it a favor, ma'am, if I may transfer my art to your servants." Vasantasenā rejects this offer and also his notion of becoming a mendicant by telling him that his place is with his master Cārudatta. The Masseur murmurs to himself that he has been refused cleverly, and remarks: *ko hi ṇāma appanā kidaṃ paccuaārena viṇāsedi*—"for who destroys his own good deed by accepting a kindness in return!" Vasantasenā dismisses him: "Go now, sir, until we meet again." The Masseur replies: "All right, ma'am!" and goes off. The text of *C* immediately continues with Vasantasenā's exclamation: *haṃ saddo viya*—"Ah, there seems to be a commotion." Enter a servant, called the Boaster (*Karṇapūraka*), who excitedly details how he has just saved a mendicant from a mad elephant.

M treats this scene as follows, after the Masseur has made his offer to teach the courtesan's servant his art, but without mentioning his intention to become a mendicant: Masseur (*to himself*): "The lady has refused me cleverly. How shall I return her kindness?" (*Aloud*) "Ma'am, out of contempt for gamblers I shall become a Buddhist monk (*śakkaśamaṇake*). May your ladyship bear in mind these syllables: 'the Masseur who gambled became a Buddhist monk!' " Vasantasenā: "No violence, sir!" Masseur: "Ma'am, my mind is made up!" (*He walks about*). Then he speaks a stanza,[5] which clearly is his exit line. But before he can exit there is noise offstage. The Masseur repeats what he hears from bystanders (he must therefore have left Vasantasenā's presence while speaking his stanza and be perhaps at the door), that a rutting elephant of Vasantasenā's has broken loose. He first wants to watch the spectacle (*aho ajjaāe gandhagaaṃ pekkhiśśaṃ gadua*), thinks better of it (*ahavā kiṃ mama ediṇā*), then decides to follow his resolution of becoming a Buddhist monk (*jadhāvavaśidaṃ aṇuciṭṭhiśśam*) and goes off. Immediately afterwards Karṇapūraka enters in *M* and reports how heroically he has just saved a mendicant from Vasantasenā's elephant. *C* does not identify the animal as Vasantasenā's.

Who is this mendicant? The *ṭīkā*[6] on *M* assures us that it is the Masseur who has just left Vasantasenā's presence. Several authors have remarked on the suddenness of the Masseur's transformation into a Buddhist friar. This sudden transition may be explained by the tendency of the Sanskrit theater to telescope the action in a way very similar to the device of dissolves in cinematography; still, since the Masseur-Friar was still on the scene when the report came that the elephant was loose, the time interval must have been very brief, certainly not long enough for the Masseur to have his head shaved, etc.[7]

Nevertheless the *ṭīkā's* information must be **[28]** correct. The version of *C* here offers a plain clue how we should account for the Masseur's transformation. In *C* the servant who reports the incident with the elephant goes out of his way to show precisely how he knew the animal's victim was a mendicant: *eṣo. . maṅgalahatthinā uttarīapaḍavirāadāe ahialakkhaṇīo kocci ppavvaido samāsādido.* The victim was identifiable as a *pravrajita* "because of his having relinquished his upper garment." In other words, this was the only indication that the man was an ascetic. Now this mere absence of an upper garment is, in an Indian street scene, almost comically inadequate to identify an unknown person as a holyman. Bhāsa must have needed some such mark of identification to make clear that the molested mendicant was the erstwhile Masseur. For if removal of the upper garment is a sufficient outward sign of ascetic renunciation (and Bhāsa makes clear that he wants to regard it so: *ahialakkhaṇīo*),[8] the Masseur, short of time as he was, had time to make this symbolic gesture. The version of *C* thus can bear out the correctness of the *ṭīkā* on *M* in identifying the Masseur-Friar with the mendicant assaulted by the elephant.

It is of interest to identify the assaulted mendicant, if we are to understand the contemporary implications of the elephant scene and to account for a curious discrepancy between the reading of the text of *M* and the reading of the *ṭīkā*. I believe that *at least* in the version of *M* there is a parody of pious Buddhist legend. The Masseur is a figure of fun, also as a Friar. His resolution to become a friar is worded with mock pomposity and reminiscent of the style of conversion stories: "May your ladyship bear in mind these Syllables: 'The Masseur who was a Gambler became a Buddhist Monk'." Very curious is Vasantasenā's reaction : "No violence, sir!" which does not at all seem in keeping with the innocuous statement just made.

Śūdraka has made a *śākyaśramaṇa* out of Bhāsa's *pravrajita* for a definite reason. After his decision to become a friar follows the commotion caused by the elephant. He inquires of bystanders what is going on and learns that it is Vasantasenā's elephant, wants to see about it, then reconsiders: "What is it to do with me? I'll do as I have resolved."

For someone who has just been done a favor and has been insisting to reciprocate, it is out of character to wash his hands of any trouble involving his benefactress; and *M* emphasizes that it is Vasantasenā's elephant. If he did not want to have anything to do with it, I imagine there were means of avoiding it, but straightaway he becomes its victim. The scene becomes much clearer when we disregard the phrase *aha vā kiṃ mama ediṇā*. What did he resolve to do? To become a friar. At that moment a must elephant breaks loose. He has not been able to repay Vasantasenā's kindness to him. Now, as a Buddhist monk, he sees his chance: "Ah, I shall go and see the lady's elephant: I shall practice as I have resolved."

To the audience the parody I suspect here must have been immediately clear. One of the most celebrated incidents in pious Buddhist legend[9] is that where the Buddha undauntedly encounters a savage elephant in a crowded street and makes the beast, moved by the saint's tranquillity, cower before his steadfast glance. Here we have an ineffectual Masseur, a gambler become friar, who sets out to repay his benefactress's kindness by taming her wild elephant with a glance on the strength of his newly resolved upon sainthood—and has to be ignominiously saved by a minor retainer of his benefactress. When the allusion was no longer [29] understood, a scribe read a contradiction between the Masseur's desire to "look to" the elephant, and his resolution to follow his new call; and thus inserted the phrase *aha vā kiṃ mama ediṇā.*

There is textual evidence to bear all this out. Precisely at the point where we suspect that the text has been tampered with, one of our oldest witnesses has a variant reading. It is found in Pṛthvīdhara's commentary on this passage. His comments on the three sentences *aho ajjaāe gandhagaaṃ pekhiśśam gadua* / *aha vā kiṃ mama ediṇā* / *jadhāvavasidaṃ aṇuciṭṭhiśśam* (*iti niṣkrāntaḥ*) are limited to the following: *galuadā gurutvam*[10] *mahāvaibhavaśālitvāt* / *yathāvavyasitaṃ pravrajyānuṣṭhānarūpam.* Clearly where we now read *gadua* "having gone" his text had *galuadāe* (*garukatayā*), which Pṛthvīdhara translates with *gurutvam* and explains with *mahāvaibhavaśālitvāt*: "on the strength of my possession of great spiritual power." This *galuadāe* now survives in *gadua,* and the word must have gone with the preceding sentence: "Ah, I will look at my ladyship's must elephant by virtue of my spiritual influence." It can hardly have gone with *aha vā kiṃ mama ediṇā*: this would conflict with the generally initial position of *aha vā* in the sense of "or rather"; also such ablatives in °*tvāt* are more likely to follow a statement as its *hetu* than to precede it. Consequently the Masseur-Friar explicitly connects his desire to look at the elephant with his newly won "guruship" as a friar; therefore there can be no contradiction between the first sentence and the third, and the intervening *aha vā kiṃ mama ediṇā,* which only makes sense when there is a contradiction must be spurious. I propose to read: *aho ajjaāe gandhagaaṃ pekkhiśśam galuadāe* / *jadhāvavasidaṃ aṇuciṭṭhiśśam*: "By virtue of my spiritual power I shall look at her ladyship's must elephant—I shall live up to my resolve." The last remark may be taken as his resolve to become a friar, but also his resolve to repay Vasantasenā's kindness.

The reason why the scene was later misunderstood, so that *galuadāe* was replaced by the curiously placed absolutive *gadua* (which we would expect to precede *pekkhiśśam*) probably was the lack of clear indication in *M* that the Masseur and the molested holyman were the same. A sentence to this effect may have dropped out, perhaps like the one surviving the *C* where the holyman was recognized by the absence of his upper garment. It is also tempting to propose that the doffing of this upper garment actually took place on the stage. The right place would be after the Masseur's solemn statement of intention, immediately before Vasantasenā's startled exclamation: "No violence, sir!" Such an exclamation is frequently addressed to someone who is doing physical violence to himself, and the partial stripping of the Masseur may quite well have inspired the courtesan's cry. A stage direction to the effect that the Masseur takes off his cloth would have been deliberately dropped when standards of stage propriety had become stricter than the *Mṛcchakaṭikà* as a whole evidences.

NOTES

1. Georg Morgenstierne, *Ueber das Verhältniss zwischen Cārudatta und Mṛcchakaṭika* (Thesis, Berlin, 1918; Halle, 1920).

2. For the purposes of this article it is not necessary to choose sides in the controversy about the plays ascribed to Bhāsa. If Bhāsa's original plays survive in the thirteen that have been found, it is clear that they have suffered changes through the ages, so that the *Mṛcchakaṭika* version in parallel passages occasionally can clarify the *Cārudatta;* if the *Cārudatta* really derives from the *Mṛcchakaṭika*, it may derive from a better version of it than we have now left, so that occasionally the *Cārudaıta* may clarify the *Mṛcchakaṭika.*

3. When Śūdraka makes the burglar Śarvilaka vow to foment a rebellion (4.26), thereby giving clearly a wholly new turn to the *Cārudatta*, he includes a reference to Bhāsa's play : *uttejayāmi suhṛdaḥ parimokṣaṇāya / yaugandharāyaṇa ivodayanasya rājñaḥ*—"I will incite...to rebellion, in order to rescue my friend, just as Y. did to rescue king Udayana". That an author writing in imitation of a play by Bhāsa could have composed these lines without giving a thought to the *Pratijñāyaugandharāyaṇa* (so Jarl Charpentier, *JRAS*, 1923, p. 585ff.) is entirely incredible.

4. Morgenstierne (*o.c.*, p. 45) suggests we read with *M ajjāe* for *ajja eva*; but this is not necessary.

5. *M* 2.17.

6. Pṛthvīdhara, whose commentary is given in K.P. Parab's edition of *M* (Nirṇayasāgara Press, Bombay, 1904) comments : *parivrājakaḥ saṃvāhaka eva bhikṣukarūpaḥ.*

7. Cf. *M* 8.5.

8. It is necessary to construe °*virāadāe* with *ahialakkhaṇīo; lakkhaṇīo* (cf. Skt. *lakṣaṇīya*, e.g. *Meghadūta* (Hultzsch) st. 77) "noticeable, remarkable", *ahia* (cf. Skt. *adhika*) "to a high degree"; the entire compound may be rendered "conspicuous". Woolner/Sarup (*The Trivandrum Plays,* I, p. 88) differ on the interpretation of *uttarīapaḍavirāadāe*; they render: "conspicuous by the red colour of his robe." This presumes apparently on an analysis °*padavi-rāadāe* (?), with *rāa* (cf. Skt. *rāga*) in the sense of "red color"; I don't see how this analysis can be defended. Meanwhile, by Skt. standards, the cpd. °*virāadāe* is curious; we would expect either *virattadāe* or simply *virāeṇa.*

9. It is one of the eight Great Events in the Buddha's life; cf. Vinaya

Piṭaka II, p. 194 ff. (Cullavagga VII. 3.11-12); Jātaka (ed. Fausbøll) V 333 ff.; also Avadānaśataka (ed. Speyer) I 177 (=Dhanapāla); Apadāna I 300 (Apadānaṭṭhakathā 114; 123); Milindapañha 349; Udānaṭṭhakathā 265; it is repeatedly illustrated in art, cf. e.g. C. Sivaramamurti, *Amarāvatī Sculptures in the Madras Government Museum* (Madras, 1942), plate XXV.1; it is tempting to connect the picturesque phrase of the *ceṭa* Karṇapūraka in *C* (*haṃ vippaḷaddho mhi / vādāaṇanikkhāmidapuvvakāāe oṇamiapaoharāe kaṇṇaūrassa paripphando ajjukāe jena na diṭṭho*) with the representations of this scene with full-breasted women looking down from upper-storey windows.

10. Parab places a question mark after *gurutvam,* but the text is not corrupt : the commentator first quotes the Pkt. word and its Skt. equivalent in the nominative, then paraphrases it with the ablative *mahāvaibhavaśālitvāt,* showing that the text had an ablative.

18

THE LARGE ĀTMAN

Throughout the older, and some of the younger, upaniṣads there recurs the expression *mahān ātmā*, which is usually rendered by "the great ātman". This rendering is doubtless correct, but on closer investigation it seems unduly to limit the intention of the adjective *mahān*. Although it is not always possible to be definite about it, in a number of cases the qualification *mahān* appears to be used in a semitechnical sense. When we pursue the more or less technical connotations, we are gradually led to later, more definitely technical, usages of *mahān/mahat* in Sāṃkhyan and comparable contexts. This semitechnical sense does not become clear from a qualification of the ātman as "great": This in our idiom is too easily understood as an honorific and slightly redundant adjective. It would, however, seem to me that the use of *mahān ātmā* is fairly precise, and that *mahān* cannot regularly be replaced by similar adjectives pointing up the greatness, importance and supremacy of the ātman, like *para, parama, uttama,* etc.

The technical connotation is better approached through such renderings as "the large ātman", for notions of spatial amplitude can be recognized. Striking also is the personal conception of this "large" being; *mahān* qualifies such beings as *ātman, puruṣa, yakṣa prathamaja.* The notion of *pratiṣṭhā* is closely connected with it, and so is that of *vijñāna.* While occasionally it can be replaced [**104**] by *bṛhat* (but this word is obsolescent in the Upaniṣads), it belongs in a context with *bahu,* "much"; *bhūman,* "muchness"; *mahiman,* "largeness"; *pūrṇam,* "fullness". And as *akṣara* has its formulaic correlate in *OṂ*, this personal principle has its own in the formula *mahas.*

This "large ātman" is first of all conceived of as a "whole". This "whole" is not necessarily a very general "everything", but a quite concrete, one would almost say, organic, whole. It is manifest and *complete*. Its completeness is realized through creation. Perhaps the most simple and fundamental summary is *bahu syāṃ prajāyeyeti* "I will be much—let me beget."— This "muchness" is its completion, and this completion is very often stated in terms of body and limbs. Illustrative is BĀUp. 1.4.17 *ātmaivedam agra āsīd eka eva / so 'kāmayata—jāyā syād atha prajāyeyātha vittaṃ me syād atha karma kurvīyeti...sa yāvad apy eteṣāṃ ekaikaṃ na prāpnoty akṛtsna eva tāvan manyate / tasyo kṛtsnatā—mana evā/syātmā vāg jāyā prāṇaḥ prajā,* etc. ("The ātman was here in the beginning, quite alone. He desired, 'let there be a wife, and then I will multiply, and then I will have riches, and then I will do rites...' As long as one does not obtain anyone of these, one feels incomplete. His completeness is: the ātman is the will, the wife is speech, the offspring is life etc."). The completeness of the ātman can also be conceived of in other than bodily terms; for instance as the completeness of the social stystem, as in BĀUp. 1.4.11ff., where the Brahman is not fully "expanded" (*sa naiva vyabhavat*),[1] until the four varṇas plus dharma have been evolved. This recalls at once the puruṣasūkta, where these varṇas were represented as originating from the creator's *body*.[2]

[105] This full expansion, this self-completion, may take place through total penetration: *sa eṣa iha praviṣṭa ā nakhāgrebhyaḥ* (1.4.7) "he has entered here down[3] to the nail-tops," fitting into the world body as a razor fits in its case (*ibid.*), so that he only can be seen as a whole: *akṛtsno hy eṣo 'ta ekaikena bhavati* "hence piece by piece he is incomplete; *ātmety evopāsīta / atra hy ete sarva ekaṃ bhavanti* "one should represent him as 'ātman'; for in him all these parts become one whole." Likewise BĀUp. 4.4.20; *ekadhānudraṣṭavyam etad aprameyaṃ dhruvam / virajaḥ para ākāśād aja ātmā mahān dhruvaḥ* "this immeasurable, this stable one must be looked upon strictly as one whole;[4] it is the unborn stable large ātman, beyond atmosphere, surpassing ether."

Unborn he may be, yet this "large ātman" is as it were physically present: *sa vā eṣa mahān aja ātmā yo 'yaṃ vijñānamayaḥ prāṇeṣu* (BĀUp. 4.4.22) "that same large unborn ātman is the one which here dwells in the prāṇas consisting in knowledge"; it is *annādo vasudānaḥ* "eater of food and giver of wealth". It is immortal, this "muchness":[5] *yo vai bhūmā tad amṛtam atha yad alpaṃ tan martyam iti* ("This muchness is the immortal; and the little is the mortal"). But it is not transcendent. The "large ātman" is the original creator who, or which, has as it were embodied himself in creation.

As long as this self-embodiment is looked upon as a *kṛtsnatā* "completeness", as an evolution away from aloneness (cf. BĀUp. 1.4–2), from dissatisfaction (*ibid.* 3), or from fear (*ibid.* 2), and creation is viewed as the self-expansion of a divine person (*vibhū*), the "large ātman" remains supreme. In an important way it **[106]** corresponds to the *sat* that arises from the *asat*, "the not-yet-existent"—hence that ŚvetUp. 3.12 can still say: *mahān prabhur vai puruṣaḥ sattvasyaiṣa pravartakaḥ* ("the large, the lord, the person") "who sets in motion the sattva", where *sattva* probably has the sense of the material world as a whole.[6] In so-called theistic upaniṣads this "large ātman" continues for a while to be highly valued. KaṭhUp. 2.22 has *aśarīraṃ śarīreṣv anavastheṣv avasthitam / mahāntaṃ vibhum ātmānaṃ matvā dhīro na śocati* ("Knowing the large, expansive ātman, bodiless, established in the unestablished bodies, the wise one does not grieve"); likewise ŚvetUp. 3.19: *apāṇipādo javano grahītā paśyaty acakṣuḥ sa śṛṇoty akarṇaḥ / sa vetti vedyaṃ na ca tasyāsti vettā tam āhur agryaṃ puruṣaṃ mahāntam* ("Speeding and seizing, without hands or feet he sees without eyes, hears without ears: he knows what can be known, but no one knows him: him they call the original, the large Person"); and 3.8: *vedāham etaṃ puruṣaṃ mahāntam ādityavarṇaṃ tamasaḥ parastāt tam eva viditvāti mṛtyum eti nānyaḥ panthā vidyate 'yanāya* ("I know that Person, the large one, sun-colored, beyond darkness: knowing him alone one goes beyond death: there is no other path to go").

But a change had already announced itself: *etāvān asya mahimā tato jyāyāṃś ca puruṣaḥ / pado 'sya sarvā bhūtāni tripād asyāmṛtaṃ divi* (" This is the extent of his largeness: but the Person is still larger. One quarter of his is all these beings; three quarters of him are immortal in heaven" [ChUp. 3.12.6]). The "really great" ātman transcends the merely "large" one: *aṇor aṇīyān mahato mahīyān ātmā*,[7] KaṭhUp. 2.20, which continues: *taṃ akratuḥ paśyati..mahimānam ātmanaḥ*. The "large one" is no longer great enough, and the *mahān ātmā* speculations now fall in line with other trends that seek to abstract the supreme from the phenomenal world. The *avyakta, avyākṛta* condition of the supreme ranks higher than its condition of *mahān*: *mahataḥ paraṃ avyaktam* "the unmanifest is higher than the large ātman" **[107]**

(KaṭhUp. 3.10–11), *aśabdam asparśam..anādy anantaṃ mahataḥ param* (Kaṭh Up. 3.15). While the "large ātman" still transcends the *sattva* (of which in ŚvetUp. 3.12 it is the *pravartakaḥ*), it, or rather he, is transcended by the *avyaktam*:...*sattvād adhi mahān ātmā mahato 'vyaktam uttamam* (KaṭhUp. 6.7). The Mahān now has found a place in a hierarchically ordered series, and from that place it will no more budge.

For the vicissitudes of the term the fundamental controversy of what will become Sāṃkhya and of what will become Vedānta, namely, whether there is a separate *prakṛti* from the supreme or not, is largely irrelevant. It holds its place, either below *puruṣa* (e.g., KaṭhUp. 3.13, cf. *infra*; 3.15) or below *avyakta* (e.g., *ibid.* 3.11). In either case it remains what BĀUp.5.4.1 called the *mahad yakṣaṃ prathamajam,* it remains the first principle of manifest creation.

As the "firstborn" this demoted large ātman had rivals. *Sattva* at one time held this position; so did *ahaṃkāra* (which in ChUp. 7.15 is on a part with *bhūman* and *ātmā*). *Sattva* is differently accommodated as the first in a triadic series of psychocosmic factors, the later guṇas; *ahaṃkāra*[8] is demoted. But there is another principle with which it has to sort out its relation, the *buddhi*. The KaṭhUp., for which the "large ātman" was still a significant concept, ranks it over the *buddhi* (KaṭhUp. 3.10; 6.7, where *sattva*∼*buddhi*); the ŚvetUp. fails to mention any relation. But in the final analysis *mahān* and *buddhi* were no rivals, as in many respects *mahān* paralleled *buddhi*.

We have seen that the creator was "large" insofar as he manifested himself, and embodied himself, in creation. But this manifestation, which is often understood as a self-creation, frequently proceeded through an act of consciousness, a self-recognition, which also could take the form of a self-formulation. Fundamental are statements like BĀUp. 1.2.1 *tan mano 'kuruta—ātmanvī syām* ("It conceived the will, 'I will be a person with a self' "); 1.4.1 *ātmaivedam agra āsīt puruṣavidhaḥ...so'ham asmīty agre vyāharat* ("The ātman was here alone in the beginning, in the shape of a man...In the beginning he uttered, 'This is I' "); 1.4.5 *so 'vet—ahaṃ vāva sṛṣṭir asmi / ahaṃ hīdaṃ sarvaṃ asṛkṣi / tataḥ sṛṣṭir abhavat,* which continues in 7: *sa eṣa iha praviṣṭa ā nakhāgrebhyaḥ* ("He knew, 'I alone am this creation. For I have **[108]** created all this'; thence creation came to be." "This one entered into it here as far as the tips of his nails"); 1.4.10 *brahma vā idam agra āsīt / tad ātmānam evāvet—ahaṃ Brahmāsmīti / tasmāt tat sarvam abhavat* ("Brahman was here in the beginning. It knew itself alone: 'I am Brahman'. From that everything came to be"). Within the context of such notions, which I elsewhere have elaborated upon,[9] this self-recognition, this self-consciousness could be singled out as the first phase of a creation process, when creation indeed was regarded as a process, completing itself through a number of phases each of which could be identified as a station and later as a principle or a rubric.

That this large ātman, this macrocosmic ātman par excellence, could acquire with such apparent ease typically microcosmic affinities is only superficially explained by the general homology of macrocosm and microcosm. This homology, true though it be, has its justification in something more precise: the conception of a creator existing as *somebody,* and as embodied in creation. This creator is the prototype of any one person, a role which he will continue to fill in different guises.[10]

Cosmogony thus may become the prototype of somatogony, and any single stage in this progressive genesis, which is autogenesis, may become the prototype of a corresponding "level" of the micropersonality. It is tempting to replace such terms as macrocosmic and microcosmic by the more pertinent macranthropic and micranthropic,[11] and also to view the process of "cosmogony" or autogenesis as it were from the head downward. The perspective from the head is forelengthened: an upside down cone, or, in the more poetic language of the Upaniṣad, an inverted *aśvattha* tree.[12] The top, to carry the image further, can be viewed as a true bottom, a *pratiṣṭhā.* The real peak of the cone is only the convergence point of a diminishing scope of attention: Undoubtedly the upward view experiences it as a huge variety, but the downward view can only see it as an ever decreasing fulness, a shrinking amplitude, an eventual evanescence beyond the horizon of substance.

That in a school of thinking so prone to hierarchical ordering as a principle of intelligibility the earliest *phase* may become the **[109]** highest *station* does not surprise. The body image of the world encouraged the specification of levels of importance: How many organs can one spare and still live? Where resides the principle of life? What is the ultimate *pratiṣṭhā*? Speculations take two closely related forms: the "rivalry" of the organs, and the problem of sleep. One may imagine a progressive "death" when sense after sense ceases functioning: What functions last and thus sustain the whole? There is the corresponding instance of the progression from wakefulness to coma: What survives so that one can awake from a comatose sleep?[13]

Effortlessly the "large ātman," itself resulting from and, in effect, identical with the creator's self-recognition, becomes involved in such speculations. No doubt there is (BĀUp. 4.4.22) "this large unborn ātman which consists in cognition among the senses" (*vijñānamayaḥ prāṇeṣu*), but by the strange vacillation of perspectives this "largeness" may also be a "tininess": "it lies within the space within the heart" (*ibid.*). This *vijñānamaya ātman* pinpoints itself there: "When this person has fallen asleep, this person consisting in cognition, where does it then stay, where has it departed from?" "Having taken consciousness with the consciousness of the organ (*prāṇas*), it lies in the space within the heart" (*ibid.* 2.1.16–17). This seeming reduction however does not decrease its amplitude: the perspective changes again: "This person consisting in consciousness among the senses, luminous within the heart, does, being total (*samānaḥ*), pervade both worlds." In this totality, this person or puruṣa or ātman equals brahman which is *vijñānamaya*, *manomaya*, *prāṇamaya, cakṣurmaya,* etc. (*ibid.* 4.4.5). Thus, however physically pinpointed (*tasya haitasya hṛdayasyāgraṃ pradyotate / tena pradyotenaiṣa ātmā niṣkrāmati...savijñāno bhavati sa vijñānam evānv avakrāmati* ["The top of his heart becomes light; and through this light the ātman departs...He becomes possessed of knowledge; and he departs after knowledge alone"], BĀUp. 4.4.2), it remains total: *yatra tv asya sarvam ātmaivābhūt. . tat kena kaṃ vijānīyāt / vijñātāram are vijānīyād iti* ("But where the ātman of him has **[110]** become everything,... whom would he know then and how? Indeed, he would know the knower"), declares Yājñavalkya.

But what is this "consciousness"? It is "larger" (*bhūyas*) than name, than speech, than will, than intent, than thought, than reflection (ChUp. 7.7.1). It heads a homogeneous series here.[14] But the old associations with creation as cognition must inevitably "place" it, as soon as thought pushes beyond the *pratiṣṭhā* of manifest creation. Is there an *ātman* "an embodiment" beyond the "large one consisting in consciousness"?

The most famous context of this *vijñānamaya ātman* is found in TaittUp. 2, which, was to become one of the important Vedānta texts. Here the *vijñāna*, which, as we saw above, was in the process of becoming "placed" in a series, finds above itself an even higher station, that of the *ānandamaya*. This TaittUp. series allows further historical analysis, as I have tried to show elsewhere:[15] At least in part it descends from older speculations centering around, or symbolized in, the *agnicayana* ritual where the three-layered universe form of old is extended to a pentadic cosmic construction, at the top of which one finds "all desires" or "bliss." Just below this there is a stage which may represent the "*yajamāna*" or a shadowy "*ātmavid*," who, although transcending the complete universe of earth, atmosphere and heaven, yet is of a more manifest nature than the highest bliss to which he may aspire.

In the context of the Taittirīya Upaniṣad, too, the treatment of the levels indicates that above the now basic triad two levels have been added; and although an attempt is made to maintain the pattern of "limbs" in the description of the *vijñānamaya* and the *ānandamaya*, these components are new and arbitrary. Whereas the earth/*annam*, atmosphere/*prāṇa*, and sky/*manas* have well-known divisions of components, disparate series of fives are associated with the fourth and fifth ātman. The *vijñānamaya* is described in terms of *śraddhā, ṛtam, satyam, yoga* and *mahas*. The first three recall a sacrificial trend of thought (still strikingly reflected in the stanza quoted thereon: *vijñānaṃ yajñaṃ tanute*, etc.); the fourth is open to speculation, while the fifth refers us back to the idiosyncratic syllable speculations of TaittUp. 1.

The word *mahas*, though once occurring in a substantive meaning in the older Upaniṣads,[16] is in the first chapter of the [111] Taittirīya best understood as a kind of mantra construct based on the *vyāhṛtis bhūḥ, bhuvas, suvas* and inspired by the technical use of *mahān* in the sense of the "large ātman." TaittUp. 1.5.1 adds *mahas* as the fourth to the three ritual utterances: *tāsām u* (sc. *vyāhṛtīṇām*) *ha smaitāṃ caturthīṃ māhācamasya pravedayate maha iti / tad brahma sa ātmā*. Here, for a brief spell, *mahas* takes the place of the Akṣara par excellence, transcending the formed and spoken universe, a place which in Sāmavedic circles and thenceforth universally will be wholly usurped by OM.[17] This "fourth" is still the highest station, supreme over universes of triads: *catasraś catasraḥ vyāhṛtayaḥ / tā yo veda sa veda brahma:*

"The *vyāhṛtis* go by fours: he who knows them knows Brahman." These "fours" are:

	Bhūḥ	Bhuvas	Suvas	Mahas
1.	earth	atmosphere	heaven	sun
2.	fire	wind	sun	moon
3.	*ṛcaḥ*	*sāmāni*	*yajūṃṣi*	*brahman*
4.	*prāṇa*	*apāna*	*vyāna*	*annam*

These series contain the usual triads which are not here hierarchically ordered; various fourths are added to them to contrive foursomes. If this adaptation of basic triads to novel tetrads is a little contrived, still it reflects an earlier stage where the fourth magnitude, the *mahas*, was the higher completer of the lower universe of the triad, still the "large ātman" and brahman. In the doubtless later section in the second chapter, this construed *mahas* is tenuously preserved as a limb of that second-grade ātman that is *vijñānamaya*.

Later though it be, the second chapter still cannot escape the persisting notions of a personified unmanifest that pervades the universe. On the *vijñānamaya* it was quoted that *vijñāna* equals *brahman*; at the same time the description of the *ānandamaya* culminates in the *pratiṣṭhā* which is also identified with *brahman*. But this *brahman* is not the ancient unmanifest, also known as *asat*, for the quoted stanza reads: "Nonexistent becomes he who knows Brahman as *asat*. If one knows that Brahman *is* (or is *sat*), one becomes existent." The sequel to this stanza is condensed or lacunous: In response to a question whether the knowing or the unknowing attain to the supreme after death, the text abruptly moves to a familiar creation account: "He (the unidentified personal creator) wished: May I be much, I will multiply. He did **[112]** *tapas*. Having done *tapas*, he created all this, whatever there is. Having created it, he entered all the way into it. Having all the way entered into it, it became both *sat* and *tyad*, uttered and unuttered, tangible and intangible, knowledge and non-knowledge, true and non-true, it became Satyam, whatever there is: They call it 'Sat-Tyam'."

Here in his full vastness reappears the "large ātman"; yet there is something higher than he, even if it seems to militate against the stanza just quoted. For the next stanza reads: "The *asat* indeed was here at first. From it was born the *sat*. This *sat* made itself into somebody (*ātmānam*); hence it is called well made." Well made, or complete? But this no longer matters: It is in the unmanifest that everything has its *pratiṣṭhā*. The "large one" is from now on in a hierarchy below this unmanifest.

The above considerations have shown us that the conceptions of a macranthropic universe, which is manifestly available, and of a knowledge-ātman, whose knowledge is creative of this universe, are closely correlated. We saw that both conceptions eventually came to be subordinated to a higher overarching conception of a primordial unmanifest from which this knowledge-person issued forth as the firstborn. The texts do not yet present us with the question whether this "unmanifest" is of a "material" or of a "spiritual" nature, and we need not address us here to the source of the later differences between Sāṃkhya and Vedānta—differences which seem to result, not primarily from a different treatment of the world, but of the "self" and "selves" within it.

The next group of texts, the philosophical portions of the Mokṣadharma corpus of the Mahābhārata, continues smoothly the speculations of the older and later Upaniṣads. The "large ātman" is peculiarly the ātman in relation to creation, whether the macranthropic creation which is the universe, or its homologon, the micranthropic body.

etad akṣaram ity uktaṃ kṣaratīdaṃ yathā jagat /
jagan mohātmakaṃ prāhur avyaktaṃ vyaktasaṃjñakam //
mahāṃś caivāgrajo nityam etat kṣaranidarśanam /

"It is called the Imperishable, as this world perishes. They call the world based on ignorance, while the Unmanifest is known manifestly. The "large one" is the firstborn: forever is this the example of the Perishable" (12.291.35–36).

But the same context had earlier shown familiar hesitations: "The *buddhi* is known as Lord Hiraṇyagarbha. [It is known as] **[113]** the "large one" in the yogas, and also as Viriñca. In Sāṃkhya doctrine this manifold one is known under various names, as "the one of diverse forms," "universal ātman", "sole Imperishable". The ātman by whom this complete universe with its multiple ātmans is enveloped is known as the "many-formed one", because it thus has many shapes" (291.17–19). It is a difference of emphasis, on the world as divine manifestation or on the divine as unmanifest, which is apparent here, rather than difference of doctrine.

The "large one" is born as a result of his knowledge:

ubhayaṃ saṃpradhāryaitad adhyavasyed yathāmati |
anenaiva vidhānena bhaved garbhaśayo mahān ||

"The puruṣa, while having had discriminate knowledge of both categories, resolves (*adhyavasāya* = *buddhi*) as he deems fit: by this very disposition the 'large one' becomes an embryo" (241.1). Here this "resolve" is the downward directed *buddhi*, which is the first station on the path of complete creation.

This "living self," later on more consistently known as *jīvātman* or *kṣetrajña*, may also be referred to as *puruṣa*, which puts us in mind of the many passages which use *puruṣa* for the macranthropos and describe Brahman, or the ātman, as *puruṣavidhaḥ*, etc. in which the notion of a whole embodied person predominates, not his abstracted immortality. "This large ātman lies there pervading this auspicious nine-gated city endowed with these three states of becoming: Hence it is called *puruṣa*." It is more than a pun on *puruṣa* = *puriśa*, for the "large ātman" is the whole person.[18] Likewise 294.35: "In many ways this ātman activates (*prakurvīta*) the generative prakṛti, and this field (*kṣetra*) is governed by the large ātman who is the twenty-fifth."

In such passages the *mahān* is primarily seen as productive. But equally illustrative are passages which view it as produced. "This (unmanifest) god first created the 'large one', and the 'large one' created the Ahaṃkāra " (175.13). Or: "I am originally issued from the Unmanifest as the triple 'large one'; higher than this ('large one') is he who is known as the *kṣetrajña*" (327.67). Here evidently **[114]** "the large one" can sum up the entire creation and in fact equals *kṣetra*.

I have taken more and more to putting this *mahān* within quotes because it becomes increasingly clear that the word is no longer to be taken in any literal sense but as a proper name which is still in search of an identity. Like *sattva* it goes through many different usages which simply reflect the fact that different milieus operated with a small vocabulary of technical terms in different ways, until as the final result of a long process of normalization one particular referend became conventional.

In the case of the *mahān* this is the *buddhi*, and, as we have seen, the early developments predisposed the term for this meaning. A creative act of (self-) cognition set in motion the process of creation; the "knowledge" associated with the "large ātman" was characteristically a knowledge directed downward toward creation. It retains, like *buddhi*, the inherent ambivalence of "knowledge": in a downward perspective it is the focusing of the unmanifest consciousness on something other than itself, the first step out of the unmanifest; in an upward perspective it is the highest form of non-knowledge and the last step before the unmanifest.

Its reduction to a principle in the hierarchically ordered scale of evolution eventually brought along a change of gender. The original personal nature of the *mahān* has been forgotten, and it survives—like many of such antique technical terms a bit perfunctorily—as a *mahat* or *mahattattvam*. Thus it is incorporated in the classical Sāṃkhya tradition[19] which made innocuous a term that in its original development of conception reflected a fundamental position opposed to the dualism of *puruṣa* and *prakṛti*, that of a supreme being, creating itself in the universe.

NOTES

1. BĀUp. 1.4.11 begins : *brahma vā idam agra āsīd ekam eva / ekaṃ san na vyabhavat*. This *brahman* becomes fully "expanded" as itself (*brahman* in the sense of "brahminhood"), *kṣatra* (*ibid.*, 11), *viś* (*ibid.*, 12), *śaudraṃ varṇa* (*ibid.*, 13). and *dharma* (*ibid.*, 14)—the whole of society with its ritual confirmation. That this "expanded" *brahman* is an ātman insofar as it is this world is stated in 15 : *ātmānam eva lokam upāsīta*, and 16 : *atho ayaṃ vā ātmā sarvesāṃ bhūtānāṃ lokaḥ*, which renders intelligible the transition to 17 : *ātmaivedam agra āsīd eka eva*, where the emphasis is on the completed (*kṛtsna*) ātman. As a result of this "spreading out," the "large ātman" will continue to be qualified as *vibhu*: *mahāntaṃ vibhum ātmānaṃ matvā* (KaṭhUp. 2.22), *apāṇipādaṃ nityaṃ vibhuṃ sarvagatam* (MuṇḍUp. 1.1.6, obviously parallel to ŚvetUp. 3.19 : *apāṇipādo javano...tam āhur agryaṃ puruṣaṃ mahāntam*), *ādidevam ajaṃ vibhum* (BhG. 10.12), *sarvātmānaṃ sarvagataṃ vibhutvāt* ŚvetUp. 3.21), *anādimattvaṃ vibhutvena vartase* (*ibid.*, 4.4).

2. RV. 10.90.12; already here the puruṣa is truly *mahān* (*sahásraśīrṣā púruṣaḥ sahasrākṣáḥ sahásrapāt* (*ibid.*, 1), encompassing the world and expanding beyond it (*sá bhū́miṃ viśváto vṛtvā 'tyatiṣṭhad daśāṅgulám*, *ibid.*, 1)' whose "largeness" (*mahimā*, *ibid.*, 3) exceeds the known world, but who is also "firstborn" *púruṣaṃ jātám agratáḥ*, *ibid.*, 7.

3. A term more concrete than, though parallel to, *vi-bhū*; the most technical variant is *anu-pra-viś*.

4. *Ekadhā* "as one" (cf. ChUp. 7.26.2 *sa ekadhā bhavati*, etc.; KauṣUp. 3.3 *asmin prāṇa evaikadhā bhavati*), but, as witness the preceding stanza (*manasānudraṣṭavyaṃ neha nānāsti kiṃcana*), this "one" is not to be understood as one in a series, but as the sum-total. Relevant is also 4.4.13 : *yasyānuvittaḥ pratibuddha ātmā saṃdehye gahane praviṣṭaḥ / sa viśvakṛt sa hi sarvasya kartā*

tasya lokaḥ sa u loka eva. "He by whom is discovered the ātman, the awakened ātman (cf. BĀUp. 1.4.10), which has entered into this deep body (deep into the body?), becomes all-creative, for he (the ātman) is the maker of all, he becomes the world, for he (the ātman) is this very world." It is the "large ātman" of the puruṣasūkta, equally master of past and future (*ibid.*, 15), which supports the entire world (*ibid.*, 17).

5. This "muchness" should in principle be understood in the terms of the often-repeated creative phrase *bahu syām*. The word *bhūmā* was early understood as an abstract to a series *bahu, bhūyas, bhūyiṣṭha*; cf. ŚatBr. 1.1.2.6 *bhūmā vā anaḥ / bhūmā hi vā anas tasmād yadā bahu bhavaty anobāhvyam abhūt*. The later emphasis on the transcendent part of the creator should not make us ignore that earlier accounts gave a positive value to the "much" to which the creator expands in creating. Even when "creation" is abstracted from the supreme being, this being still carries the attribute of plenitude in a manner quite comparable to the *sat* attributed (since Ch.Up. 6) to the supreme being *before* creation.

6. Cf. my remarks in "Studies in Sāṃkhya (iii): Sattva," JAOS 77 (1957), 95 [no. 8 in this volume].

7. *Aṇu* and *mahat* are not opposite terms. *Aṇu* in the older text has a function which is later taken over by *sūkṣma*, absent from the older upaniṣads. *Aṇor aṇīyān mahato mahīyān ātmā* translates as "the soul, subtler than the subtle and larger than the large," and the phrase means that the same soul holds the highest eminence on both the macranthropic and micranthropic levels (cf. ChUp. 8.1.3 *yāvān vā ayam ākāśas tāvān eṣo 'ntarhṛdaya ākāśaḥ*). But elsewhere we have a reduction to subtleness (*aṇimā*) of both the macrocosm and microcosm: ChUp. 6.8.6-7 *sa ya eṣo 'ṇimaitadātmyam idaṃ sarvaṃ tat satyaṃ sa ātmā*, etc. A middle position seems to be taken by those texts which ascribe *aṇimā* to the subtle channels between both worlds (ChUp. 8.6.1-2, curiously applied BĀUp. 4.3.20), in which we recognize pentadic predecessors to the three-colored *guṇas*, "threads".

8. For an intermediate case where *mahān* seems to usurp the place of the *ahaṃkāra*, cf. the discussion of E.H. Johnston, *Early Sāṃkhya* (London, 1937), pp. 60; 82.

9. Notably in my *Sattva*, pp. 105-6 [no. 8 in this volume].

10. An interesting case is provided by certain forms of quasitheistic Sāṃkhya as reflected, e.g., in the system of the Yogasūtras where "God" (*īśvara*) is an eternally released model-puruṣa, but with the typically Sāṃkhyan abstraction of *puruṣa* from all *prakṛti*.

11. So Maryla Falk, *Il Mito psichologico nell' India antica* ("Memorie delle Reale Accademia dei Lincei," ser. VI, Vol. VIII, fasc. v [1939]), pp. 289ff.

12. Kaṭh Up. 6.1.

13. Hence creation, both as autogenesis and as cosmogony can be viewed as an awakening, cf. BĀUp. 1.4.10 (after it is said that Brahman *knew* itself so that the universe came to be) : *tad yo yo devānāṃ pratybudhyata sa eva tad abhavat tatharṣīṇāṃ tathā manuṣyāṇām.* This notion lives on in purānic cosmogonies where Nārāyaṇa, etc. "wakes up" to create the cosmos, the conception of the Days and Nights of Brahmā, etc. But where the world of awakening and wakefulness, which is creation, is a lesser world, this awakening becomes a

lower creative *buddhi*, though the sage can still wake up (*buddha, pratibuddha*) to the higher reality (cf. BhG. 2.69 *yā niśā sarvabhūtānāṃ tasyāṃ jāgarti saṃyamī/ yasyāṃ jāgrati bhūtāni sā niśā paśyato muneḥ*).

14. It is clear that *vijñāna* is the intended climax of the magnitudes described in 7.1-7.7; the succeeding series *bala—anna—āpas—tejas—ākāśa—smara—āśā—prāṇa* is of a different kind.

15. *The Maitrāyaṇīya Upaniṣad : A Critical Essay* (The Hague, 1962), pp. 28-33.

16. ChUp. 3.13.5.

17. Some remarks in "Akṣara" (JAOS 79, 1959), pp. 179 ff. [no. 13 in this volume].

18. Cf. BĀUp. 2.5.18 *puraś cakre dvipadaḥ puraś cakre catuṣpadaḥ /puraḥ sa pakṣī bhūtvā puraḥ puruṣa āviśad iti / sa vā ayaṃ puruṣaḥ sarvāsu pūrṣu puriśayaḥ* "he made biped fortresses, he made quadruped fortresses; having become the bird formerly, he entered the fortresses as puruṣa [on RV. 1.27.1?] : it is this puruṣa who in all fortresses is fortress-seated." In all upaniṣadic passages *pur/pura* have the metaphorical meaning of "body"—which I can only see as inspired by a *puruṣa* known as *puriśa*—a form indeed abundantly attested to by Prākṛta; a curiously comparable case is the "etymology" *āpnoter ity ātmā*, which presupposes, not Skt. *ātmā*, but Prkt. *appā*.

19. But Sāṃkhyakārikā 22 still preserves *mahān* (*prakṛter mahān tato 'haṃkāraḥ*).

19

ON THE ARCHAISM OF THE BHĀGAVATA PURĀṆA

It is one of the paradoxes of the cultural history of India, where the final norm of orthodoxy is the acceptance of the authority of the Veda, that even the most doctrinaire texts of Brahmanistic orthodoxy betray hardly any trace of Vedic archaism. Although in cultures far less traditionally oriented a mock archaic language could lend to a verse or a prose text the vague prestige of an irrelevant past, the definite prestige of an admittedly relevant past was rarely invoked in India by language meant to suggest it. Except in some incidental and quite early cases (as in the later portions of the *Maitrāyaṇīya Upaniṣad*,[1] the *Suparṇādhyāya*,[2] the apocryphal hymn to the Aśvins in the ancient *Pauṣyaparvan*),[3] Vedic archaism in classical Sanskrit is conspicuous by its absence.

The reason is clear. When we disregard the epic language and its continuation in the Purāṇas, the norm of correct Sanskrit is Pāṇini's grammar. The entire point of writing Sanskrit at all is writing it correctly. Inaccuracies, deviations from the given norm, are not countenanced—unless their context clearly proves them to be *ārṣa*, deriving from the Ṛṣis, or *chāndasa*, hymnal, that is, in both cases, Vedic. But even this decree one might expect to find transgressed in the Brahmanistic culture, which endlessly reaffirms that its roots are in the Vedas.

The Vedas, however, were not read; they were recited. Those who knew the Vedas were primarily ritual specialists, not literati. Of any literary influence of even the *Ṛgveda Saṃhitā*, traditionally the most prestigious one, on later high Sanskrit literature, whether in vocabulary or, more telling, in exceptional nominal or verbal forms, there is very little trace.

This point, well known though it is, deserves stress, because it shows how completely the Sanskrit language, as codified and described by the three sages Pāṇini, Kātyāyana and Patañjali, had supplanted the ancient Vedic as a cultural language and how little in later times the **[24]** Veda was actually known, except by rote. By the time that Sanskrit became cultivated, the Veda was present, in a symbolic fashion, as an eternal document; it was more actively present in the erudition of Mīmāṃsā and the practice of oblations, but most pertinently present—by however indirect an affinity—in the *smṛtis* that the orthodox lived by. The archaic language, which in the fifth century B.C. already stood in need of a glossary,[4] was no longer a productive presence in the culture.

It is therefore a unique phenomenon that far later in the history of literature, when Sanskrit letters were in fact on the decline, a text purporting to belong to the Purāṇic tradition consciously attempted to archaize its language. This peculiarity of the *Bhāgavata Purāṇa* has long been recognized by scholars, but, apart from a useful philological study by F.J. Meier,[5] it has not been made the object of further investigation.

Meier, after perhaps too hastily discarding the classically permitted imperatives in *-tāt*,[6] offers two partial explanations for the archaizing tendency of the *Bhāgavata*, "*dieser eigentümiche Charakter, der es nicht nur aus den andern Purāṇas, sondern überhaupt aus der indischen Literatur heraushebt.*" He suggests that certain archaic forms may occasionally be explained by the exigencies of the meter, and that, in some other cases, archaisms may have been mediated by Middle-Indic.[7] However, though some cases can thus be accounted for, their number is negligible. Meier rightly points out, as Michelson[8] did before him, that on occasion Vedic forms are borrowed along with Vedic context, as in the Purūravas legend and the Śunaḥśepa story.[9] The results of this often ill-informed archaistic effort are picturesque: "*die Analyse solcher barocker Verse zeigt uns—und darin besteht ihr Wert—mit welcher unglaublichen Unkenntniss der Verfasser der vedischen Sprache gegenüberstand.*"[10] I would dispute, however, that this is its only value.

This unique tendency of the *Bhāgavata*, which is displayed with equal density throughout the text, irrespective of style or context, still stands in need of explanation. The question briefly stated is: Why did the author or authors responsible for the final version of the *Bhāgavata* want the book to sound Vedic?

The question is the more challenging, since the Purāṇa has a

[25] somewhat ambivalent attitude toward Vedic orthodoxy. On numerous occasions, as Thomas J. Hopkins has ably shown elsewhere in this volume,[11] the empty and conceitful formalism of the Vaidikas is unfavorably contrasted with the simple and sincere devotions of the *bhakta*. In such criticisms of Brahmanism our Purāṇa is of course not alone; it is almost a refrain in epic and purāṇa. One might go back as far as *Ṛgveda* I.164.39: "What can he bring about with the hymns who does not know the *Akṣara* in the supreme heaven where the gods are seated? Only those who know it are sitting together here."[12] This is echoed by Yājñavalkya: "If one does not know this *Akṣara*, then one's oblations, sacrifices, and austerities for many thousands of years will come to an end; and when one departs from this world without knowing the *Akṣara*, one is miserable."[13]

The interesting passage (*Bhāgavata Purāṇa* XI.21.32–34) referred to by Hopkins, is unmistakably modeled on the *Bhagavad Gītā* II.42–44:

> This flowery language [i.e., the Veda], which they proclaim without wisdom, being bent upon discussions of the Vedas and maintaining, O Arjuna, that there is nothing else to know, inspired as they are by desires and intent on heavenly pleasures—this flowery language, productive of fruits of action that spell rebirth and abounding in a variety of rites to secure joy and power, robs those who are bent on joy and power of their senses.

But, in recalling these *Gītā* stanzas, the Purāṇa does not discard the Vedas, for the text goes on:

> The Vedas deal with both Brahman and Ātman and with the three rubrics:[14] the Seers speak in mystery and mystery is dear to me. The Brahman which is Veda, very hard to know, consists in breath, senses and mind;[15] like an ocean, its shore is boundless and its deeps are unfathomable" (XI.21.35).

In fact, the orthodox formalists do not know their Veda; for in reality the Vedas celebrate the Lord; and in despising the Lord and those good people who are devoted to him, they show the depth of their ignorance.[16]

The exact date of the *Bhāgavata Purāṇa* is still unsettled, though in its case closer approximation can be achieved than in that of any other Purāṇa. The *terminus ante quem* is roughly 1000, as it was [26] known by name (but barely) to al-Bīrūnī,[17] and was quoted by Abhinavagupta.[18] The *terminus post quem* is the

Vaiṣṇava bhakti movement of South India. In a *post-factum* prophecy, the *Bhāgavata Purāṇa* (XI.5.38–40) reads:

> In the Kali Age there will be devotees of Nārāyaṇa, O King, in great numbers everywhere in Tamil country, where the Tāmraparṇī River, abundant in water, fashions a garland, where the holy Kāverī and the westerly Mahānadī flow, whose waters, O king of men, are drunk by the people, devotees of pure heart generally to the blessed Lord Vāsudeva.

Until fresh evidence turns up, it is better not to push back the date of the final version of the *Bhāgavata* too far, nor too uncompromisingly to insist on the southern origin of our text. No quotations from the *Bhāgavata* have been identified in Rāmānuja's work, although this theologian of *bhakti* cites the *Viṣṇu Purāṇa* profusely. Nor have I been able as yet to identify citations from our text in the works of Yāmuna. Both Rāmānuja and Yāmuna were South-Indian Vaiṣṇavas deeply concerned with the orthodoxy of their faith. Their reticence needs explanation, if evidence from al-Bīrūnī and Abhinavagupta is admitted. That neither appears to quote from our text may mean either that in their days it was not sufficiently known or that it was not sufficiently respectable for their orthodox purposes. But *argumenta e silentio* are never conclusive; besides, Yāmuna is incompletely and fragmentarily preserved, and Rāmānuja was very exclusive in his sources.[19]

If then, with others, we prudently prefer to keep to the tenth century as the final date of the *Bhāgavata Purāṇa*, we have in the works of Yāmuna a most interesting control. Here we have a South Indian—equally inspired by the *bhakti* movement, and neither in time nor in ambience nor, probably, in space too far apart from the authors of the Purāṇa—who presents some other aspects of Bhāgavatism, of how Bhāgavatas thought of themselves and how they were thought of by others whom they had to accommodate. For, however interesting it may be to know what the Bhāgavatas thought of orthodox and well-to-do Brahmans, it is assuredly of no less interest to see what the Brahmans thought of the Bhāgavatas. Yāmuna, our source, is unimpeachable. Here we have not a sectarian text speaking in pious and traditional platitudes about wicked adversaries, but a Bhāgavata with a fine mind who seeks to enumerate, and subsequently to invalidate, **[27]** very precisely the traditional arguments of the Smārtas against the less-than-respectable Bhāgavatas.

The context is Yāmuna's *Āgamaprāmāṇya*, a treatise meant to demonstrate the Vedic validity of Pāñcarātra. The text merits a full translation.[20] In the present passage[21] the Smārta Brahman is speaking.

Furthermore, we do not find that those who observe the rituals enjoined by scripture, like the *agnihotra*, etc., in the same manner as they observe such [Smārta] rites as mouth rinsing, initiation, etc., also follow the customs of the Tantrists. On the contrary, Vedic experts condemn those who do so. Hence, the validity asserted of the several traditions,[22] because they all have the same performers, cannot apply to heterodox traditions like Pāñcarātra, etc. For the exemplary people[23] of the three twice-born classes do not accept the content of the statements of such systems.

Objection. But Bhāgavata Brahmans, who wear the hair tuft, the sacrificial thread, etc., in accordance with the precepts of scripture and tradition, do observe the contents of Pāñcarātra day after day. Since it therefore may be deemed probable that these contents are based on Vedic injunction, how can we then assume that this tradition has its origin in error, deceit, and the like, which are the very antithesis of validity?

Reply. Well! One who argues like this renders beautiful proof of his "authority," if Bhāgavatas, who are hated by the three twice-born classes, are indeed considered to be "exemplary"!

Objection. Aren't the Brahmans, the foremost of the twice-born exemplary?

Reply. You miss the point. The Bhāgavatas are not even in the twice-born classes, let alone Brahmans! We do not hold that the Brahman is a different species, distinguishable from the human species, with defining characteristics that are found to persist in certain bodies while they are absent in others. No, the hair tuft, sacrificial thread, etc., which are enjoined upon Brahmans, etc., cannot make a man a Brahman. Nor do they convey that a man is a Brahman, for we see them inconclusively worn by crooks, Śūdras, and the like. Consequently the sole criterion of whether a man is a Brahman, is traditional nomenclature that is proved right beyond dispute.

Now, common usage does not apply the title of Brahman to a Bhāgavata without hesitation. Different appellations are used: one may be called a Brahman, or, in contrast, one may be called a Bhāgavata.

Objection. I'll grant that. Still, Brahmans may be called "Bhāgavatas," "Sātvatas," or similar names by some kind of metaphorical usage, just as they may be called "hermits"[24] and the like.

Reply. That is not the point.... A Sātvata[25] is, by definition, a member of the lowest class, descended from a tramp Vaiśya and excluded from **[28]** the sacraments of initiation, etc. As Manu[26] says: "From a tramp Vaiśya issues. . a Sātvata." It cannot be disputed that the word "Bhāgavata" denotes a Sātvata. A *smṛti* has it that "the fifth, Sātvata by name, worships the sanctuaries of Viṣṇu by royal decree;[27] he is traditionally known as a Bhāgavata." Similarly there are *smṛtis* to the effect that precisely that way of life which the Bhāgavatas are seen openly to pursue is the profession of the issue of the said tramps. Thus Uśanas:[28] ". . offering worship to a god is the occupation of *ācāryas* and

Sātvatas." Likewise in the *Brahma Purāṇa*: "[The Sātvata] shall worship the sanctuaries of Viṣṇu by royal decree." Elsewhere the same: "It is the occupation of the Sātvatas to keep clean the sanctuary of the god, to clean up the eatables offered to the god, and to guard the idol." And, likewise, to dispel all doubts about what kind of people they are, the statement of Manu:[29] "Whether they reveal or conceal themselves, know them by their deeds."

Besides, their conduct proves that they are non-Brahmans. Occupationally, they offer *pūjā* to a god, undergo a special consecration, consume the eatable offerings, observe a series of sacraments that deviate from the traditional series, which begins with the planting of the seed and ends with the cremation, fail to perform the scriptural rituals, avoid intercourse with Brahmans: these and other practices quite convincingly prove that they are not Brahmans.

The *smṛtis* hold that they are disqualified from performing Brahman duties, because they offer *pūjā* to a god. For example, "those who by heredity idolize a god by way of profession are disqualified from learning [the Veda], sacrificing or having a sacrifice performed." Likewise their own declaration in the *Parama Saṃhitā*:[30] "Whether in emergency or disaster, in terror or in straits, one must certainly never professionally offer *pūjā* to the god of gods." The very fact that they do wear the offered garlands and do eat the offered eatables—practices abhorred by all exemplary people—plainly illustrates that they are not Brahmans.

To continue: we are puzzled by the claim that the behavior of these people—at the very sight of whom all exemplary persons undergo expiatory rites like the *cāndrāyaṇa*[31]—can prove that their system is based on the scriptures. For the *smṛtis* have it that expiation is required when one has set eyes on a "godlinger";[32] and "godlingers" are those who live off a god's treasury and offer *pūjā* for a living. Thus Devala: "One is called a 'godlinger,' when one lives off a god's treasury." Also: "A Brahman who offers *pūjā* to a god for a period of three years is called a 'godlinger' and is condemnable in all his actions." Those, on the other hand, who are found to worship a god by way of hereditary profession are automatially regarded as "godlingers." The *smṛtis* lay down the expiatory rite: "A Brahman while eating should not lay eyes on. . a 'godlinger'; if he does, he must perform the *cāndrāyaṇa*." Atri likewise shows very clearly that they are not Brahmans: ". . 'godlingers'. . and those who are professional [29] Bhāgavatas are sub-Brahmans."[33] And, similarly, the venerable Vyāsa: ". . the 'godlingers' are pariah Brahmans."[34]

Thus, the very fact that Bhāgavata folk—who are apostate from the way of the Veda—accept the Pāñcarātra scriptures is sufficient ground to deny them validity.

There is no reason to distrust Yāmuna's evidence as to the esteem, or lack of it, in which the Bhāgavatas of his time were held by orthodox Brahmans. As is clear from our lengthy quotation, the Bhāgavatas laid claim to being Brahmans; it is also clear that those who made the claim were the priests among the Bhāgavatas. The Smārtas vehemently disputed their claim, because Bhāgavatas/Sātvatas were traditionally (i.e., by *smṛti*) known to be very low class: the issue in fact (according to the usual *Dharmaśāstra* system, by which caste hierarchies are made intelligible by degrees of evolution from mixed *varṇas*) of a Vaiśya Vrātya. And not only does the Bhāgavata stand condemned by his heredity but his lowliness is compounded by his sacerdotal occupation; priest to his idol he lives off his priesthood, and, whatever his social pretensions, he is a common *pūjārī*.

Before we enlarge on the relevance of Yāmuna's *Āgamaprāmāṇya* as an explanation of the archaism of the *Bhāgavata Purāṇa* we should do well to reflect on his own background. He was the second great man in the *Śrīvaiṣṇavasampradāya,* after Nāthamuni, whose grandson he is supposed to have been. At the end of his *Āgamaprāmāṇya,* Yāmuna adds a stanza glorifying the "impeccable scriptures, whose spirit has been increased by the glorious Lord Nāthamuni." These scriptures are not the Vedas of orthodoxy, but rather the Tamil *prabandham* of the hymns of the Vaiṣṇava saints of South India, the Āḷvārs, whose devotional lyrics Nāthamuni had collected and introduced into temple worship. Therefore, to conclude his treatise with such praise must have seemed most appropriate to Yāmuna. For Yāmuna had but continued Nāthamuni's work. As he now claimed validity for a class of texts that had not before been acknowledged by orthodox tradition—and claimed it by analogy to the main sources of orthodox tradition—so Nāthamuni had claimed authority for the *prabandham*. Within a couple of generations the canon of Vaiṣṇavism had been increased immeasurably. And it is of utmost significance to the cultural history of South India that Brahmanistic orthodoxy continued **[30]** to be claimed for this Vaiṣṇavism. We observe here a process of Brahmanization, or, as we shall prefer to call it, Sanskritization.

Both Nāthamuni and Yāmuna were temple priests at the recently founded Raṅganātha temple of Śrīraṅgam. P.N. Srinivasachari[35] remarks that Nāthamuni's effort in incorporating the Tamil scriptures, the "Tamil Veda", into the temple service at Śrīraṅgam introduced an "innovation [that] effected a silent revolution in temple worship, as it raised the status of the *prabandham* to the level of the Veda, and liberalized the meaning of Revelation." It is, however, doubtful whether this "revolution" was all that silent.

It is worth while to recall here that it had been the *bhakti* movement which produced the Āḻvārs and that the momentum of this same movement kept their adulation of iconic representations of the God alive among the common people. The incorporation of the Tamil *prabandham* into the sacred scriptures that served in temple worship had two effects: a *soi-disant* "orthodox" tradition in Vaiṣṇavism was thus enabled to ally itself with popular movements that had a distinct tendency to break away from Brahmanism;[36] and these popular movements themselves were given the discipline and direction that only Sanskritic tradition could impose. In the efforts of the three *ācāryas*, Nāthamuni, Yāmuna, and Rāmānuja, we discern three phases: (1) acceptance of non-Sanskritic religious literature and institutionalization of it in traditional temple worship; (2) acceptance and traditionalization of Pāñcarātra; and (3) Vedānticization of Vaiṣṇavite *bhakti*.

Yāmuna's apologia at once raises the question of how orthodox the Bhāgavatas really were. But we should change our terminology: in view of the kind of objections leveled against them, the "orthodox" were hardly, if at all, concerned with orthodoxy, but with orthopraxis, as the norm for Hinduism generally is better described by orthopraxis than by orthodoxy.

Characteristically, Yāmuna's first argument concerns the Vedic affiliation of the Bhāgavatas who observe Pāñcarātra ritual. They belong, he emphasizes, to the *Ekāyanaśākhā*[37] of the Vājasaneyins, who themselves represent the White *Yajurveda* (69). And "when one sees learned people, who day after day study the *Ekāyanaśākhā* of the Vājasaneyins, wear prominently their sacred threads and upper garments [31] and hair tufts, impart teaching, offer sacrifices, and receive priestly stipends[38] does one not know instantly that they are Brahmans?"(70).

If, moreover, the recollection of Brahmanic *gotras* makes one a genuine Brahman, so "the Bhāgavatas have the tradition: 'We are descendants of Bharadvāja, of Kaśyapa, of Gautama, of Aupagava.'[39] Nor," he hastens to say, "is their recollection of *gotra* descent unfounded or a recent matter: for the same can be argued for all *gotra* traditions. If doubt about descent were admissible, just because error could conceivably have crept in, this would confuse everybody about the authenticity of his Brahmanhood. After all, anyone might fear that he really is a *cāṇḍāla,* if he suspects his mother of having had a lover. And how, my eminent opponent, can you yourself be quite sure that your birth entitles you to Veda study! Therefore, as the Brahmanhood of the Bhāgavatas is entirely proved by their recollection of their respective *gotras,* which has been passed on from generation to generation in uninterrupted transmission and therefore stands unchallenged, there is nothing to differentiate between the Brahmanhood of Bhāgavatas and that of others."

The evidence of Yāmuna is significant, because it suggests a theory to account for the archaism of the *Bhāgavata Purāṇa.* In both cases, neither in time nor in ideology too far apart,[40] we have a conspicuous concern to persuade others, if not oneself, of one's orthodoxy, which is proved to be orthodoxy because it is based on the Veda. Briefly, Yāmuna's point is: we are orthodox on Vedic and Smārta terms, and we can prove it. The Bhāgavata's point is: I am not only orthodox in the Vedic tradition, I even sound like the Veda.

Even though much by the wear and tear of time unavoidably must escape us, neither Yāmuna's work nor the Purāṇa is alone in its Vedicism. It would be worthwhile investigating the suggestion that a similar concern in proving Vedic orthodoxy, reaching back beyond the Smārta or Vedānta traditions, motivated a Madhva, the founder of dualistic Vedānta on Vaiṣṇava religious principles, to compose the *Ṛgbhāṣya,* a commentary on a number of *Ṛgvedic* hymns. He was the first to take the *Ṛgveda* seriously as a source of metaphysical truth in the history of Vedānta. And would a similar concern contribute to an explanation of why in the Vijayanagara Empire a Sāyaṇācārya[41] [32] arose to set himself to the gigantic task of commenting on the entire Vedic corpus?

The *bhakti* movement had rung in a new period in religion as well as in the philosophical formulation of it. No one who reads either the *Bhāgavata Purāṇa*, or the *Āgamaprāmāṇya*, or any one of Rāmānuja's works, can fail to sense the utter difference of spirit that prevails. In order to bring out the contrast, the best example is not Śaṃkara; his concern with the world of process was minimal; and the *bhakta's* world is the world of process. Another Vedāntin, chronologically later than Śaṃkara no doubt, but ideologically far more naive and old-fashioned, impressively demonstrates the social conceit that Smārtas[42] could carry over into their soteriology.

In a most revealing introduction by Bhāskara to his commentary on the *Bhagavad Gītā*,[43] the learned author passes such judgments as:

It is forbidden to impart to the Śūdra, etc., knowledge of unseen things, to instruct him in *dharma* and the like. Besides, when a Śūdra, out of his own foolish desire, bypasses the instruction by Brahmans and either from a written text or from a commentary thereon learns its import and performs the rites, the rites he performs will not be of any benefit to him. On the contrary, the knowledge acquired by one who is forbidden it and who is not initiated only creates distress for him. . Since the higher and the lower classes are not equal, they likewise do not have the same *dharma*. As has been said, "If women and the Śūdras were qualified for release, the caste eminence of the Brahman would serve no purpose.". . The norm of good conduct in the land of the Āryans is conveyed solely by the Brahman's action. . In the line "wisdom, knowledge and orthodoxy are the natural functions of the Brahmans," our text will demonstrate that the Blessed *dharma* is only for Brahmans a way to Release. [How typical, his expression *bhagavān dharmaḥ!*] The Śūdra, etc., cannot be elevated . . nor can iron be made into gold by heating it some more. . Even the Kṣatriya and the Vaiśya do not have the same qualification for release as the Brahman. Therefore, only the Brahman has it. No release is possible for Śūdras, no more than it is for animals. . Since the Śūdra etc., have no release and lack qualification for the three pursuits of *dharma*, *artha*, and *kāma*, which are the goals of man, it follows that they may also not learn the doctrine of the *Bhagavad Gītā*. . Just as a bilious man who, in order to cure himself, takes medicine that is intended for a phlegmatic not only fails to be cured, but suffers even worse from the onslaught of his ailment, so indeed is it in the case of Śūdras, etc.

[33] In Bhāskara we have a spokesman for an old-fashioned Vedānta, in which the desire of knowing Brahman is compatible only with the performance of appropriate Vedic ritual,[44] which excludes all but the Brahman. This attitude was only *partly* reformed by Śaṃkara. Although he relegated all ritual performances to the realm of *vyavahāra*, or the provisional truth of process, he did not alter the spirit of exclusiveness associated with Vedānta. Precisely this uncompromising dichotomy between the realms of supreme truth and relative process encouraged an attitude summed up in the well-known dictum: *vyavahāre Bhāṭṭaḥ, paramārthe Śāṃkaraḥ* "in *vyavahāra*, a follower of Kumārila Bhaṭṭa; in respect to the supreme truth, a follower of Śaṃkara." But to be a legitimate follower of Kumārila,[45] the Mīmāṃsaka had in theory to be twice-born, in practice to be a Brahman.

It would not be difficult to multiply quotations in line with Bhāskara's views. They are important inasmuch as they show, for the age with which we are concerned, the mentality of those who traditionally regarded themselves (and, however reluctantly, were regarded by the others) as the final arbiters of *dharma* and *mokṣa*. Against their spirit of exclusiveness, in society as well as in soteriology, the rise of the *bhakti* movement placed a spirit of catholicity. This catholicity was predetermined by the movement's popular character, which gave the prime role of expression to the vernacular languages.

In spite of the long prehistory of *bhakti* (not in all respects as clear as one could wish), the southern *bhakti* movement was something new—not perhaps per se but for the first time a consistent effort was being made to place it in the Brahmanistic tradition. In the labors of a Nāthamuni, a Yāmuna, a Rāmānuja, we observe a consistent effort to promote the Sanskritization of the *bhakti* religion. The God of the *bhakta* is equated with the supreme principle of the Upaniṣads; the adoring contemplation of God in his heaven by the worshiper is equivalent to *mokṣa*; the acts of worship and veneration are on a par with the rites prescribed by scripture and tradition. Similarly, in the archaistic emphasis of the *Bhāgavata Purāṇa* we find an attempt at Sanskritization of the popular Krishna legend. Krishnaism no longer is merely a popular mythology, with its rather womanly idyl of the little boy who is also a lover, set in the rustic scene of pastures, cows, **[34]** cattle tenders and their wives. Purāṇic rather than epical, let alone Vedic in provenience, it now speaks, or at least tries to speak, in the solemn language of the Vedic seer.

Sanskritization, in the sense in which I want to use it here, is a term for a conception recently evolved by certain cultural anthropologists who are studying the factors that are active in cultural change in contemporary India. M.N. Srinivas[46] was the first to introduce the term into anthropology, and it has since been taken up by others. Its principal disadvantage is, of course, that it is a misnomer. It does not mean what it means to the Indologist—a "rendering in Sanskrit" (e.g., the Sanskritization of the Paiśācī *Bṛhatkathā* in the *Kathāsaritsāgara*), or "adoption of Sanskrit as a literary language" (e.g., the Sanskritization of Mahāyāna Buddhism since Aśvaghoṣa). More precisely the term corresponds to "rendering Sanskritic". This again is a term easily misunderstood if it is derived from Sanskrit as the name of a language. But Srinivas is an Indian; for him Sanskrit is more than the name of a language, it is the summation of a way of life. His use, and that by others, of "Sanskrit" and "Sanskritic" has reference to a rather complex notion of normative self-culture, of which it is more or less consciously felt that the Sanskrit language was its original vehicle. It carries with it associations of a sacral character. One is *saṃskārya* (to be perfected or "sacralized" by appropriate ceremonies), one observes *saṃskāras* (sacramentals)—words derived from the same root *kṛ-* with the prefixed verb *sam*. In such words a meaning of "refining or perfecting one's nature and conduct by ritual means" becomes central. Other characteristic connotations help to widen the comprehension of the concept. "Sanskritic" is that which is the most ancient, therefore the most pure, and therefore hierarchically the most elevated; it thus provides a norm for exclusive personal or group conduct—exclusive for its purity and elevation—that most effectively proves itself in securing correct descent, backward by relating oneself to an ancient lineage or an ancient myth and forward by safeguarding the purity of future offspring. It is in this comprehensive Hindu, if not in fact Brahmanistic, sense that Srinivas seems to use the term; and in this sense the term describes a significant context of cultural notions that should not be reduced too rashly. It is in this sense, too, that the term can legitimately [35] be applied to describe processes that took place in what the non-Indologist would tend to call "Sanskritic" culture,[47] known to us solely from Sanskrit texts.

Sanskritization, then, refers to a process in the Indian civilization in which a person or a group consciously relates himself or itself to an accepted notion of true and ancient ideology and conduct. His criterion for judgment of orthopraxis is likely to be the practice of those in his community whose prestige has continued to hallow their way of life. If they are Brahmans, they are likely also to be normative for orthodoxy, but here a far greater variation of norm is possible. When the person's or group's own ideology significantly diverges from the norm set by those who regard themselves as models, either a conciliation is effected, at least in orthopraxy, or a separation of tradition is accepted. Social scientists tend to find this active confrontation and the consequent change of conduct to be motivated primarily by a desire to raise one's social status. This may well be the case. But it seems to me desirable not to build this limited motivation into the conceptualization of the whole process, since other motivations may be recognized.

Despite the confusion it may create, it is worthwhile to retain the term "Sanskritization." More than other terms employed in varying, though related, contexts of conceptions—e.g., traditionalization, generalization, universalization, Brahmanization, Hinduization—it has special overtones that ought to be heard and recorded. Most audible among them is the one that rings of the past.

Central to Indian thinking through the ages is a concept of knowledge which, though known to Platonism and Gnosticism, is foreign to the modern West. Whereas for us, to put it briefly, knowledge is something to be *discovered*, for the Indian knowledge is to be *recovered*. Although doubtless a great many other factors have contributed to the reputed traditionalism of the Indian civilization, one particular preconception, related to this concept of knowledge concerning the past and its relationship to the present, is probably of central significance: that at its very origin the absolute truth stands revealed; that this truth—which simultaneously is a way of life—has been lost, but not irrecoverably; that somehow it is still available through ancient life lines that stretch back to the original revelation; and that the present can be restored [36] only when this original past has been recovered. Phenomenologically, this belief is no doubt akin to that of an original paradise on earth; but the paradise is not irretrievably lost.

One may find this belief, enacted as an attitude toward life, reflected in many different but coherent ways: metaphysically, in the assumption of the self's original universal consciousness before its implication in transmigration; ritually, in the preservation of a Vedic tradition, "continued" in Purāṇic and Tantric traditions; ethically, in the conservation of *dharma*, which itself was the way of life of the original seers who saw the light; educationally, in the teacher's pledge to transmit in full and intact his knowledge to his pupil; sociologically, in the Brahman's self-identification with the *gotra* of an ancient *Ṛṣi*; societally, in the maintenance, against all historical and contemporary fact, of a sacral prototype in the four-class system; linguistically, in the acceptance of one ancient language; and religiously, in the notion of a progressive revelation.

There is an image here of a supraculture, not to be discovered in an eventual future, but to be recovered from an available past. History, from this point of view, is not a horizontal development from event to event, with its beginnings nebulous and its end not in sight, but a vertical development, a ramification—deterioration no doubt, but with the pure roots still in sight.

Sanskrit is felt to be one of the lifelines, and Sanskritization in its literal sense, the rendering into Sanskrit, is one of the prime methods of restating a tradition in relation to a sacral past. So it was in the *bhakti* movement. Before the rather sudden rise into textual view of the great religions in the epic, *bhakti* was absent from the emerging Sanskritic tradition. The contexts in which it then arose—and the *Bhagavad Gītā*, in this respect overrated on the strength of later traditions, is certainly no exception—clearly show that the kind of religious attitude and devotion to which the term *bhakti* is more and more applied is essentially a popular one, an everyday religion of immediately existential needs, for sufferings to be alleviated, for prayers to be heard, for grace to be the only thing left, for joy to be shared, and for royal worship obediently to be demonstrated. A human dignity, a pride in achievement and in certain hope, is absent from it and the use of Sanskrit is secondary to it.

[37] It is useful to remember that, in the Sanskritic tradition, the use of Sanskrit was always secondary. The first language of anyone always was the vernacular, even if his language of preference was to become Sanskrit. The *śiṣṭa*,[48] the Indian, or rather Sanskritic, literatus, was always bilingual, speaking in a regional vernacular and in Sanskrit. And his bilingualism implied a biculturalism. Just as the bilingual man is the mediator of loans between two languages, the *śiṣṭa* was the mediator of "loans" between his vernacular culture, as small as a village or as wide as a nation, and the Sanskrit culture. On his capacity of absorption depended the free interflow. The Sanskrit culture itself is of course the product of early stages of such an interflow. But by the time the epic was concluded, to put an arbitrary date to it, a definite Sanskrit culture had constituted itself, and the future became the commentary on a basic text. This text has a context, and this context differs from region to region and from date to date. And this context is the way of life that local *śiṣṭas*, rooted in their subculture, hold to be Sanskritic.

I borrow the terms "text" and "context" from a recent article by Milton B. Singer,[49] who uses them to draw a distinction between the interests of "textualists," the philologists among the Indologists, and the interests of the "contextualists," those investigators, mostly drawn from the social sciences, who are primarily interested in the twentieth-century function of the "text" as part of a larger "context" of the social and cultural realities of those who make use of this "text".

These terms and distinctions are equally applicable to the Indian culture itself, which happens to be very textual, in the sense that a fairly limited corpus of texts was considered to be authoritative —to such an extent that thought and practice of later centuries held validity only if and when they could be shown to be in accordance with these texts.

For Bhāskara the "context" to the Vedānta "text"—literally the *Brahmasūtras* and the *Bhagavad Gītā*—is his own traditional Smārta way of life. But for Yāmuna (if we care to consider him already a Vedāntin), and certainly for Rāmānuja,[50] as later on for Madhva, the "context" was the Vaiṣṇava *bhakti* way of life. Insofar as the commentators must justify their own contexts in their text, this text must make appropriate sense. And in the explication of the text we find, if the context [38] is new, continuous Sanskritization of the context. Thus, given the "text" of the Veda, we find that the new context of the Āgamas of Pāñcarātra are Sanskritized as Veda-based, like the *smṛtis*; the Bhāgavatas are Sanskritized as Brahmans; the Viṣṇu of personal devotion, as the Brahman of the Upaniṣads; the acts of the *bhakta*, as Vedic or Smārta rites, and so on.

In this Sanskritization, some violence has to be done to reigning orthodoxy and orthopraxy. It is to be shown that the dominant norms are either not right, not really Sanskritic, or not exclusively right. In orthopraxy, the prestige of these dominant norms is often insuperable: nowhere does Yāmuna suggest that the Smārta *saṃskāras* are superseded by the Tantric ones. In other, less "textual," fields of action, the dominant orthopraxy can more easily be adapted to or accommodated. In matters of orthodoxy there is wider scope. One can go beyond the accepted norm, as Yāmuna goes beyond the *smṛtis* to the authorship of God, who in omniscience is at least equivalent to the Veda or else, as the same author does, show that one's dogma and practice are Vedic by pointing out the Vedic lifelines of the tradition (the *Ekāyanaśākhā* of the Vājasaneyins, the *gotras* that trace Bhāgavata prestige back to the *ṛṣis*). Rāmānuja writes exclusively on the level of orthodoxy (from which he silently omits Pāñcarātra, only acknowledging it in passing—a further Sanskritization), and, by widening the scope of his original texts to encompass the Vaiṣṇava *bhakti* contexts, he proves the correctness of his system. Madhva, as the first of the school founders, reaches all the way back to the *Ṛgveda* for his sources, but significantly also brings in a far greater variety of Purāṇic and Tantric materials.

I should like to suggest that in the archaism of the *Bhāgavata* we have the expression of the same concern. The Krishna legend has to *sound* Vedic because it *was* Vedic. There is a similar reaching back to the most ancient sources—however imperfectly known—to make the old foundation support the new edifice. Here Sanskritization once more takes a linguistic form. Writing in Sanskrit was not enough; to the faithful the supremacy of Krishnaism was hardly in doubt, but the high-sounding language (which often must have been unintelligible) gave appropriate notice of its Vedic orthodoxy.

The above inquiry was undertaken in order to see what precise application the "textual" Indologist can make of concepts that field [39] workers in anthropology are evolving on the basis of contemporary materials. If their concepts help to understand contemporary processes in cultural change, they may help the historian to understand previous processes. Although it is, of course, true that the materials brought together by cultural anthropologists observing present-day facts can have no documentary bearing on ages and countries beyond the time and region in which the evidence was observed, nevertheless their theories concerning cultural and social changes (sometimes, for the Indologist, too hastily hypothesized from the evidence) may have a heuristic value in general for the history of Indian culture. The historian has always taken for granted such processes as Sanskritization and cultural universalization, but the frustrating lack of "contextual" detail, in Singer's sense, often dooms attempts at specific theorizing to futility—at least for the early and classical periods.

There is, however, more hope for the middle period. Then, in greater detail of sculpture, monuments and vernacular literature, the sects arose, or, to put it more cautiously, crossed the threshold of respectability into Sanskrit. Simultaneously, the "Sanskritic" tradition itself became the issue. In this little-studied period, the canons of what is "Sanskritic" became codified from place to place. In the process, the role of the original Sanskrit culture had become negligible. After the *śiṣṭas*, the clerics had taken over.

Their knowledge is secondhand, a prestige-making product of limited erudition and no originality. It is par excellence the age in which the interflow between supraculture and subculture ceases, when the supraculture gets translated, adapted, adulterated, to conform to the subcultural standards of the clerics concerning what is deemed Sanskritic.

Before "textualists" and "contextualists" can effectively work together, greater clarity must be brought to this middle period. Sanskritists will have to modify their beliefs that much that is Sanskritic quietly persists, whereas anthropologists ought to discriminate more clearly between the various higher traditions that too frequently are lumped together as 'Sanskritic," and placed in some kind of contradistinction to littler traditions.

In spite of an increasing sophistication on the part of anthropologists in dealing with textual materials, their traditional disciplinary orientation toward a here-and-now of isolable contemporary communities [40] renders unfeasible their leisurely investigation into the significance of the texts, and the continuous feedback of this significance into the reality of here and now. The Indologist, often too uncompromisingly insisting on the primacy of a Sanskrit education, rarely gives expression to the well-known fact that the further we progress—or retrogress, as the case may be—into middle ages and modernity, the less relevant is the living Sanskrit culture of, say, the Gupta Age. Despite a growing good will on both sides, there are still to be broken down unspoken prejudices that have nothing to gain from companionable assurances of good-fellowship.

Practically, both Indologists and social scientists ought to engage in a concerted endeavor to expose the middle period. It is there that the modern "traditions," whose age is always overrated, find their origin; it is there that the Sanskritic tradition, whose pertinacity is always overrated, finds its conclusion. It would be instructive for the textualist to accompany the anthropologist to the field, however arbitrary the choice of the location may seem to him, in order to gain an understanding of the special conditions under which the material is gathered, and find out what is invisible to him. At the same time it would be most salutary for the Sanskritist to find the contextualist sitting next to him in the quiet of his study and pointing out, with similar confidence, what is inexplicably invisible to *him.*

1. On the textual layers of this text, see my study, *The Maitrāyaṇīya Upaniṣad: A Critical Essay* (The Hague, 1962).

2. Edited by H. Grube (Berlin, 1875).

3. *Mahābhārata* I.3.60 ff. (critical edition). One could also quote such deliberately vedicizing stanzas in classical Sanskrit, e.g., Bhavabhūti, *Mālatīmādhava*, stanza 5 (*kalyāṇānāṃ tvam asi*..), but the concern there is to echo rather than to identify.

4. Yāska's *Nirukta*. See Lakshman Sarup, *The Nighaṇṭu and the Nirukta* (2nd ed.; Benares, 1962).

5. "Der Archaismus in der Sprache des Bhāgaāata-Purāṇa," *Zeitschrift fur Indologie und Iranistik*, VIII (1931), 33-79.

6. *Ibid.*, 36-37. Although permitted by Pāṇini (VII.1.35) and not absent from classical literature, these imperatives regularly bring along Vedic associations, especially in the *Bhāgavata Purāṇa*. I would not exclude them from the archaistic tendency generally displayed.

7. *Ibid.*, pp. 36-37.

8. Truman Michelson, "Additions to Bloomfield's Vedic Concordance", *Journal of the American Oriental Society*, XXIX (1909), 284.

9. *Bhāgavata Purāṇa*, IX.xiv.34 ff. (from *Ṛgveda* X.95) and IX.xvi.29 ff. (from *Aitareya Brāhmaṇa*, VII.17-18), respectively.

10. F.J. Meier, *op. cit.*, p. 39.

11. Thomas Hopkins, "The Social Teaching of the *Bhāgavata Purāṇa*," this volume, pp. 3-22.

12. On the function of *Akṣara* here, see my paper, "Akṣara," *Journal of the American Oriental Society*, LXXIX (1959), 176-187 [no. 13 in this volume].

13. *Bṛhadāraṇyaka Upaniṣad* 3.8.10.

14. The *Bhāgavata Purāṇa* here reads "*trikāṇḍaviṣayāḥ*," which corresponds to "*traiguṇya-viṣayā vedāḥ*" in the *Bhagavad Gītā* (II.45). Note that the *Bhāgavata* tacitly corrects the *Bhagavad Gītā* here by adding "*brahmātma-viṣayāḥ*"!

15. Certainly to be compared with the *Taittirīya Upaniṣad* II.3 for the *prāṇamaya* and *manomaya ātmans*, the latter having *yajus*, *ṛc*, *sāman*, and *atharvāṅgirasaḥ* as its members; in oher words, the *śabdabrahman*, "the Sound Brahman, viz. the Veda" as distinguished from the "higher" Brahman.

16. Cf. *Bhāgavata Purāṇa* XI.5.9-10; discussed by Hopkins, this volume, p. 12.

17. See *Alberuni's India*, edited (in Arabic original) by E. Sachau (London, 187; al-Bīrūnī lists the *Bhagbat Purān* (i.e., *Bhāgavata-purāṇa*) and adds *alias Vāsudeva* (sc. *Purāṇa*), a title that no longer survives. It is noteworthy that al-Bīrūnī quotes the list in which the *Bhāgavata Purāṇa* figures as the alternative of a list in which it does not; this may suggest that the latter list was more authoritative at the time of his writing. The second list including the *Bhāgavata Purāṇa* he quotes on the authority of the *Viṣṇu Purāṇa* (Sachau ed., p. 63, line 10). In fact, the list tallies exactly and in sequence with that in the *Viṣṇu Purāṇa* (III.vi.21).

18. F. Otto Schrader, *The Kashmir Recension of the Bhagavadgītā* (Stuttgart, 1930), p. 7 and note. He remarks: "This passage, then, if authentic throughout, would be the earliest reference so far discovered to the *Bhāgavata Purāṇa*."

Doubt as to its authenticity is admissible: quotations from standard works are of course vulnerable to use by later scribes. One would feel more assured if the *Bhāgavata* quotation had been central to Abhinavagupta's discourse, or if several quotations had been scattered throughout the text—instead of only four and a half *ślokas* appended to another quotation in one locus.

19. See my *Rāmānuja's Vedārthasaṃgraha* (Poona, 1956), pp. 33ff.

20. My annotated translation, based on Rāma Miśra Śāstrī's edition [reprinted from the *Pandit* (Benares,1934-36)] has now been awaiting publication in India for four years.

21. *Āgamaprāmāṇya*, ed. Miśra Śāstrī, pp. 6-10.

22. Viz., those of *smṛti* and *śruti*; the basic assumption is that customs observed by the Vaidikas are thereby proved to be normative.

23. *Śiṣṭa*, the final arbiter of rectitude and correctness.

24. *Parivrājaka.*

25. *Sātvata*, apparently derived from *satvant-* (according to Pāṇini, *gaṇa* on IV.1.86, a people from the South), has occurred as the name of a people since the *Aitareya Brāhmaṇa* VIII.14 and the *Śatapatha Brāhmaṇa* XIII.v.3-21. It has become a name for Krishna and, by further derivation (?), for a Krishnaite. *Pāñcarātra* is known in the epic as *Sātvatamatam* (e.g., *Mahābhārata*, XII.cccxxii.19, crit. ed.). Perhaps because this Krishnaism was associated with classes other than Brahmans (*Mahābhārata* III.clxxxix.9-10 states that Nārāyaṇa was worshiped by *kṣatriyas* and *vaiśyas*), the name may subsequently have become the name of a low caste living off Krishna worship.

26. *Manusmṛti* X.23.

27. I.e., by occupation.

28. I have been unable to identify the quotation in the extant *Auśanasasmṛti* [in *Smṛtīnāṃ Samuccayaḥ* (Ānandāśrama Sanskrit Series, 48, Poona, 1905), p. 46 ff.] On the problem of Uśanas, see P.V. Kane, *History of Dharmaśāstra* (Poona, 1930), Vol. I, pp. 110ff. *Manu* (X.23) likewise lists the *Ācāryas* with the *Sātvatas.*

29. Not in the present vulgate. The closest statement is *Manu* IX.228, but the context is different: *pracchannaṃ vā 'prakāśaṃ vā tān niṣeveta yo naraḥ/ tasya daṇḍavikalpaḥ syād yatheṣṭaṃ nṛpates tathā.*

30. Name of a Pāñcarātra text.

31. A special fast; see *Manu* XI.106 ff.

32. *Devalaka*, a pejorative term, used in *Manu* III.152, where it is said that he (along with a physician, a meat seller, and a market trader) is to be avoided. Kullūka *ad loc.* has Yāmuna's quotation from Devala. *Manu* III.180 has it that a gift to a *devalaka* (for icon worship?) is lost.

33. *Upabrāhmaṇa.*

34. *Brāhmaṇacāṇḍāla*; quoted from *Mahābhārata* XII.77.8 crit. ed.).

35. *The Philosophy of Viśiṣṭādvaita* (Adyar, 1946), p. 511.

36. Eventually, however, a fission did occur in *Viśiṣṭādvaita*, in the Teṅkalai who favored Tamil and the Vaḍakalai who favored Sanskrit. Traditionally, the chief exponent of Tamil was Pillai Locācārya. Is it possible that the sack of Madurai by Alā'-ud-Dīn's General Malik Naib Kafur, in 1310, and subsequently the sack of Śrīraṅgam consolidated the schism?

37. Not one of the recognized *śākhās*. Although it is probable that some

early form of theistic devotion existed in late Vedic times (cf. the *Vaikhānasas*, themselves linked with Viṣṇuism), traditional accounts do not list the Ekāyana school as Vedic. The assumption of the early existence of such a school seems to be based on several mentions of it in the *Chāndogya Upaniṣad* and the *Mahābhārata*.

38. Note the orthopraxy. There is not a word about their dogma.

39. For details, see J. Brough, trans. *The Early Brahmanical System of Gotra and Pravara* (London : Cambridge University Press, 1953).

40. It is interesting to note not only that in the *Bhāgavata Purāṇa* (XI.v.27-31) obviously Pāñcarātra practices are referred to, but also that such practices occurred in the Dvāpara Age, which immediately preceded the present Kali Age. Whereas people in the Dvāpara Age worshiped the spirit as "great king" (*mahārājopalakṣaṇam*) according to Vedas and Tantras and praised the Lord of the world by paying homage to Vāsudeva, Saṃkarṣaṇa, Pradyumna, and Aniruddha (the Pāñcarātra *vyūhas*), the wise men of the Kali Age worship Krishna with offerings mainly consisting of *samkīrtanas*—as though Pāñcarātra as a decisive system of *bhakti* was, for the common people, already a thing of the past.

41. He flourished under Bukka I and Harihara; died in 1387.

42. I use Smārta in the general sense of a Brahman who traditionally practices the rites and observes the customs whose main sources are such *Dharmaśāstras* as *Manusmṛti* and *Yājñavalkyasmṛti*, and who is not "sectarian," in the sense that he has no defining theistic or Tantric affiliation.

43. So far only available in MS; an edition by Mr. Subhadra Jha, accompanied by a translation by the present writer, is due to appear in the Harvard Oriental Series.

44. Technically known as *jñānakarmasamuccaya*; it is definitely prior to Śaṃkara, who refers to another exponent, Bhartṛprapañca. See M. Hiriyanna, "Fragments of Bhartṛprapañca," in *Proceedings and Transactions of the Third Oriental Conference* (Madras, 1924).

45. Kumārila (probably sixth century A.D.) was the exponent of what since has become the principal school of Mīmāṃsā.

46. Notably in *Religion and Society among the Coorgs of South India* (Oxford, 1952), but continued in "A Note on Sanskritization and Westernization," *The Far Eastern Quarterly*, XV, No. 4 (1956), 481-496.

47. The increasing use of the qualification "Sanskritic" by Western anthropologists, who are inclined to equate it with "Sanskrit," arouses the legitimate impatience of the Sanskritist, who knows that much Sanskrit literature would not qualify as "Sanskritic" in this sense.

48. The "exemplary person" in the Smārta opposition to Yāmuna; literally, "the educated man of culture, the literatus."

49. "Text and Context in the Study of Contemporary Hinduism," *Adyar Library Bulletin* (Madras), XXV (1961), 274 ff.

50. See my *Rāmānuja's Vedārthasaṃgraha* (Poona, 1956), pp. 31 ff.

20

A CONTRIBUTION TO THE CRITICAL EDITION OF THE BHAGAVADGĪTĀ

1. *A note on Bhagavadgītā* 1.10.

In the first chapter of the Gītā occurs a stanza which has given the Indian commentators more trouble than modern interpreters have found with it. The stanza is spoken by Duryodhana:

aparyāptaṃ tad asmākaṃ balaṃ bhīṣmābhirakṣitam /
paryāptaṃ tv idam eteṣāṃ balaṃ bhīmābhirakṣitam //

Modern translators take (*a*-)*paryāptam* in the sense of "(un-) abundant, (in-)sufficient,"[1] and differ **[100]** only in whether they take (*a*-)*paryāptam* or *bhī*(*ṣ*)*mābhirakṣitam* as predicate to *balam*. Senart[2] renders it as follows: "Limitée en nombre, c'est en Bhīṣma que notre armée a sauvegarde; leur armée à eux, sous la sauvegarde de Bhīma, est immense." Edgerton[3] modifies the literal sense of this stanza by parenthetical additions, but his version is essentially the same as Senart's: "(Altho) insufficient (in number), this our host is protected by (the wise) Bhīṣma; on the other hand, (while) sufficient, this their host is protected by (the unskilled) Bhīma."

However, Duryodhana's army was not at all insufficient in number; and though Western scholars may tend to disregard the monstrous numbers of 11 *akṣauhiṇīs* on the Kaurava side and 7 on the Pāṇḍava side, Indian commentators were sharply aware of this fact. This accounts for much disagreement. Śrīdhara takes *aparyāptam* to mean *aparimitam*.[4] Nīlakaṇṭha, more fancifully, has *paryāptaṃ parita āptaṃ pariveṣṭitam* "surrounded," and he notes: "The Pāṇḍava army is in fact small, as it is limited to 7 *akṣauhiṇīs*; so it can be surrounded by his own army, which is large, consisting of 11 *akṣauhiṇīs*, but his own army cannot be surrounded by the others, thus is the sense. So theirs is *paryāptam*, *sc.* defeatable by him."[5]

The oldest commentator, Śaṅkara, does not comment on this stanza, a significant fact to which we shall revert. His commentator finds himself forced to construe the śloka as three sentences: on the basis of Ānandagiri's interpretation[6] we should split the śloka thus: *aparyāptaṃ tad* (sc. *eteṣāṃ balam*); *asmākaṃ balaṃ bhīṣmābhirakṣitaṃ paryāptaṃ tv idam; eteṣāṃ balaṃ bhīmābhirakṣitam.* The meaning of *paryāptam* is then *pareṣāṃ paribhave samartham.* As a second choice he gives for *aparyāptam* the usual *aparimitam adhṛṣyam akṣobhyam.* Rāmānuja does not here comment word by word, but has the following summary:[7] "Duryodhana, observing that the army of the Pāṇḍavas is protected by Bhīma and his own by Bhīṣma, and having conveyed to his teacher that the other army is sufficient to defeat himself but his own not sufficient to defeat theirs, was downcast in his heart." This is precisely the opposite meaning of Ānandagiri's. Commenting on Rāmānuja, Vedāntadeśika[8] offers no less than four pages of commentary on this interpretation—proof, if proof were needed, how this seemingly transparent stanza exercised the minds of eminent Indian sanskritists.

Vedāntadeśika introduces an objector, who states precisely what is the difficulty with Rāmānuja's and all modern translations: "Duryodhana does *not* consider his army inadequate, as it is protected by such warriors as Bhīṣma and Droṇa: for the eventual death of these warriors is at this point still conditional." Also, the Pāṇḍavas are outnumbered 11 to 7, and, he remarks, the very same Duryodhana will tomorrow say: *aparyāptaṃ tad asmākaṃ balaṃ pārthābhirakṣitam / paryāptaṃ tv idam eteṣāṃ balaṃ pārthivasattamāḥ*: here, as he correctly explains, we have to construe *asmākaṃ aparyāptam* "not equal to us," and not *asmākaṃ balam* "our army (is insufficient.)": for clearly "our army" is not protected by Pārtha. He goes on to suggest that our text is corrupt: Bhīma and Bhīṣma have been transposed. Restore them to their right places and "then 1. we have proper agreement in the construction 'their army, protected by Bhīma, is not equal to us,' 2. the preposition *tad* has its proper sense as remote-demonstrative, 3. there is no conflict between Duryodhana's meaning here and in the other passage."[9]

Although Vedāntadeśika brushes the argument away on unconvincing grounds, the objector is probably right on all three counts. To take his point about the pronouns first: if *paryāptam* and *aparyāptam, asmākam* and *eteṣām, bhīma* and *bhīṣma* are contrastive terms, so are *tad* and *idam.* **[101]** In these two antithetically parallel sentences we either must ignore the contrast between *tad* and *idam,* or question the contrast between *bhīma* and *bhīṣma.*

The original presence in the stanza of *tad* and *idam* is assured by the metre. Now, a confusion of the meanings of *idam* "this" and *tad* "that" (which all translators in fact assume)[10] goes against the genius of the language; but a confusion of Bhīma and Bhīṣma, neither metrically anchored, is a minimal scribal error.

Was it a scribal error? This brings up the objector's other point. Elsewhere in the epic, cr. ed. 6.47.6, Duryodhana makes a statement which, in the objector's reading makes perfect sense as to context, and also gives the obvious meaning to *tad* and *idam.*[11]

aparyāptaṃ tad asmākaṃ balaṃ bhīṣmābhirakṣitam /
paryāptaṃ tv idam eteṣāṃ balaṃ pārthivasattamāḥ//

With this relevant critical apparatus:

[b]/ K_3D_2 *balaṃ pārthivarakṣitam;* K_5D_3 (marg. *sec. m.* as in text) $G_{1\cdot3}$ *balaṃ pārthābh°.*—Da_1Ds om. 6[cd]. — [c]/ K_5 *aparyāptam idaṃ teṣām;* $D_{3\cdot4}$ *paryāptam idam e°.* — [d]/ K_4B Da_2Dn D_4-$_7$ T_1 G_4 *balaṃ bhīṣmābhirakṣitam;* K_5 *pārthivasattama.*

From the correspondences between 6.47.2-30 and BhG. 1.2-19 it is at once clear that the two text portions resemble each other very closely. Of the 59 half-ślokas of 6.47 no less than 19 correspond wholly or in part with 19 of the 36 half-ślokas of the Gītā. Although this correspondence in principle raises the question whether the Bhagavadgītā—developing within a Bhārata version, and posing and resolving a problem of kinship morality which in effect *presupposes* the actual killings in the family war—borrowed its preamble from the beginning of the Second Day or whether the latter was borrowed from the preamble to the First Day,[12] it is profitless to address ourselves to this question here: for our purposes it suffices to note that the two texts are parallel, that the two stanzas are parallel, and that the parallelism offers a basis for interpretation.

As can be judged from the quoted apparatus, the reading of 47.6*d* is less than firm. The competing reading is, remarkably, *bhīṣmābhirakṣitam,* which of course could not be accepted if the same compound is accepted in 47.6*b.* There is no better reading for *b*. On the other hand we will, like the editor, be hesitant to accept as original a superfluous vocative *pārthivasattamāḥ*, if other MSS. suggest the possibility of a corrupted reading behind the elsewhere repeated *bhīṣmābhirakṣitam*. We also note that some MSS. dropped the second half of the śloka, either by accident, or because it made no sense on account of the repeated *bhīṣmābhirakṣitam*. Still other MSS. preferred in *b*. another reading.

It is significant that the uncertainty of interpretation of 1.10, where the reading seems to be firm, is repeated in the parallel 6.47.6, where the reading is very uncertain. The reading accepted by the Editor makes no sense in the context. Duryodhana is giving his warlords a pep talk; he is supposed to be "heartening, gladdening, encouraging" (*harṣayan*),[13] and a statement that his own forces are inadequate, despite the fact that they are numerically superior and moreover directed by a great warlord, Bhīṣma, makes no sense whatever. Although the reference of Vedāntadeśika's objector has no authoritative standing, his general argument remains valid, and we have excellent evidence to uphold it.

In the critical edition of the Bhagavadgītā the remarkable fact emerges that, while the MSS. of the Śāradā Kashmir tradition are generally the most authoritative for the earliest text of the epic, including the Bhīṣmaparvan where the Gītā is found, nevertheless they are found to be late and secondary as far as the text of the Gītā is concerned.[14] This means that in Kashmir the text of **[102]** the epic was sooner fixed than elsewhere, but the text of the Gītā later. The earliest testimony concerning the Gītā is that of Śaṅkara, and the Gītā text adopted by the Editor is really Śaṅkara's text with but 14 highly insignificant variants.

It should, however, be noted that Śaṅkara does not comment on the *first* 57 *stanzas* of the Gītā, which include the *entire* first chapter. Śaṅkara therefore holds no authority for the present reading. His commentator Ānandagiri cannot be quoted as evidence: the uncommented portion in Śaṅkara's Gītā—if these stanzas were originally included at all—was as wide open to adaptation and normalization as any other uncommented Gītā manuscript.

The Editor has failed to acknowledge what then must be the most ancient testimony for this part of the text; which is curious, since the authority was known to him.[15] It is Bhāskara, the

Vedantin, who gives a scholastic word-by-word explanation of the text missing in Śaṅkara.

Now Bhāskara's text has in our stanza another reading, which is the oldest available and which eliminates all the problems found in our line. He reads:

aparyāptaṃ tad asmākaṃ balaṃ bhīmābhirakṣitam |
paryāptaṃ tv idam eteṣāṃ balaṃ bhīṣmābhirakṣitam ||

And he comments: asmākam *yathānirdiṣṭasaṃhatānāṃ* tat *pāṇḍavabalam* aparyāptam *asamartham abhibhavituṃ yato* bhīmābhirakṣitaṃ *bhīmasenena pradhānabhūtena guptam | sa ca bhīṣmāpekṣayā kiṃcin nyūnatara ity abhiprāyaḥ |* idaṃ tv *asmākaṃ* balam eteṣāṃ *pāṇḍavānāṃ* paryāptam *abhibhāvāya—vināśane samartham ity arthaḥ—yato* bhīṣmābhirakṣitam | *bhīṣmas tv anekaśastrāstrapārago nirjitānekamahāsamara ity arthaḥ ||*

There is no evidence that Bhāskara has tampered with his text; we may note in this connection that one Śāradā MS. bears his reading out.[16] May we prefer his reading? I think we must: 1. it has the authority of the most ancient authority; 2. it removes the inexplicable anomaly of *tad* and *idam*; 3. it does justice to the universally accepted superiority of Bhīṣma to Bhīma as a warlord; 4. it fits the tongue of Duryodhana addressing his columns, who are superior in numbers, on the first day of battle; 5. it explains the recurrence of the same line in what is evidently an exhortatory address by Duryodhana in 6.47.

Finally, it helps to explain the variety of readings in 6.47.6. We can now more clearly see why *pārthivasattamāḥ* is uncertain: compared to the repeated *bhīṣmābhirakṣitam* in 6*d* of many MSS., it represents an early emendation by an easy vocative to meet an anomaly which other MSS. solved by dropping 6*cd* entirely. The reading *bhīṣm°* in 6*b* necessitated taking *aparyāptam* in the artificial sense of "*aparimitam*" (cf. Nīlakaṇṭha *ad loc.*), which other scribes could not understand, so that in 6*b bhīṣmābhirakṣitam* was changed to *pārthivarakṣitam* (possibly under the influence of *pārthivasattamāḥ* in 6*d*), which in turn may have given rise to *pārthābhirakṣitam*, though this may have been an independent emendation of *bhīṣm°*. The original source of all later difficulties was of course a proleptic dittography of *bhīṣmā°* for *bhīmā°* in 6*b*. This original *bhīmā°* is still evidenced for the Gītā by Bhāskara and one Śāradā MS., until in the Gītā "vulgate" transmission too the two compounds were transposed. This may have been influenced by the very general *bhīṣmā°* reading in 6.47.6*b*; or a deliberate change to account for *tasya saṃjanayan harṣam* in 12,[17] or sheer coincidence of repeated dittography. By Rāmānuja's time the reading was definitely established.

On this showing we must conclude that Bhāskara's reading is the correct one, and that the translation of the stanza should read: "That army, guarded by Bhīma, is not equal to us; on the other hand this army, guarded by Bhīṣma, is equal to them."

2. *The Text of Bhagavadgītā Ch.* 1

Since Bhāskara is the oldest authority for those portions of the Gītā which Śaṅkara left uncommented upon, his evidence surely demands more **[103]** consideration than it has received. Belvalkar, the editor of the Bhagavadgītā makes mention of him, but has made no study of what on even superficial enquiry reveals itself to be the earliest testimony to part of his text: "Bhāskara's variants are reported in our Critical Apparatus on the authority of T. R. Chintamani," "who has given some details and extracts."[18] This is an error of method. The relevant portion, principally comprising the first chapter, may be negligible as far as doctrine is concerned, a mere preamble, and therefore usually rushed through or forgotten (as Śaṅkara did); but for the purpose of textual criticism it is of great importance. If it can be shown that a number of Bhāskara's readings are distinctly superior to those of the Vulgate (V), there is at least room for the presumption that variants elsewhere are also significant. Incidentally, it must be pointed out that for this portion we cannot really speak of a "Vulgate" before Rāmānuja. We can have no certainty about the readings Śaṅkara had in that portion of the text which he skipped through.

In judging the quality of Bh.'s readings we have additional support: for we have a good part of Gītā ch. 1 in the parallel text of MBh. 6.47. In effect, 6.47 is our most ancient, though indirect, authority for Gītā ch. 1, whether it preceded the Gītā in time (as is likely) or not. We find that in a number of instances Bh.'s text is closer to 6.47 than V is.

Finally, on the basis of the principle of chronological priority, as adopted by the critical edition in the case of Śaṅkara's text, we may assume the greater correctness of Bh.'s text there where there is little to choose between two variant readings.

* * *

1.1. *sarvakṣatrasamāgame* for *samavetā yuyutsavaḥ*. Bh. has the advantage of greater stylistic effect:-*kṣetre -kṣetre -kṣetra-*.
1.7. *nāyakān* for *nāyakā*. V demands a tortuous construction, but has the advantage of being a *lectio difficilior*. We must assume an omitted (*ye*) *nāyakā*.
1.8. *kṛpaḥ śalyo jayadrathaḥ* for *kṛpaś ca samitiṃjayaḥ*; a *jayadrathaḥ* in this stanza is probably original, though it is hard to make out where it occurred. Nīlakaṇṭha reads a *jayadrathaḥ* in 8*d* for the meaningless *tathaiva ca*.
1.8*d*. *saumadattiś ca vīryavān* for *saumadattis tathaiva ca*. Bh. is no doubt preferable, with the typical strengthening of the last item in a series by means of an adjective; but considering the probability that a *jayadrathaḥ* occurred in the stanza, not Bh. but Nīlakaṇṭha may have preserved the more authentic reading.
1.9*a*. *anye'pi* for *anye ca*.
1.9*d*. Bh. *nānāyuddhaviśāradāḥ* presents an interesting case. V here has *sarve yuddhaviśāradāḥ*. 6.47.4*d* in a parallel stanza has a variety of readings apparently stemming from an original *sarvaśastrāstravedinaḥ*, with reasonable support for *sarve* instead of *sarva*°. If we accept that 1.9 is a calque of 6.47.4 we surmise an original *nānāyudhaviśāradāḥ* behind *nānāyuddha*°, with a variant *sarvāyudha*°. Possibly to avoid repitiousness after 9*c* or by mistake, *nānāyudha*° was changed to *nānāyuddha*°, *sarvā/sarve-yuddha*°.
1.10. For Bh.'s undoubtedly correct reading, cf. supra.
1.11*a*. *tu* for *ca*.
1.14*a*. Bh. appears to read *śvete* for *śvetair*, a likely error.
1.18.*ab*. Bh.'s *pāñcālaś ca maheśvāso draupadeyāś ca pañca ye* is completely parallel to 6.47.18 (where v. l. *pāñcalyaś*) and distinctly superior to V with the stanza-fillers *sarvaśaḥ pṛthivīpate*.
1.19*d*. *vyanunādayat* for V *vyanunādayan*. V here has an obvious *lectio facilior* for the augmentless imperfect; the latter Bh. reading has however been preserved in 6.47.29.
1.21*a*/24*a*. Bh. *ubhayoḥ senayor* for *senayor ubhayor*.
1.23. Bh. omits this stanza, which is in fact a repetition of stanza 1.22.
1.27*ab*. Bh. lists this as a separate half-stanza. Probably this

half-stanza was an additional 26*ef*. The stanza division in V. is anomalous: 27*cd* obviously goes with 28 *ab*, after which *arjuna uvāca,* and 28 *cd* with 29 *ab*. Bh. then reads another supernumerary stanza, 29*cd*-30*a-d*. We may assume the following original division: A. 26-27 *ab*; B. *cd*.-28*ab*; C. 28*cd*-29*ab*; D. 29*cd*-30; this gives the best sense.

1.28. Bh. *sīdamāno 'bravīd idam* for V *viṣīdann idam abravīt*; V looks like an "improvement," meant to bring out not merely that Arjuna sat down, but sat down *despairing*.

[104] 1.28. Bh. *svajanān...yuyutsūn samavasthitān* for *svajanaṃ...yuyutsuṃ samupasthitam.*

1.29. Bh. *sraṃsate gāṇḍīvam* for V. *gāṇḍīvaṃ sraṃsate*. Bh. is stylistically superior, esp. in the correct stanza division: there we have the sequence *romaharṣaś ca jāyate / sraṃsate gāṇḍīvam.*

1.33. Bh. *ta eva naḥ sthitā yoddhuṃ prāṇāṃs tyaktvā sudustyajān* ("they stand arrayed to fight us") for V's facile *ta ime 'vasthitā yuddhe*. Belvalkar's argument for *dhanāni ca* in d fails to convince.

1.43*cd*. *utsadyate jātidharmaḥ kuladharmaś ca śāśvataḥ* for *utsādyante..°dharmāḥ..°dharmāś ca śāśvatāḥ*.

1.47*c*. *utsṛjya* for *visṛjya*.

* * *

It is clear from the above comparison that Bh.'s Gītā readings which for this portion of the text are the oldest available are in a number of instances preferable to those of "V." This being the case, Bh.'s readings elsewhere deserve close attention. As will become clear, Bhāskara, writing within a century of Śaṅkara and knowing Śaṅkara's text, had before him another text which he used. Since his commentary frequently engages in polemics with Śaṅkara, we may presume that the *quality* of Bhāskara's readings were not in question: Bhāskara does not simply have recourse to another text in order to combat Śaṅkara's interpretation; for his contemporaries it could not be an issue which text he used. This should prove that very close to Śaṅkara's date there existed two variant texts that were equally authoritative. Therefore the question of the "critical edition" of the Bhagavadgītā can again be raised legitimately.

3. *Bhāskara and the so-called Kashmir version*

Before we can address ourselves to the question of how far Bhāskara's readings contribute to our knowledge of the "original" text of the Gītā, we have to raise the prior question of his relationship to the Kashmir version. Schrader has the distinction of having brought this version to light.[19] But his argument that this version contains a number of preferable readings has not convinced scholars. Edgerton[20] and after him Belvalkar[21] have argued that on the contrary in the majority of significant cases the Vulgate is superior.

In the critical edition of the Mahābhārata the singular paradox came to light that while for the epic in its entirety the Kashmir recension was on the whole superior to other versions, this is not true for the episode of the Bhagavadgītā. This seemed merely due to the fact that we have a more copious and older apparatus for the Gītā than for the entire epic. On the assumption of the existence of one single Vulgate against which the variations of the Kashmir version could be measured, a Vulgate version moreover which is the oldest known text, Edgerton could come to the belief "that the variant readings of the Kashmirian text are without exception late and secondary, and have no bearing on the determination of the oldest form of the Gītā."[22] With the evidence of Bhāskara this judgement will now have to be revised. Instead of the assumed relation O→V→K, we must now accept the more complicated relation:

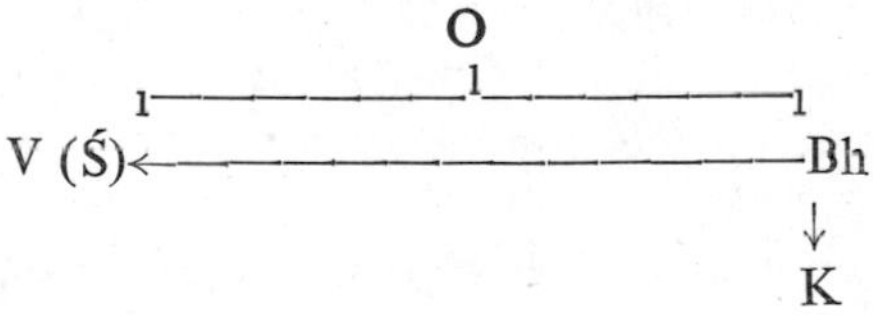

This relation is required by the fact that Bh. had, besides Śaṅkara's Vulgate, another text which must be considered a *Vorlage* of what now survives as the Kashmir version. It is, however, not identical with it, an important fact not recognized by Belvalkar.

Belvalkar's treatment of Bhāskara's evidence has been inconsistent and inadequate. He writes: "the commentator Jayatīrtha, *apud* 6.7b, records the ingenious manner in which the scholiast Bhāskara (whom, it seems, even Abhinavagupta has mentioned with reverence) changed the traditional text of a stanza from the BG. with a view to get from it a more suitable sense. Where such "pious" tampering with the original is actually recorded in the case of one noteworthy Kashmirian writer, one would be justified in viewing with suspicion most of the other "Kashmirian" variants in the Bhagavadgītā portion of the Bhīṣmaparvan, which seems [105] to be obviously due to some partisan's over-zeal at simplification."[23]

This argument is entirely circular as well as aprioristic. It supposes that Jayatīrtha was right, which supposes that his text was right and that Bhāskara did not have a text equally right. On this presupposition, which should have been investigated, to base the sweeping generalization that other Kashmirian writers would have tampered likewise and that therefore Jayatīrtha's text was right in the first place closes a circle unworthy of the learned Editor.

There is in the first place the question of the identity of the Bhāskara mentioned by Jayatīrtha and the Bhaṭṭabhāskara listed by Abhinavagupta. Jayatīrtha reacts to Bhāskara's reading in 6.7, *parātmasu samā matiḥ* for V. *paramātmā samāhitaḥ*, which he calls "fabricated" (*kṛtrimaḥ pāṭhaḥ*). Jayatīrtha knew Bhāskara's commentary, and the Bhāskara whose commentary he knew is the *bhedābhedavādin* author of our present Bhāskara MSS. This Bhāskara has a considerable number of readings in common with the Kashmirian version, which has in 6.7 the very reading to which Jayatīrtha objected. Of the Bhaṭṭabhāskara mentioned by Abhinavagupta we know only that he had commented on the Gītā, but unless we assume that there were two Bhāskaras who commented on the Gītā we may safely conclude that Jayatīrtha's Bhāskara and Abhinavagupta's were the same person. Unfortunately we lack the final evidence of Bhāskara's comment on 6.7, which is lost.

The fact that Bhāskara was known to Abhinavagupta does not make him a Kashmirian. The use of the qualification "Kashmir version" is misleading, if it is taken to mean a version known only in Kashmir and nowhere else. We do not know whether Bhāskara was a Kashmirian. We do know that he had a text different from, sometimes superior to, the Vulgate of Śaṅkara and prior to, and consistently superior to, a version of the Gītā now known from Kashmir sources. We do not even know whether Abhinavagupta himself had firsthand knowledge of Bhāskara's commentary. His statement that "previous commentators, Bhaṭṭabhāskara, etc., have studied the text in great detail" would on the face of it make it likely that he knew Bhāskara's commentary. But this is difficult to rhyme with Schrader's assertion that Abhinavagupta as well as Rāmakaṇṭha "must have been completely ignorant of what is now the Vulgate text of the Bhagavadgītā, for Bh. has a number of "Vulgate" readings. If anything, Schrader's plausible conclusion that "the Vulgate of the Bhagavadgītā was still unknown in Kasmir by the end of the tenth century" would place Bhāskara well out of Kashmir. For the consequence is that Śaṅkara's *bhāṣya* was also not known in Kashmir, and Bhāskara knew that very well indeed.[24]

Bhāskara knew, and thus authenticates, three works of Śaṅkara, the Brahmasūtrabhāṣya, the Gītābhāṣya and the Upadeśasāhasrī. While he is very familiar with the two bhāṣyas, which he attacks time and time again, he is not proven to be familiar with any other work in the Śaṅkara tradition, a fact pointed out by Hacker[25] and very relevant for his date. Elsewhere I have raised the question whether Śaṅkara and Bhāskara were not contemporaries—there is one bit of evidence to suggest that[26] in which case his home would be likely to be South-India. If this evidence be considered insufficient, we can show at least that Bhāskara was known to Vācaspatimiśra, who devotes several pages to the refutation of his philosophy in the Bhāmatī on 1.1.4 and elsewhere. This would place him, if we accept the traditional dates, at least within a century of Śaṅkara.

I believe that the conclusion is unavoidable that in the ninth century there existed a text of the Bhagavadgītā which had equal authority with that used by Śaṅkara; that it existed outside Kashmir; and that it is the prototype of the so-called Kashmir version. The consequence of this conclusion is that the Kashmir version is late and secondary, not to the Vulgate, but to Bhāskara's text. A further consequence is that as far as critical criteria are concerned, the Bhagavadgītā portion is **[106]** not really an exception within the Mahābhārata tradition: that for the Bhagavadgītā too the K tradition carries on a text, however deteriorated here and there, that was authentic and of which we have the earliest record in Bhāskara's *bhāṣya*.

4. *Bhāskara's Gītā text*

The commentary on the Bhagavadgītā by Bhāskara, entitled in full Bhagavadanuśayānusaraṇa, survives incomplete in two partly overlapping manuscripts, one from a London Library, the other now deposited in the Sarasvatī Bhavan Library in Benares.[27] The London manuscript is written in Kashmiri script, the Benares one in devanāgarī.

Between them the manuscripts cover the following portions of the text of the Bhagavadgītā: 1. 1-47; 2.1-57*ab*; 3.3-43; 4.1-42; 5.1-29; 6.1-2 and 26-47; 7.1-30; 8.1-28; 9.1-33.

Up to and including 3.31 the Gītā stanzas are written out in full; thereafter by *pratīka* with the exception of (the supernumerary) 3.40-42; and of 5.29 and 6.29. In most cases the literalness of the commentary permits us to recover the reading of Bhāskara's text even though it is only given *pratīkena.*

I list hereunder the variants of Bhāskara's text, following the numbering of V, omitting the variants of ch. 1 (cf. supra).

2.		
1*c*.	*sīdamānam*	*viṣīdantam*
3*a*.	*mā klaibyaṃ gaccha kaunteya*	*klaibyaṃ mā sma gamaḥ Pārtha*
5*b*.	*śreyaś cartum*	*śreyo bhoktum*
6*d*.	*te naḥ sthitāḥ*	*te 'vasthitāḥ*
10*d*.	*sīdamānam*	*viṣīdantam*
11.	*tvaṃ mānuṣenopahatāntarātmā viṣādamohābhibhavād visaṃjñaḥ / kṛpāgṛhītas samavekṣya bandhūn abhiprapannān mukham antakasya*	(omitted; in Bh. the numbering now differs)
18*c*.	*vināśino*	*anāśino*
26*d*.	*nānuśocitum*	*nainaṃ śocitum*
29*b*.	*tathaivaṃ*	*tathaiva*
30*d*.	*nānuśocitum*	*na tvaṃ śocitum*
40*a*.	*nehātikrama*° but V is quoted as variant	*nehābhikrama*°
41*b*.	*ekaiva*	*ekeha*
43*d*.	*gataṃ* (?)	°*gatiṃ*
50*a*.	*jahātīme*	*jahātīha*
52*ab*.	*yadā tvaṃ mohakalilaṃ* (*buddhyā*?) *vyatitariṣyasi*	*yadā te mohakalilaṃ buddhir vyatitariṣyati*
54*b*.	lacuna in text and commentary	
55-	(here an interpolation has intruded upon the text : *aiśvaryasya sa*(*ma*)*grasya dharmasya* (*ya*)*śasaḥ śriyaḥ / vairāgyasyātha mokṣasya saṇṇāṃ bhaga iti dhvaniḥ* //)	
57*cd*-	3.3 (lacuna)	
3.		
12*a*.	*kāmān*	*bhogān*
18*b*.	*vākṛteneha*	*nākṛteneha*
22*d*.	*vartāmy eva*; but V is quoted as variant	*varta eva*

23*a*.	*yadi tv ahaṃ na varteya*	*yadi hy ahaṃ na varteyaṃ*
23*c*.	*anuvarteran*	*anuvartante*
27*b*.	*bhāgaśaḥ*	*sarvaśaḥ*
31*b*.	*anuvartanti*	*anutiṣṭhanti*
31*d*.	*te vimucyanti*	*mucyante te'pi*
32*b*.	*nānuvartanti*	*nānutiṣṭhanti*
	(from 32 onward stanza is quoted by *pratīka*)	
35*d*.	*paradharmodayād api*	*para-dharmo bhayāvahaḥ*
38.	*bhavaty eṣa kathaṃ śṛṇu* *kathaṃ caiva vivardhate /*	
[107]	*kimātmakaḥ kimācāras* *tan mamācakṣva pṛcchataḥ //* (this stanza is quoted by *pratīka* but not commented upon) *śrībhagavān uvāca—* *eṣa sūkṣmaḥ paraḥ śatrur* *dehinām indriyaiḥ saha /* *sukhatantra ivāsīno* *mohayan pārtha tiṣṭhati //* *sa eva kaluṣaḥ kṣudraś* *chidraprekṣī dhanañjayaḥ/* *rajaḥpravṛtto mohātmā* *mānuṣāṇām upadravaḥ //* *kāmakrodhamayo° mayo ghoras* *stambhaharṣasamudbhavaḥ/* *ahaṃkārābhimānātmā* *dustaraḥ pāpakarmabhiḥ //* *harṣam asya nivartyaiṣa* *śokam asya dadāti ca /* *bhayaṃ cāsya karoty eṣa* *mohayaṃs tu muhur muhuḥ //* (These four stanzas are quoted in full with the concluding comment : *iti sāṃkhyamatānusāriṇaḥ kecanādhīyante / te ca pañca ślokā na vyākhyātāḥ*)	
39*d*.	*vā*	*ca*
4.		
2*a*.	*paramparākhyātam*	*paramparāprāptam*
3*b*.	*sanātanaḥ*	*purātanaḥ*
14*b*.	*mām evaṃ yo* (?)	*iti māṃ yo*
23*c*.	*yajñāyārabhataḥ*	*yajñāyācarataḥ*
5.		
2*b*.	*naiḥśreyasakarāv*	*niḥśreyasakarāv*
5*ab*.	*yad eva sāṃkhyāḥ paśyanti* *yogais tad anugamyate*	*yat sāṃkhyaiḥ prāpyate sthānaṃ* *tad yogair api gamyate*

8*d*.	*bhuñjan...śvasan svapan*	*aśnan...svapan śvasan*
21.	(omitted?)	
23*b*.	*vimocanāt*	*vimokṣaṇāt*
24*a*.	*antaḥsukho*	*yo'ntaḥsukho*
24*c*.	*sa pārtha paramaṃ yogam*	*sa yogī brahmanirvāṇam*
6.		
28*a*.	*evaṃ yuñjan*	*yuñjann evam*
28*c*.	*brahmasaṃśleṣam*	*brahmasaṃsparśam*
28*d*.	*atyanta*° (?)	*atyantam*
29*c*.	*paśyate*	*īkṣate*
37.	(adds, but fails to comment on supernumerary half-stanza) *anekacittovibhrānto mohasyeva vaśaṃ gataḥ*	
38*a*.	*kaścid* (?)	*kaccid*
38*b*.	*śāradābhram* (hypermetrical) (?)	*chinnābhram*
39*a*.	*etaṃ me*	*etan me*
40*d*.	*tāto* (but probably *tāta*)	*tāta*
41*b*.	*jāyate dhīmatāṃ kule*	*kule bhavati dhīmatām*
43*b*.	*pūrvadaihikam*	*paurvadehikam*
43*c*.	*tato yatati bhūyo'pi*	*yatate ca tato bhūyo*
45*b*.	*avaśo 'pi san* (?)	*avaśo 'pi saḥ*
7.		
1*b*.	*mām āśritaḥ / madāśritaḥ*	*madāśrayaḥ*
11*a*.	*balavatāṃ cāham*	*balavatām asmi*
18*b*.	*me mataḥ*	*me matam*
20*b*.	*āśritya*	*āsthāya*
23*c*.	additional half-stanza, uncommented.	
28*a*.	*antaṃ gataṃ*	*antagataṃ*
[108]		
8.		
5*b*.	*tyaktvā* (?)	*muktvā*
8*b*.	°*vṛttinā*	°*gāminā*
12*d*.	°*dhāraṇam*	°*dhāraṇām*
20*b*.	*'yaṃ vyakto 'vyaktāt*, or *'nyo 'vyakto 'vyaktāt*	*'nyo 'vyakto vyaktāt*

5. *The two texts compared*

As will be clear from the above list of variants, differences between Bh. and V are matters of detail; Edgerton's remark about the K version, that "differences are relatively very slight and rarely affect the essential meaning of even single stanzas, never of the work as a whole,"[28] applies fully to Bhāskara's text as well. Its interest lies principally in the help it gives to clarify the crucial relationship between K and V.

In a number of cases Bh. seems to me to be superior to V. 2.1*c* Bh. *sīdamānam* was more likely to be changed to the more emphatic *viṣīdantam* than vice-versa; cf. 1.28.

3*a*. Bh. *mā* with imperative not countenanced by Pāṇini; which might possibly account for the Pāṇinean *mā gamaḥ* of V?

5*b*. V *śreyo bhoktum* may be a *lectio facilior* for Bh. *śreyaś cartum*.

6*d*. Bh. *te naḥ sthitāḥ pramukhe*, cf. 1.33; V *te 'vasthitaḥ* is more easily explained out of *te naḥ sthitāḥ* than vice-versa; V continues to presuppose a *naḥ* or *asmākam* (Edgerton: "they are arrayed in front of us").

3.22*d* Bh. prefers the less regular active *vartāmy eva* to *varta eva* which he also knows. Similar cases: 31*b*. *annuvartanti*; ib. *d vimucyanti*; 32*b*. *anuvartanti*; 43*c*. *yatati* these irregularities are normalized in V.

35*d*. Although one hesitates to change this famous stanza, Bh. sequence "death in one's own duty is more salutary than prosperity through the duty proper to someone else" makes better sense of *śreyaḥ*; runs nicely parallel to ab. *śreyān svadharmo*.. *paradharmāt*; and does away with the lame ending *paradharmo bhayāvahaḥ*. The close resemblance of *paradharmodayād* api to *paradharmo*bhay*ā*vahaḥ renders it likely that a corruption of Bh. underlies the variant of V.

39*d*. Bh. *vā* has to be taken in the obsolescent sense of *iva*, and thus makes better sense than V *ca*, which might quite well be a "correction" of a misunderstood *vā* "or." Bh. translates "knowledge is obfuscated by this perennial foe, in the form of Desire, which is like an insatiable fire" instead of V (Edgerton) "by this constant foe in the form of Desire and an insatiable fire."

4.23*c*. *ārabh* with *karman* "undertaking, initiating acts" seems slightly preferable as *lectio diff*. to V *ācar* "performing acts."

5.2*b*. *naiḥśreyasa*, less common than V *niḥśreyasa*.

5.5*ab*. V appears to be a reinterpretation of Bh.: "that which the followers of the reason-method (Edgerton) see is followed by the application of yoga discipline." This would suggest that "Sāṃkhya" presents a view, which is thereupon acted upon through yoga; the two are therefore complementary and thus "one" (*ekam*). V suggests that both s. and y. as such, independently of each other, lead to the same goal (*sthānam*), and are therefore identical from the point of view of their result. V commits us to taking *yogaiḥ* in the sense of *yogibhiḥ*, for which I cannot find other attestations except 12.289.2-3 and 298.8.

5.24*a*. V *yo'ntaḥsukho* looks like a facilitation of *antaḥsukho... yaḥ*, but it is a border case.

24*c*. It is easier to explain V *sa yogī brahmanirvāṇam* as a re-interpretation of V. *paramaṃ yogam,* inspired by the *labhante brahmanirvāṇam* of 25*a*, than to treat *paramaṃ yogam* as a gloss of *brahmanirvāṇam*. The vocative *Pārtha* where V has *yogī* need not make us suspicious; just in this didactic situation where great emphasis is required the alliterative vocative makes fine sense.

6.43*c*. Bh. *tato yatati bhūyo 'pi,* normalized in V *yatate ca tato bhūyo*.

6. *Conclusion*

I have refrained from entering into too great detail in comparing V and Bh.—apart from the first chapter where this detail was required by Bhāskara's seniority—, because I see little profit in arguing for one reading over another in the numerous cases where there is little to choose. We shall never recover an "original" Bhagavadgītā [**109**] on the basis of the available textual evidence, including Bhāskara's.

The comparison of Bhāskara's variants with Śaṅkara's *textus receptus* is, however, enlightening in so far as it shows how relatively minor the variations still were in a fairly late period, at least five centuries after the final redaction of the text. Clearly, the text of the Cītā was stabilized quite early and apparently sooner than that of the large mass of the great epic. This stands to reason. The very fact that Śaṅkara felt impelled to comment on the Gītā, a text far from congenial to his central doctrines, should sufficiently show in how high an esteem the Gītā was held as a quasi-philosophical, moralistic and religious discourse. Such an esteem supposes separate commentatorial—and therefore editorial— treatment. Already Śaṅkara refers to conflicting interpretations of evident predecessors (2.11, 21; 3.1; 4.18, 24; 18.6) and such references presuppose a commentatorial tradition antedating Śaṅkara by at least several centuries. Thus Śaṅkara himself must have found an already firmly established text, close to a Vulgate, so well known that he did not feel the need to comment on the beginning portions. If Bhāskara, who quite obviously knew Śaṅkara's text, thought nothing of using variant readings, this demonstrates that this was mostly a matter of piety of traditional affiliation with one school of commentators rather than another and that the Gītā interpretation was no longer a matter of textual criticism: the variants were compatible and hermeneutically irrelevant. Therefore I strongly doubt if the remaining portions of his bhāṣya, if they ever come to light, would change the picture offered by what is extant. The significance of Bhāskara's text thus is that it proves the existence of a generally accepted Gītā text well before both him and Śaṅkara.

The variations between Bhāskara's text and the "Kashmirian" manuscripts seem to me to indicate that in Kashmir the Bhagavadgītā was not so stabilized; in other words, that a firmly established separate existence of the text, in the form of one or more authoritative commentaries, was unable to check the natural deterioration of the readings until far later. This would well agree with the relatively late date when distant Kashmir begins to participate in "Indian" philosophy.

But in spite of the deterioration, natural under the circumstances, changes took place on the basis of a sound text which we find earlier represented in the transmission out of which Bhāskara wrote. The "Kashmirian" variations, when compared with Bhāskara's text which is so far older than our oldest mss. and must itself rest on a yet older commentatorial transmission, illustrate by their comparative insignificance the excellence of the preservation of the Mahābhārata; and even though we are unable to recover the authentic original of the redacted epic, we are once more assured that the Kashmir transmission brings us closest.

NOTES

1. cf. PW I, 651 *paryāpta* "erfüllt, zum Abschluss gebracht, das volle Maass habend, ein hohes Maass erreichend, geräumig, voll, hinreichend, genügend."
2. Emile Senart, *La Bhagavad-gītā* (Paris, 1944²), p. 1.
3. Franklin Edgerton, *Bhagavad Gītā* (Cambridge, Mass., 1946), I, p. 5; cf. also his note p. 180.
4. Śrīdhara, *Śrīmad-Bhagavadgītā* (ed. K.S. Agāśe), Poona (*ĀSS*) 1901.
5. *Śrīman Mahābhāratam* vol. III, with *Bhārata-bhāvadīpa* by Nīlakaṇṭha (Poona, 1931), part VI *Bhīṣmaparvan*, p. 43.

6. *Śrīmadbhagavadgītā Ānandagiri-kṛtaṭīkāsaṃvalita-Śāṅkara-bhāṣya-samavetā*, ed. Kāśīnāth/Āpṭe, ĀSS 34 (Bombay, 1936), p. 11-12.

7. *Śrīmadbhagavadgītā*, *Vedāntācārya-Śrī-Veṅkaṭanāthakṛta-Tātparyacandrikākhyaṭīkāsaṃvalita-Śrīmad-Rāmānujācārya-viracitabhāṣyasahitā*, ed. M.R. Śankara and V.G. Āpṭe, ĀSS 92 (Bombay, 1923), p. 34-35.

8. *o.c.*, p. 29 ff.

9. *o.c.*, p. 30 : *tatra bhīṣmabhīmaśabdayor viparyāsāt pāṭhabhedaḥ | tadā ca bhīṣmābhirakṣitaṃ tad balam asmākam aparyāptam ity anvaye sāmānādhikaraṇyaṃ tad iti viprakṛṣṭanirdeśasvārasyaṃ duryodhanābhiprāyāvirodhaś ca sidhyati*. The same objector also puts forward Ānandagiri's interpretation : *vākyabhede tv evaṃ yojanā*, etc. (*ib.*).

10. *so 'yaṃ ghaṇṭāpathāt pātaccarakuṭīrapraveśaḥ* "this is like a robber entering a hovel by way of the belfry," that is to say, creating and solving a problem that does not exist, *ib.* 30.

11. Edgerton's "this our host" for *tad asmākaṃ balam*, and "this their host" for *idam eteṣāṃ balam*, actually translates as though *tad* and *idam* were transposed. I doubt strongly whether English *this their host* could be rendered with Skt. "*idam.*"

12. S.K. Belvalkar, *Mahābhārata*, cr. ed., *The Bhīṣmaparvan* (Poona, 1947), p. 788 notes on 6.47 "this chapter..may well belong to the pre-Gītā stage in the evolution of the epic."

13. consequently the men of Dhṛtarāṣṭra "rejoice excitedly" : 6.47.21-22.

14. I refer to the discussion of Belvalkar, *o.c.*, Intr. civ ff. on the evidence for the Bhīṣmapravan as a whole compared with *ib.* lxxviii ff. for that of the BhG.

15. *o.c.*, Intr. lxxvii.

16. MS *siglum* $Ś_3$.

17. apparently understood as *tasya*, sc. *Duryodhanasya*, which presumes that D. was less than happy before. Bh. comments : *tasya prakrāntasya balasya Duryodhanasya vā*, which at least offers a reasonable alternative : it is quite intelligible that after Duryodhana had ordered his troops to defend their mainstay Bhīṣma the latter wishes to inspire confidence by blowing his horn. It is likely that the BhG. has here condensed the corresponding portion of 6.47 which in 21-22 reads: *tatas te tāvakāḥ sarve hṛṣṭā yuddhāya Bhārata | dadhmuḥ śaṅkhān mudā yuktāḥ siṃhanādāṃś ca nādayan || teṣāṃ śrutvā tu hṛṣṭānāṃ kuruvṛddhaḥ pitāmāḥ | siṃhanādaṃ vinadyoccaiḥ śaṅkhaṃ dadhmau pratāpavān.*

18. *o.c.*, Intr. lxxvii.

19. F. Otto Schrader, *The Kashmir Reccension of the Bhagavadgītā* (Stuttgart, 1930).

20. Review of Schrader's *o.c.* in *JAOS* 52 (1932), p. 68 ff.

21. "The so-called Kashmir Recension of the Bhagavadgītā" *NIA* II,4 (1939-40), p. 211-251.

22. *The Bhagavad Gītā*, Intr. xiii.

23. *Bhīṣmaparvan*, Intr. lxxxii f.

24. I do not believe that we should take references to predecessors mentioned in passing too seriously: Bhāskara may have been known traditionally as an important commentator and Abhinavagupta's reference might well be a courtesy to an author he had not read or whose text he had not available.

25. Paul Hacker, *Vivarta* (Ak. Wiss. u. Lit., Mainz., Abh. G. u. S.-w.Kl. 1953, 5; Wiesbaden 1953).

26. See my "Relative dates of Śaṅkara and Bhāskara," *Adyar Bulletin*, 1962 [no. 15 in this volume]; B.N. Krishnamurti Sarma in "Bhāskara—a Forgotten Commentator on the Gītā," *IHQ* IX (1933), p. 663 f., also suggests that Ś and Bh. were contemporaries, but I find his belief that Bh. is attacked by Ś. in his Gītābhāṣya and that Bh. rejoined in some additions to his own bhāṣya hard to follow.

27. The London MS. was discovered by Dr. V. Raghavan while searching for his monumental *Catalogus Catalogorum*; a preliminary edition of both MSS is under preparation by Dr. Subhadra Jha.

21

THE SPECULATIONS ON THE NAME "SATYAM" IN THE UPANIṢADS

Several years ago, when restudying the old crux *vācārambhaṇam* of the sixth chapter of the Chāndogya Upaniṣad,[1] it became apparent to me that the phrase *nāmadheyam..iti satyam,* which forms part of the double formula *vācārambhaṇaṃ vikāro nāmadheyam..iti satyam*, could, if so analysed, meaningfully be fitted in a series of speculations concerning the Name "Satyam". Whatever the ultimate significance of the phrase *vācārambhaṇaṃ vikāraḥ* the remaining phrase *nāmadheyam..iti satyam* had a comparatively rich, if varied, background in Upaniṣadic speculation. For the purposes of the earlier inquiry the Satyam speculations were only briefly dealt with.[2] We may now return to them with greater detail.

What strikes us at once is that in the "Satyam" speculations the Upaniṣadic thinkers are not primarily concerned with *satyam* as a word with an accepted lexical meaning. Rather than elaborating on a meaning of "agreed-upon truth, the truth as spoken or observed",[3] they depart from the sounds as such and find in its syllables a wealth of hidden elements that only indirectly seem to be related to the meaning of *satya*. In dealing with the significance of "Satyam" we are not in the first place concerned with the upaniṣadic meaning of the lemma *satya*, but with the speculative content attributed to the word-symbol "Satyam".

This symbolic content of "Satyam" is clearly illustrated by BĀUp. 2.3.1: *dve vāva brahmaṇo rūpe mūrtaṃ caivāmūrtaṃ ca / martyaṃ cāmṛtaṃ ca/sthitaṃ ca yac ca/sac ca tyac ca.* Here Brahman has two modes (*rūpa*), *sat* and *tyad,* which together constitute Brahman as "Satyam." That the sequel in BĀUp. 2.3.6 seeks to transcend this "Satyam" with a "Satyasya Satyam" is for the time being irrelevant.

The text of 2.3.1 states that in Brahman-Satyam are summed up a higher "disembodied, immortal and moving"[4] component as well as a lower "embodied, mortal and inert" component. The latter is resumed as "Sat", the former as "Tyam." The use of "Sat" in this meaning of, or reference to, the existing [55] world of embodied and mortal beings must derive from the ancient speculations about the *sat* "this which is here and now" which evolved from the *asat.*[5]

The primacy of the *asat* out of which *sat* arose, did not continue unchallenged; and if not already in the Nāsadīyasūkta,[6] it was most explicitly challenged and rejected in ChUp. 6.2.2.: *kutas tu khalu somyaivaṃ syād iti hovāca/katham asataḥ saj jāyeta/ sat tv eva somyedam agra āsīd ekam evādvitīyam*: "But how could it really be like this? How could the existing spring from the non-existing? On the contrary, it was the existing which was here at the beginning, alone and without a second."

If we are right in connecting the "Sat" analysed from "Satyam" with the *sat* that occurs in more ancient creation accounts, we shall expect to find a similar re-evaluation of "Sat" in other "Satyam" speculations. And such a re-evaluation we find indeed. ChUp. 8.3.4.f. reads: *tasya ha vā etasya brahmaṇo nāma "Satyam" iti / tāni ha vā etāni trīṇy akṣarāṇi sat-ti-yam iti / tat yat "sat" tad amṛtam / atha yat "ti" tan martyam / atha yad "yaṃ" tenobhe yacchati / yad anenobhe yacchati tasmād "yam"*. In this analysis "Sat" has taken over the content of "Tyad" in BĀUp. 2.3.1; the element "tyam" is replaced by a new analysis of "ti" and "yam". The word-symbol has remained the same, but the interpretation has changed considerably: an unreal "ti", a quite mortal *svara-bhakti,* has been discovered in it, whereas an element "yam", associated with the root *yam,* is invoked to establish the connectedness of the immortal and the mortal: Brahman, whose name is "Satyam", still encompasses both.

The Taittirīya Upaniṣad still departing from the analysis of "Sat" and "Tyad", does not hesitate to equate "Tyad" with the untrue and "Sat" with the true: *sac ca tyac cābhavat..satyaṃ cānṛtaṃ ca*; but still the universe which the creator has become comprises both: "*satyam*" *abhavad yad idaṃ kiṃ ca / tat "satyam" ācakṣate.* In this context we should not try to render "*satyam*" as a word with the meaning "real, true", but as a word-symbol summing up the entire universe, created and uncreated, a proper name of the creator. This passage thus retains the inclusiveness of "Satyam", but with the roles of the components neatly reversed.

The word-symbol "Satyam" which is considered a name (*nāman, nāmadheya*) or esoteric teaching (*upaniṣad*)[7] of the Brahman refers to the supreme in his two modes, created and uncreated. It occurs in several passages where it has not been noticed, and its recognition helps our understanding. An interesting case is BĀUp. 5.4: *tad vai tad / etad eva tad āsa satyam eva*: "It was both *that* and *this,* namely "Satyam.' " The text continues: *yo haitan mahad yakṣam prathamajaṃ veda satyaṃ brahmeti jayatīmāṃl lokān / jita in nv asāv asad ya evam etan mahad yakṣaṃ prathamajaṃ veda satyaṃ brahmeti,* which I should prefer to translate as follows: "he who knows this great Spirit which is the first-born, with "Brahman is 'Satyam' ", conquers these worlds. Would he indeed be conquered who knows this great first-born Spirit with "Brahman is [56] 'Satyam' ?" No other translation makes good sense. The unaccented *asat* must be a surviving subjunctive of *as,* auxiliary to *jita,* while the inversion of *jita,* supported by *in nu,* makes it almost certain that the sentence is interrogative. Hence Böhtlingk[8]: Könnte wohl der besiegt worden, der.." But I cannot follow Böhtlingk when he renders *yo haivam* (*ya evam*) *etan mahad yakṣaṃ prathamajaṃ veda satyaṃ brahmeti* with "der in diesem grossen, übernatürlichen Wesen, in der erstgebornen Wahrheit, das Brahman erkennt" : here in connecting *prathamajam* with *satyam* he leapfrogs the verb *veda,* which we would hardly expect just there. Deussen's solution[9] is no better : "welcher also jenes Wunderding als Erstgebornes weiss, und dass das Brahman das Reale ist." Still another solution in Senart[10]: "celui qui connaît le grand génie premier-né, qui sait que *brahman* et le réel;" he notes : "traduction d'un sens tres douteux. A revoir." Instead I suggest to regard the clause *satyaṃ brahmeti* as precisely the content of the esoteric knowledge by which one "knows" the *mahad yakṣaṃ prathamajam.* As I have argued elsewhere, we should understand this "large first-born Spirit" within the general context of the speculations on the *mahān ātmā* in the Upaniṣads. This "Large Ātman"[11] is the supreme who creates himself in the creation of the world and hence is capable of being summed up in the compositum "Satyam" which is both *tad* and *etad.*

This explanation finds further support in the surrounding sections of the chapter. This section is preceded by two which speculate on *da-da-da* (5.2) and *hṛ-da-ya* (5.3) and followed by one concerning "Satyam" as *sa-ti-yam*. The very occurrence of our passage in this environment encourages us to recognize here the same sort of speculation as we have noticed before, a speculation which refers to a dual Brahman which is both "That" and "This" (*tad, etad*), namely "Satyam."[12]

Harder to analyse is BĀUp. 5.5.1-2. Here again "Satyam" occurs in a creation account: *āpa evedam agra āsuḥ / tā āpa Satyam asṛjanta / Satyaṃ Brahma Prajāpatim / Prajāpatir devān* : "the Waters were here at first. The Waters created Satyam, Satyam Brahman created Prajāpati, Prajāpati the gods." Is the occurrence of Brahman so singular here? Senart prefers to translate "les eaux produisirent le réel, le réel *brahman,* brahman Prajāpati", but this means emending the text.[13] It seems more natural to assume that, after the previous passage stating the equivalence of Brahman and "Satyam," this Brahman is still understood as "Satyam," the one that bridges the uncreated and created, after which the (self-) created creator Prajāpati occurs.

That here, too, the symbolic "Satyam" predominates, the creator viewed as both "this" and "that," the lower and the higher, out of whom a further stage, that of Prajāpati, can be separated, may be presumed from the sequel which once more exploits "Satyam." As the text continues : "the gods knew (*upāsate*) [57] 'Satyam.' This is trisyllabic: *sa-ti-yam*. .The first and last syallbles are 'true' (*satyam*), with in the middle the 'untrue' (*anṛtam*). The untrue, being on both sides encompassed by *sat-yam* becomes "*Satyam.*" We again meet here with the notion that "Satyam" contains the 'unreal, untrue', while at the same time the meaning of *satya* "true" is invoked.

"Satyam" here is to all intents and purposes a proper name, a *nāmadheya*. This appears from *ib.* 2 : *tad yat tat Satyam asau sa ādityaḥ*. This interesting passage (like already 5.5.1) shows that "Satyam" is no longer the sum total, there is something beyond it. "That person who is in that (solar) disk and this person who is in this right eye (note the careful "this" and "that"), those two are based one upon the other. That one is based on this through the (sun's) rays, this one is based on that one through the prāṇas."

We now find a person within "Satyam," ensouling it as it were, and transcending, the "Satyam" just identified with the Sun.

And just as the Sun may be equated with a now humbler "Satyam," so the Sun's homologon, the Eye, may be equated with it. In one of those discussions at Janaka's where Yājñavalkya shines so confidently, the king quotes Barku Varṣṇa as saying that Brahman is the eye.[14] Yājñavalkya replies : "Varṣṇa was talking as anyone with a mother and a father and a teacher might talk. For what of a man without eyesight ? But did he tell you its abode, its base?" "No, he did not." "Then it is incomplete, great king!" "You tell us then, Yājñavalkya." "The abode is the eye, the base is *ākāśa*. One should know it as Satyam." "What makes it Satyam?" "The eye, great king," he said.[15] "To one who sees through the eye they say 'Did you see?' and he says : 'I did see' : that is Satyam." In a similar vein with again the conflation of "Satyam" with *satya* "truth," *ib.* 5.14.4: "that fourth *pāda* of the gāyatrī is based on "Satyam." The "Satyam" is the eye, for the eye is indeed true. Therefore, when two come squabbling, the one saying, "I saw it," and the other "I heard it," we will credit the first one."

This equation of sun/eye with "Satyam" is also indicated in the sequel of BĀUp. 2.3.1 with which we began our exposition. A further classificatory division has here, however, been introduced between sun/eye and "Satyam." In 2.3.2 it is said that the Sun is the inner essence of "Sat," the lower, and the solar person is the inner essence of "Tyad." In a typical fashion the dual classification of Sun/Satyam on the one hand and the Person on the other is distributed over the dual classification Sat-Tyam, but since Sat and Tyam had already been accounted for, a deeper level is distinguished, that of a Sat essence and Tyad essence. But, meanwhile, we have progressed farther from a Sun = Satyam equivalence. Also the homology of Sun—Solar Person = Eye—Person-in-the-Eye has become more of a problem and has to be made explicit : *ity adhidevatam* // 4 // *athādhyātmam.* From the point of view of the human person (*adhyātmam*) the eye is the Sat essence, the Person in the right eye the Tyad essence. The reason why they are called "essences" (*rasa*), instead of Sat and Tyad respectively, seems to be that another principle *vāyu/prāṇa* has preempted the place of "Satyam :" *prāṇā vai satyam* (2.3.6), although this does not follow at all from 2 and 3. But ultimately this is [58] irrelevant, for obviously the question no longer is : what is "Satyam," but: what is *beyond* "Satyam," what in fact is the *satyam* of Satyam. Hence the new doctrine: *atha nāma-dheyaṃ satyasya satyam iti / prāṇā vai satyam / teṣām eṣa* (*sc. puruṣaḥ*) *satyam*: "Now then the Name: "Satyasya Satyam:" for while the *prāṇas* are Satyam, he is the Satyam to them." This new doctrine stands by no means alone: likewise 2.1.20 *tasyopaniṣat satyasya satyam iti,* etc..[16]

We may fairly say that now the old "Satyam", summing up the universe both on its unmanifest and its manifest levels, has been superseded. How completely it has been superseded is shown by 1.6.3, which simultaneously states the more advanced triad of *nāman, rūpa* and *karman : tad etat trayaṃ sad ayam ātmā/ ātmā ekaḥ sann etat trayam/tad etad amṛtaṃ satyena channam/ prāṇo vā amṛtaṃ nāmarūpe satyam / tābhyām ayaṃ prāṇaś channaḥ* : "this which is three is this ātman; the ātman which is one is this triad. That which is immortal is concealed by the Satyam. That which is immortal is the Prāṇa; the Satyam is name-and-form. By these two is concealed this Prāṇa." The word *ātman* here apparently refers to the embodied, created person, while Prāṇa is the higher "soul". The Sat-Tyam complex has now become the lower, entirely discrete world, opposing itself to the higher and immortal. Henceforth the manifest and unmanifest must be summed up in *sac cāsac ca tatparam.*[17]

Limiting ourselves to the evidence of the BĀUp., ChUp. and TaittUp. we are able to distinguish thus far the following stages of development in the speculations concerning the "Name Satyam :"

(1) A vestigial stage, in which "Satyam" as a name for a supreme being like Brahman sums up both a higher component identified with Tyad/Tyam, and a lower component Sat. This Sat corresponds to the *sat* which in earlier Vedic and Upaniṣadic texts was used to describe the manifest created world which originated from a higher principle called *asat* or "non-*sat*, not-yet *sat*;" this *asat* is reflected in the element *tya* of the binomium *sat-tya.* But already at this stage the non-manifest is not the uncreated; it is concretely identified with such un-substantial (*amūrta*), volatile (*yat*) and undying (*amṛta*) entities like *prāṇa/ vāyu/antarikṣa.* These are entities of the second level in the typical triadic universe. In the contexts where these vestiges are preserved there is already assumed a level higher than "Satyam", in the first place of Sat essence and Tyad essence; in the second place,

in part overlapping of Satyasya Satyam. Still, the ancient functions of *sat* "this which is here and now" and non-*sat* persist.

[59] (2) A development in which the element Sat is reinterpreted as the truly original and higher one, under the influence of the Sat-only doctrine most explicitly stated by ChUp. 6.2. It takes various forms: 1. a complete reversal of the significance of Sat and Tyad, where Sat is the "true" (*satya*), Tyad the "untrue" (*anṛtam*); 2. Sat as the "true", while *-tyam* is reinterpreted as *ti-yam,* where the element Ti, the "Unreal", *svarabhakti* syllable represents the untrue and an element Yam is further analysed and interpreted. This is an advance of the vestigial Satyam (1), but it retains the dyadic value of Satyam.

(3) A devaluation of the Satyam dyad, which continues the Sat-tyam interpretation of (1) where the "higher and unmanifest" was already identified with second-level entities like *prāṇa/vāyu/antarikṣa* with extensions toward sun/eye. More and more the dyad refers to the created creation, instead of both to the created and uncreated. It demands a higher principle transcending it.

(4) The consequent formulation of a principle transcending this "Satyam", described by the cumulative term Satyasya Satyam. This principle may be the "person in the sun/eye", or the "soul" in a still more microcosmified opposition to *nāmarūpa* and *karman.* The name Satyam as a word symbol now has lost its real significance. It no longer sums up the sum-total, only the manifest creation to which a principle from without opposes itself. This opposition is not merely a restatement of the Sat-Tyad contrast of stage (1), where fundamentally complementary phases were subsumed under the same word symbol. Now it is the transcendence of the supreme principle which prevails, a transcendence so absolute that an apparent dichotomy has taken place which can no more be stated in one unifying symbol.

In Uddālaka's account in ChUp. 6, which so far we have deliberately left out of consideration, the Name Satyam recurs. Its function there is essentially a variation of (3) and (4), with the emphasis on the Satyam complex as a *natura naturans*. A further innovation is that this Satyam is not described as a dyad, but as a triad, of *tejas, āpas* and *annam,* which corresponds to the triad of sun, atmosphere and earth. This triadic pattern no doubt was encouraged by the trisyllabifications of *sa-ti-yam,* which, although not evidenced in our sources outside ChUp. 6, could as easily carry triads as *gā-ya-trī*,[18] *ud-gī-tha*[19] etc.

But a more far-reaching innovation has been introduced in this easily understood triad : the component members are no longer only horizontal levels which form a hierarchy of principles; they are characteristics which cut *vertically* through the entire creation. Each of them has three products. However, it is clear that these three series of three products really belong on only two levels : *tejas* produces 1. *vāc*; 2. *manas*; 3. bone; *āpas* produce 1. *prāṇa*; 2. blood; 3. urine; *annam* produces 1. *manas*; 2. flesh; 3. feces.

The *manas* seems to be repeated because the author worked with a series of eight, while he needed nine items. If we reduce the three series of three vertical productions to horizontal levels we get the following sequence :

[60]1. *tejas—vāc* (*manas*)
2. *āpas—prāṇa* (*manas*)
3. *annam*—bone/blood/flesh/urine/feces.

If we compare these products to the dyadic Satyam, we have in the first place the *amūrta* level of *prāṇa*, and in the second place the *mūrta* level, embodied, mortal and stationary. Uddālaka's Sat transcends its three primary emanations, the three *rūpas* that are "Satyam,"[20] and his Sat too no doubt was a Satyasya Satyam.

We may call this "Satyam" stage (5), but the "Satyam" speculations are really quite dead. The "Satyam" as the three *rūpas* still pretends to sum up the entire world, but they are reduced to general rubrics of classification of products which they themselves evolve. Other rubrics, like those of the five elements, are already competing, while a new approach to evolutionary derivation is being developed.

From now on we find *satyam* persisting as an adjective. But so powerful was the ancient Sat-doctrine, of which the Satyam speculations are one offshoot, that vestiges linger on far later in *sattva*, the vicissitudes of which we have traced elsewhere.

In spite of the comparatively small corpus of texts dealing with "Satyam", it does within its limited compass reflect the momentous changes that took place during the few generations the older Upaniṣads comprise. The notion that creation arose *e nihilo*, the *sat* out of the *asat*, is only vestigially preserved,[21] and only in a context where interest is centered on a much newer development. The doctrine of an "original Sat" as the substantial cause of creation is accepted and will continue to haunt both Sāṃkhya and Vedānta. Simultaneously an element of opposition is introduced into the "Satyam" dyad. The interpretation of Sat as *satyam* "true" insinuates a component that is "untrue" within the "Satyam". Certainly in part due to this assumption, which makes a polarity out of the dyad and therefore must break up "Satyam" as a comprehensive symbol, the "Satyam" complex is removed from the Supreme and the Supreme made transcendent over it. On the one hand "Satyam", summing up the created world (*nāma, rūpa, karman; tejas, āpas, annam*) may symbolize the factors which constitute creation; on the other hand, by that very token, it may be considered something negative and hostile, by which the true is hidden (*channam*). There where the postulate of Sat as substantial cause prevails, the "Satyam" can be a direct emanation of Sat, as in Uddālaka's view and an immanentism prevails. But there where the polarity between the supreme and the created world is emphasized, as in the reformulation of Satyasya Satyam, a transcendentism wins out: the supreme has no direct relations with a world or a body that only conceals it, and a dualism will arise of a spiritual order and a creational order.

[61] At the same time, this limited corpus also demonstrates how closely in touch these thinkers were with tradition, even while they began to formulate such diverging views. That one and the same *ādeśa*, "The Name of the Supreme is Satyam", continued to be resorted to as a word symbol in order to render their interpretations of the Supreme and the Created must go to show that there existed a school erudition in which they all participated; and whatever outside influences they were exposed to, a number of them at least drew on their school erudition to state their views.

NOTES

1. "Vācārambhaṇam reconsidered", *IIJ*, II (1958), p. 295 ff.; note also "Correction", *ib.* IV (1960), p.67 [no. 10 in this volume].

2. *IIJ*, II, p. 300 ff.

3. It is, of course, indisputable that the great importance of the *ṛtam/satyam* conceptions in the preceding period prepared the way for this word to become the vehicle of later esoteric interpretations.

4. It is likely that the qualification of *yat* "moving" is inspired by another analysis of "Satya" into *sat* and *yat* : elsewhere we also find *yam* (cf. below). Perhaps we can recognize this *yat* already in Śat Br. 7.4.1.6. : *tad yat satyam*

āpa eva tat/āpo hi vai satyam/tasmād yenāpo yanti tat satyasya rūpam ity āhuḥ/ āpā eva tad asya sarvasyāgram akurvaṃs tasṃād yadaivāpo yanty athedaṃ sarvam jāyate yad idaṃ kiṃ ca. Here is prefigured the relation between a "higher" (the *satyasya rūpam,* which makes the water flow), and the "lower", or consequent—the creation brought about by the flowing of the waters.

5. cf. RV. 10, 72.2; TaittBr. 2.2.9; BĀUp. 1.2.1; ChUp. 3.19.1; TaittUp. 2.7.1.

6. RV. 10.120, where we find an attempt to push beyond the *sat-asat* conception of the origin of the universe.

7. BĀUp. 2.1.20 (of *satyasya satyam,* see below).

8. *Bṛhadāraṇyaka Upaniṣad.*

9. *Sechzig Upanishad's des Veda* (Leipzig 1905[2]), p. 490. I am inclined to agree with Deussen in seeing in the speculations reflected in this passage the origin of the repeated formula *etad vai tad* of KaṭhUp. 4.5.

10. *Bṛhad-āraṇyaka-Upaniṣad* (Paris 1934), p. 93.

11. cf. my "The Large Ātman", *History of Religions,* 1964 [no. 18 in this volume].

12. As was recognized by Śaṅkara in his *bhāṣya* on 5.4 and 5.5.1.

13. Senart, *op. cit.,* p. 94, cf. note 1.

14. BĀUp. 4.1.4.

15. cf. also my *The Maitrāyaṇīya Upaniṣad* (The Hague, 1962), pp. 36, 41.

16. In form the expression *satyasya satyam* was not new: cf. the material collected by Hanns Oertel "Zum altindischen Ausdruckverstärkungstypus *satyasya satyam* 'das Wahre des Wahren' = 'die Quintessenz des Wahren'," *Sitzungsber. Bayer Ak. d. Wiss.,* Phil. hist Abt. 1937, 3, p. 28 f. Oertal remarks: "... 'das Wahre' des Nominativs *satyam* (liegt) auf einer ganz anderen Ebene als 'das Wahre' des Genitivs *satyasya.* Das letztere bezeichnet das empirische, mit den Sinnesorganen wahrgenommene 'Wahre;' das erstere ein ausserhalb des Bereichs der Sinne liegendes metaphysisches 'Wahres'." As a summary statement this is true enough; but it does no justice to the historical development which presumes a "Satyam" that summed up the two levels, higher and lower, within one symbol. Later reflection superseded this, not just by postulating a higher level beyond it, but by positing an entity completely apart from the erstwhile comprehensive "Satyam," giving up the continuity of the world and the creator immanent in it in favour of the transcendence of the supreme.

17. cf. SvetUp. 4.18 (*yadā...na san nāsac chiva eva kevalaḥ*); MuṇḍUp. 2.2.1. *sad-asad-vareṇyaṃ param*); PraśnUp. 2.5 (*sad asac cāmṛtaṃ ca yat*); ib. 4.5 (*sac cāṣac ca sarvaṃ paśyati,* implying some knower beyond it); BhG. 11.37 (*tvam akṣaraṃ sad asat tatparaṃ yat*).

18. ChUp. 3.12; BĀUp. 5.14.1.ff.

19. ChUp. 1.3.6. f.

20. ChUp. 6.4.1 *nāmadheyaṃ trīṇi rūpāṇīty eva satyam* : it is here that we have the principal use of the *nāmadheyam..satyam* formula, to which the uses in ChUp. 6.1 anticipate in an exemplifying fashion. As these examples of 6.1 show, the *satyam* is seen as the substantial cause; thus in 6.4 the *rūpas* are immanent in the various products which they together constitute and parts of which are thus classifiable by them.

21. That is, within the Satyam complex; elsewhere the old-fashioned notion survived (cf. ChUp. 3.19.1; TaittUp. 2.7.1).

22

THE SĀMAVEDA IN THE PRAVARGYA* RITUAL

The presentation of the office of the *Sāmaveda* priests in the Pravargya is, as we find it in the *Lāṭyāyana* and *Drāhyāyaṇa śrautasūtras*[1], at first sight confusing. Both sūtras present it as part of the *Soma* office. Since the two sūtras run almost wholly parallel and incidental differences between them are not important for our argument, I shall quote from the Lāṭyāyana. The *Jaiminīya śrautasūtra* will be considered later.

Lāṭyāyana presents the office in 1.6. The order of the description is as follows. The precepts begin, curiously, with the function that occurs at the end of the series (normally six) of Pravargyas, namely at the point when the *udvāsana* takes place (C-H 77)[2]. Sūtras 1.6. 1-12 are entirely clear. Then follow two sūtras which state variations. While sūtras 1-12 state clearly that the sāmans are 1. the *tyagnāyiḥ*, 2. the *vārṣāharam,* 3. the *iṣṭāhotrīyam,* and 4. the *śyaitam,* sūtra 13 quotes the authority of Master Dhānaṃjayya to the effect that the priest "having approached by way of the eastern door of the *prāgvaṃśa* hut, and passed by the fires on the northern side, should then take his stand to the West of the *gārhapatya* fire and gaze upon the Mahāvīra sanctuary, while chanting the *vāmadevyam*". Sūtra 14 reverses this by stating the superseding authority of Śāṇḍilya to the effect that the sāmans end with the *śyaitam.*

[180] Dhānaṃjayya's precept makes little sense at the point where it is quoted. At this time of the ritual the paraphernalia of the Pravargya have already been brought out of the *prāgvaṃśa* hut and arranged on the *uttaravedi.* Is the priest to return to the bamboo hut and gaze on a sanctuary that is no longer there? It is far more likely that the statement of sūtra 13 referred to the first appearance of the priest on the scene of the Pravargya; it clearly parallels a similar precept for the first appearance of the Hotar[3]. The later sūtra compiler, finding sūtra 13 as it were appended to the previous 12 as a footnote, must have misunderstood its import, as though it were an option to what had been stated, namely that the *śyaitam* was to be followed by the *vāmadevyam,* and then invoked Śāṇḍilya to show that the sāmans really ended with the *śyaitam.* In my interpretation Dhānaṃjayya did not really conflict at all; he simply proposed a sāman at the *beginning* of the Pravargya.

Lāṭyāyana thus primarily deals with the concluding rites of the Pravargya; this is the point when the *Sāmaveda* begins to participate in the Soma ritual—the shifting of the action from the provisional bamboo hut to the *mahāvedi.* At this juncture the *agnipraṇayana* occurs at once (C-H 79), and this rite is ruled upon in Lāṭyāyana 1.6.38. We may therefore reconstruct a more original sequence: 1.6.1–12, followed by 1.6.38 ff.

Sūtras 13-14 and 15-37 then appear to be an insertion; and this is how the text presents them—if not as an insertion, at least as an optional addition. The sequence 15-37 is introduced as follows : *gaṇaḥ sāmāny uttarāṇi //15// abhirūpyāt kartavyāṇīty eke //16// na vā kuryāt //17// sve vā yajñe kuryād ity eke* //18. "The following sāmans constitute the (supererogatory) group. Some hold that they should be done for the sake of propriety; others hold that the priest should not do them, or do them at his own sacrifice."

This supererogatory group comprises all the sāmans chanted at the *agniṣṭoma* prior to the removal of the Pravargya. The evolution of custom seems transparent enough: 1. the group was not done at all; 2. a sacrificer belonging to the *Sāmaveda* might choose to do them at his own sacrifice; 3. the custom might be extended to all sacrifices for the sake of "propriety", or sacerdotal equity.

At that it is a hefty group: at the *dīkṣaṇīya iṣṭi* either the double *Tārkṣyasāman* or the *tyam ū ṣu* (C-H 15)[4]; at the *prāyaṇīya iṣṭi* the *pravad bhārgavam* (C-H 28); at the *ātithya iṣṭi* the *gāyatrī auśanam* **[181]** (C-H 44); and at the *udayanīya iṣṭi* the *udvad bhārgavam* (C-H 255). These are the preliminary *iṣṭis* of the *upasad* days; the last one is the concluding *iṣṭi* of the *agniṣṭoma.* We do well to note that the *Sāmaveda* participates in the *iṣṭi* only at the Soma sacrifice; it is absent from the *darśapūrṇamāsa.*

The remainder of the "group" comprises the sāmans chanted at the Pravargya before the concluding rites dealt with in Lāṭyāyana 1.6 1-12. The sūtras 22-37 contain the following precepts:

1. When the anointing of the Mahāvīra takes place, one should chant the *śārga* (or *śārṅga*) (Āp. 15.7.3)[5]
2. When the golden and silver disks are put in place, the *śukra* and *candra* (silver disk Āp. 15.7.3; golden disk *ib.* 15.8.5a).[6]
3. When the fanning of the fire takes place, the *gharmasya tanvau* (*ib.* 15.8.6-10).[7]
4. When the priests pronounce that the pot is red, the *gharmasya* or the *indrasya rocanam* (*ib.* 15.8.13).[8]
5. When the cow and goat are milked, the *dhenu* (*ib.* 15.9.8-9).[9]
6. When the milk is being brought in, the *payas* (*ib.* 15.9.11-12).[10]
7. When they pour out, the *Sindhusāman* (*ib.* 15.10.1).[11]
8. When they grasp the pot with the tongs, the *vasiṣṭhasya śaphau* (*ib.* 15.10.6).[12]
9. When it is being carried to the fire, the two *vratapakṣas* (*ib.* 15.10.8).[13]
10. When the *gharma* is being offered, either the two *vratas* of the Aśvins or of Day and Night (*ib.* 15.10.11).[14]
11. When the two *rauhiṇa* cakes are brought forward, the *rajanam* and the *rauhiṇakam* (*ib.* 15.10.10 and 11.5).[15]
12. When they place the paraphernalia on the throne, the *ārūḍhavad aṅgirasam*, with *svaḥ* at the *nidhana* (15.12.2).[16]

[182] Although, as we saw, Lāṭyāyana presents all these sāmans as forming part of the optional group, the question whether they are really optional is in the end resolved by decree: "He says that the Gharma is accompanied by Ṛk, Yajuṣ, and Sāman."

My argument that sūtras 13-37 are a later addition and thus show the growth of *Sāmaveda* participation in the Soma sacrifice during the period of the compilation of the Sūtras is supported by the way the *Jaiminīya śrautasūtra*[17] treats the Pravargya ritual. It treates it in two different places, once in chapter 5 and once more in chapter 23. In chapter 5, the text gives the sāmans that are done at the disposal rite (*udvāsana*), as in Lāṭyāyana 1.6 1-12; while in chapter 23, as an appendix to the main corpus of the *śrautasūtra*, the sāmans prior to the concluding rite are entered. Since Dieuke Gaastra's Dutch translation is not accessible to everyone, nor always correct, it may be useful to enter here a translation of the short sections.

Chapter 5. "When they dispose of the Pravargya, they call on him (viz. the Prastotar). Having put on the sacrificial thread and sipped water, he remains about. When the Adhvaryu summons him : "Prastotar, sing the sāman!" he sings the last sāman of the series built on *agniṃ hotāraṃ manye dāsvantam*[18] three times with the *hiṃkāra*; at every *pāda* he repeats the *stobha*; all join in the finale, including the sacrificer's wife. Indeed, at this time the gods were set upon by the Rakṣas'. Agni saw the "Rakṣas-slaying" sāman. The Rakṣas' were beaten off. That they join in the finale is for the beating off of the Rakṣas'. They carry (the paraphernalia of) the Pravargya, while putting it down three times. He sings the sāman every time it is put down. Indeed, these worlds are three, (thus they do it) for the differentiation of these worlds. While he (the Prastotar) stands in the West, (the Adhvaryu) joins (the paraphernalia of) the Pravargya together. When he circum-irrigates for the second time, (the Adhvaryu) says to him: "Prastotar, sing the sāman." He chants the *vārṣāhara* sāman three times with the *hiṃkāra*. Standing in the same place he sings the *iṣṭāhotrīya* with the *hiṃkāra*. They fall in with the finale of the *iṣṭāhotrīya,* not of the *vārṣāhara*. Then the Prastotar takes the cloth with which the Wife was screened off. When returning he sings the *śayitam*."

Chapter 23. "We shall teach the times of chanting at the **[183]** Pravargya. After putting on the sacrificial thread and sipping water, he enters (the *prāgvaṃśa* hut) between *vedi* and *utkara*[19], passes around behind the Hotar and sits down to the South, while facing the Gharma. Then he performs the *śānti* with the *vāmadevyam* with the boiling water. When the Adhvaryu gives the summons: "Brahman, we shall proceed with the Pravargya!" "Hotar, praise the Gharma!" "Prastotar, chant the sāmans!" (Āp. 15.6.1), he sings the first of the two sāmans built on *brahma jajñānam*[20] three times. When the Pravargya is anointed, the *śārṅga*. When the (silver) disk is put on (the *khara*), the *śukra*. When the other (golden) disk is put on top (of the Mahāvīra), the *candra*. At the fuelling of the gharma, the two tanu's of gharma and the two vratas of gharma. When (the pot) is ablaze, the *gharmasya rocanaṃ*. The *rajanam* when the first *rauhiṇa* cake is offered. When (the calf) is let loose to the cow, the *dhenu* or *kakubh* (Āp. 15.9.6). When the cow is proffered to the calf[21], the first *śyavaśya* built on *gaur dhayati marutām*. When she is miled, the *dohādohīya*.

When the milk is brought in, the *payas*. When the milk is poured out, the *sindhu*. When the pot is encompassed (with the tongs), the two *śaphas* of Vasiṣṭha. When it is carried forward, the *brāhmaṇaspatyam* or the two *vratapakṣas*. When the Gharma is offered, the two *vratas* of the Aśvins. When the other *rauhiṇa* cake is offered, the *rauhiṇakam*. When the Gharma is set together (on the throne), the *ārūḍhavad aṅgirasam* three times, or the *kava*. Having done the *śānti* with the *vāmadevyam* with the boiling water, he departs the way he entered; and when the *upasad* is set up, he stands at the *utkara*; and on the calling of the Subrahmaṇyā invocation[22], he goes forth as his task demands."

Two things strike us in the Jaiminīya account: the strict separation of the disposal rites of the Pravargya from the rites of the actual performance of the Pravargya, each in a different chapter; and the varying sāmans in what Lāṭyāyana and Drāhyāyaṇa call the "group". It is clear from the presentation that the Jaiminīya treats the sāmans of chapter five as an intrinsic part of the Soma office; while the appended chapter 23 seems less mandatory.

The Jaiminīya treatment indicates the correctness of my assumption that Dhānaṃjayya's intention, in Lāṭyāyana 1.6.13, was not that the entire Pravargya ceremonial was concluded with the *vāmadevyam*, but rather that each twice-daily performance began **[184]** with it as a *śānti*; Jaiminīya takes this further and prescribes the same sāman also at the end of each performance. This practice makes intelligible the misunderstanding of the compiler of Lāṭyāyana that the series of Pravargyas at the disposal rite is concluded with the *vāmadevyam*; we saw that Jaiminīya also concludes the ritual with the *śyaitam*.

I am in general agreement with Dieuke Gaastra's thesis that the *Jaiminīya śrautasūtra* is an ancient text; it may well be that for the main *agniṣṭoma* part of the sūtra it is older than Lāṭyāyana-Drāhyāyaṇa. In the Pravargya chapter five we meet with an old construction (*pratiṣṭhāpam* as gerund) and brāhmaṇa-like insertions (the "rakṣas-slaying" sāman, etc.) that indicate its antiquity. But this is not necessarily true of the appended chapter 23, which is far drier in style, and gives all appearance of having been added later to the already completed sūtra.

It is curious that the "group" contained in chapter 23 does not, as in Lāṭyāyana, comprise the sāmans sung at the various *iṣṭis* of the *agniṣṭoma*. We also note that the Pravargya repertoire there is even larger than that of Lāṭyāyana. These facts do not permit of certain conclusions.

That the execution of the Pravargya sāmans incorporated in the "group" was a relatively later addition to the ritual seems to find further corroboration in Āpastamba. This śrautasūtra mentions that the Adhvaryu summons the Prastotar—and in the last place—with the blanket order: "Prastotar, sing the sāmans!" No specific sāman is, however, recognized until the udvāsana takes place and the Adhvaryu gives the summons: "Prastotar, sing the sāman." This is the sāman that figures first in the lists of both Lāṭyāyana and Jaiminīya; it is the *tyagnāyiḥ* which is the sāman on which the concelebrating priests take action—we might call it the first operational sāman of the Pravargya. It is interesting that in the *SV.* tradition this sāman is simply known as the *Pravargyasāman.* Āpastamba also specifically recognizes the *iṣṭāhotrīyam* and the *vārṣāharam.* Thus, although Āpastamba at the very beginning acknowledges that sāmans are chanted during the rite, the fact that only the concluding sāmans are in any way ritually incorporated contributes to the argument that the earlier sāmans were to some extent supererogatory and not significantly part of the ritual.

In Kātyāyana, finally, we find an intermediary stage between the few sāmans mentioned in the sūtras of the *Black Yajurveda,* and those described in the "group" of Lāṭyāyana-Drāhyāyaṇa. This *White Yajurveda* sūtra takes for granted that the *Sāmaveda* participates throughout. This is interestingly shown by the fact **[185]** that, while in 26.2.11 the priest is named Prastotar (here Kātyāyana follows the *Vājasaneyi Saṃhitā*), in 26.7.44 it is the Udgātar who receives the *dakṣiṇā*; there seems to be little doubt that the entire Sāmaveda choir participated. Again different from the *Black Yajurveda* sūtras and surely indicative of its later date, Kātyāyana treats of the Pravargya within the context of the *agniṣṭoma,* only very casually indicating that the rite is optional: *upasadā cariṣyaṃś cariṣyan pravargyena carati sapravargye* (26.2.1) "..at a sacrifice entailing the Pravargya, he proceeds with the Pravargya whenever about to proceed with the *upasad.*" The impression left is that the Pravargya is a definite part of the Soma sacrifice and that the Udgātar and presumably his choir take part in it. Kātyāyana takes more cognizance of the *Sāmaveda* by including more formal summons for specific sāmans than the other *Yajurveda śrautasūtras.* He calls for the *śukram* (26.3.1), the *candram* (*ib.* 4.1). the *gharmasya tanvau* (*ib.* 4.10), the *dhenu* (*ib.* 5.2), the *payas* (*ib.* 5.9) and the *vasiṣṭhasya śaphau* (*ib.* 5.13) in addition to the regular concluding sāmans. We do not yet have the complete list of Lāṭyāyana, but many on it.

While much escapes us, we can trace the following development in the participation of the *Sāmaveda.* At first the *Sāmaveda* only participated in the disposal ceremony (*udvāsana*) and the three concluding sāmans were chanted. The repertoire, however, grew, as Kātyāyana shows. Lāṭyyana and Drāhyāyaṇa give a full list and, while formally leaving an option, state clearly that the Pravargya is accompanied by the *Sāmaveda.* The appended chapter 23 of the Jaiminīya gives an even longer list for its *śākhā*; and while the separate treatment in chapters 5 and 23 permits us to conclude that the full list was later, it gives no explicit option any more.

That the *Sāmaveda* originally only participated in the *udvāsana* and not at the actual twice-daily performances and that even so this participation was a secondary one, is shown by the fact that only an acolyte of the Udgātar, the Prastotar, is called upon. While the *Vaitāna śrautasūtra* does mention the Udgātar as the priest, the other sūtras are unanimous in citing it the Prastotar's office. So, even if the *Sāmaveda* for propriety's sake (*ābhirūpyāt*) partook in the Pravargya, it was in a nominal fashion: side by side with such principal priests as Hotar, Adhvaryu and Brahman, only a secondary *Sāmaveda* priest figures.

This nominal participation is underscored by two further facts. In the first place, this ritual office is not recognized in the *Sāmaveda Brāhmaṇas* whose business is with the large Soma rituals—the Pravargya is ignored. In the second place, the Prastotar is not among those invited to partake of the gharma draught.

[186] In conclusion we may say that the Pravargya was not a Sāmavedic rite, just as the *darśapūrṇamāsa*, the *cāturmāsya* and the *paśubandha* are not Sāmavedic rites. That the *Sāmaveda* eventually began participating was probably due to mere presence of its priests. As it were arriving at the sacrificial area for the Soma pressings and rituals proper, they became involved in the *udvāsana* ritual which marks the end of the preliminary rites of the *upasad* days and the beginning of the *mahākarman.* Then gradually, by a progression still dimly visible, they began chanting their

sāmans during the *upasad* days themselves. If the chanting of sāmans signifies the peculiar importance of the rite, the progression shows that the Pravargya itself, as part of the *agniṣṭoma*, grew in stature. For while the sūtras remember an option for the Prastotar not to perform, once he does so it is with a massive array of sāmans.

NOTES

*This paper is one in a series of preliminary studies toward an interpretation of the *Pravargya*; they will eventually form an introduction to a complete description of the *Pravargya* ceremony, intended to supplement W. Caland and V. Henry on the *Agniṣṭoma.*

1. *The Śrautasūtra of Lāṭyāyana*, ed. by A. Vedāntavāgīśa (Calcutta 1872); *The Śrautasūtra of Drāhyāyaṇa*, ed. by J.N. Reuter, Part 1 (London 1904).
2. W. Caland et V. Henry, *L'Agniṣṭoma*, 2. vols. (Paris 1906-7); numbers refer to sections.
3. *ŚāṅkhŚS*. 5.9.4; *ĀśvŚS* 4.6.1.
4. C-H only mention the double *Tārkṣyasāman.*
5. For the sake of brevity I only quote Āpastamba, who is followed closely by Hiraṇyakeśī and Vārāha; the variations of Mānava and Kātyāyana are not relevant for our present purpose. The Śārṅga is found in Sāmasramin's edition of *SV*. in the Bibliotheca Indica, II, 167, iii.
6. Bibl. Ind. II, 271 and II, 462.
7. Bibl. Ind. II, 443.
8. Bibl. Ind. II, 515.
9. Bibl. Ind. II, 449.
10. Bibl. Ind. II, 449.
11. Bibl. Ind. I, 426.
12. Bibl. Ind. II, 269.
13. I have been unable to identify this sāman in the Bibl. Ind. edition; it is to be found in the Poona ed. (*Sāmaveda-kauthumaśākhīyaḥ grāmageya (veya, prakṛti) gānātmakaḥ*, Poona 1942), *Āraṇyageyagāna* 2.1.5-6.
14. Bibl. Ind. II, 491 and 475 respectively.
15. Bibl. Ind. II, 486.
16. Bibl. Ind. I, 251.
17. Ed. by Dieuke Gaastra in *Bjjdrage tot de kennis van het Vedische ritueel: Jaiminīyaśrautasūtra* (thesis Utrecht, Leiden 1906).
18. This is the *tyagṇāyiḥ* or Pravargyasāman.
19. That means: keeping to the three fires; the *utkara* is in the north-eastern corner of the hut.
20. The ṛks on which these and other sāmans are built are found in Gaastra, *o.c.*
21. So as to make the milk flow.
22. C-H 49.

23

SOME NOTES ON THE UTTARA-YĀYĀTA

Embedded in the Ādiparvan of the *Mahābhārata*[1] is a text of apparently Upaniṣadic intentions which deserves to be noticed. Sukthankar, the editor of the Ādiparvan, disagrees: 'The..eschatological discourse between Yayāti and Aṣṭaka..is in part most obscure and incoherent, and so clumsily worded as to be almost unintelligible.' He proceeds to dismiss it as an 'old interpolation'. This, however, does not mean more than that it is an old text which was inserted rather early into what was to become the *Mahābhārata*; *a priori* it might well be older than the text with which it became combined.

This text, the Uttara-yāyāta, is found in *MBh.* I. 81-8. It follows immediately after the *yayātyupākhyāna*, hence apparently its name: 'Latter Days of Yayāti'. It seems to me likely that the Story of Yayāti was adopted into the text first, for its contents are of primary concern to this part of the Ādiparvan which deals with genealogies. It gives the story of Devayānī and Śarmiṣṭhā, who by Yayāti become the mothers of the famous Five Nations named after their **[618]** sons Yadu, Turvaśu, Druhyu, Anu and Pūru. It is the descendants of Pūru who prevail and the Bhāratas of the epic derive from the Pauravas.

Even though the Story of Yayāti may be prior as far as the text of the *Mahābhārata* is concerned, it cannot be said that the Uttara-yāyāta is simply a later appendix to it. It is conceived of as a text in its own right: the theme is completely new and not prepared in any way by the Story of Yayāti; except for Yayāti himself all the persons who figure in it are different; although *ślokas* occur, it is largely composed in another metre; and the style is markedly different. I believe it is justified to assume that two different texts existed, the Story of Yayāti and the Uttara-yāyāta, that the former was incorporated into the Saṃbhavaparvan because of its genealogical interest, and that the latter was brought along, or later added, because of the identity of its hero.

The Story of Yayāti proper ends with I.80; this is clear from the final *śloka* I.80. 27, which contains a benediction: 'But from Pūru springs the Paurava dynasty, in which you yourself have been born, O King (Janamejaya), to rule this kingdom mightily for a thousand years'. The following chapters, 81 and 82, give the appearance of being transitional. Chapter 81 is the kind of summary chapter which so often precedes the fully developed story in the epic: after consecrating Pūru, Yayāti departs for the forest, goes to heaven, falls from heaven back to earth, remains suspended in the sky, and returns to heaven in the assembly of the **[619]** Kings Vasumat,[2] Aṣṭaka, Pratardana and Śibi. This occasions a question from Janamejaya, to whom the story is being told, whereupon Vaiśaṃpāyana promises to tell him *yayāter uttarāṃ kathām*; the remainder of the chapter describes Yayāti's dire mortifications in the forest.

In ch. I. 82 it is described how Yayāti is much honoured in heaven. Śakra[3] appears and questions him about the words he used when he transferred the kingdom to Pūru. Yayāti does so in one *śloka* (I.82.5), then launches into praise of gentleness of temper and speech. All this seems prefatory to the main 'narrative' of I.83-8.

Synopsis of I. 83-8.

I.83. Indra asks Yayāti : who is his equal in *tapas*? Y. declares that no one is. Indra says that because of this disdain Y.'s worlds are coming to an end[4] Y. requests him that he then may fall among the good (*sat*). Indra consents. Y. falls and on the way is sighted by Aṣṭaka, who asks who he is.

I.84. Y. identifies himself[5] and states that he is falling; he declares his superiority over the others. Aṣṭaka remarks that knowledge bestows seniority. This occasions a discourse by Y., apparently to establish his knowledge. Fate (*diṣṭa*) is stronger than acts, and this **[620]** insight leads to equanimity. Hereupon Aṣṭaka recognizes him as a *kṣetrajña*, a guide who knows the country, and he asks about the *dharmas*. Y. describes how after a thousand years[6] each time he moved from 'great worlds'[7] to the world of Indra, to the world of Prajāpati, to the world of God after God. Then the Envoy of the Gods said three times 'Fall!'. His merit having been used up (*kṣīṇapuṇya*) he falls[8] lamented by the Gods, to Aṣṭaka's ritual site.

I.85. Aṣṭaka asks why he fell. Y. replies that once one's merit is used up, Indra and the Gods desert one. A.: how does one use up one's merit, where does one go? Y. : to the hell-on-earth (*bhauma naraka*).[9] A.: what becomes of the creatures when they have died? Y.: after their last gasp they spend countless eons —sixty or eighty thousand years—then they are pushed out by the Rākṣasas of the *bhauma* hell.[10] A.: after falling, how do those who are dead (*bhūta*) become embryos? Y. now embarks on a difficult discourse, which we shall analyse below (I.85.10-20). A. asks: how can a mortal find the best worlds? Y. extols equanimity.

[621] I.86. A asks about the acts of the various *āśramas*. Y. describes them. A. : how many kinds of hermits are there? Description by Y.

I.87. A. asks: by whom have you been sent, where is your kingdom? Y.: I have been cast to the *bhauma* hell; I chose to fall among good people. A. implores him not to fall, offering him his own worlds. Y.: no one but a Brahman can accept gifts; being a Kṣatriya he declines. Pratardana then enquires what worlds are coming to him and offers them to Y., who declines.

I.88. Vasumanas asks about his worlds and wants to give them to Y., or to sell them for a stalk of straw. Y. declines any false bargains. Śibi asks about his worlds and offers them; Y. declines. Then five golden chariots appear which take them to heaven by way of the sun's rays.[11] Because of his generosity, Śibi outpaces them all. A. once more asks Y. to identify himself; Y. is revealed as the maternal uncle of them all. He had conquered the earth, and given it to the Brahmans.

*Analysis of I.*85. 10-20.

It would seem that Sukthankar's strictures apply particularly to this 'eschatological discourse'; still, on closer analysis it becomes far more intelligible than Sukthankar held. The key to the understanding of the **[622]** text is that it is based on a naturalistic and folkloristic account of transmigration which in essentials is closely related to that presented in *Chāndogya Upaniṣad* V. 2-8. Once this parallelism is observed, the interpretation falls effortlessly into place.

In I. 85. 9 Aṣṭaka asks: 'How do they become (*bhavanti*), how do they become a new being (*ābhavanti*), how do those who have been before (*bhūtāḥ*) become embryos?' We should read *kathaṃ bhūtā* for the meaningless *kathaṃbhūtā* adopted in the critical edition.

In I.85.10 Yayāti replies :

asraṃ retaḥ puṣpaphalānupṛktam
anveti tad vai puruṣeṇa sṛṣṭam |
sa vai tasyā raja āpadyate vai
sa garbhabhūtaḥ samupaiti tatra ||

'A drop, clinging to a flower of a fruit, goes into the sperm; that is ejaculated by the man. He indeed falls into the flux of the woman; there he enters as an embryo.'

This corresponds exactly to *ChUp*. V. 10.6: the souls on their downward route have become mist (*abhra*); then they become the rain cloud (*megha*), and 'having become a cloud, it rains. They are here [on earth] born as rice and barley, herbs and trees, sesamum and beans. From these, to be sure, the departure is very difficult. Now, if a man eats that as his food, if he then emits his sperm, then he (the "soul") becomes once more.' The *asra* of our text **[623]** should be understood as '(rain) drop)', instead of the normal 'tear'. The parallelism of our text and *ChUp*. offers for *puṣpa* the intention of 'vegetable'. The genitive *tasyāḥ* must refer to the woman with whom the man cohabits. *Rajas* 'menstrual flux' is either used metonymically for the womb, or might refer to the woman's orgasmic emission. *ChUp*. V. 10. 7 has simply *yonim āpadyeran*; the same verb is used here: *āpadyate*. The *sa* in c and d must refer to the being that is reborn; cf. in *ChUp*. V. 10.6, *tad bhūya eva bhavati,* where *tad* is not the subject of *bhavati,* but an adverbial 'then': in the next line the subject is masculine: *te. . . . yonim āpadyeran.* Apart from the curious usages of *asra* and *rajas* (no doubt deliberate to sound enigmatically Upaniṣadic), the message of the verse is clear enough.

I.85.11:

vanaspatīṃś cauṣadhīś cāviśanti
āpo vāyuṃ pṛthivīṃ cāntarikṣam |
catuṣpadaṃ dvipadaṃ cāpi sarvam
evaṃ bhūtā garbhabhūtā bhavanti ||

'They enter the trees of the forest and the herbs, water, wind, earth and sky; [and thus] the entire two-footed and four-footed creation: thus those who have been become embryos.'

The words *vanaspati* and *oṣadhi* parallel the same in *ChUp.* V.10.6; similarly *vāyu* and *antarikṣa* are given in V.10.5, the latter as *ākāśa*. The verse elaborates the previous one, as is shown by the repetition of **[624]** *garbhabhūta*. As in verse 9, the text in d makes much better sense if we read *bhūtā* separately, instead of *evaṃbhūtā* adopted in the critical edition.

I. 85. 12:

Aṣṭaka uvāca :
anyad vapur vidadhātīha garbha
utāhosvit svena kāyena yāti /
āpadyamāno narayonim etām
ācakṣva me saṃśayāt prabravīmi //

'Aṣṭaka said : "Does the embryo take on another shape, or does it transmigrate with its own body, when it enters this human womb? Explain to me, I speak from doubt." '

I see no justification for critical ed. *kāmena* (marked doubtful), while there is good manuscript authority for *kāyena*; graphically the difference between the two characters is often minimal or nonexistent. Also, *utāhosvit* indicates a contrast: 'or else?'—'either a new body or its own', make sense; 'either a new body or by its own desire' makes none. Aṣṭaka's question is well taken; that it is raised implies that there must have been an inchoate notion of a permanent transmigrating 'subtle body'.

I.85.13:

śarīradehādisamucchrayaṃ ca
cakṣuḥśrotre labhate kena saṃjñām /
etat tattvaṃ sarvam ācakṣva pṛṣṭaḥ
kṣetrajñaṃ tvām tāta manyāma sarve //

[625] 'In which way does it obtain the full growth of bones, body and so forth, eyesight and hearing, consciousness. Explain this entire fact at my question; for we all deem you, friend, as one who knows the country.'

Śarīra in contrast to *deha*! While it is possible that a distinction between *sūkṣmaśarīra* and *sthūladeha* is intended, I prefer *śarīra* in the older sense of the hard part of the body. *Cakṣuḥśrotre* stands *pars pro toto* for all the senses. 'Consciousness' for *saṃjñā* is not to be taken too literally; it probably corresponds to *manas* or *buddhi*. *Tattvam* has a competitive variant *tvaṃ naḥ*; but *tattvam* 'basic fact, or principle in individuation' makes good sense just in this context of speculations where especially Sāṃkhya likes to use *tattvāni*; *tattvaṃ sarvam* might be translated 'all the *tattvas*'. The word *kṣetrajña* here *does* make one pause in this context; after all, Yayāti, on his way to rebirth, is technically a *kṣetrajña*. While it may possibly be a pun, assuming that the word already had acquired its technical sense, its use elesewhere in the Uttara-yāyāta makes me choose the older meaning of 'guide'. But this word bears watching.

I.85.14 :

Yayātir uvāca:

vāyuḥ samutkarṣati garbhayonim
ṛtau retaḥ puṣparasānupṛktam /
sa tarta tanmātrakṛtādhikāraḥ
krameṇa saṃvardhayatīha garbham //

[626] 'Yayāti said: "Breath draws up into the embryo's womb, at the [mother's fertile] season, the germ that had been mixed with the juice of flowers. It, carrying out its task with the *tanmātras*, in this, gradually brings the embryo here to growth." '

I take °*yonim* here as accusative of direction, *retaḥ* as object. *Vāyuḥ* no doubt stands for *prāṇa*, which later in Sāṃkhya accompanies the subtle body in transmigration. Here, too, it is not identical with the 'soul' that becomes the *garbha* but accompanies it. The *retaḥ puṣparasānupṛktam* is the *asraṃ puṣpaphalānupṛktam* of verse 10, the vital drop clinging to the vegetable which has become mixed with the *puṣparasa*, which in turn makes up the sperm. *Tanmātrakṛtādhikāra* permits of several translations. If taken as a noun it is a Karmadhāraya 'the qualification effected by the *tanmātras*'; but this would provide a new subject, whereas the *sa* of c idiomatically resumes *vāyuḥ* of a; also, such an *adhikāra* seems hard to understand as operating independently. If adjectival and a Bahuvrīhi, it means either (the wind) 'by which the *adhikāra* is effected by means of the *tanmātras*', or 'for which an *adhikāra* is effected by the *tanmātra*'. The choice rests on the meaning of *tanmātra*. Does it have the Sāṃkhyan meaning of 'those objects whose realm is one of the five elements that are perceived by the senses (light—visible object—eyesight)'? It is clearly already a factor in the evolution of the senses. In origin, the word is a Bahuvrīhi 'that of which the measure is that [sense]', namely, the sense which is [627] the 'measure' or *pramāṇa* of the object sensed. I take it that here *tanmātra* is loosely used as 'factor accompanying the evolution of a sense', and the entire compound then means '[the breath], which functions at this point (*tatra*) by means of those factors'.

I.85.15:

sa jāyamāno vigṛhītagātraḥ
ṣaḍjñānaniṣṭhāyatano manuṣyaḥ /
sa śrotrābhyāṃ vedayatīha śabdam
sarvaṃ rūpaṃ paśyati cakṣuṣā ca //

'When born, when his limbs are stretched out, man, possessing the bases on which the six perceptions are founded, perceives sound here with his ears, and sees all that is visible with his eyesight.'

Vigṛhītagātra, namely when the limbs have been loosened from their foetal position. The *āyatanāni* of course are the senses among which here the *manas* is included.

I.85.16:

ghrāṇena gandhaṃ jihvayātho rasaṃ ca
tvacā sparśaṃ manasā veda bhāvam /
ity aṣṭakehopacitiṃ ca viddhi
mahātmanaḥ prāṇabhṛtaḥ śarīre //

'With his nose he knows smell, with his tongue taste, with his skin touch, with his mind thought. Thus, Aṣṭaka, know from the great-spirited one the augmentation of the breathing creature in the body.'

[628] *Bhāva* might equally be translated by 'feeling', since the *manas* is the faculty of both thoughts and emotions. *Upaciti,* lit. 'increase', here refers to the growth of the body and the faculties of the person born. The question is wheteher *mahātmanaḥ* is a genitive appositional to *prāṇabhṛtaḥ* (in which case, as applied to a new-born baby, *mahātman* means even less than it usually does in the epic), or to be taken as an ablative dependent on *viddhi.* The evidence of a reading *mahātmanaḥ prāṇabhṛtāṃ* (to which *mahātmanaḥ*—abl.—and *prāṇabhṛtaḥ*—gen.—is a *lectio difficilior*) makes me decide for the second alternative.

I.85.17 :

Aṣṭaka uvāca:

yaḥ saṃsthitaḥ puruṣo dahyate vā
nikhanyate vāpi nighṛṣyate vā |
abhāvabhūtaḥ sa vināśam etya
kenātmānaṃ cetayate purastāt ||

'Aṣṭaka said: "The embodied person who is burnt or buried or ground has become a nothing when he has come to his death. In which way does he know himself from before?"

Saṃsthita 'properly constituted'. *Nikhanyate* 'is buried', a practice known in the Veda; *nighṛṣyate* 'is ground to dust', namely the bones surviving from the cremation. No answer will be forthcoming to the question of d.

[629] I.85.18:

Yayātir uvāca:

hitvā so 'sūn suptavan niṣṭanitvā
purodhāya sukṛtaṃ duṣkṛtaṃ vā |
anyāṃ yoniṃ pavanāgrānusārī
hitvā dehaṃ bhajate rājasiṃha ||

'Having relinquished his spirits, like a man asleep, having gasped his last breath, having set before him his good and evil acts, he follows after the Breath to another womb; having shed his body, he enjoys another, O lion among kings.'

Niṣṭanitvā, epical gerund of *ni-stan,* surely here 'to give forth the death rattle, to expire'[12] *Puro-dhā* 'to place before, as a guide', the meaning being that his *karman* sets the way. *Pavana* is the *vāyu* of above. *Anyāṃ yonim* dependent on *anusārī* with verbal government.

I.85.19:

puṇyāṃ yoniṃ puṇyakṛto vrajanti
pāpāṃ yoniṃ pāpakṛto vrajanti |
kīṭāḥ pataṅgāś ca bhavanti pāpā
na me vivakṣāsti mahānubhāva ||

'To a good womb go those who have done good, to a bad womb go those who have done evil. The evil become worms and flies. I do not wish to speak [of them], O majestic one.'

[630] On this cf. *ChUp.* V.10.7; perhaps the *pāpāḥ* of c (apparently different from those who are merely *pāpakṛt*) correspond to the low (*kṣudrāṇi*) constantly reappearing (*asakṛdāvartīni*) creatures that go by neither of the two routes, the third order of 'Be born! Die!' of *ChUp.* V.10.8, about which nothing is further said.[13]

I.85.20 :

catuṣpadā dvipadāḥ ṣaṭpadāś ca
tathā bhūtā garbhabhūtā bhavanti |
ākhyātam etan nikhilena sarvaṃ
bhūyas tu kiṃ pṛcchasi rājasiṃha ||

'Four-footed, two footed, and six-footed—thus do those who have been become embryos. This has now all been told entirely. But what more do you ask me, O lion among kings?'

Again, read *tathā bhūtā* for *tathābhūtā*. The *pāda-s* a and b, like 11 c and d, echo 9 c and d, where the governing question was asked. Thus the instruction I.85.9–20 is precisely bracketed.

The Uttara-yāyāta as a 'baronial' Upaniṣad.

I trust the reader will agree that there is little that is obscure, incoherent, or even clumsily worded in this discourse. Within the Uttara-yāyāta as a whole it forms a tight little text, which in a straightforward, [631] though still primitive way describes the process of transmigration, and describes it through a person who is about to go through it. While I have placed due stress on the relations with *ChUp.* V. 10, and thus by implication *BĀUp.* VI.2, we have no evidence that the author actually knew these Upaniṣads. We should rather prefer to look upon the Uttara-yāyāta section as a narrative dramatization of beliefs which also found expression in the Upaniṣads. From this point of view, the text appears to be of a *genre* with such texts as the *Kaṭha Upaniṣad*, metrical and narrative and even bardic in style, where the bardic tradition, in an admittedly later age, intersects with the Upaniṣadic tradition.

On reflection there is nothing surprising in the thought that there must have existed numerous exemplifications in the bardic tradition of 'Upaniṣadic' questions and answers, which, embedded as they were in the rhapsodic repertory, might with some justice be called 'baronial lore'. Now, it is peculiarly interesting that just the transmigration account of the Uttara-yāyāta that parallels those of the *Chāndogya* and *Bṛhadāraṇyaka* is by the Upaniṣads themselves declared to be baronial in origin. *ChUp.* V. 3. 7 has: *iyaṃ na prāk tvattaḥ purā vidyā brāhmaṇān gacchati* 'this lore has not gone to the Brahmans before you', and *BĀUp.* VI. 2.8 reads: *iyaṃ vidyetaḥ pūrvaṃ na kasmiṃś cana brāhmaṇa uvāsa* 'this lore has not lodged before this with any Brahman'. These two statements make it quite clear that it was part of the tradition of this particular *vidyā* that it belonged to the baronial lore.

[632] I do not intend here to revive the old question of whether there was any special Kṣatriya wisdom from which the Brahmans were excluded, but rather to suggest an answer to the questions which the quoted Upaniṣadic statements must raise and to place the statements in a meaningful context.

It is hard to believe in the existence of 'two cultures', a Kṣatriya and a Brahman one. Rather do the epics and Upaniṣads present the picture of an intimate interrelationship between Brahman and baron. Yet, when we compare the epic with the previous Vedic literature, it is clear that we can make a distinction between on the one hand the baronial entourage with his *purohitas,* surely reinforced by the village Brahmans, and on the other hand the true Brahman experts, highly trained specialists in a difficult and recondite lore which found its superb expression in the really grand Śrauta rituals which they conducted. However, sharply competitive with one another at times, they did constitute a community of specialists separate from the local baronial estates. To be sure, the grand Śrauta rituals of Rājasūya, Aśvamedha and Vājapeya were eminently the celebrations of barons, still they were occasional affairs. Many of the priests were almost constantly on tour and away from their communities for extended periods. On these tours they universalized their knowledge—and thus the variations between *śākhās* in a Veda remained really very minor—, but this knowledge remained of a highly specialized character. Higher speculation, as we begin [633] to meet it in the later Brāhmaṇas, Āraṇyakas and Upaniṣads, would be expressed in the universe of discourse that their occupation and preoccupations had provided. These priests were by no means mythopoets; a patron interested in the myths behind the rites must often have been disappointed by their specialized accounts: thin, not at all fleshed out to a baron accustomed to headier stuff by his own bards.

Far more striking than the presence of kings in the Upaniṣads is their absence in the Brāhmaṇas. It is here that one might expect proudly flaunted names of superb regal patrons who helped institutionalize special liturgies. We must conclude that this 'prescientific science' was simply beyond the ken of the barons; baronial interest in liturgy was strictly practical and they left the priests to their own devices. However, when their speculations began to touch on the after-life and the heaven to which the barons since the *Ṛgveda* had so confidently looked forward became at least problematic, we find the barons at once participating in the discussions. There is good reason to suppose that the barons were at least as interested in their own hereafter as their priests and had quite possibly more questions to ask of their own conduct, if this conduct predetermined their future life. While only a few names are mentioned in the Upaniṣads—which remained Brahmanic texts transmitted in specialized groups—it can be safely assumed that there existed a thriving oral literature which raised the same questions and provided the same answers, but to a different audience and in **[634]** a different style. We can look upon them as a kind of bardic counterpart to the Brahmanic Upaniṣads. It is a text like the Uttara-yāyāta which gives us an insight into its contents and forms.

While the parallel Upaniṣadic passages give an abstract account of the *devayāna* and the *pitṛyāna*, the bardic text dramatizes it as the story of one who actually travels the way. All the discussants are kings themselves.[14] There is no intimation that the eschatological lore presented needs a priest for its promulgation; it is the report of a royal eye-witness. The protagonist is Yayāti, a grand baronial hero. He is little known in earlier literature; *ṚV*.I.31.17 and X.63.1 know him as the son of Nahuṣa and a patron of sacrifices. In the genealogies of the Ādiparvan he is made into a great ancestor, the eighth from Dakṣa himself, the father of the Five Nations, among whom the Pauravas predominate.

It would seem to me that we can understand the so-called baronial provenance of the Upaniṣadic *vidyā* best if we, with the aid of the Uttara-yāyāta, accept the existence of a well-known bardic story with royal heroes in which the facts and progress of transmigration was described. It may, for that matter, have even been an early form of the Uttara-yāyāta itself. The present text displays a number of discrepancies and inconsistencies which are best understood as the result [635] of varying versions which at a fairly late date were consolidated into one version. And a variety of versions should point to both antiquity and popularity.

While it would be rash to extrapolate from this instance—though on closer reading of the epic more may appear—we find good reason to accept that side by side with the Upaniṣads there existed a bardic literature seized with similar concerns. It is not necessary to assume that that literature always would have had to wait on the problems and solutions provided by the Brahmans. They may well have been mutually reinforcing, so that there may have been some cause for Pravāhaṇa's contention in the *Chāndogya* that this was a baronial lore: that very much the same conceptions return in the typically baronial Uttara-yāyāta is at least very curious. But this is probably as far as we may go. That the Upaniṣadic accounts and the Uttara-yāyāta deal with transmigration should not seduce us to the conclusion that the baronial literature produced this basic philosopheme exclusively.

NOTES

1. Vishnu S. Sukthankar, *The Mahābhārata:* the Ādiparvan (Poona 1933), Addenda et Corrigenda, p. 992. Of course all *Mahābhārata* quotations are from the critical edition.
2. Sic; the king's name will later be Vasumanas.
3. But later the name Indra will be used.
4. But in I.84 it is the 'Envoy of the Gods' who tells him to fall.
5. He will be asked to identify himself twice more, I.87 and 88.
6. In the Story of Yayāti, too, the millennium is the usual time unit; Yayāti belonged to the Kṛta Yuga (I.85.1).
7. On the notion of 'world' now see J. Gonda, *The Sanskrit Word Loka* (Transactions of Amsterdam Academy 1967).
8. This must derive from a different version that I.84, where the reason for Yayāti's fall is his self-glorification.
9. I.e. the *saṃsāra.*
10. In *bhaumā rākṣasāḥ* (85.8), *bhauma* stands for *bhaumanaraka.*
11. Cf. *ChUp.* VIII.6.5; the notion is accepted in *Vedāntasūtra* IV.2.17.
12. Not recorded in this sense by Monier Williams.
13. And which are called *kīṭāḥ pataṅgā yad idaṃ dandaśūkam* in *BĀUp.* VI.2.16.
14. Among whom Pratardana, himself connected with a *vidyā* (*KauṣUp.* III.9).

24

TWO NOTES ON THE MEGHADŪTA

Kālidāsa's Meghadūta has been translated some eighteen times since the first translation by H.H. Wilson in 1813, which came to Goethe's attention. In spite of this hermeneutic activity, it cannot be said that all the problems of this famous poem have been solved. At another occasion I suggested a more precise translation for M.36;[1] we may here return to two other stanzas which I think have not been clearly understood.

pratyāsanne nabhasi dayitājīvitālambanārthī
jīmūtena svakuśalamayīṃ hārayiṣyan pravṛttim/
sa pratyagraiḥ kuṭajakusumaiḥ kalpitārghāya tasmai
prītaḥ prītipramukhavacanaṃ svāgatam vyājahāra//

The word *nabhas* is commonly taken in the sense of the month "*śrāvaṇa*," principally on the authority of the Indian commentators. Before Kālidāsa, this meaning is only attested for some Vedic texts;[2] and its occurrence here is, to say the least, unexpected. Unlike other and later *kāvya* authors, Kālidāsa does not go out of his way to puzzle his reader with obscure and erudite words and meanings.

Besides, and this is a worse offense, the phrase *pratyāsanne nabhasi* becomes redundant. In stanza 2 the author had set the time of the appearance of the monsoon cloud *āṣāḍhasya praśamadivase*, There is a variant *prathamadivase*, obviously a lectio facilior, which has rightly been rejected in what is so far the best critical edition of the text, that of Hultzsch.[3] The word *praśama* is nicely chosen; primarily it means "extinction"; taking into account that *āsāḍha* is a very hot month, the description of the last day of *āṣāḍha* as "the day when the summer month is extinguished" is both elegant and appropriate

This reading is known on the authority of Vallabhadeva (tenth century), who is the oldest commentator on our text. It is not quite right to present it as a conjecture of Vallabhadeva.[4] He writes "certain (commentators), however, confused by the similarity of the writing of *śa* and *tha*, read *prathama* and with great difficulty make sense of the meaning. But 'first day' is completely excluded, since the rainy season is beginning." The most recent translation follows Vallabhadeva's reading.[5]

If we accept *praśamadivase,* the meaning of *nabhas* "śrāvaṇa" is unacceptable because of its redundancy. It is totally out of character for a poet like Kālidāsa to **[169]** continue, after having said in stanza 2 that it was the last day of one month, to say in stanza 4 that the next month was at hand. The Edgerton translation hedges here a bit; the absolute locative is translated by "the rains now at hand," in which he seems to take *nabhas* in a derived sense from "mist, clouds" to "rainy season". This is certainly not unreasonable; however, such a meaning is only recorded by lexicographers,[6] and, for all we know, perhaps reconstructed from exactly this passage.

I think another interpretation commends itself. As is well known, the word sequence in Kālidāsa is extremely important for the overtones of his intention. A typical example is M. 1a where *svādhikārapramattaḥ* is immediately preceded by *kāntāviraha-guruṇā;* even though the words have no grammatical relation to each other, the very pairing of them immediately suggests that if Kubera's curse that exiled our Yakṣa was "the more painful because of the separation from his beloved," the fact that the Yakṣa had been negligent in his duties was caused by his passion.

In stanza 3 it is indicated that the Yakṣa, living on the mountain when he saw the cloud embracing the mountain peak (*āśliṣṭa-sānum*, 2), then took himself to the peak, though not without difficulty, emaciated as he was by the pains of separation: *tasya sthitvā katham api puraḥ* "taking his stand with difficulty before the cloud." The Edgertons misread the text here, I think: "Before that fountain-head of yearning (i.e. the cloud), Kubera's henchman stood with an effort restraining his tears, . ." But in the clause *tasya sthitvā katham api puraḥ, tasya* and *puraḥ* obviously belong together and thus bracket off the clause, enclosing *katham api*. Besides, the idiom *katham api* "somehow, i.e. always with difficulty" is far more generally used with verbal forms than constructed with an adjective like *antarbāṣpaḥ*.

The Yakṣa then has moved up to the peak from Rāma's hermitage where he had been living. And this point, picayunish as it may seem to be, helps us to understand *nabhas* in 4. In my opinion, the most common meaning of the word, "sky, heaven," makes the best sense here. Having climbed to the mountain peak to greet the cloud that perches there, the Yakṣa has approached the sky in a very literal sense. And this pedestrian fact is neatly twisted by Kālidāsa: *pratyāsanne nabhasi dayitājīvitālambanārthī*. The nearness of heaven puts the Yakṣa in mind of death. The poet elaborates here on the well-known euphemism for dying as "going to heaven" (*svargaṃ gā, āsthā, āpad*; *svargīya* etc.). And this thought of death inspires the Yakṣa, who has his beloved constantly in mind, to "support the life of this beloved." In this interpretation the translation reads "being desirous to support the life of his beloved now that heaven was so close at hand.." Vallabhadeva's own preference is śrāvaṇa for *nabhas*, noting that thus stanza 4 repeats the meaning of stanza 2 with his reading of *praśama*. He notes however the interpretation of "others" who take *nabhas* in the sense of *gagana* "sky," "the sky being brought near since it is overcast by the cloud." This sense can well be adapted to the interpretation given above. The translation of the entire stanza then runs :

[170] Wishing the cloud to take a message of his own good health as he became anxious to support the life of his beloved now that heaven was so close by, he spoke affectionately an affectionate word of welcome to it after offering it a guest gift with fresh jasmine flowers.

* * *

pādanyāsakvaṇitaraśanās tatra līlāvadhūtai
ratnacchāyākhacitavalibhiś cāmaraiḥ klāntahastāḥ|
veśyās tvatto nakhapadasukhān prāpya varṣāgrabindūn
āmokṣyanti tvayi madhukaraśreṇidīrghān kaṭākṣān||

The problem here is the meaning of *vali*. The word quite commonly is attested in the meaning of "a fold of skin, a wrinkle." The stanza describes the temple dancers in the Mahākāla temple of Ujjayinī who are engaged in a fan dance; the fans (*cāmaras*, chowries) are said to be *ratnacchāyākhacitavalibhiḥ*. Since the stanza dwells on the voluptuousness of the dancers there is a priori no reason to dismiss the attested meaning for *vali*, and particularly of *trivali* "the three wrinkles about a woman's navel" which are considered a mark of beauty. If we take it in this sense, then *khacita* becomes a problem; it means "studded, encrusted." The commentators generally do injustice to the meaning either of *vali* or of *khacita*. Vallabhadeva, retaining the meaning of *vali*, glosses *khacita* as *prakaṭīkṛta* "made visible," which is not only unattested but also farfetched. Mallinātha[7] invents for *vali* the meaning of *cāmaradaṇḍa* "the fan handle," apparently borrowing from Dakṣiṇāvartanātha[8] who paraphrases the entire compound with *ratnacchāyāsaṃbaddhacāmaradaṇḍavalibhaṅgaiḥ* "(the fans), the fold-like bends of whose handles are fashioned with the hues of jewels." A similar interpretation is given by Sthiradeva[9] who has *taddaṇḍamaṇḍalībhūtaparvavicchitti* "the edge of the knot which circles around the fan's handle." The latter commentators here have in mind a handle made of cane with the knots encrusted. These knots would then be metaphorically described as *vali* in the common sense; this interpretation is not unreasonable but rather farfetched. Of the recent translators, de Pompignan follows Mallinātha, the Edgertons (probably) Dakṣiṇāvartanātha: "the handle-rings studded with bright gems."

I believe the solution is quite simple: *khacitavali* is a bahuvrīhi compound of the type that is a favorite of Kālidāsa in the Meghadūta, with the first member a past participle; the bahuvrīhi analysis either as "by whom (which) something is done" or "for whom (which) something is done." *khacitavalibhiś cāmaraiḥ* then translates "the chowries by whom the navel-folds of the women are encrusted." It is the boldness of this expression which has led the commentators to their various variations.

It can escape no one how much Kālidāsa in this poem delights in describing colors and reflected colors; one of the charms of the Meghadūta is just this glittering play of all kinds of light in all kinds of ways. Here we have, I think, another example. The temple dancers are waving the fans about as they dance, holding the handle of the fan no doubt at waist height as the most obvious place to hold them. The handles of the fan are certainly encrusted with jewels, and the most natural way to [171] read the entire compound is that the reflection of these gems (*ratnacchāyā*) on the waists of the dancers seem to stud their navel folds.

The closest to come to this interpretation was Sthiradeva who gives an alternative paraphrasis to the one mentioned above:

athavā khacitāḥ chūritāḥ tāsām eva cāmaragrahiṇīnām udaralekhā yaiḥ.

The translation of the entire stanza then runs as follows:

There (in the temple court) [the courtesans [whose girdles tinkle as they make their steps, their hands tired by the playfully waved chowries which seem to stud their navel folds with reflections of their gems, will cast at you, when they receive from you fresh rain drops that soothe their nail scratches, sidelong glances which are lengthened by a string of bees.[10]

NOTES

1. "The Gajasaṃhāramūrti in Meghadūta 36," Festschrift Munshi [no. 14 in this volume].
2. E.g. Śatapatha Brāhmaṇa 13.15.22.31.
3. *Kālidāsa's Meghadūta*, by E. Hultzsch (London, 1911), with Vallabhadeva's commentary.
4. *Meghadūta (le Nuage Messager)*, poème élégiaque de Kālidāsa, traduit et annoté par R.H. Assier de Pompignan (Paris, 1938), p. 2, note on stanza 2: "correction de V. . La leçon ancienne, conservée par M et la plupart des commentateurs, a dû être *prathama*. Elle accorde mieux avec 61." Neither of the statements convinces. The author prints *praśama* and translates *prathama.*
5. *Kālidāsa, the Cloud Messenger*, translated from the Sanskrit *Meghadūta* by Franklin and Eleanor Edgerton (Michigan, 1964).
6. Cf. PW s.v. *nabhasa.*
7. *The Meghadūta of Kālidāsa with the commentary* (*Sañjivinī*) *of Mallinātha*, ed. N.B. Godbole and K.P. Parab (Bombay, 1902).
8. *The Meghasandeśa of Kālidāsa with the commentary Pradīpa of Dakṣiṇāvartanātha*, ed. T. Gaṇapati Śāstrī (Trivandrum, 1919).
9. *Kālidāsīyam Meghadūtam, Sthiradevāvyakhyāsanātham*, ed. V.G. Paranjpe (Poona, 1935).
10. Thus I would take *madhukaraśreṇidīrghān*; it is a common conceit that a women's eye is so much like a lotus flower that bees mistake it for one; thus the eye, already long, is even lengthened by a string of bees in pursuit.

25

THE SEVEN CASTES OF MEGASTHENES

One of the most curious problems presented by Megasthenes' *Indika* as preserved principally by Strabo, Arrian and Diodorus Siculus[1] is that of the seven population groups in which, according to him, Indian society was divided. It has been pointed out frequently that these seven groups make no sense. They obviously cannot be identified with the *varṇas,* which are four. It is also out of the question that the seven groups exhaust the number of *jātis* that existed in Candragupta's time.[2] In the best study, to my knowledge, on the subject of Megasthenes' account of Indian society Barbara Timmer comes to the following conclusion:[3] "The mutual sequence of the seven classes is therefore determined by different motivations: first, by Indian conceptions; second, by their social functions; third, by incidental qualities such as number; and for the rest by the author's whim." These "Indian religious conceptions" amount to the fact that the Brahmins are placed first and are declared to be the most highly honored group. The division into seven groups she attributes to a partially mistaken application by Megasthenes of the common Brahministic notion that class and profession coincide, so that he identified every professional and vocational group as a class or caste.[4] While this is a fetching notion, it is hard to understand why Megasthenes identified [229] only *seven* vocations; physicians and lawyers, for instance, are not recognized among them.

While many of Miss Timmer's results should be retained, it may be worthwhile to return to this old problem and suggest a new interpretation which may bring some clarity to it. It has become customary to translate Megasthenes' *groups* by "class, caste,"[5] and we may well wonder whether this is not a misnomer, since the groups correspond to neither.[6] The only *varṇa* discernible is that of the Brahmins, but in his description Megasthenes clearly refers to only a small group among the Brahmins, namely, the professional priests. To identify the soldiers with the kṣatriyas is stretching the point beyond reason; and if we identify the artisans and tradesmen with the vaiśyas, are we to consider all the peasants śūdras? And that these seven groups were the only castes of the time militates against historical evidence. It therefore prejudices the question by calling these groups "castes."

On the other hand, it is true that Megasthenes himself identifies them in caste terms when he says that the groups do not intermarry, that members of the groups are not permitted to adopt the vocation of another group, and that vocations thus are hereditary.[7] Also, from his description of the manners of India, it is clear that he observed the lack of commensality which we would attribute to their differences in caste.[8] We are thus faced with the fact that Megasthenes knew about caste and erroneously assumed that the seven groups corresponded to castes. I am inclined to go a step further than Miss Timmer and submit that the application of caste to the groups was *completely* mistaken and that, if one of the groups happened to be a caste also, it was by accident.

This leads us to assume that the application of notions of class **[230]** and caste to the seven groups can only be confusing and that we should look for another principle of classification in order to understand why Megasthenes mentioned just these groups. For even if they were not castes, they might still be a correct division of society, however rough.

He enumerates them in this order: philosophers, peasants, herdsmen (including hunters), artisans-tradesmen, soldiers, inspectors, and officials; and, though incomplete, this looks like a rough and ready inventory of population during Candragupta's time. It is possible to argue that Megasthenes himself has drawn up these groups from personal observation, but there is an important argument against it. He mentions carefully the relation of each group to the treasury; and though such information could no doubt have been acquired by interviewing the groups once he had listed them, it is far more likely that he simply went to a treasury official and asked for the information.

Megasthenes, after all, was an ambassador, and envoys are rarely courtesy visits. He was sent by Seleukos Nikator, who spent most of his life warring for Alexander's bequest of the

Middle East. In 307 or 306 Seleukos had invaded Northwest India, no doubt to claim Alexander's old conquests. Troubles elsewhere forced him in 304 to stop his campaign, and in fact he completely abandoned all claims to the territory in a treaty with Candragupta in which he actually ceded the Paropanisadic country, Arachosia, and Gedrosia for five hundred elephants. It was after concluding this treaty that Megasthenes was sent to India, to keep a check, one cannot help thinking, on Candragupta's own intentions. An army of 400,000 men, as Megasthenes attributes to the Maurya,[9] is a considerable force on a warring neighbor's flank. A country's military power depends on its revenues, and one may safely assume that Megasthenes, himself a general, investigated the tax basis of the country.

Looked at from this point of view, Megasthenes list makes excellent sense. It is an official list: the seven groups are in fact seven *treasury or tax categories.*

1. Philosophers: tax-exempt and occasionally to be paid out of the treasury.

[231] 2. Agriculturalists: free from military service and in theory tenants of the king's land as Crown demesne, paying 25% in rents.

3. Herdsmen: pay cattle taxes, but may receive grain grants for clearing the jungle of game.
4. Artisans-tradesmen: pay taxes, with the exceptions of weaponsmiths and shipwrights, who are paid out of the treasury.
5. Soldiers: including horses, elephants and their handlers, entirely paid out of the treasury.
6. Inspectors:[10] entirely paid out of the treasury.
7. Officials: entirely paid out of the treasury.

We have therefore two basic groups: those who pay taxes *into* the treasury, and those who receive money *from* the treasury—respectively, (2), (3) and (4); and (5), (6) and (7). This leaves the category of the philosophers, who are in neither category, being tax-exempt and not paid out of the treasury, except in incidental cases at New Year.

This classification of the population by people who neither pay nor receive, those who only pay (with specific exceptions), and those who only receive,[11] seems to me a very sensible one from the point of view of the fiscus, and at the same time resonant of

[232] Indian classification. There is A, there is B, and there is neither A nor B; the last group could as easily have been placed last in the list, but it is obviously put first as a sign of respect either by Megasthenes' informant or by Megasthenes himself.

It is noteworthy that after the description of the seven groups Megasthenes resumes the topic of the philosophers in greater detail.[12]

Miss Timmer curiously rejects this interpretation because "members of the same class often relate differently to (the treasury)."[13] This is true, but every tax category usually has its minor exceptions. Again in the listing there seems to be sensible order: those who all pay taxes (2); those who all pay taxes, but may be recompensed for special services (3); those who all pay taxes with the exception of weaponsmiths and shipwrights. Of the last one it is at once noted with typical accountant's precision what happens to the products; the weapons go to the general for distribution, the ships go to the admiral for rental.

I see a similar order in the categories (5), (6) and (7). First, no doubt the largest recipent of expenditures is the Army,[14] followed directly by Intelligence, which surely was military as well as fiscal, and finally the Government.

The only mistake Megasthenes made was to think of these fiscal population groups as castes and to apply to them what he knew of caste. The mistake is understandable, especially since the groups obviously included castes. And it might have been a simple misunderstanding. *Jāti* may mean any group[15] that can be classed together, and Megasthenes, upon asking a revenue official, "How many *jātis* are there in the countty?" could well have received the answer, "These seven."

NOTES

1. For the reader of Dutch the most convenient compilation of the materials here discussed is found in Barbara C.J. Timmer's *Megasthenes en de Indische maatschappij* (Thesis, Amsterdam 1930); others will have to rely on J.W. McCrindle, *The* Indika *of Megasthenes and Arrian*, now reprinted as *Ancient India as Described by Megasthenes and Arrian* (Calcutta 1960) and *Ancient India, As described in Classical Literature* (Westminister 1901); the Greek and Latin sources are collected in E.A. Schwanbeck, *Megasthenis Indica* (reprinted Amsterdam 1966).

2. Arrian reports, somewhat incredulously, that according to Megasthenes there were 118 "tribes" in India (McCrincle, *The* Indika, pp. 198-99), which may well correspond to castes; the number itself may be based on the usual 108 in the sense of a hundred, or fairly large indefinite number.

3. Op. cit., p. 68.

4. P. 67.

5. Particularly since McCrindle; more recently, A.L. Basham, *The Wonder That was India* (London 1954), p. 101, spoke more cautiously of Megasthenes' "seven occupational classes."

6. Among others and most recently, R.C. Majumdar, "The Indika of Megasthenes," (JAOS, 1958), pp. 273ff., finds in these "castes" an occasion to impugn Megasthenes' veracity: "His description of the seven castes, which are unknown to Indian literature or tradition, may be cited as an example (sc. of Megasthenes' unreliability), where, on a few basic facts, he has reared up a structure which is mostly inaccurate and misleading." But translating them as "castes" in the first place produces the inaccuracy; cf. also his note p. 231, in reprint of McCrindle, *Ancint India.*

7. Timmer, op, cit, pp. 53-55 for the sources.

8. Cf. Timmer, p. 263, corresponding to Strabo, 15.1.53.

9. Strabo I, 53, p. 709; H.L. Jones, *The Geography of Strabo* (New York 1932) translates "40,000,"' which Majumdar wants to accept; but Arrian 12, 2-4 says that the solders are the second most numerous group (after the peasants), which makes us prefer 400,000.

10. To translate *episkopoi/éphoroi* as "spies" is to narrow unduly the significance of this group; they constitute a government service which, since it is listed separately, was clearly budgeted separately from Army and Ministries, as secret services usually are. Their use of prostitutes as "stool pigeons" (for which Kauṭilya also allows) is not at all surprising. The information thus elicited would be of at least three kinds: on criminal underworld activity generally, even though prostitution itself was legal; on the amount of discretionary income of possibly undertaxed citizens (these kinds of information would no doubt emerge from the city courtesans who, according to Strabo, are distinguished from camp-following prostitutes); and on unrest in the army (from camp followers). The service as a whole is approximately that of a police force—criminal, political as well as military—a service not accounted for among Megasthenes' three principal government departments (Timmer, pp. 177-78); Strabo, 15-1.50-52.

11. It is revealing to what extent Megasthenes' account is saturated with what one might call fiscal attitudes: the army is really overpaid and makes merry in peace-time on government money (Timmer, pp. 155-56); Strabo 15.1.47; of the three principal departments, the first, the agoranómoi, collects revenues from lumber-jacks, carpenters, smiths and miners; the second, the astunómoi, includes a *pañcāyat* to encourage the flow of foreign money, one for vital statistics "for the sake of taxes," one for commerce which makes sure that merchants dealing in more than one product are doubly taxed and one that supervises the 10% sales tax. This consistent interest in taxation should point to the preoccupation of both Megasthenes and his informant.

12. Which may indicate that the description of the philosophers was the last one; but the point is tenuous.

13. P. 69.

14. According to Arrian, the second largest group of the population.

15. Megasthenes seems to have used only *meros* and *genea*, or "parts" and "kinds" in his original account; both words are sufficiently neutral and both are translatable by *jāti*, when speaking of population groups.

26

ON THE STRUCTURE OF THE SABHĀPARVAN OF THE MAHĀBHĀRATA

It is somewhat surprising that the critical edition of the Mahābhārata, which has provided us with as clean a text as will probably ever be within our reach, has not so far inspired to more research on the great epic. It would now seem to be the time to investigate what the text edition contributes to, or takes away from, the multifarious views proposed about the origin and development of the Mahābhārata, and to give a fresh evaluation of the holistic approaches of the analytic, synthetic and inversion schools.

It is not now our intention to take up this pressing task. In this article I should like to study in particular one of the central books of the epic proper, the *Sabhāparvan*. It appears to me that closer investigation into the structure of this book reveals a definite design and that some of the incidents in it, in particular the anomalous dicing game, can be more clearly understood from this design.

For the development of the plot that underlies the Mahābhārata as we have received it, the second book, the *Book of the Assembly Hall is,* of course, of signal importance.[1] The epical portions of the preceding *Ādiparvan* have done no more than set the scene: Dhṛtarāṣṭra's holding down a precarious regency for not clearly identifiable heirs to the kingdom of Hāstinapura,[2] the rivalry between the young Pāṇḍava and Kaurava princes; the thinly disguised banishment of the Pāṇḍavas to Varaṇāvata; their escape there from Duryodhana's assassination attempt in the lacquer house; their disappearance from which they emerge at Draupadī's Bridegroom Choice, which leads to their alliance with the Pāñcāla king Drupada and indirectly to a tentative solution of the fundamental inheritence problem by the partition of Kurukṣetra into a Hāstinapura and an Indraprastha branch. The same *Book of the* [69] *Beginning* also establishes the close connection of Kṛṣṇa Vāsudeva with Yudhiṣṭhira and especially Arjuna. The latter association is sealed in the *Burning of the Khāṇḍava Forest*—which to me appears a burning of the woods to make room for the agriculture that must make Indraprastha viable;—and from the same forest emerges the shadowy Maya[3] to build the assembly hall from which the second book derives its name.

The *Sabhā* consists in the following minor[4] parvants: (1) the *Building of the Assembly Hall,*[5] (2) the *Descripton of the Halls of the World Guardians,*[6] (3) the *Council,*[7] (4) the *Slaying of Jarāsaṃdha,*[8] (5) the *Conquest of the World,*[9] (6) the *Royal Consecration,*[10] (7) the *Taking of the Guest Gift,*[11] (8) the *Slaying of Śiśupāla,*[12] (9) the *Dicing Game,*[13] (10) the *Sequel to the Dicing.*[14] The first one establishes Yudhiṣṭhira as king *de facto*. The following one presents Nārada, who instructs the king in just policy, then embarks on a description of the halls of Indra, who governs the East; of Yama, regent of the South; of Varuṇa, regent of the West; and of Kubera, who rules the North. To these quarters there is added, in usual fashion, a fifth *diś*, the zenith, over which Brahmā presides. Although this description is surely secondary to the epic, it is not a fortuitous insertion; it has a real function in that it magnifies Yudhiṣṭhira's hall, which on earth as it were epitomizes the celestial five, and thus borrows from them a universal totality.[15] In conclusion, Nārada glorifies King Hariścandra who attained to his high estate because he celebrated the *rājasūya*. This gives Yudhiṣṭhira thought of himself performing the Royal Consecration.

It is from *this intention* that all the further events of the epic derive. As far as the *Sabhāparvan* is concerned, I wish to argue [70] hereunder that the circumstances of the *rājasūya* have lent their design to the parvan as a whole and that the parvan is an epic dramatization of the events of the *rājasūya*. To be sure, we shall no more expect complete fidelity to the sūtras here, than of the epic Aśvamedha to the Vedic one.[16] On the contrary, we expect that extra dimension which is so sadly lacking in the ritual texts: the royal dimension. The king is not lilely to be seen only as a *yajamāna,*[17] but as a potentate. To avoid misunderstanding, I want to make it clear that I do not want to argue that "originally" the *Sabhāparvan* was just a description of the *rājasūya*, though certainly a number of events of the *rājasūya* form a central part of it. My main point will be that those responsible for the composition of the *Sabhā* found in the *rājasūya* a ready model for their composition and that they designed the book on it.

This hypothesis helps to explain the anomaly of the dicing game. Yudhiṣṭhira, honored by the entire baronage, which has brought him tribute, and secure in his own kingdom, seemingly succumbs to his passion for dicing and responds to a challenge to a game at which he loses everything, including his freedom. It has upset many scholars that he, the King Dharma, could be celebrated as law-abiding and still depicted as flagrantly flying in the face of morality[18]. Tḥis is not the only anomaly. The matter of the game is brought up abruptly and laconically by Śakuni to Duryodhana: "Yudhiṣṭhira is fond of gambling, but does not know how to play".[19] But in all the previous six hundred pages of the epic, not a single reference to this addiction is found.[20] Further, it is automatically assumed that Yudhiṣṭhira, if challenged, cannot refuse to play. Yudhiṣṭhira holds forth on the evils of gambling. Dhṛtarāṣṭra allows the game, because it is *diṣṭa* "destined".[21]

Held, in his ethnological study of the epic, *The Mahābhārata* tries to argue that the dicing in the *Sabhā* is to be seen as a *potlatch.* I do not believe so, but I wish to retain the notion that it is ritually inspired. That makes it easier to understand the inevitability of the [71] game; if it is ritually decreed that, after his coronation, the king shall gamble, then that is that, not as a matter of course, but as a matter of fact.

And, as it happens, it *is* so decreed. The ritual texts prescribe that after the Unction, surely the high point of the *rājasūya,* the king must engage in a dicing game. Now, it can hardly be a coincidence that in the epic *rājasūya* likewise a dicing game almost immediately follws upon the solemn installation of the king. If we may assume, as I think we must, that this sequence was inspired by the same sequence in the Vedic *rājasūya,* it also suggests why fundamentally Yudhiṣṭhira's morality was not affected by engaging in the gaming. In fact, it was his dharma, once having performed the one rite, to continue to the next. In the Vedic rite the dicing is completely *pro forma*; the entire game is reduced to the king's holding five dice which symbolize the five regions: "He is become king of the regions"[22] In the epic, however, the game is in earnest.

If we then have reason to assume that in the composition of the *Sabhā* the paradigm of the Vedic *rājasūya* played a role, it is worthwhile to investigate whether other events can be fitted into that underlying frame. These events then should start with the Council, which in other versions is styled the *rājasūyārambha*; an appropriate name, for the Council is in fact the counsel to undertake the *rājasūya*.

For a proper understanding of the epic *rājasūya*, we must keep in mind that it does not merely purport to bestow kingship on a local ruler, but *sāmrājya* "universal sovereignty" (cf. 2.12.11 f. and *passim*). Hence it is said in ib.13: *tasya yajñasya samayaḥ svādhīnaḥ kṣatrasampadā* "the covenant for this sacrifice is dependent on oneself, with the fullness of the baronage". As soon becomes clear, this *kṣatrasampad* means the full concurrence of the other kings. This baronial consensus of consent is central to the epic *rājasūya*. Yudhiṣṭhira at once sends for Kṛṣṇa who counsels him to defeat [72] Jarāsaṃdha who holds many kings captive in Girivraja,[23] and has driven Kṛṣṇa's own tribe of Vṛṣṇis from Mathurā to Dvārakā; allied with Jarāsaṃdha is Śiśupāla of Cedi,[24] his "marshal". The goodwill earned by the release of the kings will provide the baronial consent required (13.60 ff.; 14.20).

It is tempting to connect this consent to the *rājasūya*, the question of which is raised immediately, with the very first rite of the Vedic *rājasūya*: it is an oblation to Anumati, who is, of course, nothing but Consent personified.[25] The need for Consent recurs when Yudhiṣṭhira is at last ready to offer up the *rājasūya*: then he prays for Kṛṣṇa's assent (2.30.22):

māṃ vāpy abhyanujānīhi sahaibhir anujair vibho |
anujñātas tvayā Kṛṣṇa prāpnuyāṃ kratum uttamam ||

Kṛṣṇa gives him formal permission (ib. 23/24)

tvam eva rājaśārdūla samrāḍ arho mahākratum |
yajasvābhīpsitaṃ yajñaṃ mayi śreyasy avasthite |

This Consent of the barons is interesting from more than one point of view. It takes into account the historical hegemony of Magadha. When it is said that Jarāsaṃdha of Magadha "holds captive" 84 of the 101 kings living, this is surely one way of saying that they are his vassals (even though this "captivity" is then again taken literally, for he is herding them to sacrifice to Paśupati). Also the fact that he dispossessed Kṛṣṇa of Mathurā, not very flattering to the glorified hero, may well reflect an actual raid up the Yamunā by Magadha. One might read an inconsistency in the fact that the *Slaying of Jarāsaṃdha* is followed by the *Conquest of the World*, as though the release of the captive kings was, after all, not sufficient to provide the "baronial consent", but I think the inconsistency is only apparent. As will be seen below, the World Conquest was again taken from the Vedic *rājasūya*, and is likely to be original in one form or other in the present composition of the Sabhā. That Jarāsaṃdha must be killed is not only because he is the present *samrāj en titre*, but because no "world conquest" would make any sense to the contemporaneous audience, well [73] aware of the Magadhan hegemony, without the prior reduction of Magadha.

There is one complexity about Jarāsaṃdha's defeat which deserves notice. It is undertaken by Yudhiṣṭhira and executed by Kṛṣṇa, Bhīma and Arjuna (in fact Bhīma kills him), yet the blame is later laid at Kṛṣṇa's door,[26] as it is also he whom the released kings honor for it.[27] This may explain Yudhiṣṭhira's need to seek Kṛṣṇa's consent later, as though the consent of the kings was, as it were, proxied to Kṛṣṇa.[28]

The *digvijaya* of the Pāṇḍavas on behalf of Yudhiṣṭhira can, in my opinion, not reasonably be separated from the *rājasūya* rite of *digvyāsthāpana*, "the separate establishment of the quarters", which precedes the unction.[29] In the sūtras the rite consists in the following action: the king makes a step into each of the five directions. The universal sovereignty obtained by this rite is symbolized by relevant parts of the Veda, the pantheon, the year, and the people. The rite is a study in ritual reductionism; not only are the relevant parts of the Veda reduced to meters, stomas and sāmans, and the pantheon to five Gods; in the Black Yajurveda the king does not even have to make these steps physically, but takes them mentally.[30]

One of the exasperating things about the Vedic *rājasūya* is that one hardly ever sees the king as *king*. It is scarcely fair to blame our sacerdotal authors for that; one imagines that if the *prayoga* of the Archbishop of Canterbury's office at the British coronation were given as the complete description of the ceremony, it would read as bloodless and fleshless as the Vedic counterpart does. Such a *prayoga* exists in the form of the Westminster *Liber*

Regalis (14th century), and a glance at it confirms my contention; it is of real interest only to the priest and the religiously minded.

Another example from the same British ceremony may be quoted as illustrative of the reduction of rites. There is an early, rather martial, addition: after the church service a banquet was held in Westminster Hall; and during the first course a champion rode [74] on horseback into the hall and challenged all dissenters by throwing down the gauntlet; he did this three times. The new king then drank to the champion from a silvergilt goblet and handed it to him in reward. The later development of this rite is illustrative: it was done last in 1821; the champion's claim was admitted as late as 1902, when, however, the banquet had fallen into desuetude, and the champion henceforth was reduced to the bearer of the standard of England.

Thus, the martial panoply that ought to accompany a royal consecration may be either unacknowledged in the ritual manual, or, in actual practice, reduced to a ceremonial which, without historical evidence, would be rather less than transparent. On the other hand, the events that give the coronation practical substance, the parade that presents the king to the populace, the receptions that provide the homage of the nobles, the visits of neighboring royalty—and the constant, institutionalized jockeying for precedence among the guests—are evanescent in the bald descriptions.

The Vedic *rājasūya* provides examples of a comparable kind. Compare with the British champion, for instance, the "chariot drive" of the newly anointed Vedic king: as we now have it, the king mounts a chariot, drives it off, raids a baron who has taken up a position "somewhere to the east or north of the sacrificial compound". The king shoots arrows at the baron, makes the chariot turn right and returns to his starting point. We see the banquet canceled, and the life-risking champion holding a flag.

Heesterman sagely remarks,[31] "From the point of view of the Vedic ritualist, it (the *rājasūya*) consisted of a series of *ekāhas*, alternating with *iṣṭis* and an occasional animal sacrifice, all of a common type and only modified by the simple insertion of special rites such as the unction, the chariot drive, the dicing ceremony and the use of some special formulas". As a result, in the descriptions the king to be anointed moves through the ritual as a hieratic shade; but it is beyond need of proof that for the king's party the matter lay rather differently. Thus the epical *rājasūya* gives a very relevant picture of different concerns: actual dominion, actual tributaries, actual precedence, and its attendant strife; while the barons leave to the priests their concerns with *ekāhas* and *iṣṭis*. [75] Typically the guest barons appear at the sacrificial terrain only for the Unction and the assignment of the Guest Gift.[32]

Neither priest nor baron obviously gives the full story; but the priest's story might occasionally be fleshed out with the baron's meat. Thus, as the significance of the *digvijaya* is attenuated in the sūtras, so it is no doubt exaggerated in the Mahābhārata.[33] Still, this declaration of dominance over the quarters must at some time have had *some* substance to it; there must have been attending royalty and tribute-paying potentates,[34] for whom the ritual expression of dominion was a little more than five steps taken, physically or mentally. In the introduction to the *digvijaya*, however grandiose, we still see the recognition that any pretense to to sovereignty must take into account the actual hegemony of Magadha; and a king, making himself sovereign, must have made *some* conquests.

In all its exaggeration, the epic *digvijaya* leaves enough options to the conquering king. There are actual raids on other potentates, and battle points scored; frequently the defeated "enemy" will join the victor in further raids. But often the means is diplomacy, and the tribute is token in intention.

There remains some uncertainty about he way in which the killing of Jarāsaṃdha and the *digvijaya* were supposed to dovetail. As mentioned, Kṛṣṇa names Śiśupāla as Jarāsaṃdha's marshal. Yet we do not hear of him when Jarāsaṃdha is slain. When Bhīma conquers his part of the world, his reduction of Śiśupāla is polite in the extreme: the latter smilingly asks him what he is up to, and the other explains that it is Yudhiṣṭhira's *rājasūya*. Śiśupāla willingly accommodates him and Bhīma winds up staying as his guest for thirty days.[35] Nevertheless, Śiśupāla will be very much in hostile evidence at the ceremony.

The *digvijaya*, in which I see an epic dramatization of a baronial exploit also reflected in the Vedic *digvyāsthāpana*, is followed in the epic by the *rājasūya* proper, as it is in the sūtras by the *Unction*. [76] The epic is highly unspecific in its terms,[36] but, as noted, again begins with a request for Consent. That this consent is a matter of fact is not only amply proved by Duryodhana's description of the riches that tributary kings brought in,[37] but significantly also by the serene acquiescence of the Kauravas of Hāstinapura. Considering past strained relations which necessitated the establishment of the Pāṇḍavas as a junior branch at Indraprastha, one should have expected some comment on the junior's pretensions. But they all come happily enough. True, Yudhiṣṭhira seems to be pleading for a truce "at this sacrifice",[38] yet the good faith with which they attend the sacrifice—at which they are charged with responsibilities, or "stride like masters"[39]—is evident enough. It is noteworthy how Yudhiṣṭhira with customary punctilio defers to Bhīṣma when the Guest Gift is to be offered.[40] The entire house once more acts as a unit. It is important to note that from now on there is going to be *one* kingdom, which will vacillate, beginning with the dicing, between the Hāstinapura and Indraprastha Kauravas.[41]

If our hypothesis that the *Sabhā* is intentionally patterned on the Vedic *rājasūya* is correct, we may expect an important rite involving a gift immediately after the Unction,[42] where this episode is called the *arghābhiharaṇa*, the *Taking of the Guest Gift*. While all the guests are assembled at the *vedi*, Bhīṣma tells Yudhiṣṭhira that the guest gifts be fetched and adds, "First bring the gift for the one who is the most deserving of them!" Yudhiṣṭhira seeks Bhīṣma's advice and the latter decides that the one be Kṛṣṇa Vāsudeva. Śiśupāla, the late Jarāsaṃdha's marshal, protests and rises to leave the *sadas* with other kings; he is stopped by Yudhiṣṭhira and berated by Bhīṣma, whom he answers in kind. At last his insults are too much for Kṛṣṇa, who beheads him with his discus.

In the Vedic *rājasūya* there occurs at this point the gift of the [77] remaining unction water.[43] This consecrated water is given to the heir apparent. According to the Black Yajurveda this takes place away from the sacrificial terrain, either at the heir's mother's, or at the heir's; the White Yajurveda however lays down that it takes place on the sacrificial terrain.[44]

I believe that the epic and Vedic episodes are parallel. The epic guest gift is never described and is therefore likely to be the usual water.[45] The honor involved is not that accorded to an heir, as in the sūtras, but to the most important personage present. Obviously, Kṛṣṇa is not Yudhiṣṭhira's heir; still we have to keep in mind that in the epic *rājasūya* we do not have a simple royal consecration, but an installation of a *samrāj*, a unique position that is not strictly inheritable. If, after Yudhiṣṭhira, Kṛṣṇa stands first, the implication is likely that the purple might next well descend on *him*. It is therefore understandable that Śiśupāla's protests against the honor are, first of all, pronounced by *him*, the late Jarāsaṃdha's marshal, who clearly has his own pretensions; and, secondly, focus on the fact that Kṛṣṇa is not a king, and, is moreover, the assassin of Jarāsaṃdha.[46] Recognition of such a one as probable "heir" to the sovereignty is repugnant to him, as it is to others.

Śiśupāla by now must obviously die; and he does, by Kṛṣṇa's hand. Here, perhaps, we are pushing the analogy too far; but it does occur to one to wonder whether Kṛṣṇa in killing Śiśupāla is not substituting in the epic account for the king in his Vedic "chariot drive',[47] which is in fact an attack, and presumably successful, against another baron, presumably a challenger.[48]

To resume for the nonce. Starting from the striking parallelism between the *Sabhāparvan* and the Vedic *rājasūya* in that both have the unlikely sequence of a royal installation and a dicing game, we [78] have pointed to other parallel episodes. These parallels are, by their nature, episodes that are open to epic dramatization and provide a baronial interpretation of stages in the royal ceremony, which in the priestly manuals might well be understated; conversely, sacerdotally important events, the *iṣṭis* and *ekāhas*, are likely to be outside the attention of the barons. We have distinguished a number of such parallels: the important Consent, which leads to the overthrow of Jarāsaṃdha, palely reflected as an *iṣṭi* to Anumati on the sūtra side. The *digvijaya*, as dramatization of the actual dominion implied by the ritual *digvyāsthāpana*. The Unction is, of course, identical with the *abhiṣeka*. Next, the giving of the guest water to Kṛṣṇa and the giving of the Unction water to the heir. And finally, as possibly inspired by the chariot drive, and presumably directed against a baron, the killing of the rival Śiśupāla. I submit that this clustering of analogues, in rather predictable order, cannot be coincidental. Again, I do not pretend to propound that our present *Sabhā* 'grew" out of a baronial account of the *rājasūya*, but only that the composers of the parvan were aware of the sequence of events in the Vedic *rājasūya* and used it in building the narrative analogously.[49]

This brings us to a more detailed enquiry into the dicing game. While the composers used the Vedic *rājasūya*, they had a facility in substituting for the "king" in his various exploits other members of his own party. Kṛṣṇa, Bhīma and Arjuna defeat Jarāsaṃdha; Bhīma, Arjuna, Nakula and Sahadeva conquer the world; Bhīṣma decides to whom the guest water should go; Kṛṣṇa kills Śiśupāla. But in substituting, they are not replacers but lieutenants, acting on the express authority of Yudhiṣṭhira. In the principal moments, the *anumati*, the *abhiṣeka*, and the dicing game, it is Yudhiṣṭhira, and no one else, who is the agent.

In the sūtras, the dicing is no less attenuated and ritualized than the *anumati, digvyāsthāpana* and chariot drive; and nothing in the references gives us a certain idea of its purpose in the *rājasūya*.[50] [79] The epic cannot throw too much light on the original intention, since it is reworked to suit its own purposes. It may either be a survival, in so far as it is quite possible that in the epic circles memories lingered on that at one time the *rājasūya* game was in earnest; or a revival, in so far as the paradigm of the *rājasūya* was deliberately seized upon to provide the structure of the *Sabhāparvan*, and to contribute to the plot of the Mahābhārata as a whole. The epic is a series of precisely stated problems imprecisely and therefore inconclusively resolved, every inconclusive solution raising a new problem; until the very end, when the question remains: whose is heaven and whose is hell? This point counterpoint is typical also of the sequence: royal installation and dicing for kingship; but as all the other dubieties, they strictly remain within the family.

In this instance I think the composers have seized upon the dicing rite in the Vedic ceremony as a ritually legitimate, even prescribed, way of swinging the doubt from Yudhiṣṭhira's apparently unassailable position to the Kauravas' claims. The dead letter of the Vedic game is dramatically revived; and, while there is running protest that this is not fair, that the rite should have remained as dead and buried as the sūtras have it, once challenged Yudhiṣṭhira can hardly refuse to complete the perilous course of the *rājasūya*, about which he earlier had voiced doubts.[51]

Now to the game itself. Considering the varieties of gaming, and the superstitions about them, I am rather doubtful whether an attempt to recover "the" ancient Indian game is worthwhile, and whether any statements about its mythic or cosmic function are representative. But this much can be said. The epic evidence strongly suggests that the game was one more of skill than chance. This skill, attributed to Śakuni,[52] is not further described. One solitary place suggests that a fairly large number of dice were used.[53] [80] As the mode is clearly a yes-or-no game, with no scores being kept from play to play, every one throw decides the play; terms like *kṛta, tretā, dvāpara* and *kali,* which require score-keeping, do not occur.

A peculiarity of the game is that both parties begin by staking a similar sum. Who plays is important on the king's, that is Yudhiṣṭhira's, side; for although he likes to delegate tasks, this he must do. It is not important on his adversary's side; the king plays against a challenging party. The one who primarily challenges him is the one who puts up the stake—Duryodhana; that Śakuni plays for him elicits only a mild remark from Yudhiṣṭhira.[54]

The game presented shows an interesting structure. It goes on in two sessions, each of ten throws. This parallism between the two sessions cannot be accidental; and I take it that, actually, or in the intention of the composer, it was to last for twenty throws exactly. This number is easily seen as the multiple of four and five; but, while we may point to the fact that both these numbers are important in early Indian dicing and that both represent totality,[55] the typical obsession with number combinations in gaming anywhere, inclines me to discount any specific significance. But this much is certain, the game was to last twice ten throws.

Clearly this is not necessarily an attempt at verisimilitude on the part of the composers, as though this type of game would last for twenty throws only, but a deliberate attempt at dramatic tension. An audience,used to symmetry as no other, would, after the first ten throws[56] are demarcated by a passionate plea that the game be stopped,[57] only expect that the second phase would last for the same number of throws. Yudhiṣṭhira's losing streak after ten throws is obvious to the audience; Vidura's unsuccessful attempt at intervention only increases the tense excitement about how the second half will be resolved.

During the first half the stakes are increasing; Yudhiṣṭhira gambles away (1) the initial stake; (2) multiples of one thousand [81] *niṣkas*; (3) his chariot; (4) a hundred thousand serving wenches; (5) a thousand male servants; (6) a thousand bull elephants; (7) a thousand chariots; (8) his horses; (9) ten thousand bullock carts with their teams; (10) four hundred *nidhis*. These huge riches, while still credible to an epic imagination that had just been stirred by the description of Yudhiṣṭhira's wealth, incite a happy sense of doom and disaster if the unlucky streak continues. As it does.

In the second half,[58] Yudhiṣṭhira stakes and loses untold millions, in fact all his riches in chattels; (2) all his cattle; (3) all his land; (4) his pages; (5) Nakula; (6) Sahadeva; (7) Bhīma; (8) Arjuna; (9) himself.

At the tenth throw of this phase he stakes his wife Draupadī. The audience groans and protests, but does nothing to stop the game, which, falling just one short of the necessary number of throws, must run its inexorable course. The game evidently is going to have to be a total one, with a total winner and total loser, just as Yudhiṣṭhira earlier had been the total sovereign. But we keep being reminded that this is a family game, a *suhṛddyūta*,[59] and whatever the outcome, the family's power will remain total. Having lost everything else, Yudhiṣṭhira stakes Draupadī and, with her, the alliance with Pāñcāla. The throw is lost; but at this point, when the pendulum seems to have swung totally to the Kauravas' side, the composers introduce one of their usual and artful dubieties: was Yudhiṣṭhira, who had lost his freedom, at liberty to stake Draupadī, whom, as a slave, he no longer owned?

There is much argument, but it remains inconclusive. Even the Kauravas are divided. In the end Dhṛtarāṣṭra decides that the last throw was indecisive, and that therefore the game as a whole has neither been won nor lost. Meanwhile the Pāṇḍavas have gone through so many indignities, particularly on Draupadī's account, molested as she was by Duḥśāsana and insulted by Duryodhana, that the breach, mournfully predicted by Vidura, cannot possibly be prevented. Since the game was neither lost nor won, the Pāṇḍavas depart free and rich men. But only nineteen throws have been made; and this number demands completion, as does the final breach of Pāṇḍavas and Kauravas.

At this point it becomes predictable not only that the game must [82] be concluded, but that it must be concluded with a single all-or-nothing stake between the two family branches. Promptly there follows the *anudyūta*, the follow-up game, in which Duryodhana with his father's consent, decides to stake Hāstinapura against Indraprastha. Again, Yudhiṣṭhira cannot refuse, since this game is but the completion of the preceding one. To keep the dubiety in the chain of events, the authors decree that this should not be *quite* an all-or-nothing throw, but a bet against thirteen years in exile, with the playful and adventurous element thrown in that during the thirteenth year the losing party should live "among people", and not be found out; leaving, even at this seemingly final point, all the options open.

It would seem to me that we have sufficient reason to accept that the *Sabhāparvan* is not a meandering improvisation from one event to another, but a fairly tightly structured narrative; and that it borrowed its structure from the Vedic *rājasūya*. While it would seem to me unprofitable to speculate on the "original" form of this parvan, it does appear that two events in this book are so basic that they must have been given from the beginning: the *Unction* and the *Dicing*.

The *Unction* legitimizes Yudhiṣṭhira as the paramount king of the Kauravas, after all the preceding dubieties of the Ādiparvan as to who is the real heir. This legitimacy is required if we are to justify the final internecine war. The period of exile is, after, all, only an interruption in Yudhiṣṭhira's reign. The fact that his rightful kingdom is withheld from him after the exile is a just *casus belli*.

No less can we imagine a Bhārata without the *Dicing* and the events it sets into motion. This would mean that the narrative would have ended with the *Unction*. In itself this would have meant the satisfactory ending to a different story: how after many tribulations the uncertain, but now vindicated, heir succeeds to his patrimony, and is definitely installed. It is irrelevant whether or not this kind of narrative—which in certain respects recalls the Rāmāyaṇa—was a building block in the Bhārata story. The design that we have to work with is that of the grand infrastructure of the stories of a Bhīṣma, Droṇa, Vidura, Dhṛtarāṣṭra, Pāṇḍu and his vicarious paternity through Dharma, Vāyu, Indra, and the Aśvins; an infrastructure too complex to support a simple succession legend. Built into the plot from the beginning is a genuine genealogical uncertainty [83] about the legitimacy of the succession, which leaves, after Yudhiṣṭhira's successful *rājasūya*, still the claims of the senior Hāstinapura branch to be accounted for. Thus I cannot see in the present design of the epic an *inde-*

pendent story, in need of no completion, of Yudhiṣṭhira's enthronement.

It follows, for me at least, that the Dicing was a necessary part of the design, necessary to demonstrate the Pāṇḍavas' virtue in abiding by the terms of the game, and their virtuousness in exile, and the unfitness of the Kauravas who refused to abide by the same terms and to give back the kingdom. From the Pāṇḍava side the game was an honest one, since they abode by the rules and the consequences; from the Kaurava side it was a dishonest one, since they did neither. The Pāṇḍavas have accepted everything, Pāṇḍu's curious self-exile to the forest, their own semi-exile to Varaṇāvata, the devilry of the arson in the Lacquer House, their self-exile until their reappearance at Draupadī's Bridegroom Choice; and, after the *Dicing*, the stipulated thirteen-year exile of the Āraṇyaka and Virāṭa parvans. Their actions, in the *Dicing* and afterward, demonstrate their worthiness as heirs, *de facto* proved by the *Unction*, *de jure* by the consequences of the *Dicing*.

Therefore I see the *Unction* and the *Dicing* indissolubly intertwined in the narrative of the *Sabhā*, and the rest of the Bhārata story. In this carefully structured *Books of the Assembly* all the other events are made to relate to the basic theme. The beginning finds Yudhiṣṭhira installed in his Hall and prosperous. His justice in Indraprastha is emphasized by Nārada's politic interrogation, the centrality of his Hall by Nārada's description of the five celestial Halls, which his mirrors on earth; while the same sage's mention of Hariścandra's glory by *rājasūya* inspires Yudhiṣṭhira with the desire to offer up the same Royal Consecration. Granted that all these preliminaries may be secondary, they all subordinate themselves to the principal event of the eventual *Unction*. Also, they remain in character with the cosmic scope of the *rājasūya*, on which Heesterman rightly insists so much, but they somehow come better off in the epic than in the saṃhitās and sūtras. Thereafter, if I am right, a number of the components of the Vedic *rājasūya*—however this ceremonial was precisely reflected on the baronial level, but in any case with more pomp and circumstance—have been drawn upon to further the story, and with great flexibility. With all its agglutinations **[84]**—and rather few they are—the entire *Sabhā* builds up to the climax of the *Unction*, and it in turn to the climax of the *Dicing*. In my opinion, the ritualists of the *rājasūya*—if that rite can be separated from royal concerns—provided the royal bards with the sequence; but look what those bards did with it!

NOTES

1. All the references are to the critical edition of the *Sabhāparvan* by Franklin Edgerton (2 vols. Poona 1943-44), in Visnu S. Sukthankar, *The Mahābhārata.*
2. Please note that this is the correct spelling, *not* Hastināpura, which is unknown to the Mahābhārata. When the latter scansion is needed, the epic has *Gajāhvaya* etc.
3. A study on this intriguing Asura Architect is needed.
4. For the sake of convenience I follow, with (book) (I) etc. the parallel division of the Mahābhārata into 100 parvans.
5. 2.1-4.
6. 2.5-11.
7. 2.12-17.
8. 2.18-22.
9. 2.23-29.
10. 2.30-32.
11. 2.33-36.
12. 2.37-42.
13. 2.43-65
14. 2.66-72.
15. If Brahmā's Hall is in the zenith, Yudhiṣṭhira's is in the nadir, that is, the earthly mirror image of Brahmā's.
16. Cf. P-E. Dumont's partial analysis and translation of the epic account in *L'Aśvamedha*, Paris-Louvain 1927, 375 ff.
17. The word is missing in the epic account,
18. This incident in fact provided A. Holzmann with the starting point of his 'inversion' theory.
19. 2.44.18.
20. Nor is he at all eager to accept the challenge : 2.52.10 ff.
21. 2.45.55.
22. J.C. Heesterman, *The Ancient Indian Royal Consecration* (Thesis Utrecht), The Hague 1955, ch. XVII. Āpastamba and Hiraṇyakeśin have the king play with a brahmin, *kṣatriya, vaiśya* and *śūdra*, for parts of a cow (=earth?); Baudhāyana mentions brahmin, *sūta, grāmaṇī, kṣattar* and *saṃgrahitar*; Kātyāyana mentions no players, but indicates that the king plays with his kinsmen: (he plays "so that the king may be the centre of his kinsmen (*sajāta*)" and "he gives the losing combination (*kali*) to the kinsman:" Heesterman 143 ff. (On this also cf. the Nala story). There are other indications that the epic ritual follows the White Yajurveda, see below.
23. The older name of Rājagṛha (which seems to have been in the plain), the capital of Magadha before the shift to Pāṭaliputra.
24. 2.13.9.
25. Heesterman, II, 15 ff.
26. 2.39. I ff.

27. 2.22.30 ff.; also, Kṛṣṇa inherits Jarāsaṃdha's chariot: 2.22.11 ff.

28. In ib. 35 ff. Kṛṣṇa demands that the kings support Yudhiṣṭhira's claim to sovereignty, in return for their freedom, which they promise.

29. Heesterman, XII, 103 ff.; I do not know why he renders the compound "Mounting the Quarters of Space".

30. Heesterman, XVI, 127 ff.

31. O.c. p. 3.

32. 2.33.1.

33. The conquest includes Rome and Antioch! cf. Edgerton, JAOS 58, 262 ff.

34. Cf. the descriptions in 2.31.1 ff., 45.19 ff., and esp. 47.1-43 for the importance attached to the tribute brought, and compare the simple corresponding rite of the *ratnins* (Heesterman, VI, 49 ff.), where *ratnin* no doubt be understood as "holder of *ratna*/tribute" rather than "office-holder".

35. 2.26.11-16.

36. The only rite mentioned by name (the *sūtra's* name) is the *abhiṣeka.*

37. 2.47.1-43.

38. 2.32.2.

39. 2.33.3 ff.; 7.

40. 2.33.26.

41. Some other correspondences with the Vedic *rājasūya* may be noted here. The Unction Water, a mixture of many sources (Heesterman, 84-85), is brought by the "bucket-like" ocean in a conch shell and is gathered from the three oceans (2.45.26-29; 49.14.-18). The preparation of the sacrificer (= king) corresponds with 2.49.5-10.

42. For the Vedic Unction, cf. Heesterman, XIV, 114 ff.

43. Heesterman, XV, 123 ff.

44. As it is done in the epic: at the *vedi* (2.33.1) and the *sadas* (ib. 29). We should keep in mind that the *adhvaryu* was Yājñavalkya (2.30.35), who belonged to the White Yajurveda.

45. Cf. PW. s.v. *argha, arghya.*

46. 2.34.14 ff.

47. Heesterman, XVI, 127 ff.

48. The analogy may seem remote, but it would seem that the avoidance of challenge is a significant part of a coronation. Such a challenge might at some courts have been avoided by the king himself, at others by his champion.—The importance of the chariot is clearer from the epic account (2.49.5ff.); on the same chariot Yudhiṣṭhira drives out to meet the challenge of the game at Hāstinapura (2.52.20), and he loses it at the game (2.54.4 ff.)

49. And understandably so: the Sabhāparvan *is* after all the story of Yudhiṣṭhira's attempt at paramountcy in the Kaurava kingdom by means of the *rājasūya.*

50. The original function of the dicing game at the Vedic *rājasūya* still awaits satisfactory explanation. Heesterman is not convincing. Is it after all not possible that at one time a competition for leadership among rivaling tribal chieftains, or among dynastic princes, might have been decided by the dice as well as by chariot races? In any case, before we can symbolize the thing, we must have the thing.

51. Śakuni suggests the match to Duryodhana in a very matter-of-fact way : *dyūtapriyaś ca Kaunteyo na ca jānāti devitum/samāhūtaśca rājendro na śakṣyati nivartitum.* In 2.53.13, Yudhiṣṭhira states simply: *āhūto na nivarteyām iti me vratam āhitam:* in other words, no challenge should go unheard. His objections in 2.52.10 ff. hardly accord with his being *dyūtipriya*! It all has the inevitability about it best summed up by Dhṛtarāṣṭra (2.45.58) *pravartatāṃ suhṛddyūtaṃ diṣṭam etan na saṃśayaḥ.* And this inevitability I attribute to the ritual prototype in the Vedic *rājasūya.*

52. Who is called *atidevin* "playing for too high stakes," *kṛtahasta* "of trained hands," or "whose hands deliver the *kṛta*," and *matākṣa* "knowing the dice" (2.52.13). The last term is known to Baudhāyana (Heesterman, 145).

53. 2.45.47: *tataḥ saṃstīrya ratnais tāṃ (sabhām) akṣān avopya sarvaśaḥ* "having bestrewn the (hall) with jewels (= dice?), and having sown out the dice altogether." On the numbers in the *rājasūya.*, cf. Heesterman, 143 ff.

54. 2.52.14: *mahābhayāḥ kitavāḥ saṃniviṣṭā māyopadhā devitāro'tra santi* "very dangerous gamblers have been brought in; they are sure to gamble here with wizard tricks".

55. Heesterman, 145 ff.

56. 2.53.15-54.29.

57. 2.55-57.

58. 2.58.

59. This seems to be the correct translation; a *suhṛd* in the epic is most often a family member.

27

ĀNANDA, OR ALL DESIRES FULFILLED

It is quite a few years ago now that I was grappling with a particularly confusing passage in the Vulgate version of the *Maitrāyaṇīya Upaniṣad* and found that a celebrated section of the *Taittirīya Upaniṣad* provided the necessary clues to amend the *Maitrāyaṇīya* corruptions satisfactorily.[1] Not only that, the comparison of the two Upaniṣads made clear that the *Maitrāyaṇīya* also shed needed light on the *Taittirīya*, that one was not the epigone of the other, and that therefore the sections of the two texts had to be studied in one context. The purpose of my *Maitrāyaṇīya* study was mainly to contribute to our understanding of the textual history of that Upaniṣad, and I did not pursue too far the implications of the context it shared with the *Taittirīya*. I should now like to return to one issue it raises.

[28] *Taittirīya Upaniṣad*, chapter 2, is well known on two counts: it propounds the so-called Five-Sheath[2] doctrine of the *ātman*, and it defines *brahman* as bliss and bestower of bliss,[3] *ānanda*. This definition of *brahman* as *ānanda* became central to later Vedānta thought which defined the supreme as *saccidānanda*, "existent, spirit and bliss." Also, when the road to release from the bondage of *karman* in transmigration became viewed as the road to knowledge of *brahman*, the bliss that was *brahman* placed a highly positive value on this release: for not only was release merely desirable as an escape from the miseries of life, death, and rebirth, it was a state of bliss by itself, over and beyond the escape from the misery of bondage.

How was this notion of bliss prepared? How was this bliss regarded; or, what was regarded as blissful, and why? An investigation of the early contexts of *ānanda*, before it was viewed as the opposite of bondage, provides interesting answers.

Ṛg Veda 9.113.6 gives early notice:

yátra brahmā́ pavamāna chandasyā̀ṃ vā́cam vádan /
grā̄vṇā sóme mahīyáte sómenānandáṃ janáyann–
índrāyendo pári srava //

"O thou now purified, Soma in whom the *brahmán* priest, while speaking the words of the hymns, rejoices with the pressing stone, generating *bliss* through Soma—swirl around for Indra, O drop!"

The scene here is of the soma sacrifice when the soma stalks are being pounded with the pressing stones and the pressed-out juice swirls around the cowhide on which this pressing takes place.[4] The purification takes place while the pressing goes on by straining the juice through a cloth into the *droṇa* trough underneath.[5] It is clear from *Ṛg Veda* 11 how this bliss is seen. Still addressing Soma, the poet says

yátrānandā́ś ca módā́ś ca múdaḥ pramúda ā́sate /
kā́masya yátrāptā́ḥ kā́mās tátra mā́m amŕ̥tam kr̥dhi—
índrāyendo pári srava //

"Thou in whom the *blisses*, joys, pleasures and raptures are sitting, in whom the desired objects of desire are obtained, make me immortal in thee—swirl around for Indra, O drop!"

[29] While no doubt the soma was pressed for Indra, its principal recipient, the priest drank it too, and it is obvious that he, not Indra, asks for the immortality in the draught in which *bliss* rests and desire's objects are obtained. The word *ānanda* here, paraphrased by "joy, pleasure and rapture," and paralleled by the phrase *kāmasya...āptāḥ kāmāḥ*, signifies the joyous state of (drug-induced) ecstasy in which the ecstatic may hope for immortality. Three points may be kept in mind from the beginning: the use of the word *ānanda*, its association with the fulfilment of the greatest desires,[6] and its potential for immortality.

Once more in praise of the soma about to be offered, the *adhvaryu*, the priest of the Yajurveda, invokes it according to the *Vājasaneyi Saṃhitā* 19.8,[7] as follows: *upayāmágr̥hīto 'sy āśvináṃ téjaḥ sārasvatáṃ vīryàm aindráṃ balám / eṣá te yónir módāya tvānandā́ya tvā máhase tvā:* "Thou hast now been taken in the ladle,[8] (thou) glory of the Aśvins, might of Sarasvatī, strength of Indra: this (ladle) is thy womb—(I take) thee for joy, for bliss, for largeness."

Again *ānanda* is coupled with *moda*, but also now with *mahas* "largeness," on the creative implications of which I have commented before in this journal.[9] It may here signify a "swelling with joy," for there is no clear indication yet that *ānanda* (or for that matter *moda*) meant anything more than the exuberance following the drinking of the soma. The same *Saṃhitā*, 30.6, in a series of persons who contribute to human activities, good or bad ("for dancing a bard, 20.5), for singing a songster," 30.6, so *kā́māya puṃścalū́m* "for lust a harlot," lists *ānandā́ya strīṣakhám* "for bliss a friendly woman"[10] and later in the same context *ānandā́ya talavam* "for bliss a musician" (30.20). The meaning of the word *ānanda* is not summed up by "sexual bliss", though it is no doubt among the joys included in it. *Vājasaneyi Saṃhitā* 20.9 has a list of answers to the question, "Who are you, what are you, for what (man), for what (woman) do I take you?" the following one: *ānandanandáv āṇḍáu me bhágaḥ sáubhāgyam pásah:* "My testicles pleasure me to bliss; vagina, penis are my delight."

While the occurrences so far give us little reason to assume any [30] specific refinement of meaning for *ānanda* (although we should keep the *Ṛg Veda* passages in mind), the *Śatapatha Brāhmaṇa* employs it with a broader and higher intention, 10.3.5.13: *ānanda evāsya vijñānam ātmānandātmāno haiva sarve devāḥ sa haiṣaiva devānām addhāvidyā sa ha sa na manuṣyo ya evaṃvid devānāṃ haiva sa ekaḥ* : "bliss, (that is to say) knowledge of it (sc. the *brahman*) is his self: indeed, all gods are ensouled by bliss: that is the peculiar knowledge of the gods; the very (person) who has this knowledge is not a human, he is one of the gods." Here the scope of *ānanda* is certainly broadened: knowledge of the "eldest (= supreme) *brahman*" (*Śatapatha Brāhmaṇa*, ibid., 10) equals bliss, which equals soul. Moreover, this conception of *ānanda* might well be called a special knowledge (*vidyā*), for it was important enough to be signed by a sage in the immediate sequel:[11] *etad dha sma vai tad vidvān Priyavrato Rauhiṇeya āha / vāyuṃ vāntam ānandas ta ātmeto vā vāhīto veti sa ha sma tathaiva vāti tasmād yān deveṣu āśiṣa icched etenaivopatiṣṭhetānando vā ātmāsau me kāmaḥ sa me samṛdhyatām iti saṃ haivāsmai sa kāma ṛdhyate yatkāmo bhavaty etāṃ ha vai tṛptiṃ etāṃ gatim etam ānandam etam ātmānam abhisambhavati ya evaṃ veda* : "This is what Priyavrata Rauhiṇeya, who knew exactly this, said to the blowing wind: 'Your soul is bliss, now blow this way or that!' So the wind blows these ways. Therefore the blessings which a person wishes from among the gods, let him attend (on the gods) with: 'Your soul is bliss. What I desire is this...It must succeed.' For him that desire indeed succeeds, whatever desire he has. He who knows this obtains this contentment, this course, this bliss, this soul."

Here, as in the *Ṛg Veda* verses quoted, the idea of *ānanda* is connected with the fulfilment of wishes, and it is important to note that it is a divine attribute, which is however within the reach of man: *etam ānandam etam ātmānam abhisambhavati.* There is also a creative part to *ānanda*, for the god is by his *ānanda* moved to create. This creativeness easily blends into procreativeness, as in *Śatapatha* 6.2.2.6: *Prajāpatiḥ prajāḥ sṛṣṭvānuvyaikṣata tasyātyānandena retaḥ parāpatat*: "Prajāpati, having created the creatures, looked about; because of his supreme bliss his semen spilled."[12] Here the bliss is both the result of creation and the cause of procreation. This perception of *ānanda* [31] will persist, although this bliss does not necessarily equal orgasm. A hasty reductionist might depart from a basic meaning of "orgasm" and leave the history of *ānanda* there, blissfully content that further blisses must be derivative or sublimative of orgasms, but the texts do not.[13] They use *ānanda* as a quasitechnical term indicating a state in which all desires are fulfilled so that no desires are left, and in which all other realms of desire are transcended.

The quoted *Śatapatha* passage of 10.5.2.11 stresses that the bliss which is knowledge elevates a person: he is no longer a man, he is one of the gods. This vaguely recalls *ṚV.* 9.113.11 where having obtained all desires (=*ānanda*) is a condition for immortality. What the texts appear to assume is that the bliss of *ānanda* is of a different order altogether from other pleasures that human beings may experience, and that sexual bliss is at best a metaphor for it. Even in its sexual connotation the scope of *ānanda* is rather different from what one might expect. There are six such occurrences in the *Kauṣītaki Brāhmaṇa Upaniṣad*, all of which have the same context where the penis (*upastha*) is treated as one of the motoric faculties (the *karmendriyas* of later texts). In 1.7 it reads: *kenānandaṃ ratiṃ prajām* [*āpnoṣi*] *ity upastheneti*: "He said, 'With what (do you obtain) bliss, sexual pleasure, offspring?' 'With the penis.' " So also in 2.15, 3.5–8. The sequence *ānandaṃ ratim* is noteworthy: *rati* reads like a gloss on *ānanda*: "bliss, that is to say, sexual pleasure," as though by this time that connotation of the word needed explanation. In the same context of sensory and motoric faculties *ānanda* occurs in *Bṛhadāraṇyaka Upaniṣad* 2.4.11.

The *Bṛhadāraṇyaka* in 4.1.6 indicates a convergence point of this, rather abstracted, sexual bliss and divine bliss: *mano brahmeti..mana evāyatanam ākāśaḥ pratiṣṭhānanda iti..kānandatā Yājñavalkya / mana eva samrāḍ iti hovāca manasā vai samrāṭ striyam abhihāryate tasyāṃ pratirūpaḥ putro jāyate sa ānando mano vai samrāṭ paramaṃ brahma nainam mano jahāti sarvāṇy enam bhūtāny abhikṣaranti devo bhūtvā devān apyeti*: " '*brahman* is thought,' he said..'Thought is its domain, space its foundation, its bliss,' he replied. 'In what consists this bliss, Yājñavalkya'? 'Thought, Sire,' he said: 'by thought, sire, [**32**] one is fetched to a woman:[14] from her a son in his image is born: that is bliss. Thought, sire is the highest *brahman*; thought does not desert him, (but) all things flow into him; having become a god he joins the gods.' " Despite the esoteric language the old idea shines through: *brahman* equals knowledge, which equals bliss—which is like the bliss that is the son born to a man by a woman fetched by desire. We reencounter also the *Śatapatha* notion that bliss follows creation and causes semen to flow. We are far removed from *ānanda* as sexual pleasure; *BĀ Up*. 3.9.28 repeats: *vijñānam ānandam brahma*: "*brahman* is knowledge, bliss."

Here it becomes necessary to look more closely at the formation of the word *ānanda*. It is not, as at first sight it might seem, a nominal derivative from the root *nand-* with preverb *ā*; the verb *ānandate* is not recorded until much later.[15] Rather should it be regarded as a verbal noun *nanda* with prefixed *ā*, and thus to belong to a fairly large group that often goes unrecognized: *ā* indicates the *place where* the verbal action occurs, for example, *āśrama,* where one toils; *ārāma,* where one enjoys oneself; *ākara,* where things are scattered; *ālaya,,* where things lie, etc. The word *ānanda* thus implies a locus: *that in which* one finds bliss, be it a son, the fulfilment of a wish, the knowledge of *brahman,* the *ātman*, the *brahman*; or, as in the case of the wind, in blowing where it lists. *Ānanda* then is not just a free-floating unfocused bliss, a state of beatitude; it has an implied object.

Where, now, does one find this bliss? In *BĀ Up*. 2.1.19 King Ajātaśatru holds forth on deep, dreamless sleep and what happens to the "soul" there: through the 72,000 veins of the body which lead to the pericardium "he creeps toward the pericardium and lies in it; as a young prince, or a great king, or a great brahmin would lie having reached the pinnacle of bliss, so he lies there." And this leads us back to the *Taittirīya* and its five sheaths of the person, for Ajātaśatru's description of the "souls" contracting to the center of the body where it finds the pinnacle of bliss closely resembles the "soul's" progression through *ātman*-sheaths until it reaches the pinnacle where it is bliss.

[33] The *Taittirīya* pictures the human person as consisting of five layers called *ātman*, which increase in subtleness. Each of these *ātmans* is described as *puruṣavidha* "personlike" with a head, two sides (or wings), an "*ātman,*" and a foundation (or tail). About this later. These "personlike *ātmans*" are *annamaya*, "made of food"; *prāṇamaya*, "made of breath"; *manomaya*, "made of mind"; *vijñānamaya*, "made of knowledge"; and *ānandamaya*, "made of bliss." The *annamaya* is the visible body whose parts the teacher can point to.[16] The *prāṇamaya* has as its parts the five *prāṇas*, the *manomaya,* the four Vedas and their instruction. The *vijñānamaya* has *śraddhā,* "faith"; *ṛta,* "=dharma"; *satya*, "truthfulness"; *yoga*, "enterprise"; and *mahas*, largeness." At the pinnacle, or, if you will, the center, is the *ānandamaya*, which has as its parts pleasure, delight, rapture, bliss, and *brahman*.

The image is a complex one: it comprises a hierarchy of *ātmans* that rise from the visible body to the universal *brahman* which is bliss; a hierarchy of faculties rising from physical subsistence (*anna*), vitality (*prāṇa*), learning (*manas*), ethics [17](*vijñāna*), to ecstasy (*ānanda*); and elements of a bird-symbol, with a head, two wings, a trunk and a tail. The complexity of the image shows that the different hierarchies and pentads are brought together in an attempt to unify them.

Whence this bird? A parallel *Maitrāyaṇīya* passage[18] points to the road we now have to take back. It too has five layers: (1) fire=earth with its seasons (~food); (2) wind=*prāṇa* and its five forms; (3) sky (=*ākāśa*) with Indra=Sun, with the five Vedas including *itihāsapurāṇa* (~*manas*); (4) the knower of the *ātman* (~*vijñāna*); and (5) *brahman*, where one becomes blissful. The first three layers have heads, wings, trunks, and tails but not the fourth and fifth, whereas the *Taittirīya* carries on the image to the last two levels with the consistency of one who completes what was left out. As though all this imagery were not enough, the *Maitrāyaṇīya* has additional, more archaic features: the head, etc., are altar-building bricks (*iṣṭakā*), and the first three levels are the first, second, and third layers of an altar built by Prajāpati, clearly in the shape of the bird well known from the ritual of the *agnicayana*.[19] While the *Taittirīya* postpones the description of a [34] journey of the "soul" till 2.8,[20] the *Maitrāyaṇīya*[21] has this journey right in the altar-layer context: the soul is here the *yajamāna*, the sacrificer, who is passed on to the fourth level of the *ātmavid*, "the knower of the *ātman*," and finally to *brahman*, where he becomes *ānandin* "filled with bliss."

This is upaniṣadic statement at its most compact: archaic structures are retained but to them are added new elements that are yet felt to fit comfortably into those structures. It departs from older speculations on the cosmic homologies of the laying of the three fires and the building of the bird-shaped altar of the *agnicayana*. The three fires, or the three layers, represent the familiar three-leveled world of earth, sky, and heaven. Each level is then filled: the first is the fire on earth through the year, which means food; the second is the sky with the wind, which micranthropically[22] is the *prāṇa*; the third is heaven with the sun and is also the space, which is the medium of sound, that is, the Vedas.

But this world was no longer enough. In *Śatapatha* 10.5.4.3 Celaka Śāṇḍilyāyana announces: *ima eva lokās tisraḥ svayam ātṛṇṇavatyaś citayo yajamānaś caturthī sarve kāmāḥ pañcamī imāṃś ca lokānt saṃskurva ātmānaṃ ca sarvāṃś ca kāmān ity eva vidyād iti*: "One should know that the three pierced-brick layers are these three worlds themselves, the *yajamāna* himself is the fourth,[23] all objects of desire the fifth: he perfects these worlds, himself, and all objects of desire." Although the fulfillment of all desires, for which the Vedic poet prayed at the soma sacrifice, may be the logical goal of all wish-fulfilling ritual, it is clear that these speculations have left the actual ritual performance behind, while borrowing from it the old hierarchy of the cosmos and expanding that. At the pinnacle appears *ānanda*, which is all desires fulfilled; but "all desires" are now epitomized in the knowledge of *brahman* and of *ātman*, the knowledge which *is* the *brahman* and the *ātman* itself. The *Taittirīya* text goes on to say: "This is the inquiry into bliss. If there were a young man, a fine young man, studious, very prompt, very stable, very vigorous, and if all this earth were his, filled with wealth—that is one human [35] bliss."[24] A hundred such blisses is one bliss of human Gandharvas, a hundred such one of divine Gandharvas, a hundred such one of the Ancestors, etc., up to Indra, a hundred of whose blisses are one of Bṛhaspati, whose hundred are one of Prajāpati, whose hundred, finally, are but one of *brahman*. This paean to *ānanda* ends:

yato vāco nivartanta aprāpya manasā saha /
ānandaṃ brahmaṇo vidvān na bibheti kutaścana //

"Whence words return along with the mind without reaching it—he who knows that bliss of *brahman* has nothing to fear from anywhere."

This verse gloriously concludes a chapter in the history of *ānanda,* to open a new one in Vedānta, of *brahman,* and *ātman*, and God and his grace, and the soul and its bhakti.

In following the course of the uses of the word *ānanda* we have seen it pause at the landmarks in the development of religion and thought. It was the high joy of drinking the soma and of offering it, the climax of the ritual building of the universe, the unhindered happiness of gods, the orgasm that begets a son in one's image as a metaphor for one's self-renewal as one of the gods, the joyous knowledge of oneself and the eldest *brahman*, and the bliss that is the *brahman* and the *ātman*. It appears as a value completely outside the context of transmigration, in its own right; this seems to me very important.

It often appears as though the "joy" one is told to find in the *ātman* when it is released from transmigration is not much more than the absence of the misery caused by the thirst for life and the bondage of *karman*. But it is clear now that this is not so. There was a conception of the possibility of a bliss that transcended all that is pleasurable in this world well before, and apart from, the need for it that arose from the gloom of interminable existences. Kṛṣṇa's use comes to mind of *brahmanirvāṇa*, which is [36] the *brāhmī sthitiḥ* in the *Bhagavadgītā,*[25] the *nirvāṇa* that is *brahman*, which is the stance in *brahman* that opens not on a void but a fullness.

NOTES

1. J.A.B. van Buitenen, *The Maitrāyaṇīya Upaniṣad* (The Hague, 1962), pp. 29 ff.

2. *Pañcakoṣavidyā* is the traditional name in Vedānta; the word *koṣa* is not used by Taitt Up. in this context.

3. Taitt Up. 2.7.1 *ānandayāti*.

4. Willem Caland and Victor Henry, *L'Agniṣṭoma*, 2 vols. (Paris, 1906-7), §129, I, pp. 157, ff.

5. Ibid., § 133 f., I, pp. 168 ff.

6. *Kāmasya kāmāḥ* may be read as a superlative idiom; but note that *kāma* regularly occurs in two meanings side by side: "desire" as a craving, and "object of desire," its objective.

7. I quote from the *Mādhyaṃdina* version, which I have at hand.

8. *Upayāma* is the name of the ladle with which soma is offered into the fire.

9. "The Large Ātman," pp. 105-10 [no. 18 in this volume].

10. The compound by its accent should be read as a *karmadhāraya.*

11. *Śat Br*. 10.3.5.14.

12. It becomes a white, hornless, bearded he-goat (and is described as the sap of life), which upon being sacrificed is returned to Prajāpati as his life breath, (ibid., 7).

13. Nor do the Pāli texts cited in the *Copenhagen Dictionary* indicate such a connotation; the synonyms quoted for *ānanda* are *tuṭṭhi, pīti, nandi, pamoda, pamāda, somanassa*. Besides, the many uses of the word as a proper name, beginning with that of the Buddha's favorite disciple, indicate its high meaning.

14. Cf. *Chāndogya Up*. 8.2.9: *atha yadi strīlokakāmo bhavati saṃkalpād evāsya striyaḥ samuttiṣṭhanti*; in the *BĀUp*. passage too *manas* has the sense of "purposeful thought."

15. The *Petersburg Dictionary* cites the *Bhaṭṭikāvya* and *Gītagovinda* for the earliest attestations of *ānandate; ānandayāti* (*Taitt Up*. 2.7.1) and *ānandayate* (*Praśn Up*. 4.2, hence *ānandayitvam*, ibid., 8) are to be regarded as denominatives from *ānanda*. The *Copenhagen Pāli Dictionary* cites *ānandati* only from the late prose of the *Jātakas*.

16. As he does in *Taitt. Up*. 2.1.1.

17. I do not intend this as a meaning of *vijñāna*, only as the use the author makes of the word.

18. *Maitr Up*. 6.33.

19. Cf. my remarks in *The Maitrāyaṇīya Upaniṣad*, p. 29-33.

20. Where the "*puruṣa*" travels from the *annamaya ātman* to the *ānandamaya*.

21. *BĀ Up*. 2.1.19 knows of a comparable journey.

22. I happily borrow this term from Maryla Falk, *Il Mito psichologico nell' India antica*, Transactions, Lincean Academy, ser. 6, vol. 8, fasc. 5 (Rome, 1939), pp. 289-738; it is much more useful in the Indian contexts than "microcosmic."

23. The *yajamāna* as the prototype of the journeying soul deserves further study.

24. *Taitt Up*. 2.8. This "human bliss" is well chosen: Vedic students probably were rarely fine, studious, prompt, stable or vigorous; besides, they were paupers, living off begging. For them to be such paragons and to have all of earth with its wealth would be bliss indeed. Remember that a teacher is talking to his student, with apposite irony. A similar idea, namely, that all ordinary human pleasures culminate in and symbolize the pleasure that is the *ātman*, explains, I think, the curious passage in *BĀ Up*. 2.4.5: "It is not for the desire for a husband that the husband is dear to one, but for the desire for the *ātman*." This is repeated in identical phrasing with wife, sons, wealth, brahminhood, *kṣatra*, worlds, gods, (all) creatures, and "everything," which equals "all objects of desire" that are thus transcended by the *ātman* as object of desire.

25. *Bh G*.2.72.

INDEX